BRAQUE

The Papiers Collés

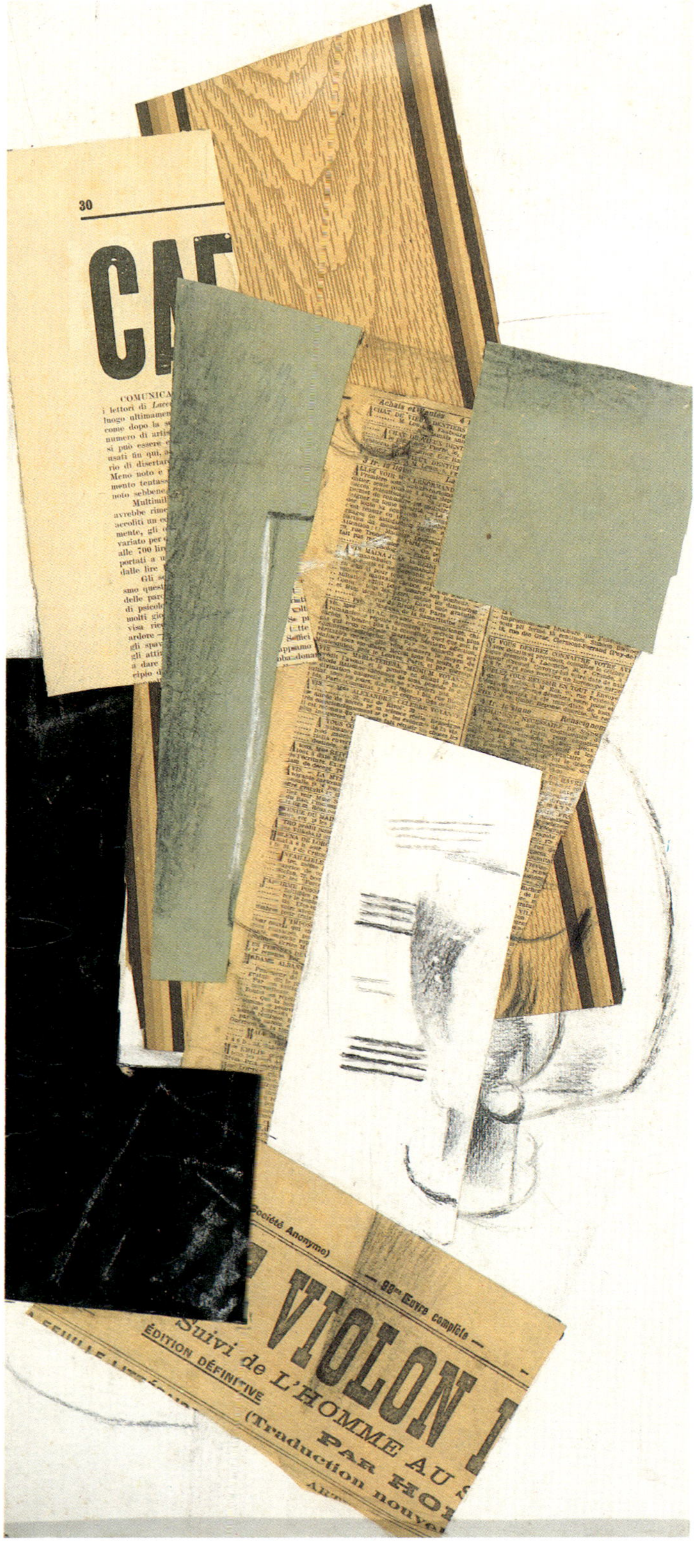

Plate 1 *Glass, Bottle and Newspaper (Le violon)*, 1914. Cat. no. 46. Private collection.

BRAQUE
The Papiers Collés

Isabelle Monod-Fontaine
with
E. A. Carmean, Jr.

Contributions by
Trinkett Clark
Douglas Cooper
Pierre Daix
Edward F. Fry
Alvin Martin

National Gallery of Art, Washington 1982

This catalogue was produced by the Editors Office, National Gallery of Art, Washington. Printed by Garamond/Pridemark Press, Inc., Baltimore, Maryland. The type is Trump Medieval set by Hodges Typographers, Inc., Silver Spring, Maryland. Cover and text papers are Warren's Cameo Dull. Designed by Susan Lehmann.

Exhibition dates at the National Gallery of Art: 31 October 1982-16 January 1983.

Most of the material in this catalogue was originally prepared for publication in *Georges Braque: les papiers collés,* which accompanied the exhibition at the Centre Georges Pompidou, Musée national d'art moderne, 17 June-27 September 1982.

Photo credits: Michael Tropea, Chicago (plate 5)
Bruce C. Jones, Rocky Point, N.Y. (plate 7)

Cover: *Aria de Bach,* 1913. National Gallery of Art, Washington. Collection of Mr. and Mrs. Paul Mellon, 1982. Cat. no. 24.

Library of Congress Cataloging in Publication Data:

Monod-Fontaine, Isabelle.
Braque, the papiers collés.
Catalog of an exhibition held at the Musée national d'art moderne, Centre Georges Pompidou, Paris, and at the National Gallery of Art, Washington, D.C.
Translation of French texts with additional notes and articles in English.
Bibliography: p. 165-171
1. Braque, Georges, 1882-1963—Exhibitions. I. Braque, Georges, 1882-1963. II. Carmean, E. A. III. National Gallery of Art (U.S.) IV. Musée national d'art moderne (France) V. Title.
N6853.B7A4 1982 709'.2'4 8-14176
ISBN 0-89468-056-0

CONTENTS

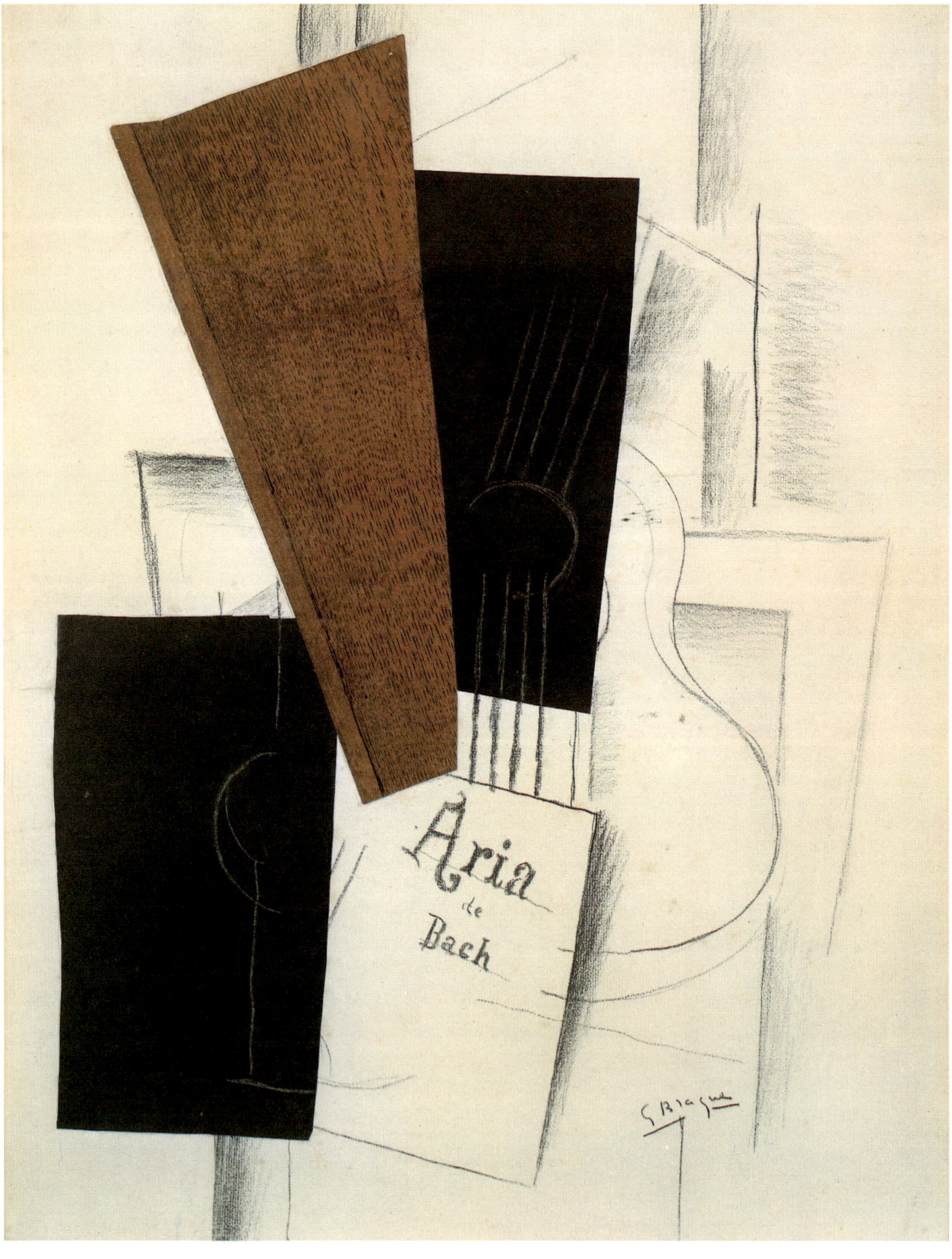

Plate 2 *Aria de Bach,* 1913. Cat. no. 24. National Gallery of Art, Collection of Mr. and Mrs. Paul Mellon, 1982.

FOREWORD

THE YEAR 1982 MARKS THE CENTENARY of Georges Braque's birth. In addition, it coincides with the seventieth anniversary of the making of his first *papier collé,* truly a watershed invention in the art of this century. To celebrate these two occasions the National Gallery is presenting an exhibition, *Braque: The Papiers Collés,* which has been organized with the Musée national d'art moderne at the Centre Georges Pompidou in Paris.

Braque's works have played an important role in the history of the National Gallery's involvement in twentieth-century art. In 1952 Chester Dale lent this institution his collection of paintings, including superb examples by Braque and his cubist colleague Picasso. Ten years later the Dale bequest added these works to our permanent collection, five major oils by Braque and eleven by Picasso. A lacuna in our holdings, however, has been the representation of Braque's work in *papier collé.* This omission has now been rectified by the recent generous donation by Mr. and Mrs. Paul Mellon of *Aria de Bach,* dated 1913. In the present exhibition, *Aria de Bach* joins a comprehensive gathering of Braque's other collages to provide an in-depth study of his invention and articulation of this medium.

The exhibition opens with the very first *papier collé* and reveals how Braque rapidly pursued its implications. His paring down of formal elements, in 1913, is also shown, as is the subsequent development of works which are complex in composition and rich in both texture and color. The exhibition concludes with a collage of 1917, one of Braque's initial works in the style of later cubism.

In Washington this exhibition follows *Mondrian: The Diamond Compositions; Picasso: The Saltimbanques; Kandinsky: The Improvisations;* and *Bellows: The Boxing Pictures* as part of a series of gallery projects devoted to key aspects of twentieth-century art. The Paris version of this exhibition was organized by Isabelle Monod-Fontaine, curator at the Musée national d'art moderne; the Gallery's version by E. A. Carmean, Jr., curator of twentieth-century art, and Trinkett Clark, assistant curator in that department. A team of scholars from both museums, led principally by Mme. Monod-Fontaine, has prepared the *catalogue raisonné* of Braque's *papiers collés* which appears in this publication. Four other scholars, Douglas Cooper, Pierre Daix, Edward Fry, and Alvin Martin, have contributed to this research, and each has written an informative essay as well. Our colleague, Dominique Bozo, Director of the Musée national d'art moderne, has been most generous in all aspects of this project. To the many staff members, both at the Centre Georges Pompidou and the National Gallery, who were involved with this exhibition and catalogue, we extend our grateful appreciation.

We also wish to thank M. and Mme. Claude Laurens, who have been supportive of this exhibition from its conception. The Laurens have given much assistance to the Braque research team, making available many invaluable documents from their archives.

Finally, we are most grateful to the lenders who have allowed their rare and fragile *papiers collés* to be included in this exhibition. Their generosity permits us to span the seventy-year interim and approach the very moment of invention and discovery of this significant new form of cubist art.

J. CARTER BROWN
Director

LENDERS TO THE EXHIBITION

The Art Institute of Chicago
Ernst Beyeler, Basel
The Cleveland Museum of Art
Mr. and Mrs. Sidney E. Cohn
Columbus Museum of Art, Ohio
John R. Gaines
Galerie Rosengart, Lucerne
Mrs. Thomas J. Hardman
Kunstmuseum Winterthur
Los Angeles County Museum of Art
Menil Collections, Houston
Musée national d'art moderne, Paris
The Museum of Modern Art, New York
Philadelphia Museum of Art
Saidenberg Gallery, New York
Yale University Art Gallery
Private Collections

ACKNOWLEDGMENTS

THIS EXHIBITION AND STUDY is a joint project between the Musée national d'art moderne at the Centre Georges Pompidou and the National Gallery of Art. *Braque: The Papiers Collés* did not begin that way, however. Unbeknownst to the other, each museum embarked on its own *catalogue raisonné* project, first concentrating upon the collages on its own continent. When Dominque Bozo and I finally learned that we were not only organizing the same exhibition, but also had independently undertaken the identical research project, we quickly agreed that our two institutions should join together in this centenary exhibition of Braque's work.

Unlike that of his colleague Picasso, whose oeuvre has been studied in great detail, Braque's, while greatly admired, remains largely unstudied both in its totality and specific development. Thus the research behind this project must be pioneering in character. Neither the exhibition nor this study would have been possible without the time and efforts of many people. From the French side, our colleague Isabelle Monod-Fontaine prepared the *catalogue raisonné,* published concurrently with the exhibition at the Centre Georges Pompidou in June. She was assisted by Nathalie Brunet. In Washington, Trinkett Clark, assistant curator in the Department of Twentieth-Century Art, aided in all aspects of the exhibition. In particular, she made additions to Mme. Monod-Fontaine's catalogue, and she contributed the greatly expanded chronology of Braque's career. Douglas Cooper, the senior scholar of cubism, very generously offered his own notes on the collages to the *catalogue raisonné.*

We are especially thankful to the authors who shared their knowledge of this crucial moment in the history of cubism. In addition to the studies by Mme. Monod-Fontaine and Mr. Cooper, essays by three other scholars appear here. Pierre Daix, author of the *catalogue raisonné* of Picasso's cubist work of this same period, drew upon his detailed knowledge of the movement for his text on the two cubist colleagues. In a similar manner, Edward Fry's longtime study of cubism and its literature lies behind his essay on the French tradition. Finally, Alvin Martin has added new insights to Braque's work and the emergence of the synthetic cubist style.

Central to the realization of this combined project has been the participation of M. and Mme. Claude Laurens, M. Laurens being the son of Henri Laurens, Braque's lifelong friend and fellow cubist. In addition to making available invaluable documentary material from the Laurens archives, they have devoted countless hours of insight, advice, and support to this study, and we wish to acknowledge them in particular. Through our many conversations, M. Laurens, who from his childhood knew not only Braque, but also Picasso, Léger, and Gris, has given me a special feeling for the cubist artists, and for the invention of collage, which is celebrated here.

Several other people were also important to this project: in Basel, M. and Mme. Ernst Beyeler; in Paris, Heinz Berggruen, Nicole Genetet-Morel, and Maurice Jardot; and in Mougins, Jacqueline Picasso.

Many members of the National Gallery staff contributed. In the library, Thomas McGill and Delores Stachura were especially helpful. The translation of the French texts was undertaken by Margaret Morgan Grasselli, with assistance from Jacqueline D'Amecourt. In the photography laboratory, Richard Amt made many necessary prints, while the organization of all supplementary illustrations was coordinated by Laura Coyle, of the Department of Twentieth-Century Art. Also in this department, Caren Hammerman, a summer intern in 1979, conducted research on this topic. Mei Su Teng edited this publication, clarifying several points. The presentation of the exhibition is the work of the Department of Installation and Design.

E. A. CARMEAN, JR.

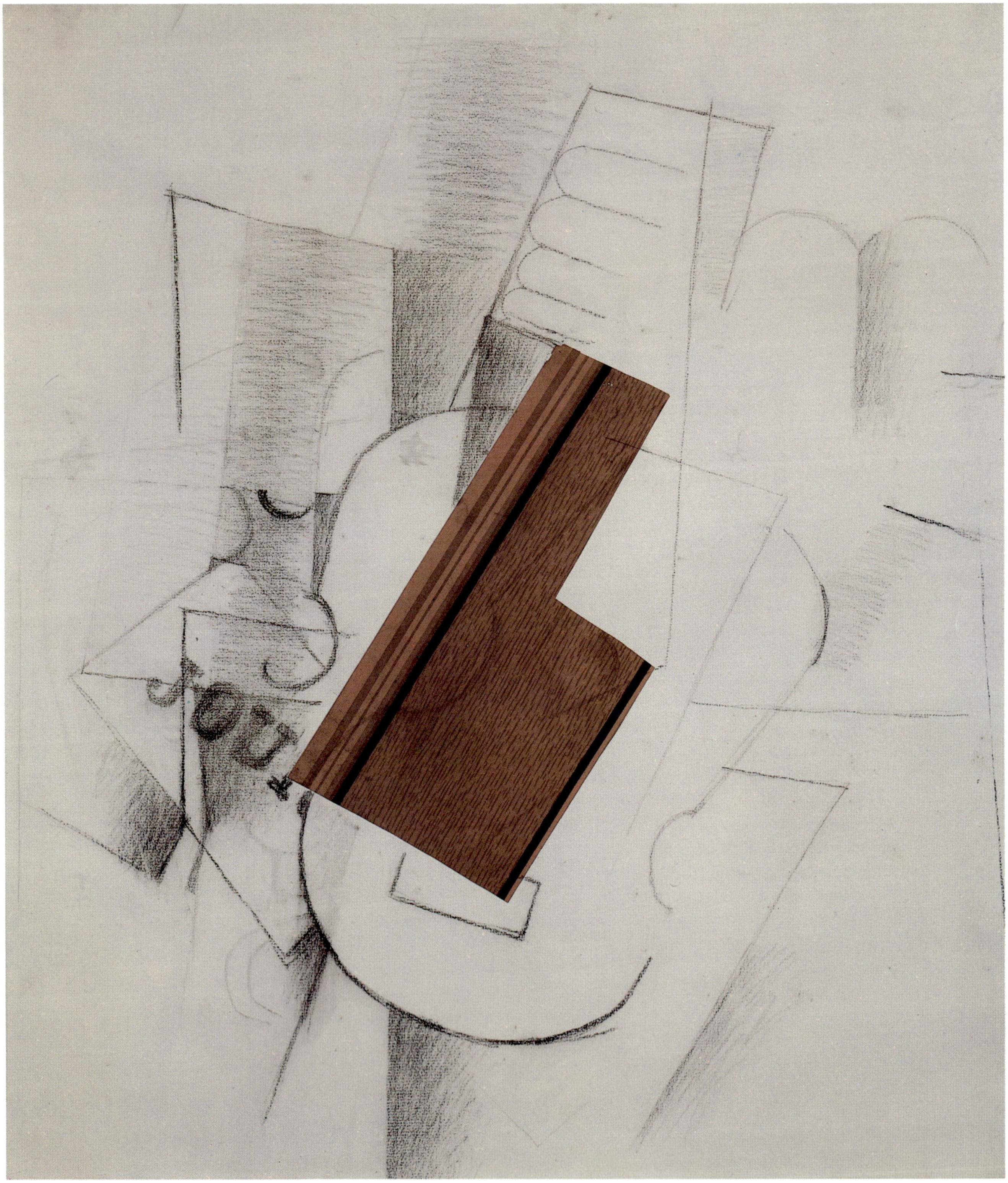

Plate 3 *The Guitar (La guitare),* 1912. Cat. no. 4. Private collection.

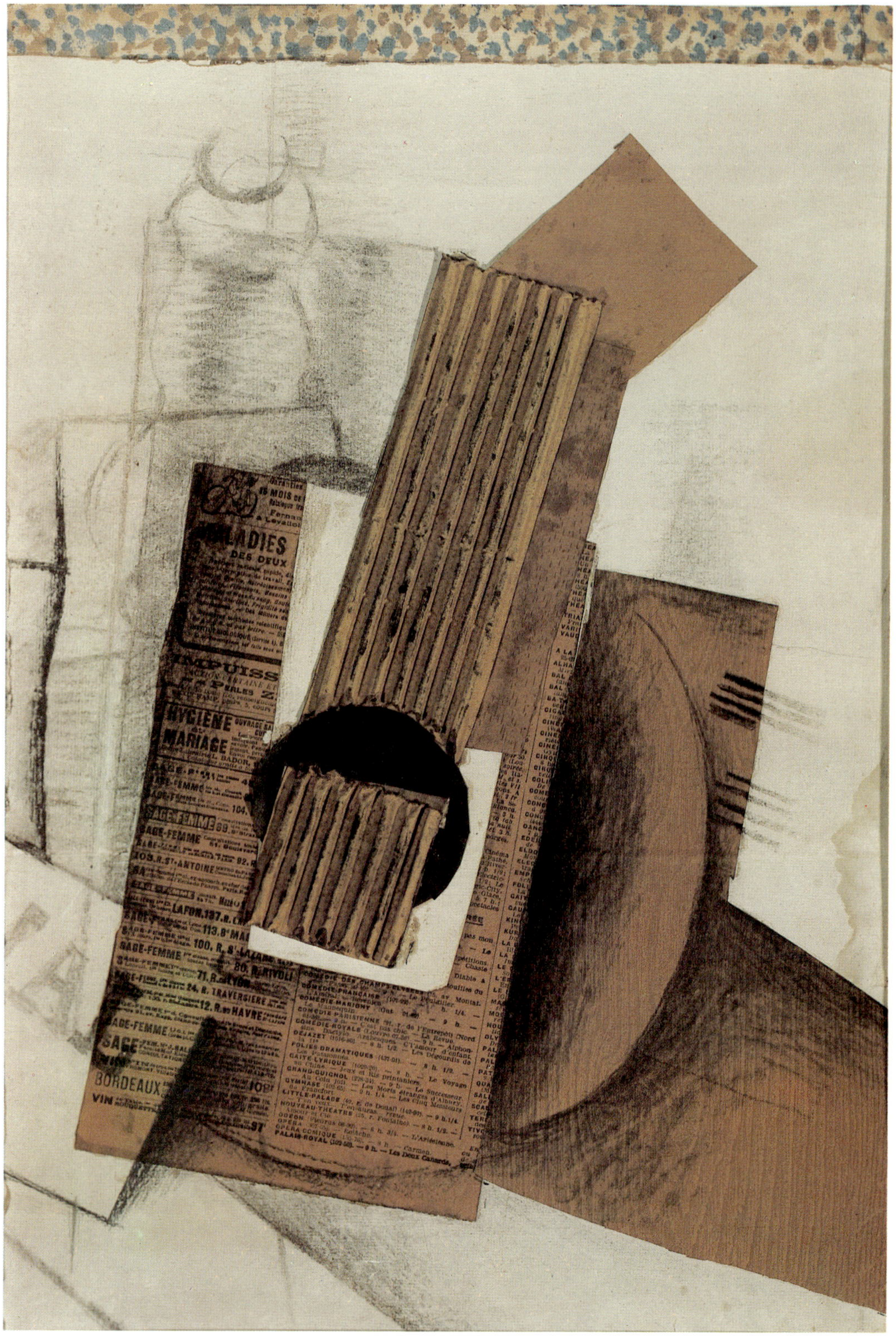

Plate 4 *The Mandolin (La mandoline)*, 1914. Cat. no. 52. Ulmer Museum, Ulm.

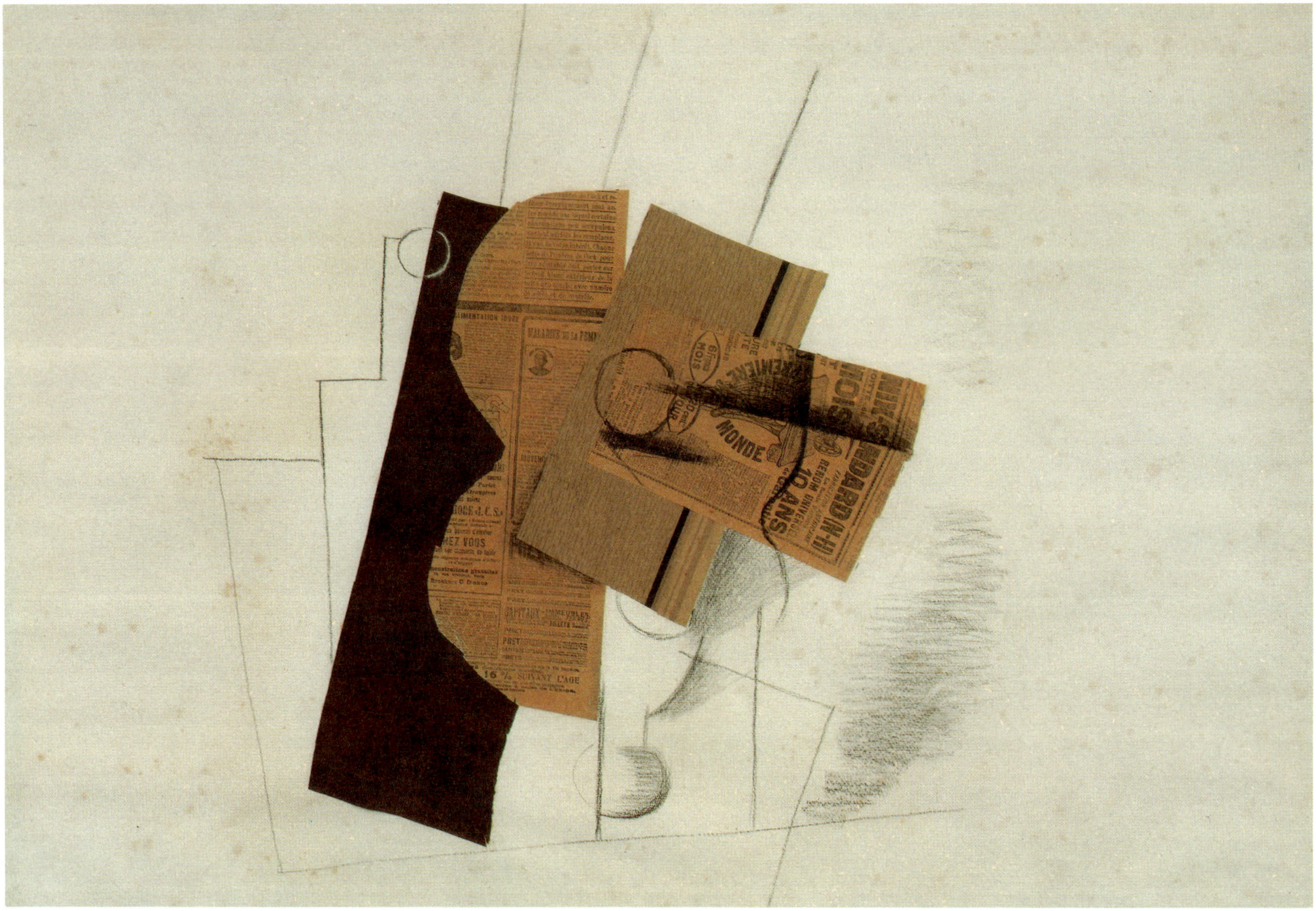

Plate 5 *Guitar and Glass (Guitare et verre),* 1913-1914. Cat. no. 33. Private collection.

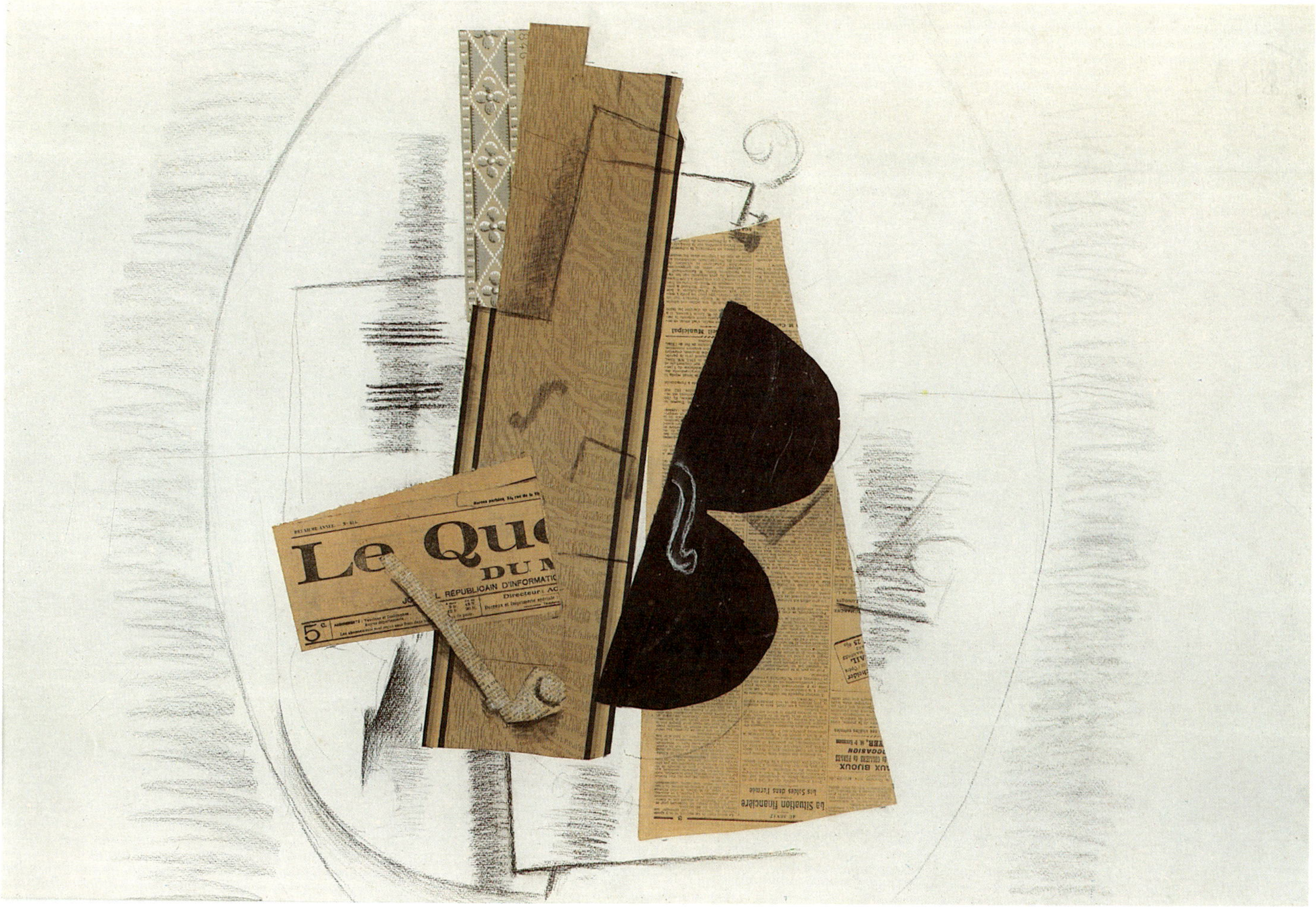

Plate 6 *Violin and Pipe ("Le Quotidien"),* 1913-1914. Cat. no. 38. Musée national d'art moderne, Centre Georges Pompidou, Paris.

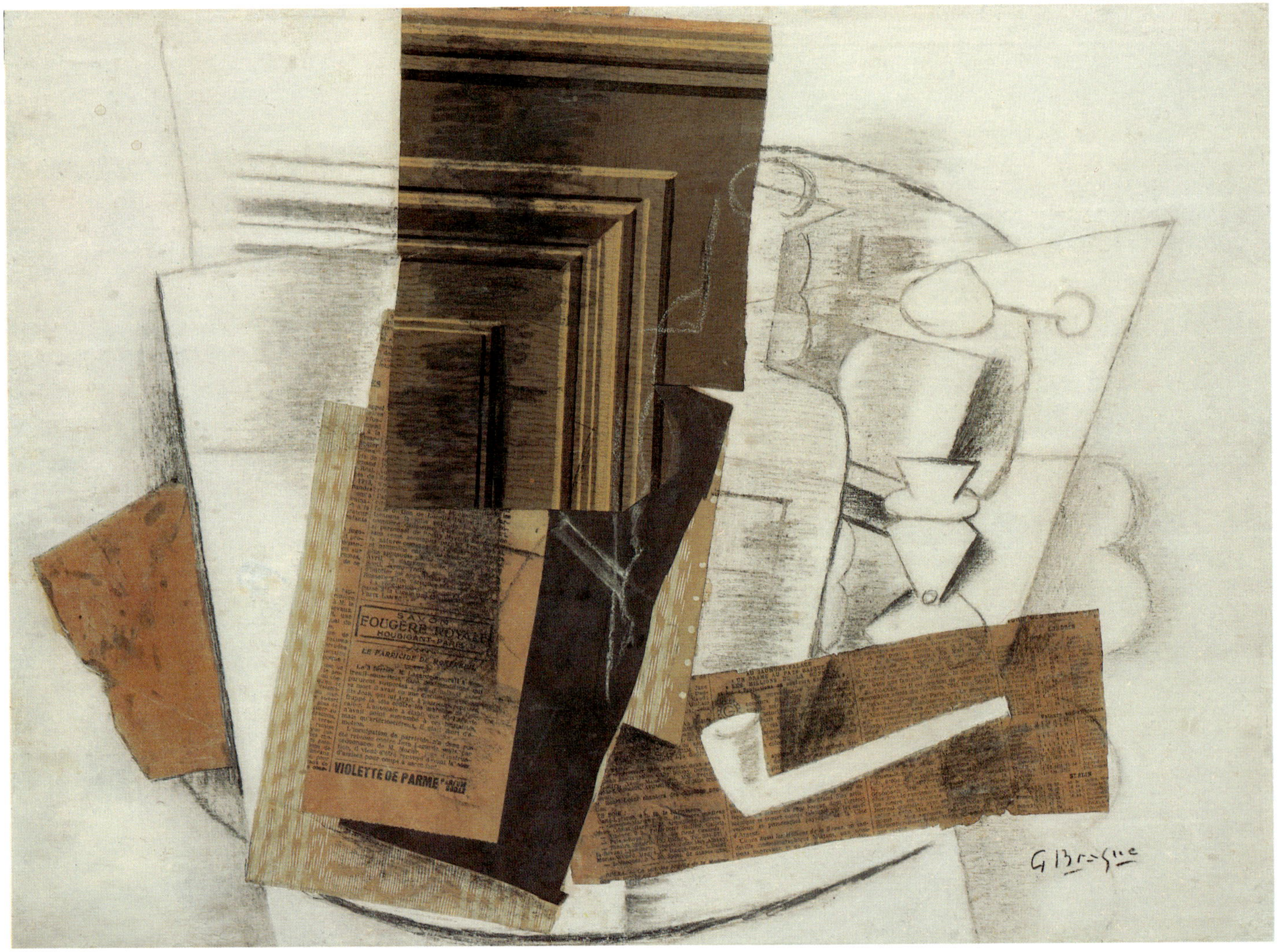

Plate 7 *Still Life with Packet of Cigarettes (Nature morte au paquet de cigarettes),* 1914. Cat. no. 40. John R. Gaines.

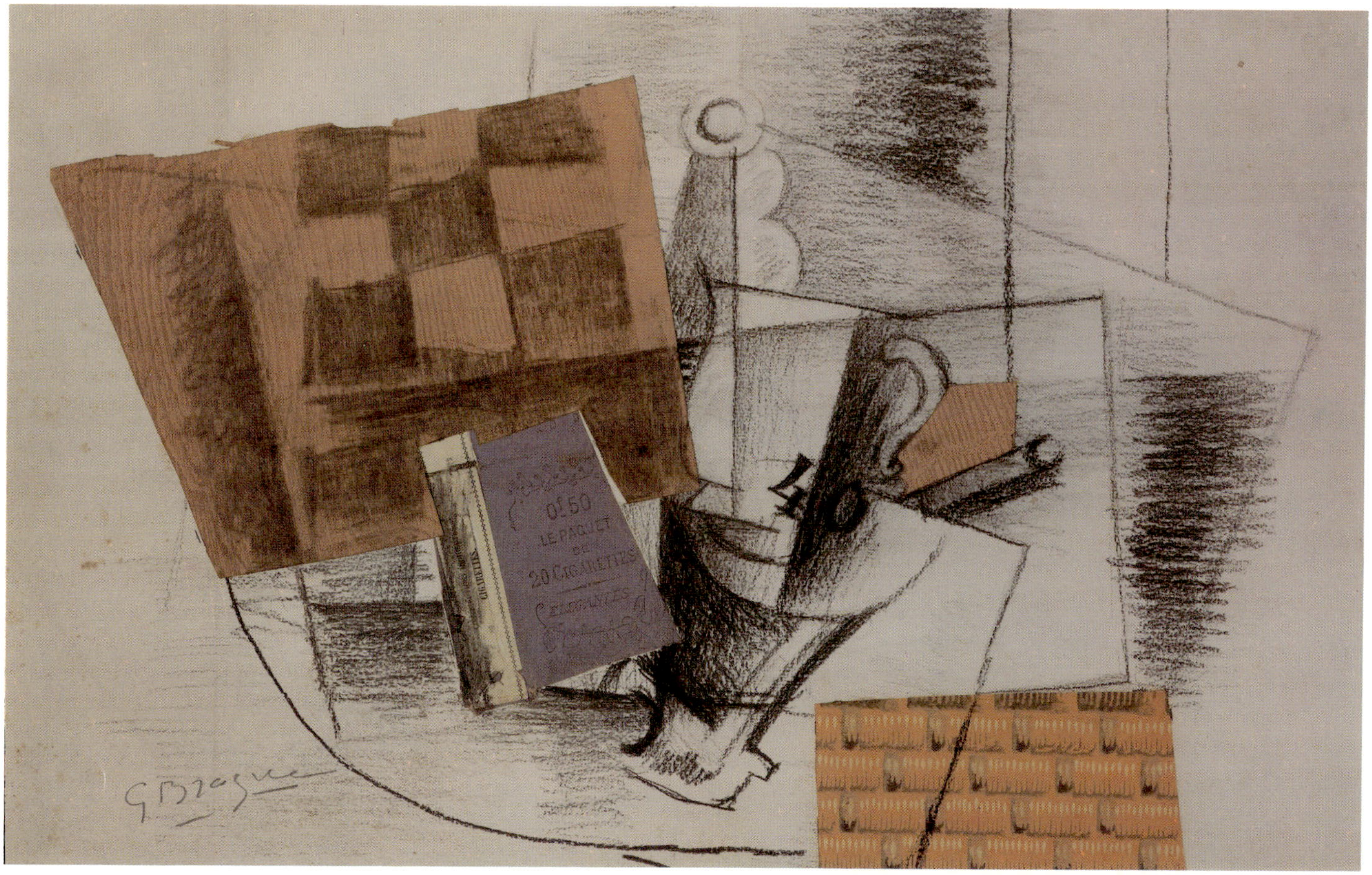

Plate 8 *Bottle, Glass and Pipe ("Violette de Parme")*, 1914. Cat. no. 44. Private collection.

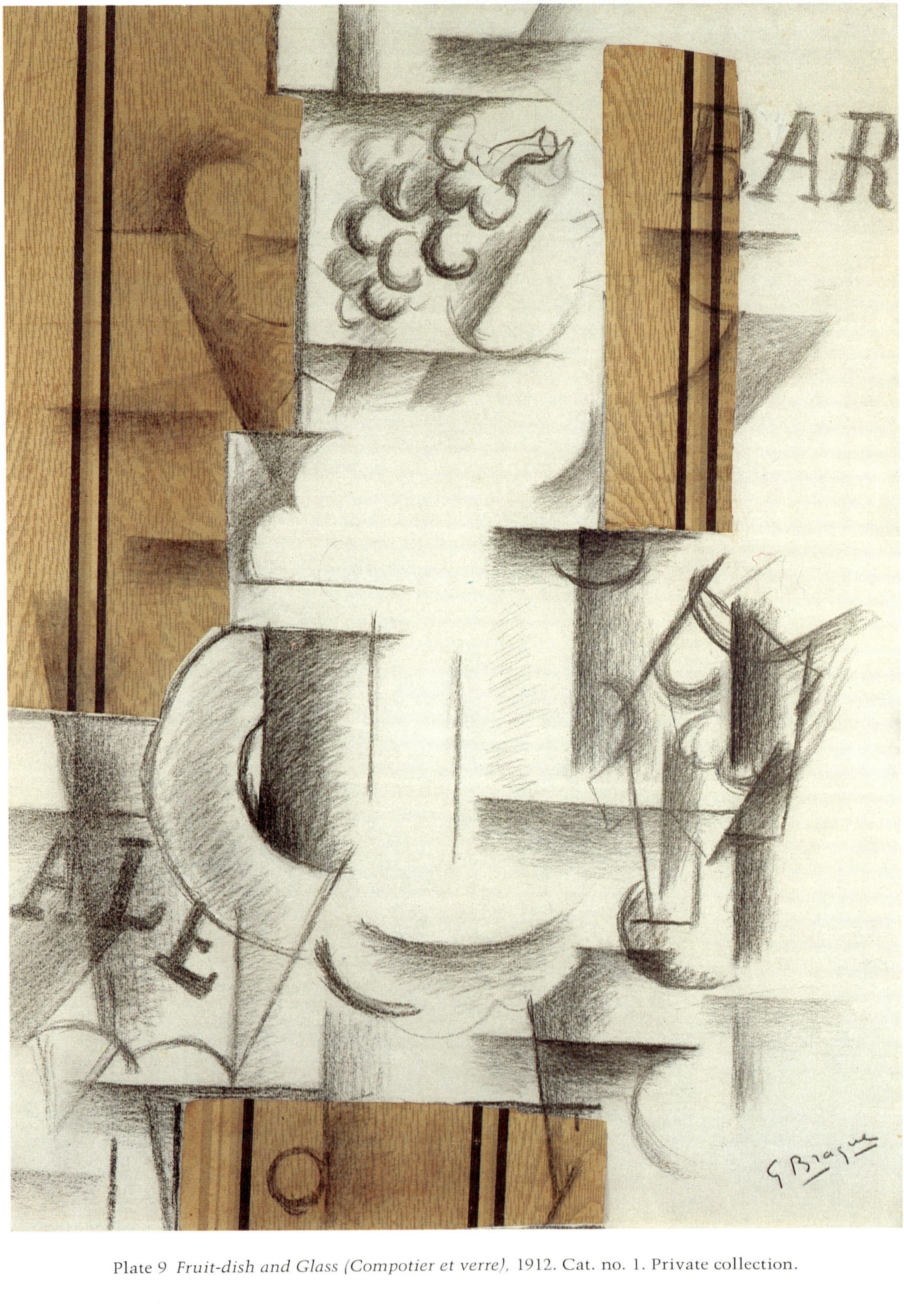

Plate 9 *Fruit-dish and Glass (Compotier et verre)*, 1912. Cat. no. 1. Private collection.

BRAQUE AS INNOVATOR: THE FIRST *PAPIER COLLE*

Douglas Cooper

For Gary Tinterow

ONE DAY IN THE WINTER of 1946-1947, I met by chance in London a runner I knew from Paris, who offered me a *papier collé* by Braque: *Fruit-dish and Glass.* Though signed, this work was not dated. I quickly saw, however, that it must have been executed in 1912. It was a particularly fine example and in excellent condition, so I bought it right away. Thus it became the first *papier collé* by Braque which I added to my collection of, predominantly, works by the four great cubist artists.

I recognized this *papier collé* as one that I had seen reproduced in various publications, specifically among the plates of the small book by Maurice Raynal published by *Valori Plastici* in Rome in 1921, and in 1924 in a French edition of which it was on the cover. But I knew nothing about the past history of this *papier collé,* not even the names of any dealers, galleries, or collectors who had owned it previously. I looked it up first of all in the rather summary *Braque Catalogue* by Georges Isarlov (Paris, 1932), which is little more than a none too accurate list of titles, measurements, and dates compiled from the stockbooks of Braque's principal dealers: Kahnweiler (before 1914), Léonce Rosenberg (1917-1923), and Paul Rosenberg (from 1924 onward). There, I soon identified my newly acquired *Fruit-dish and Glass* with no. 144, although there was a discrepancy in the measurements (62 x 48 cm. instead of 62 x 44.5 cm.). Before 1914, it appeared this *papier collé* had been included in the stock of the Galerie Kahnweiler, by whom it had been acquired, under the terms of a contract with the artist, in the winter of 1912-1913.

At that time, collectors were understandably in doubt as to the lasting properties of the pieces of paper pasted (or sometimes pinned) onto the basic sheet of paper or cardboard which acted as the support. Would they lose their original color with the passage of time? And if so, how would this unbalance the pictorial effect of the artist's original conception? Were *papiers collés* to be regarded as works complete in themselves, or were they no more than an intermediary stage in the evolution of some oil painting?[1] Considerations such as these tended to militate against the saleability of *papiers collés.* Moreover, there was less demand in those days for works by Braque than for works by Picasso,[2] even among those who championed cubist painting, because people tended to think of Braque as a sort of lesser Picasso.

Nevertheless, early in 1913 the Galerie Kahnweiler sold *Fruit-dish and Glass* to Wilhem Uhde, a collector-dealer living in Paris, who was one of the first supporters of Braque and had begun buying his works in 1907. Uhde, like Kahnweiler, was of German nationality, and as a result any pictures belonging to him which were in Paris when war was declared were sequestered by the French State as "Enemy Property." They were offered at public auction when the war was over. Thus *Fruit-dish and Glass* reappeared on the Paris market as no. 69 in the Uhde Sale at the Hôtel Drouot on 30 May 1921. It was then bought for 235 francs by Léonce Rosenberg, owner of the Galerie de l'Effort Moderne, where a major show of recent works by Braque had been held in March 1919. Evidence of this purchase still exists in the form of a Galerie de l'Effort Moderne label stuck on the cardboard backing of this *papier collé* which shows a stock number and the date 30 May 1921. Yet for a long time I hesitated to identify *Fruit-dish and Glass* positively with no. 69 in the Uhde Sale—the only *papier collé* by Braque included in the catalogue—because its measurements were given as 70 x 53 cm., and it was said to be unsigned. I was prepared to account for the strange measurements either by carelessness[3] or by the work's having been measured in a frame. There remained, however, the problem of the signature, which was ultimately clarified when I discovered that *Fruit-dish and Glass* had not been signed by the artist in 1913, when it had been photographed at the Galerie Kahnweiler. Indeed, no matter in what publications I looked, even as late as the 1930s and 1940s, I could find no alternative photograph showing the artist's signature at the bottom right of the sheet as we know it today. I have now been convinced by Madame Monod-Fontaine, who researched the provenance of this *papier collé* independently, that the solution given here is correct.

However, I still do not know at what date Braque signed *Fruit-dish and Glass,* nor at whose request. But I have found out that Léonce Rosenberg sold it to André Breton, from whom it passed, when they separated, to his wife Simone (later Simone Collinet, who became a dealer in the 1950s with a gallery in the rue Furstenberg) and lent it to the Braque exhibition at the Kunsthalle in Basel in April 1933 (cat. no. 60, with a reproduction showing no signature). Maybe it was Simone Collinet who asked Braque to sign the sheet and who was the seller in 1946: I have found no trace of another owner between these two dates.

So much for the past history of *Fruit-dish and Glass.* But when Braque and his wife Marcelle came to dinner at the Château de Castille, where I then lived, on 7 September 1957, I was fascinated and amazed to learn from the artist himself that this was the first *papier collé* he had made, and what is more that it had preceded by at least a week the first *papier collé* executed by Picasso.

During the summer of 1912, these two artists had been trying out different technical means—variations of texture, imitation wood-graining, self-explanatory details and lettering, for example—to make it easier for the eye to interpret objects or figures represented in their pictures. For Braque and Picasso were genuinely concerned that despite their new manner of representation, an apparent connection between the appearance of reality as we know it and the visible content of their paintings should continue to exist. They set out to create and establish a new and strictly pictorial reality, distinct from the reality we know, a reality which would exist in its own right and on equal terms with any other form of reality. And they regarded this pictorial reality as irrefutable because it was a vital part of a newly created "picture-object"[4] existing as a thing in itself. What Braque, as much as Picasso, sought to avoid was that, through paying too much attention to the representation of spatial relationships and details of structure, their pictures might appear even against their will, to be simply figurative abstractions.

To counteract this possibility and to ensure that the spectator would read what was in their pictures both correctly and completely—and not see something different—Braque and Picasso began, in 1911, to include a few realistic and descriptive details—a watch with its chain, a coat-button, a hat; a pair of breasts or a moustache—as recognizable indications. Braque, drawing on his early experience as a house-decorator, used paint in appropriate places to imitate wood-graining or the veins and flecks in marble, while with a paint-comb he simulated the fibrous texture of a beard or the hair on a head. Short or truncated words, musical references and figures, which are easily read, serve to identify certain forms and evoke the setting. But Braque and Picasso found that this lettering was also a useful compositional element, because it provided fixed points within the pictorial space to which the eye could refer as it deciphered the whole composition.

After that, it was only a short step to include in a picture some "real" element representing itself where previously there would have been a re-creation of it in paint. Picasso was the first to take this step when, at the end of May 1912, he pasted a piece of American cloth over-printed with a design of chair-caning onto a small oval canvas and, by means of some well-devised over-painting, integrated it into a still-life composition as the seat of a chair. This procedure is known as *collage*—something pasted—and is distinguished from the technique known as *papier collé,* which was invented three months later, by the fact that the pasted element does not have more than a strictly concrete significance.

Picasso's first collage led to intense discussions between Braque and Picasso, a few weeks later, around other problems whose solutions offered a further challenge to their imaginations. Two of these were particularly pressing: by what means and on what terms it would be possible to revert to using a wide range of colors in their pictures, and how they could overcome a certain "visionary" aspect that was present in order to make them more concrete. A solution to the second of these problems was found through *papier collé* because it offered a way of introducing into a picture what Braque referred to as "certainties," that is to say specific and familiar elements taken straight from the "real" world. These they situated within their picture using a wholly different kind of perspective than if they had been dealing with the same object re-created or imitated in paint. It seemed more difficult to find a new method for working with a range of pure colors. Since 1909, both Braque and Picasso had employed only neutral tones because impressionist and fauve painting had shown them that color was an unstable element subject to disturbing modulations resulting from the play of light or reflected emanations from other colored elements. In 1911-1912, both artists had attempted in a few paintings to enliven the general effect by including passages of pure color which had no descriptive or other purpose: for example, Braque in *The Bottle of Rhum* and *The Violin,* Picasso in *Notre avenir est dans l'air.* But with the invention of the technique of *papier collé,* involving elements which had a given color of their own, the artists learned that form and color exist and function independently of each other. And this discovery led them next to cut out in a sheet of colored paper—which thus assumed a descriptive function—the silhouette of some object they wished to represent, and according to the manner in which they pasted it into the composition could create a contrast which gave it the value of a colored plane.

Undoubtedly Braque, who was of a more rational temperament than the impulsive Picasso, thought a great deal throughout the summer of 1912 about how he was going to proceed in the light of all that he had learned about picture-making in the past few months. That is how he was led to conceive the new technique of *papier collé,* of which he produced the first example, *Fruit-dish and Glass,* in September 1912.

As I go on looking at this picture today, seventy years later, and bearing in mind all that we now know about the stylistic development of cubist painting, from which this picture sprang, I am still amazed by the lucidity of the artist's conception and by the precision of his execution. For, after all, Braque was trying out a new technique for the first time and the conception of this, to my mind, faultless and beautiful *papier collé* can hardly be described as elementary. Subsequently, he was to execute quite a few *papiers collés* which were simpler, less perfect, and less astonishing. But this first example is, I think, a major artistic achievement.

It now turns out that Braque had been preparing in advance to deal with the use of color by a new means. He himself told me—clearly relishing still the gentle irony of the situation and pleased with himself for his wiliness—that a few days before he started on *Fruit-dish and Glass* he was wandering around Avignon when his eye was caught by a roll of paper printed as *faux bois* (oak grain) displayed in the window of a wallpaper shop in the rue Joseph Vernet. His imagination was fired and he began to think about how this *faux bois* paper could help him find a solution. But Braque did not buy a length of it right away: he thought he would wait to do so until Picasso had left for Paris— which he intended to do in the next few days—to organize the move of his belongings into a new studio-apartment at 242, boulevard Raspail. "I had bought the paper and completed *Fruit-dish and Glass* before he returned," Braque added. This little story, which was recounted spontaneously in front of the work itself, is of historical value because it enables us to determine rather exactly the date at which Braque made this *papier collé.* For we know, by the dates on some letters written by Picasso, that he was away from Sorgues between the 3rd and the 12th of September 1912.

The next time Picasso came to the Château de Castille, which was not very long after Braque's visit, I told him what I had heard. "Well, if that's what Braque told you," he remarked, "then it is certainly true and I won't dispute it."

When he saw Braque's latest work, soon after he got back to Sorgues from Paris, Picasso too started to make *papiers collés.* But right from the start the two artists approached the technique in a different spirit, each seeing in it different pictorial and expressive possibilities in accordance with their different temperaments and the nature of their inventive and imaginative inspiration.

Fruit-dish and Glass is a still-life group of two objects standing on a wooden table in front of a wall with wood-paneling. The fruit-dish, in which there is a bunch of grapes, is in the center of the composition. To the right of it stands a stem-glass. The word *ALE* appears at the bottom left, while in the top right corner is the word *BAR:* both words suggest something seen in a café and thus situate the subject within a context. The basic elements of the composition are three pieces of *faux bois* paper cut out and shaped to the artist's needs, the two pieces at the top representing the paneled back wall, while the third piece at the bottom affirms that the table is made of wood and also indicates the drawer (its knob is visible) which fits in beneath the overlapping edge of the table. The fruit-dish, the glass, and the table are drawn in charcoal (with heavy modeling in places) partly on the white surface of the paper, but also partly right over the pieces of pasted paper. These diverse elements are thereby related to each other, while a structural notation determines their relative positions within the imaginary pictorial space. The pasted elements here have only a literal and a descriptive significance, which is true of all of Braque's *papiers collés* made before the spring of 1913: a change of conception becomes evident in *Aria de Bach, Still Life with Guitar,* and *Guitar* (nos. 24, 23, and 27 in this catalogue) in which the pasted papers were selected to make color contrasts and to establish layers of planes.

During the six months that followed the execution of *Fruit-dish and Glass,* Braque investigated the potential structural uses and the coloristic roles that could be extracted from his new technique. At the same time, he observed the freedom which Picasso found in it to release his powers of invention and imagination. Encouraged by all of this activity, Braque ventured in early 1913 to undertake *papiers collés* in which he represented a greater number of objects and used different types of pasted elements—two sorts of *faux bois* paper in the same picture; drawing used to turn a piece of *faux bois* paper into the representation of checkerboard; pieces of newspaper or pieces of black and colored papers (sometimes with a bold decorative pattern over-printed); or wrappings from a packet of tobacco. Thus he became involved in more elaborate compositions. Then in the winter of 1913-1914 Braque made some unexpected innovations: he introduced a topical note in his pasted elements, featuring newspaper advertisements, and including the program from opening night of the Tivoli Cinema in Sorgues (31 October 1913), for example. And a few months later he used corrugated cardboard to evoke the strings of a mandolin. Then in 1914 Braque's *papiers collés* underwent another significant change of character as he began to cultivate a decorative conception. Thus we find him using light colors, generally applied in the *pointillé* technique, to create a sense of space between planes and to give surface animation. At the same time, Braque sets off these light colors against heavy dark tonalities in the background, thus enhancing an illusion of relief.

Braque's use of the technique of *papier collé* was always markedly personal and differs significantly from that of Picasso. For instance, drawing plays a much greater role in Braque's *papiers collés,* because he uses it to define objects as well as to establish spatial relationships between them. One never finds in a *papier collé* by Braque, as one does in a work by Picasso, a piece of newsprint cut and shaped to represent the quantity of wine in a bottle. Braque seems never to have pasted in as a "real" element a playing-card, a piece of music, or a visiting-card: he always chose to draw them. Even the head of a man in a hat, smoking a pipe, is entirely represented by a drawing which establishes its position between two strips of *faux bois* paper, representing the background wall, and spreads across them on both sides. Lastly, there is no *papier collé* by Braque in which one finds a double meaning, a witticism, a sudden touch of fantasy, a malicious thrust or a flash of irony such as one comes across constantly in *papiers collés* and other works by Picasso.

I have ranged far afield from my starting point in *Fruit-dish and Glass.* But I wanted to make clear that when Braque made his first *papier collé* he was not acting on a sudden impulse and had no thought of mockery. That is why I wanted to establish this work, first of all, in the perspective of Braque's stylistic development during the preceding four or five years and went on to examine some pictorial developments that followed from it. But after the end of the war Braque's initial experience with the technique of *papier collé,* which was his personal invention, exerted a new and very considerable influence on his style of painting, and we can follow the workings of this influence throughout the whole of Braque's later oeuvre. Unlike Picasso who, by virtue of his Spanish nationality, was able to pursue his artistic development unhindered throughout the war years, the continuity in Braque's work was broken at the end of July 1914 when he was mobilized in the French army. This fact is important, more especially so because in May 1915 Braque was severely wounded in the head and was unable for that reason too to do any painting during a convalescence that lasted virtually two years. Thus, when he started to work again in 1917-1918 he was without orientation and had to pick up the threads of cubist pictorial developments as best he could. Braque looked back, of course, to the last group of works he had executed in the spring and early summer of 1914. But he was also to find valuable new guidance in *papiers collés* and sculpture which were then being produced by his close old friend Henri Laurens. There is evidence too that Braque was to some extent influenced by the later and more severe cubist idiom of another old friend, Juan Gris.

It is not surprising, therefore, that a new note is sounded in Braque's painting of 1917-1918, especially in some *papiers collés* composed with a greater variety of pasted elements and in which the forms are bolder, the colors stronger, subtler, and more contrasted, and the composition built up on a complex arrangement of overlaid planes. At the same time, Braque developed a firmer and more geometrically determined set of forms and compositional structure while, picking up on a characteristic of some of his last prewar works, he developed a conception akin to sculptural relief. Only subsequently, in 1918-1919, did Braque embark on a series of large-scale still-life compositions which are characterized by large relaxed forms, an overall looseness in the handling, and a richer, more varied, descriptive use of color attached to large planes—just as it had been in some of his *papiers collés* of 1913 and 1914. Thus within two years of starting to work again, Braque had evolved, through a fusion of the past and the present, a wholly new and very personal late cubist idiom.

Fruit-dish and Glass had been made some six years previously and it was the root from which sprang a whole period of Braque's stylistic development leading up to this extraordinary later phase. That is what gives an unexpected degree of significance and importance within Braque's oeuvre to this first *papier collé* and justifies its being described as one of his major imaginative achievements.

NOTES

1. Of course, Braque and Picasso continued to make oil paintings simultaneously with their works in *papier collé,* and it is undeniable that, quite soon after September 1912, there is evidence in their paintings of a stylistic change which is related to their experiences with *papier collé.* However, each *papier collé* was conceived individually as something complete in itself. Neither Braque nor Picasso ever transposed or even attempted to translate one of their own *papiers collés,* as a whole or in part, into terms of an oil painting. Even the *Still Life with an Ace of Clubs* by Braque (1913; Musée national d'art moderne, Paris), the subject matter of which has elements in common with *Fruit-dish and Glass,* the *papier collé* under discussion, is in fact quite a different picture. It was executed perhaps some six months after the *papier collé,* many more objects are represented in it, while its composition and structure are much more elaborate.

2. A comparison between the contracts signed individually by the two artists (Braque's dated 30 November 1912 and Picasso's dated 18 December 1912) with the Galerie Kahnweiler, in which the purchase prices of their ongoing works are specified, makes this quite clear. For whereas Braque received 40 francs for a drawing, Picasso received 100. Moreover, whereas Braque was paid on a graduated scale for his oil paintings from the smallest (less than size 6) at 60 francs per point to size 20 at 200 francs per point, Picasso received 250 francs per point up to and including size 6, and 500 francs per point from then on up to size 20. At sizes 50 and 60 the gap between the two artists was even more marked, Braque receiving only 400 francs per point for either size, whereas Picasso received 1500 and 3000 francs per point. Yet Picasso's output was about three times that of Braque.

3. There are innumerable examples of this in the catalogues of the Kahnweiler and Uhde Sales, as well as in the Isarlov catalogue.

4. *"Tableau-objet"* was a French expression coined in 1911 by Braque and Picasso to designate their intention to create pictures which were not meant to be imitations of any natural models but, instead, new objects added to the "real" objective world and existing there autonomously in their own right.

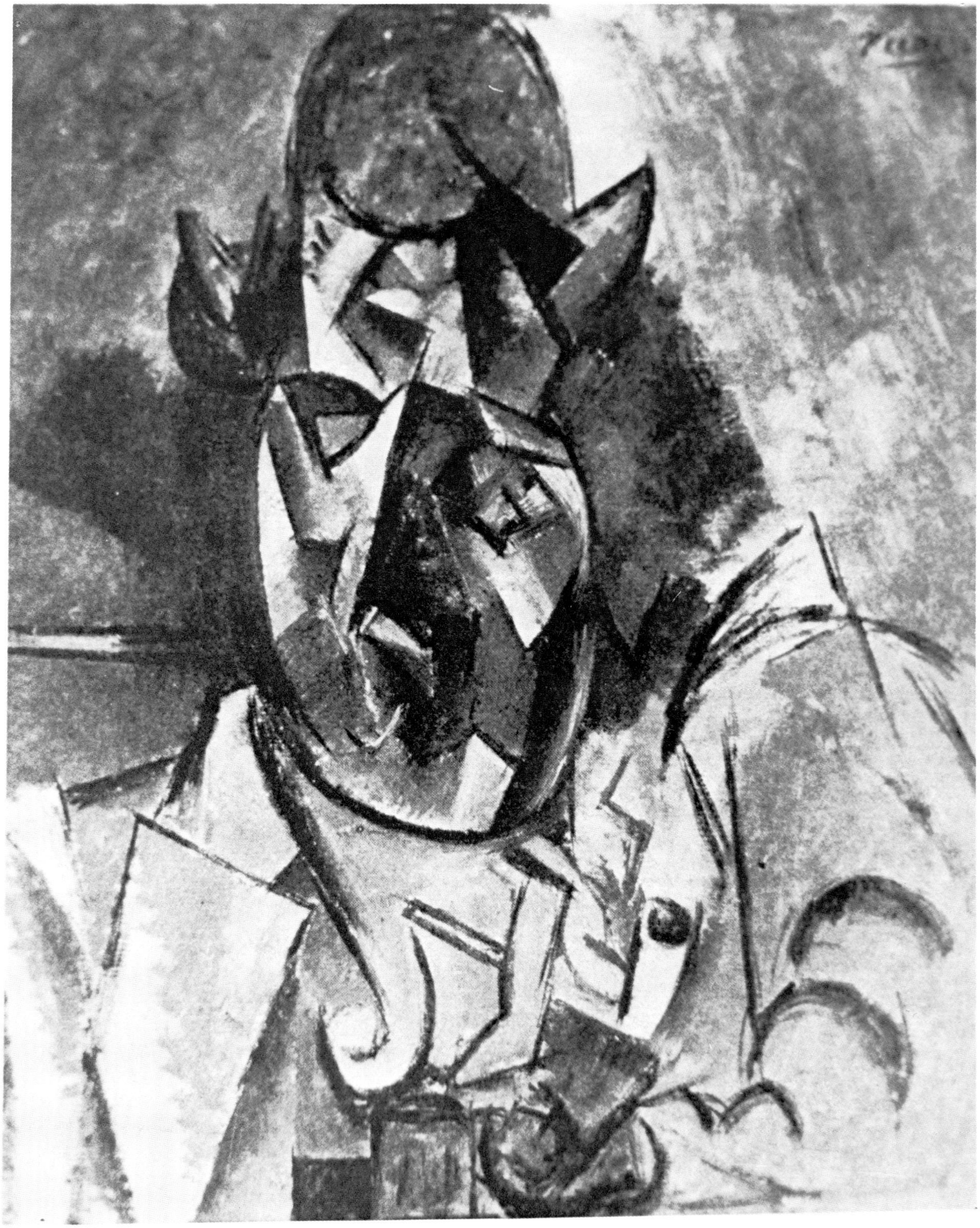

1. Pablo Picasso (Spanish, 1881-1973), *Portrait de Braque,* 1909, oil on canvas. Collection of E. Brageline, New York.

BRAQUE AND PICASSO AT THE TIME OF THE *PAPIERS COLLES*

Pierre Daix

TO DEFINE THE RELATIONS between Braque and Picasso during that astounding revolution which they achieved in concert—the invention and exploration of a radically new medium, *papier collé* —could seem to be, some seventy years later, an academic exercise, indeed a conventional celebration. It is by no means so. That leaps to the eyes in the fact that an exhibition of Braque's *papiers collés* is a clearing up which reviews from top to bottom the established data. The paradox is even more striking in that it is well established that it was Braque who was at the origin of the invention. Indeed, it is the very status of *papier collé* as medium and as creative innovation which is at cause here. It benefited very early, thanks to Aragon (as early as September 1918) and to the surrealists, from an aura of scandal, but its notoriety diverted in some ways, the serious reflection and the concrete study of the works and of their meaning. One will have an idea of this when I point out that, because of a systematic error by Zervos in 1942, in the first general inventory of Picasso's *papiers collés,* his exploration of the medium was completely turned around, with the *papiers collés* of 1913 placed before the initial experiments of the autumn of 1912. This chronological reversal, which prevented all understanding of Picasso's creative processes during such a decisive period, had been accepted without criticism up until the beginning of the 1970s and it is only just during the last years that a coherent order has been reestablished.[1]

Put in another way, until now it has been practically impossible to grasp the cooperation between Braque and Picasso at this precise moment when they were exploring together the medium of *papiers collés.* However, Picasso's work offers the inestimable advantage that, by its utilization of newspaper clippings, not only title fragments or advertisements, but also fairly long strips of printed text—treated as a new color—they allow an easy enough discovery of the newspaper's date of publication, establishing each time an irrefutable *terminus a quo.* Braque not only used newspaper clippings more rarely, but also his style of usage was more discreet. That rendered the search for the newspapers that he included more ticklish, but it must be admitted that this search is still just beginning. Similarly, the collecting of archival data about Braque is way behind as compared to what has been done for Picasso. Let us hope that the reevaluations which are sure to mark this centenary lead to the necessary resumption of scientific study.

The Realism of Cubism

In September 1912, when Braque "invented" his first *papier collé,* it was four full years since the beginning of his "rope climbing party" with Picasso, since their return to Paris in the autumn of 1908 and the discovery that their landscapes made during the summer at La Rue des Bois and l'Estaque put into practice the same lessons of Cézanne. It was also then just five years since their meeting at Bateau-Lavoir when Braque had been impressed by *Les demoiselles d'Avignon* (fig. 3), as tradition has it, but just as much by *Le nu à la draperie (The Nude with a Drapery)* from which he directly derived his *Grand nu (Large Nude)* of 1908 (fig. 2).[2] They therefore already had behind them a long collaboration and a practice of exchanging ideas. However, very remarkably, what is common to them— that is to say what would separate itself from their production if one brought together what they owed to each other and what they evidently discussed together, while eliminating what was peculiar to each— forms a kind of diagram of the history of cubism, if one means by that term the process of breaking away from the perspective and illusionism of the Renaissance.

Let us say, to grossly oversimplify —but so as to adapt ourselves to include the *Nu bleu, souvenir de Biskra (Blue Nude, Souvenir of Biskra)* of Matisse and the *Baigneuses (Bathers)* of Derain in the Salon des Indépendants of 1907, to the *Demoiselles d'Avignon* of Picasso and the *Grand nu* of Braque between 1907 and 1908—that although the two

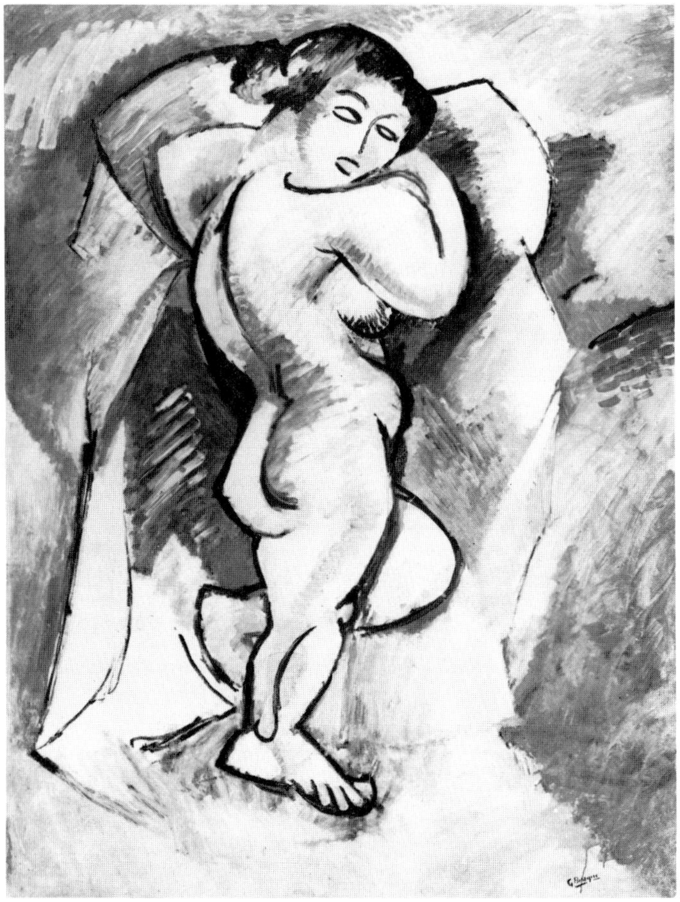

2. Braque, *Grand nu,* 1907-1908, oil on canvas. Collection Alex Maguy, Paris.

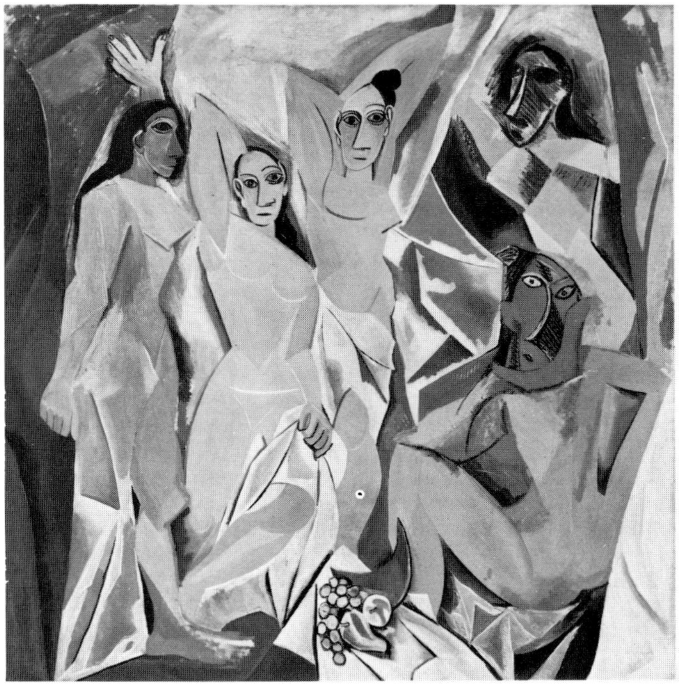

3. Pablo Picasso (Spanish, 1881-1973), *Les demoiselles d'Avignon,* 1907, oil on canvas. The Museum of Modern Art, New York. Acquired through the Lillie P. Bliss Bequest.

generations from Manet (born in 1832) to Seurat (born in 1859) had not ceased to struggle between the preeminence of the exterior reality over painting and that of the practical reality of the latter, cubism settled definitively in favor of the second. If the *Demoiselles d'Avignon* takes on the value of a clap of thunder, and Alfred Barr would see in it the birth of cubism, it is because it proclaims the break of painting from nature—let us be more precise, from "exterior" nature. If Picasso there bluntly overturns the natural appearance of his prostitutes, he also learns to respect the natural physics of the space which appears on the canvas, the physics of contrasts of graphic rhythms, contrasts of imagined, and imaginary, colors. In the last anaylsis, for the illusionist representation of the actual physical reality of his group of female nudes he substitutes the physical realities, analyzed optically, of the outlines and the fields of colored pigments which his gestures have disposed on the sized rectangle of his large canvas. Realism is passed, during the realization of this painting, from the illusory representation of exterior reality to the optical communication of material modifications worked by the artist on his canvas. Reality, too. Art, in one blow, is no longer the access to a transcendency of which the craft and the material contingencies are only the interpreter (which pushes to conceal them), but at first work with the material in order to force the latter to produce a signification, indeed the transcendency. The language of painting is more important than its representation. It is necessary therefore to conserve its accidents, its hesitations, its corrections, indeed its slips.

The *Demoiselles d'Avignon* scream it. The difference between Picasso's landscapes at La Rue des Bois and Braque's at l'Estaque mark, in the autumn of 1908, how much the two painters had refined their understanding of the syntax of this language during that year. They had simplified natural forms reduced to their geometry—what was to make Vauxcelles speak of "schemes" and of "cubes" before Braque's houses—and recreated Cézanne's inversions of perspective which project the forms toward the spectator from the material surface of the painting, achieving an optical depth rather than an illusionist one. They perceived the impact of architecture, opposing curved "organic" rhythms of trees to the rectilinear cadences of the houses, and knew how to explore the "passages" induced by the rhythms between the spatial container/holder and identifiable forms. What distinguishes them is that Picasso challenged the third dimension only by the accumulated contrasts of volumes against each other, which eliminated "air," the atmospheric sensation of natural space and led to a certain dryness in the oppositions of colors. Braque, by contrast, knew how to recapture Cézannesque gradations of tone, that is to say the fine vibrations of the colored surface which allow the planes to be turned under our gaze, to make an atmosphere quiver, and to engender an internal dynamic in the painting, to animate the "passage" from a simple overture to a communication, and the inversion of perspective to a mobile invasion of forms toward the spectator.

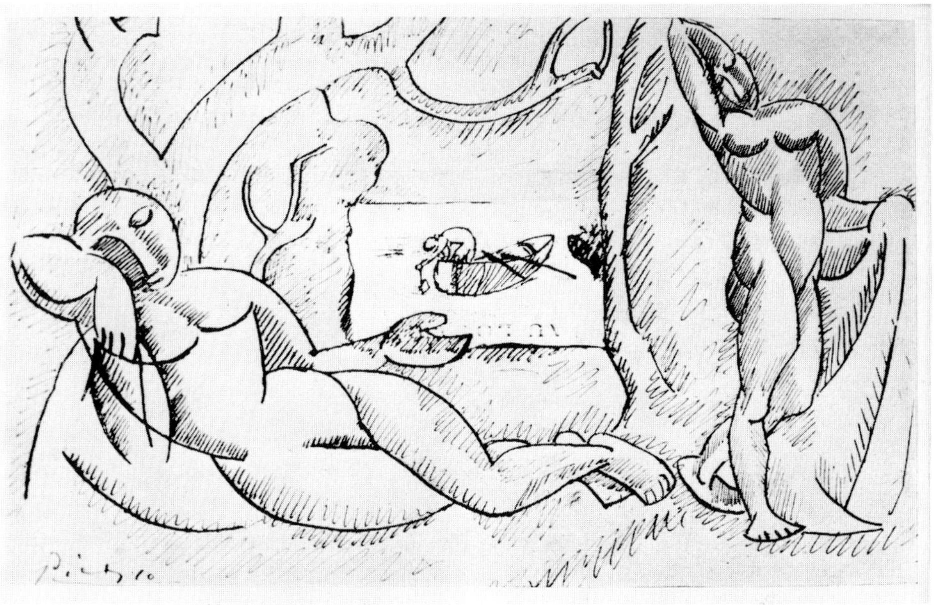

4. Pablo Picasso (Spanish, 1881-1973), *Study for "L'Offrande,"* 1908, drawing. Location unknown.

It is this which authorizes William Rubin to speak of an "advance" on Braque's part over Picasso in matters of Cézannism during the summer of 1908, and as he showed in his article "Cézannisme and the Beginnings of Cubism,"[3] one confirms that Picasso felt this advance and in consequence modified his large canvas *Trois femmes (Three Women)* by removing the contrasts of hatched rhythms and primitive deformations in favor of the introduction of gradations allowing the geometricized planes to turn and to reestablish rhythm by the very dynamics of the volumes. The solution was not found in the deepening of the reference to exterior reality, but in the optical expression proper to painting, in the autonomous grammar of painting.

Certainly, I am trying to rationalize and translate into the language of the end of the twentieth century an experience which the painters of the time, like Cézanne himself, could only conduct by feeling their way and without the support of adequate intellectual equipment nor of a theory of vision. But, if examination of the gradations and passages in Braque's works shows us that it is indeed at this level that he knew how to read Cézanne, we have with Picasso other proofs which teach us that, independently, he knew how to spot other deviations of Cézannesque pictorial expression of space from traditional illusionist representation and that he also had asked himself the question about purely optical effects capable of provoking the sensation of depth. Curiously enough, this reflection will lead us to the first known collage by Picasso, a collage without a follow-up, which is certainly not a *papier collé* in the strict sense, even though it broaches the problem.

In the series of studies on the theme of *L'offrande (The Offering)* which he finished in the beginning of 1908 (fig. 4), Picasso is seen creating depth by darkening the figures of men in the foreground and violently illuminating the nude woman in the distance, which is a reprise in reverse of the classical lighting of the young Cézanne in *Une moderne Olympia (A Modern Olympia)* or *L'après-midi à Naples (Afternoon in Naples)*.[4] However, in a contemporary drawing,[5] which repeats the same problem of opposing horizontal and vertical figures, but this time with two nude women against a forest background, one finds the same contrasted lighting, realized with great power by a collage gouached with white. The recognized reference is this time no longer to Cézanne, but rather to the *Déjeuner sur l'herbe* of Manet and to its central gap of light, especially since the third person, indifferent to the two women in the foreground, is also on a river. This collage has all the characteristics of a guidepost and therefore from the start has an effect of chance due to the use of a brighter paper, but Picasso heightened this effect with gouache, without in any way annulling the intrusion of collage, since one can still see that it is an entry ticket . . . to the Louvre. This points up already the effects of humor taken in 1912-1913 from the misappropriation of newspaper titles and advertisements. Of course one can think that this repair is later than the drawing. But Zervos dated it to the beginning of 1908, as did Thannhauser, who had Picasso sign it much later in 1939. It is most likely that this discovery was then accidental. It was too early in 1908 for Picasso to know how to make the most of it.

Optical realism then manifested itself to Picasso mainly by impossibilities. Kahnweiler relates, that in 1909, doubtless at about the time when he began to "break" the three

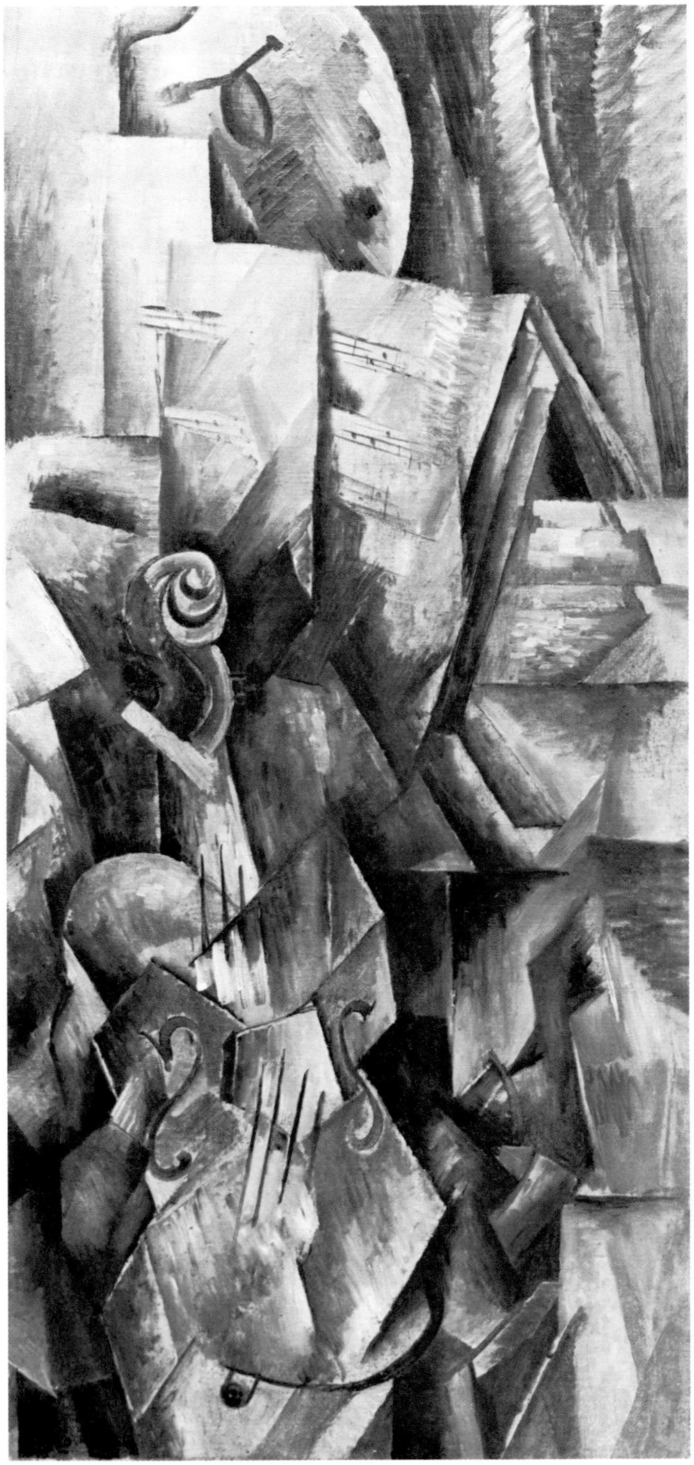

5. Braque, *Violon et palette*, 1910, oil on canvas. The Solomon R. Guggenheim Museum, New York. Photo: Robert E. Mates.

dimensional forms of the *Tête de Fernande (Fernande's Head)* or the *Pomme (Apple)*, Picasso tried to make projections on his paintings that would articulate his painted planes under the gaze, but he failed.[6] The refinement of the fragmentation of form, then its discontinuity required monochrome painting, almost without color. Each time Picasso tried in 1910 to introduce color into a painting, "with equal right" as Kahnweiler put it, that is to say for itself without blending or gradations, he had to cover it over because it destroyed his composition. In truth, by the fragmentation of surfaces, Picasso and Braque had arrived at using a unitarian pictorial handwriting, capable of expressing in the same fashion a figure or an object and the spatial container. One of the masterpieces of this kind was the *Portrait de Vollard (Portrait of Vollard)* from the spring of 1910. In this way the figure or the object is nothing more than a modulation of the space, a condensation of the discontinuity.

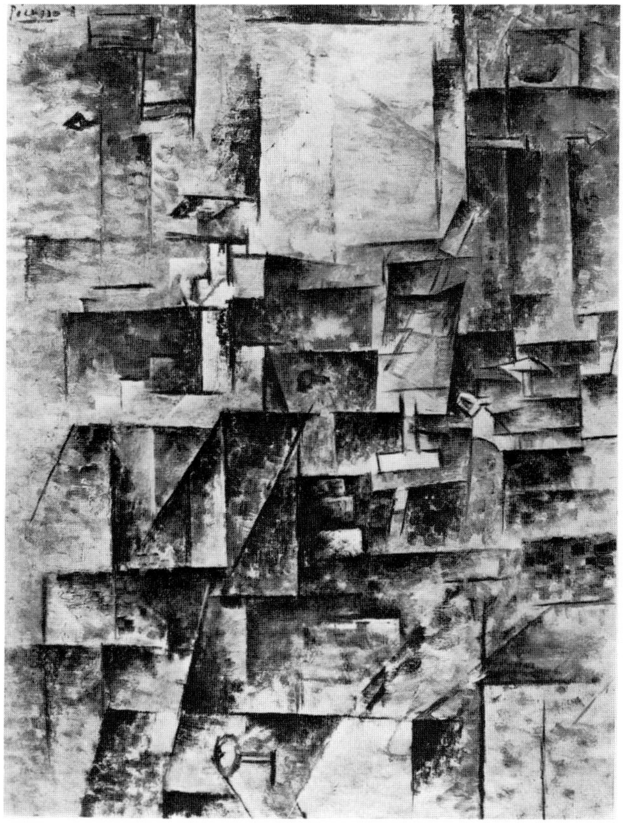

6. Pablo Picasso (Spanish, 1881-1973), *La table de toilette*, 1910, oil on canvas. Location unknown.

The key was elsewhere than in the optical effects and it is Braque who found it. He was looking for something completely different, essentially to anchor in space still-life compositions that were so finely fragmented that one's gaze could no longer articulate the space. He then made up a way to paint a form which could not be fragmented, but which would still identify the articulations of the space—the famous nail in *trompe l'oeil* in his large vertical still lifes such as *Violon et palette (Violin and Palette;* fig. 5*)*, and *Broc et violon (Jug and Violin)*.

Instead of adding physical information, as Picasso was trying to do, Braque, in sum, had the idea of introducing intellectual information, "conceptual" as Apollinaire would later say. The nail, contrary to the projections or fields of pure color, did not disrupt the total grasp of the painted space, but it modified our mental interpretation of it and in the same way our deciphering, our reading, our penetration of a work which, while offering itself in one stroke to our gaze, compelled it to numerous exploratory courses.

This was a discovery of instinct that no theory of vision could yet support. It is no more so today. Henceforth we know that our vision does not passively receive an imprint of objects, but that our brain treats the information received by an optical sweep of our eyes, that it confronts it with the stock of information coded in our memories, in such a way that our vision depends not only on the contrasted stimuli of wavelengths, but also on the fact that the outlines are accepted or not as identifying known objects. Picasso went too fast. Unexpected color did not pierce the canvas because of its rupture with the surrounding monochrome, but because it was abstract; its information did not belong to the stock in our memory.

It is this which explains Braque's second breakthrough at the time of his meeting with Picasso at Céret during the summer of 1911. In the interval, the two friends had multiplied the inventory of informative landmarks. The nail could be replaced by a key in its lock: *La table de toilette (Vanity Table;* fig. 6*)*

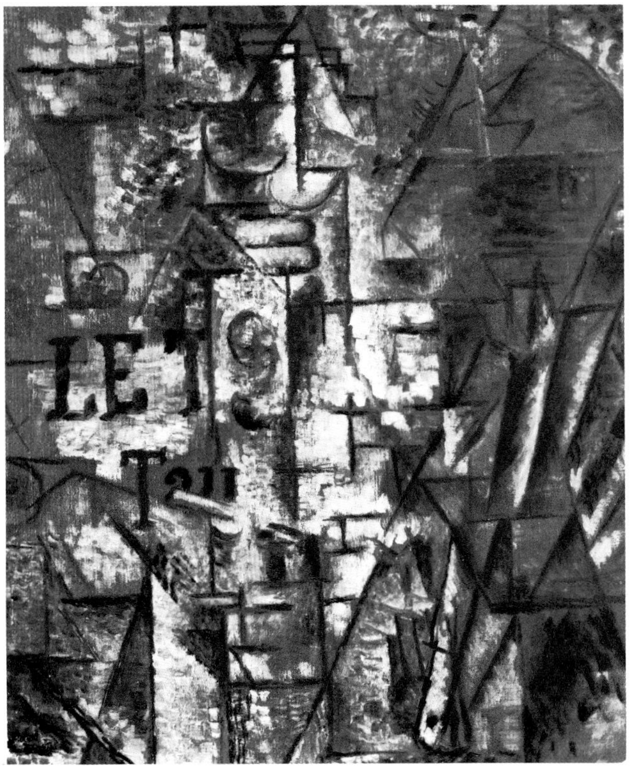

7. Pablo Picasso (Spanish, 1881-1973), *Le Torero,* 1911, oil on canvas. Private collection.

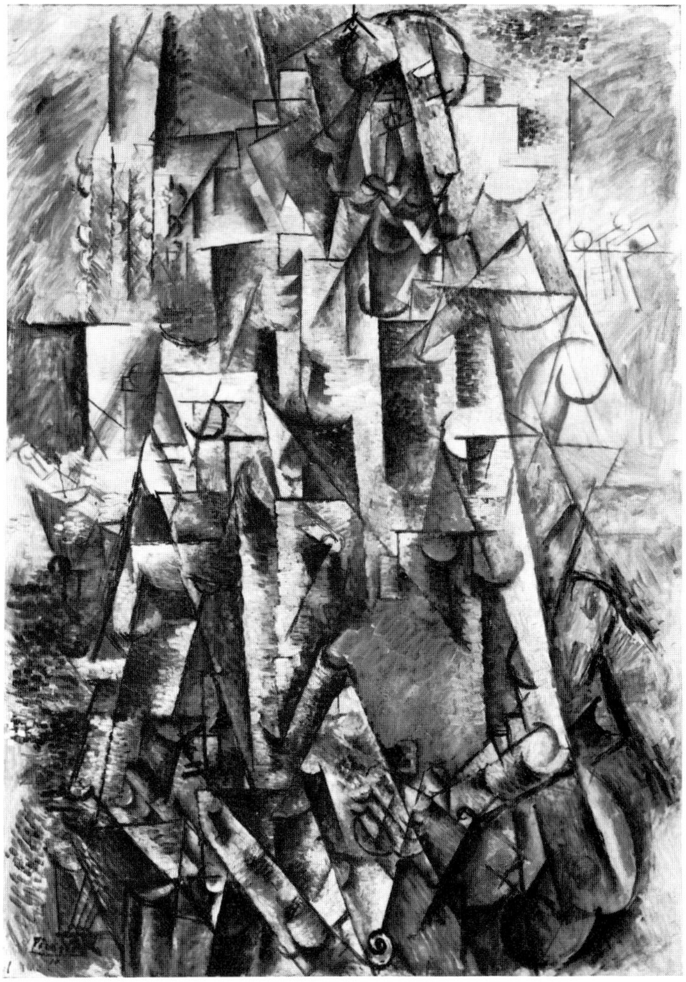

8. Pablo Picasso (Spanish, 1881-1973), *Le poète,* 1911, oil on canvas. The Peggy Guggenheim Collection, Venice; The Solomon R. Guggenheim Foundation, New York.

(Picasso, Cadaquès, 1910);[7] then by an anchor, the handle of a cup, a curtain-loop, the stem of an apple, the fringes of a rug, which would lead to the hole of the violin and the circle of the guitar. Braque, on his side, took up again the spatial guidelines already discovered by great predecessors: in *La table (The Table)* of 1910,[8] the drawer knob dear to Cézanne, the oblique line of a knife coming from Manet, a fan or the verticality of the bottle; in *Le pyrogène et Le Quotidien (The Pyrogène and Le Quotidien),* the newspaper in the fan of its folding with the marks of its painted letters as they were before in van Gogh.[9]

It is exactly this that Picasso takes stock of at Céret, adding to it the pipe and clarinet, but detaching the letters from the surface of the newspaper title in *Le Torero* (fig. 7) and *La bouteille de rhum,*[10] that is to say, treating them as pure signs outside of the object.

He then felt himself strong enough to pass from still lifes to figures in which he organized, on a pyramidal armature, information that, in the *Portrait de Kahnweiler (Portrait of Kahnweiler)* of the preceding winter, was still spread over the canvas according to the order of appearances. *L'homme à la pipe (Man with a Pipe), Le poète (The Poet;* fig. 8*)* of the Peggy Guggenheim Foundation, and *L'accordéoniste (The Accordionist),*[11] are successes which must have impressed Braque since he answered them with his large canvas of *Le Portugais (The Portuguese;* fig. 9*),* a guitar player. But he there made a step of extreme importance in completely dissociating the informative guidelines from the composition. To do this, instead of remaining tributaries of the paint-

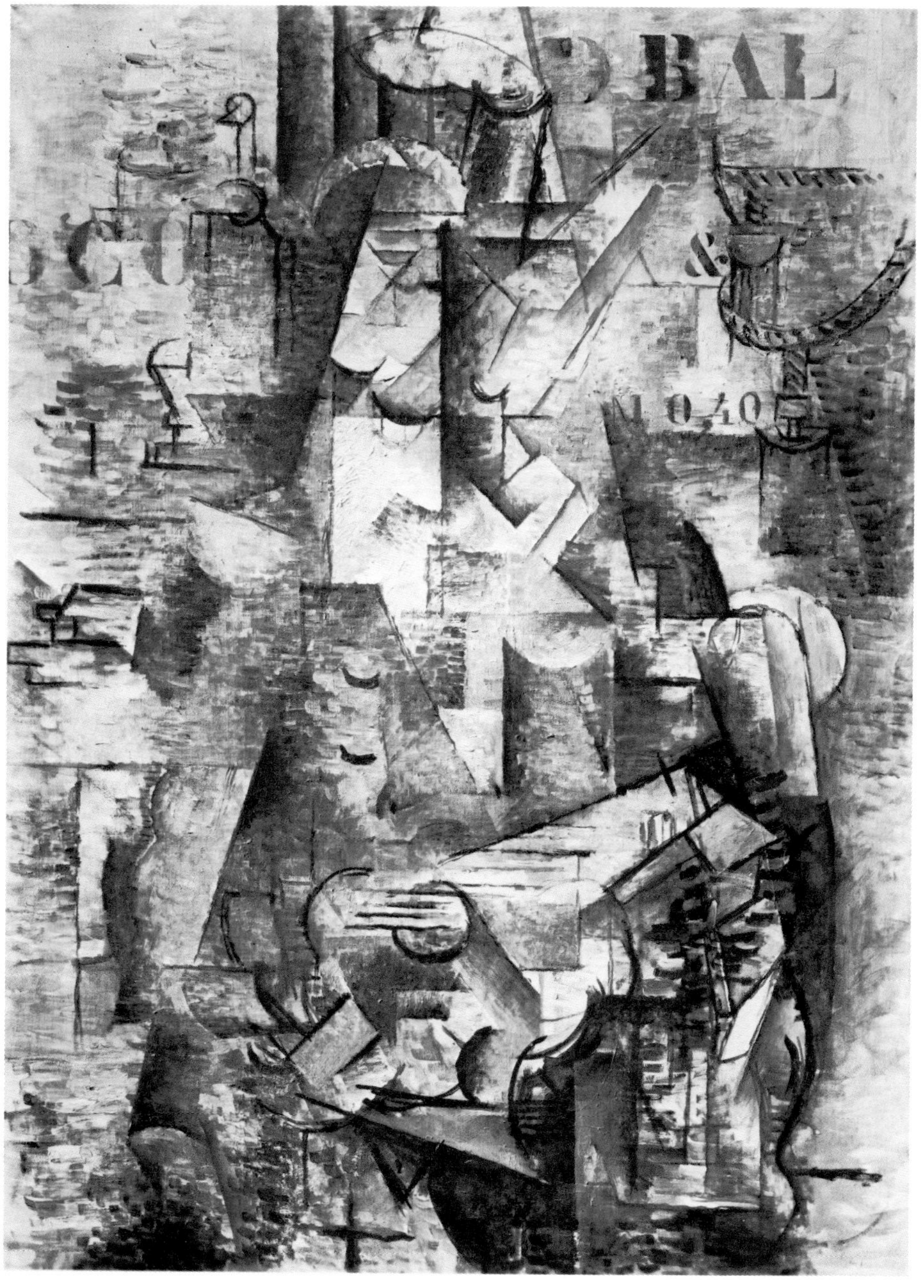

9. Braque, *Le Portugais,* 1911, oil on canvas. Offentliche Kunstsammlung-Kunstmuseum, Basel.

er's hand and of *trompe l'oeil,* they were exteriorized, objectivized, by the standardized form of the letters and numbers painted with mechanical stencils.

The effect of contrast, of rupture, was then no longer produced only by the identification of optical information, but by the fact that, even though painted, this information no longer belonged either to the subjectivity nor to the hand of the artist. It took on the value of an inclusion of the exterior world and of an intrusion. And even though Picasso, to signify the spatial environment of his still lifes and his figures, had not progressed much since the unitarily fragmented handwriting of the *Portrait de Vollard* and the reference points of the *Portrait de Kahnweiler,* reusing for example in the background of *Le poète* the Cézannesque pipe-rack which had served him since 1907, Braque by his stenciled inscriptions, created by allusion a bistro window with its advertisements in block letters. He thus created a difference of levels in the painting, a difference of levels in the pictorial handwriting which neutralizes and objectifies itself; a difference of levels in the information by the presence of an exterior reality, independent of "art."

From the Discovery of Collage to the Invention of Papier Collé

The stencil effect would practically not be repeated by Braque, and Picasso would wait until the winter of 1911-1912 and even, no doubt, till the beginning of spring to use it in his turn in *Le bouillon kub (The Bouillon Cube),* Prague's *Violon, verres, pipe et ancre (Violin, Glasses, Pipe and Anchor;* fig. 10*),* and the large recapitulatory still life in the Berggruen collection (fig. 11).[12]

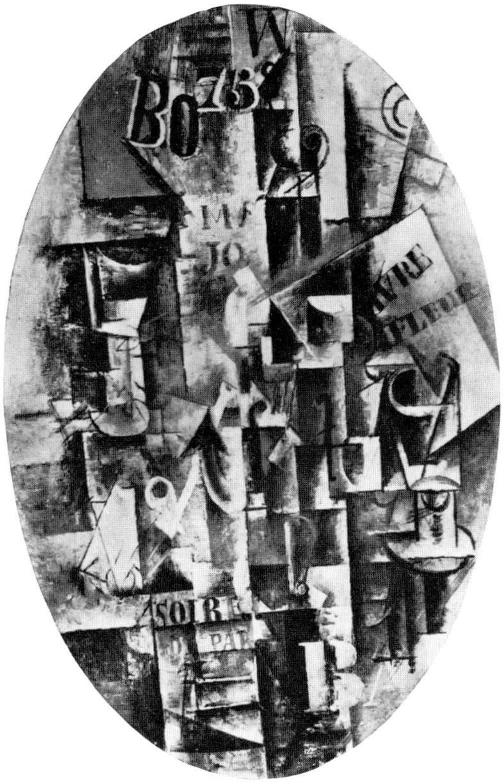

10. Pablo Picasso (Spanish, 1881-1973), *Violon, verres, pipe et ancre,* 1912, oil on canvas. National Gallery of Prague.

In return, he then used the stencil effect to accentuate the intrusion of exterior information by painting the numbers of *Violon, verres, pipe et ancre* in red. Color, which could not be introduced as evidence of obvious appearances, could be if it was conveyed by the informative rupture. This was Picasso's great concern at the beginning of 1912. He placed some blue in the streamers of *Souvenir du Havre*[13] and, at the top of the canvas, the colors of the French flag (fig. 12). Above all, he imitated a sample of raw reality with pieces of imitation wood. This use of a decorative painter's technique reveals the influence of Braque (whose father and grandfather ran a painting business) and involves him in the search for pieces of painting which seem to be beyond the painter's hand.

If, in the *Bouteille de Pernod et verre (Bottle of Pernod and Glass;* fig. 13*)*,[14] the imitation wood indicates the surface of a table, in *Souvenir du Havre* it is dissociated

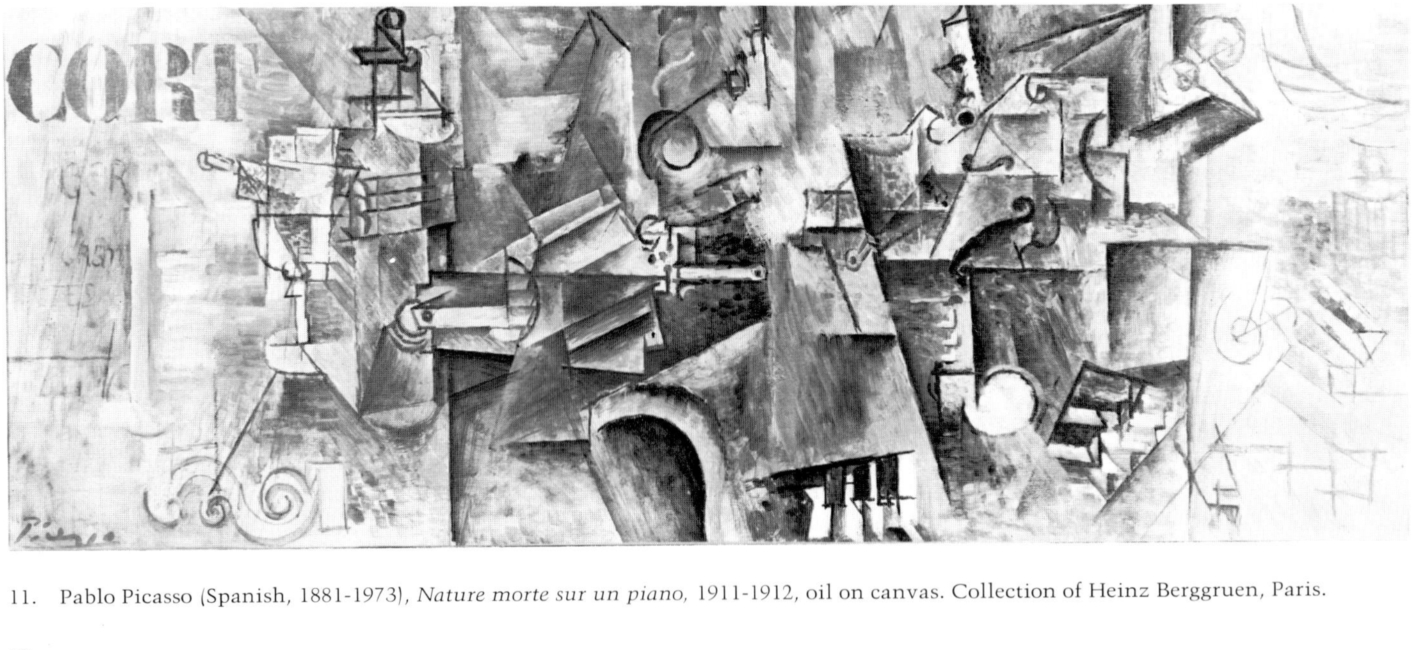

11. Pablo Picasso (Spanish, 1881-1973), *Nature morte sur un piano,* 1911-1912, oil on canvas. Collection of Heinz Berggruen, Paris.

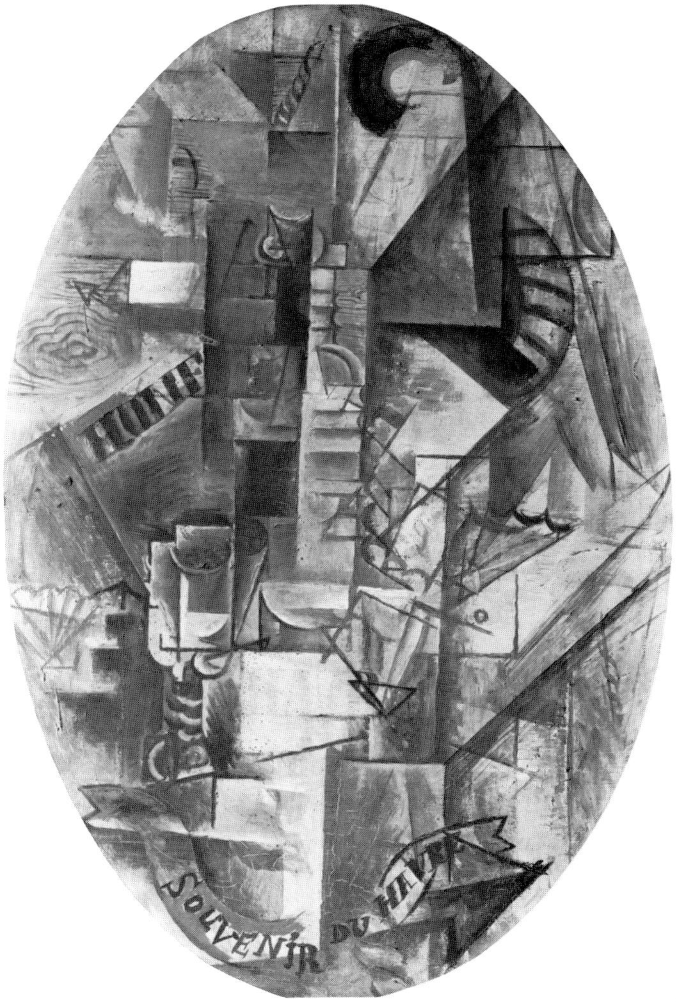

12. Pablo Picasso (Spanish, 1881-1973), *Souvenir du Havre,* 1912, oil on canvas. Private collection, Basel.

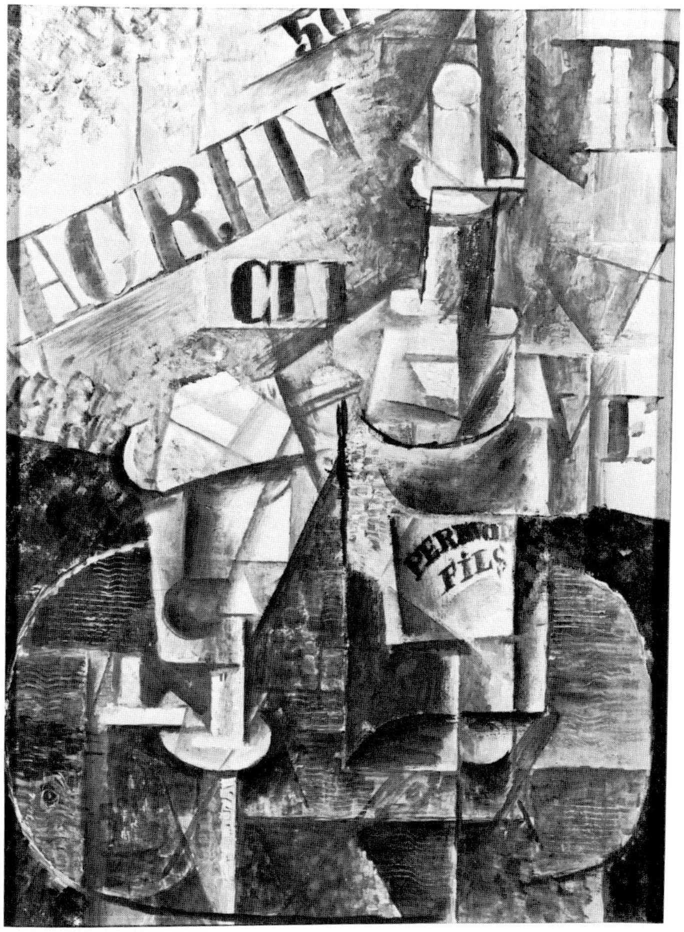

13. Pablo Picasso (Spanish, 1881-1973), *Bouteille de Pernod et verre,* 1912, oil on canvas. The Hermitage Museum, Leningrad.

from all objects, pure information like the inscriptions or the French flag. The small oval canvas, *La lettre (The Letter),* bears a real pasted stamp and, still in the oval format, the *Nature morte à la chaise cannée (Still Life with a Caned Chair;* fig. 14*)*,[15] framed with rope, contains a piece of waxed canvas bearing an imprinted caning motif from a still life painted in the figuration of the moment.

This first collage introduced an effect of undeniable reality, but Picasso, far from using it to create the illusion of a support of canework for his objects, contented himself with placing on it a part of the base of his glass, taking great care to signify with a horizontal stroke a border which separates it in two and dissociates the information from the representation of a chair. I emphasize this dissociation because it is of utmost importance. The inscriptions can overlap and be broken up in a like manner—they are never complete. Not only to conserve their allusive force and mystery, but also because, to contribute from the outside to the composition, they must show themselves at the same time both independent and open to integration in the painting. The French flag in Picasso's series of still lifes on the theme *Notre avenir est*

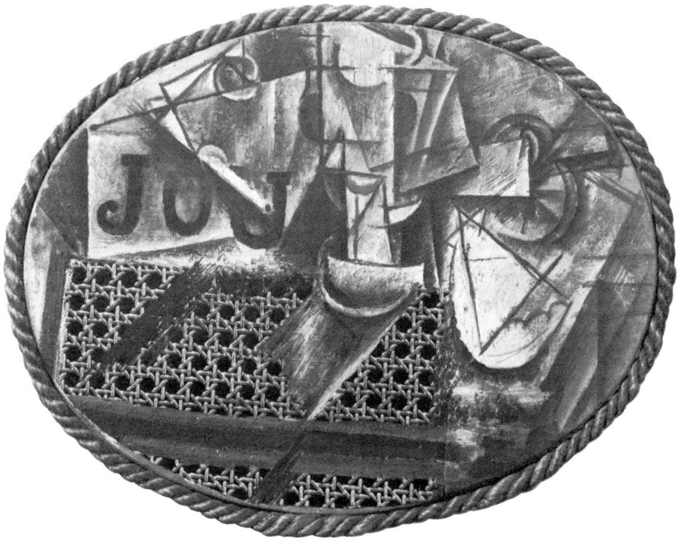

14. Pablo Picasso (Spanish, 1881-1973), *Nature morte à la chaise cannée,* 1912, oil and oilcloth on oval canvas, encased with rope. Musée Picasso, Paris.

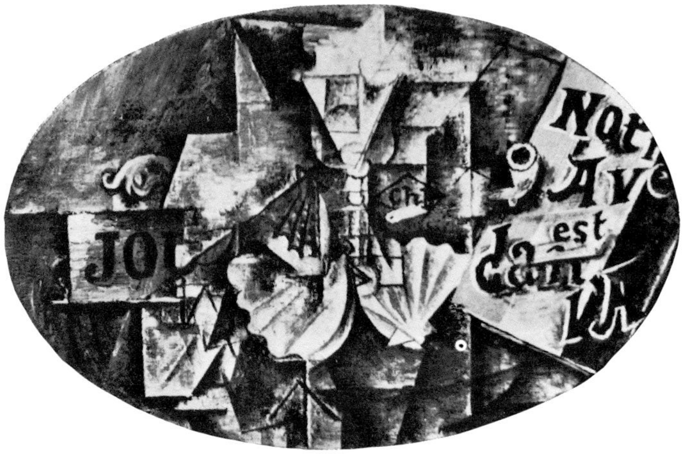

15. Pablo Picasso (Spanish, 1881-1973), *Notre avenir est dans l'air,* 1912, oil on canvas. Private collection, New York.

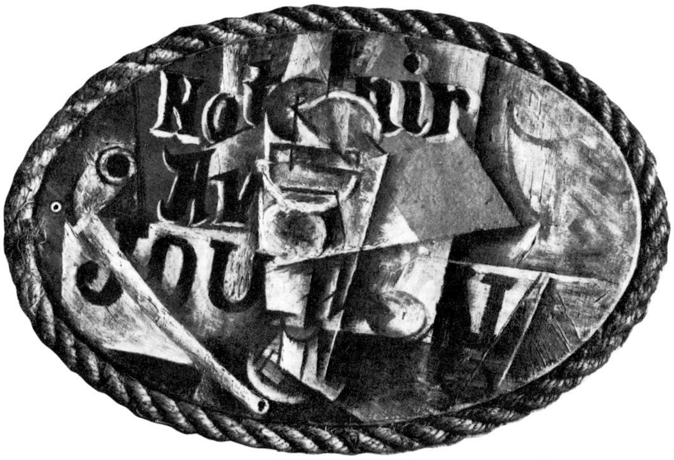

16. Pablo Picasso (Spanish, 1881-1973), *Notre avenir est dans l'air,* 1912, oil on canvas. Location unknown.

17. Pablo Picasso (Spanish, 1881-1973), *Nature morte espagnole,* 1912, oil on canvas. Private collection, France.

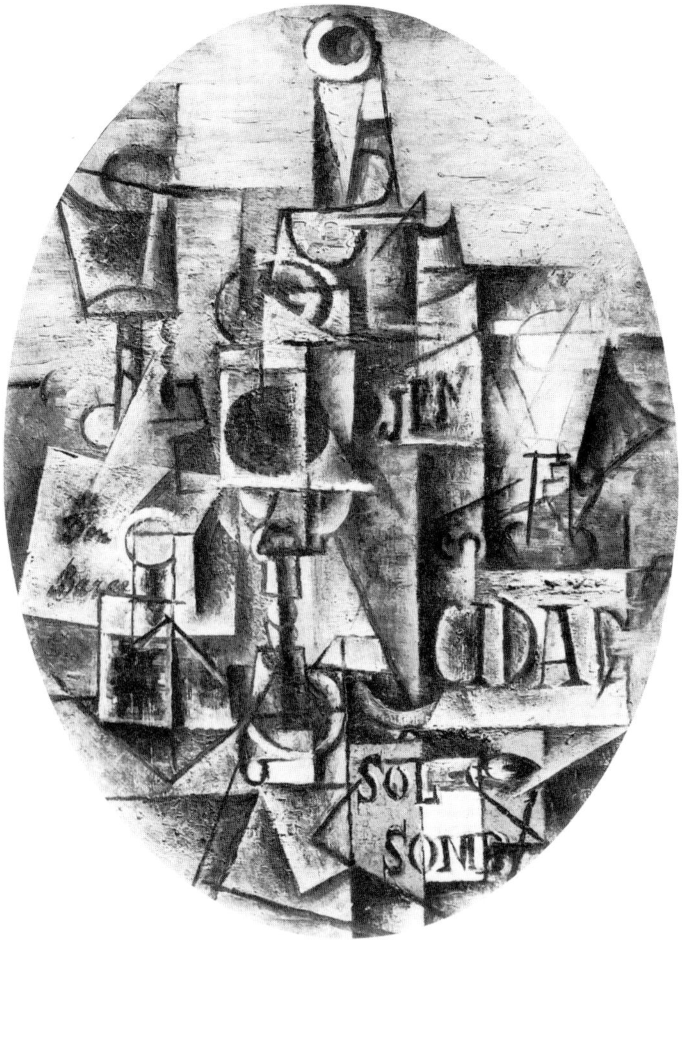

dans l'air (Our Future Is in the Air; figs. 15-16*),*[16] if it henceforth screams its tricolor fields, is integrated by the very defects of the inscription which covers it. It is not closed on its entirety.

This breakthrough on Picasso's part is deeply marked by Braque's contributions, not only following reflection on the effect of stenciling and the use of techniques taken from decoration, but also by the use of oval formats which eliminate all the dead angles of the spatial container and allow, by tightening up the composition, the neutralizing of the imbalance which the introduction of pure colors could produce.

After the eventful interruption of his trip to Céret with Eva, his new companion, Picasso moved to Sorgues, near Avignon, where Braque joined him in July 1912 with his young wife. It was there, in their shared solitude, that the two painters would be able to define these effects of dissociation which stenciled letters and numbers, fragments of pure color, pieces of imitation wood, and collages provoked equally in their compositions. Picasso, in his *Nature morte espagnole (Spanish Still Life;* fig. 17*)*,[17] made at Céret, thought of including Ripolin (enamel paint). This is commercial painting in "great" painting, but also a new effect of lacquer which gives the red and yellow bands of the ticket for entry to the arenas the value of collage even though they are painted. Thus can one imitate by the various means of painting the optical unevenness of collage, translate it as it were. At Sorgues, he would introduce a completely alien element, unfortunately now lost, into a guitar: a gingerbread heart bearing the inscription *"J'aime Eva"* ("I Love Eva"),[18] which confirmed that the painted indication of relief could support an actual and exterior relief (fig. 18). Moreover, in the Pushkin Museum's *Le violon (The Violin;* fig. 19*)*,[19] he came to introduce a horizontal white stroke in slight relief which "brings out" the volumes of the instrument's case from the plane of the canvas by its optical power alone.

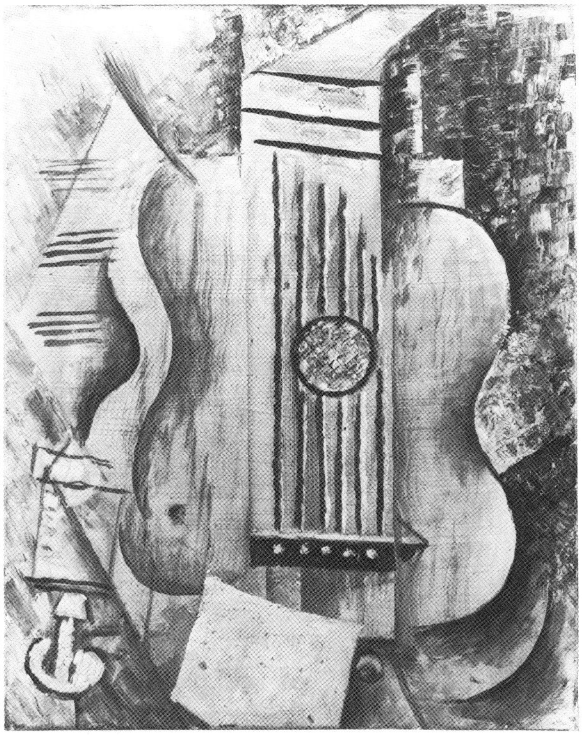

18. Pablo Picasso (Spanish, 1881-1973), *"J'aime Eva,"* 1912, oil on canvas. Musée Picasso, Paris.

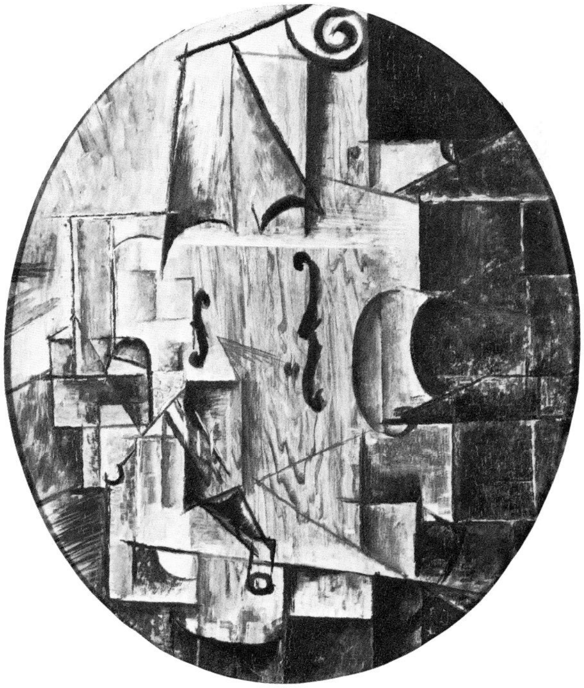

19. Pablo Picasso (Spanish, 1881-1973), *Le violon,* 1912, oil on canvas. Pushkin Museum, Moscow.

Thus from Braque's *trompe l'oeil* nail in 1909 to this stroke in relief, one can follow all the experimentation with the inclusion of different information, which by the rupture that it brought to a painting more and more liberated from imitation—or if one prefers, less and less illusionist—created at the same time the presence of an exterior reality and signs of space, signs of volumes independent of the formal indications of the composition. We know from Kahnweiler that Braque's and Picasso's concern was at that time to escape "from what was bothering them so much in painting, namely the need to use illusionist means to signify volume." These nonillusionist means were there. But Kahnweiler informs us that it was the Wobé (African) mask that Picasso owned "which was at the origin of the upheaval which was then taking place."[20] Independently, Edward Fry arrived at the conclusion that it was probably during the trip to Marseilles made during the stay at Sorgues that Picasso had acquired his Wobé mask.[21] Whatever the case, contrary to what Kahnweiler says, the stages that I have analyzed show that the presence of the Wobé mask could have crystallized the process of understanding the signs of space and volume, but it surely did not set it in motion. Wobé masks, as we know, are remarkable for the fact that they represent relations in volumes by nonimitative signs, that they provoke inversions of reliefs. The eyes, instead of being set in hollows in the face, are cylinders which project, while the forehead is curved back.

The Sorgues sketchbooks make us understand how Picasso, from this mask, extracted the new degree of figurative freedom which would characterize his heads made of dissociated planes during this period of the *papiers collés* at the end of 1912 and the beginning of 1913 (fig. 20).[22] As Kahnweiler has already emphasized, the inversion of relief of the guitar's hole became a projection in his construction of a guitar hanging on the wall of the boulevard Raspail studio among the *papiers collés* whose spacial relations it had sometimes induced.[23]

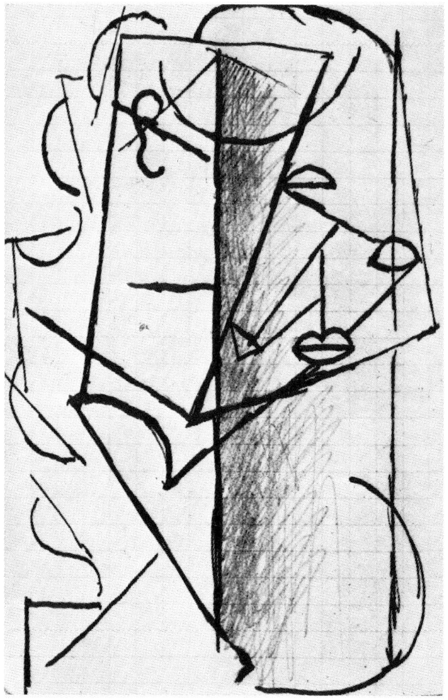

20. Pablo Picasso (Spanish, 1881-1973), drawing from Sorgues sketchbook, n.d., ink and pencil on paper. Location unknown.

As for Braque, whose paper reliefs executed at Sorgues and noted by Kahnweiler unfortunately no longer exist, his work in the summer of 1912, at least inasmuch as it involved innovations, is along the lines of stencil effects and the optical inclusions and unevennesses of Picasso. *La nature morte à la grappe de raisins (The Still Life with a Bunch of Grapes),* which surely did not remain in Kahnweiler's private collection only by chance,[24] repeated the theme of the fruit dish already painted by Picasso at Céret, but in a canvas where, contrary to Braque's custom, the writing is very disengaged from a painting reduced to light monochrome almost without color. The volumes are brought out by the addition of sand to the pigments, thereby changing completely the optical appearance by the creation of impastos and reliefs in place of transparency. However, these slight reliefs act in opposition to imitation, making the impastos recede and bringing out the transparencies. The volume of the bottle, the roundness of the compote, the relief of the grapes are entrusted to drawing.

It is not only a new optical differentiation, but also a new dissociation of form and color. Contrary to what I thought when I wrote my catalogue on Picasso's cubism, it now seems to me that the small canvas *Compotier (Fruit-dish;* fig. 21*)*,[25] which reduces the theme of the *Nature morte à la grappe de raisins* to the presence of the fruit dish on the table with the glass, a newspaper, and a pipe, derives directly from the *Nature morte* and prepares the way for *papier collé.* Indeed, it repeats the opposition between sanded pigments and transparencies, but, except for the grapes, the writing is lighter, more allusive, in order to provoke the contrast with the blackness of the fragment of newspaper title. Above all, it frames the subject with fragments of painted imitation wood in a manner succinctly imitative used by Picasso in *Souvenir du Havre,* without employing the comb.

However, setting aside the disappearance of the newspaper title, replaced by two inscriptions even more detached from the objects, the

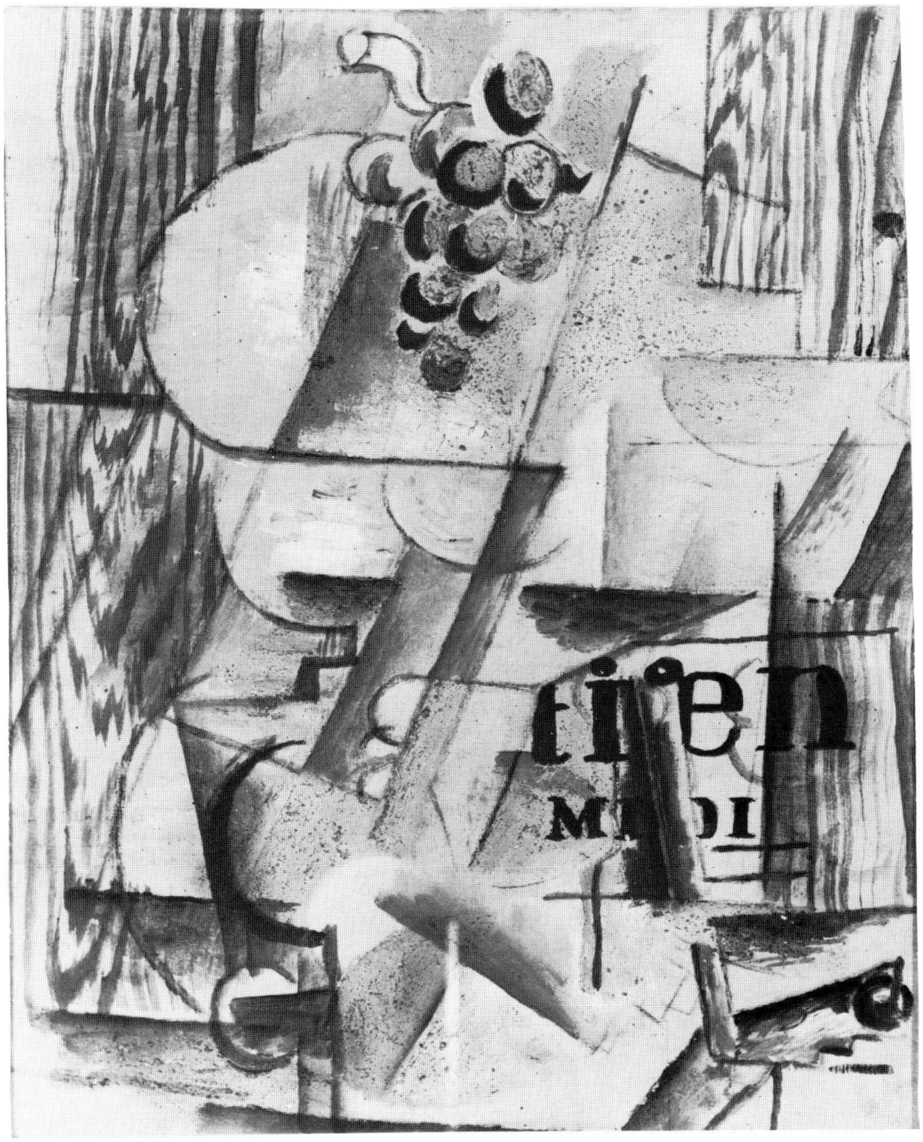

21. Braque, *Compotier,* 1912, oil on canvas. Private collection. Photo: Archives Leiris.

first *papier collé* invented by Braque is the exact transposition of the theme of this canvas, the painted imitation wood being replaced by a printed strip of paper imitating wood. The only change is that Braque has placed a horizontal band of the printed paper at the bottom. Reliefs are created by the shadows of the drawing, but in a manner which is as allusive and nonimitative as the sanded paints. It is this which makes one think that the *Compotier* was the "machine à voir" ("seeing machine") as Jean Paulhan put it, of *papier collé,* and not the reverse. Toward the end of his life, Braque, better than anyone else, commented on the importance of the invention: "With that we arrived at dissociating cleanly color from form and at seeing its independence in relation to form, because that was the main concern. Color acts simultaneously with form, but has nothing to do with it." *Papier collé* revealed, in effect, that it is the brain which brings about the fusion of colored and formal information and there is absolutely no need, to obtain this fusion, to bring information in order, with the appearances and cut outs of exterior reality. The *papier collé* legitimized the autonomy already gained by the painting of the two friends and the liberties they attempted, exactly like the Wobé mask. Since the date of the trip to Marseilles was 9 August, *papier collé* five weeks later could well have benefited from its impact.
directly from the *Nature morte* and prepares the way for *papier collé.* Indeed, it repeats the opposition between sanded pigments and transparencies, but, except for the grapes, the writing is lighter, more allusive, in order to provoke the contrast with the blackness of the fragment of newspaper title. Above all, it frames the subject with fragments of painted imitation wood in a manner succinctly imitative used by Picasso in *Souvenir du Havre,* without employing the comb.

However, setting aside the disappearance of the newspaper title, replaced by two inscriptions even more detached from the objects, the first *papier collé* invented by Braque is the exact transposition of the theme of this canvas, the painted imitation wood being replaced by a printed strip of paper imitating wood. The only change is that Braque has placed a horizontal band of the printed paper at the bottom. Reliefs are created by the shadows of the drawing, but in a manner which is as allusive and nonimitative as the sanded paints. It is this which makes one think that the *Compotier* was the "machine à voir" ("seeing machine") as Jean Paulhan put it, of *papier collé,* and not the reverse. Toward the end of his life, Braque, better than anyone else, commented on the importance of the invention: "With that we arrived at dissociating cleanly color from form and at seeing its independence in relation to form, because that was the main concern. Color acts simultaneously with form, but has nothing to do with it." *Papier collé* revealed, in effect, that it is the brain which brings about the fusion of colored and formal information and there is absolutely no need, to obtain this fusion, to bring information in order, with the appearances and cut outs of exterior reality. The *papier collé* legitimized the autonomy already gained by the painting of the two friends and the liberties they attempted, exactly like the Wobé mask. Since the date of the trip to Marseilles was 9 August, *papier collé* five weeks later could well have benefited from its impact.

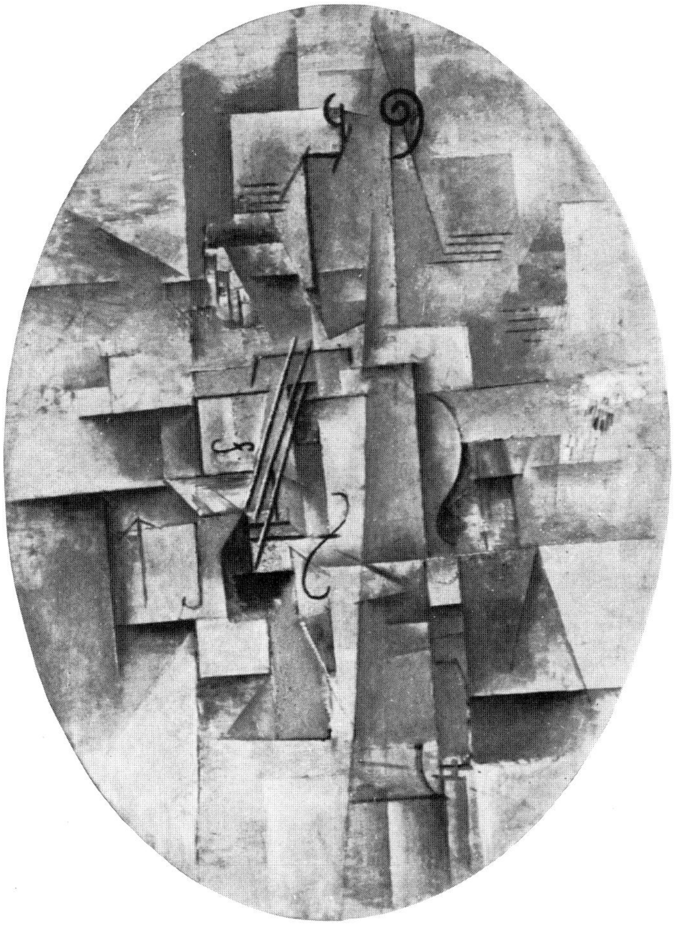

22. Pablo Picasso (Spanish, 1881-1973), *Le violon,* 1912-1913, oil on canvas. Rijksmuseum Kröller-Müller, Otterlo, The Netherlands.

Picasso's sketchbook from Sorgues reveals also how the presence of the Wobé mask pushed him to a drawing style which, instead of continuing to define the form of objects, summed itself up in an element of information, that is to say, instead of remaining dependent on the architecture of the object and married to it, he aimed to give information about its rhythmic virtualities, about its identifying signs, abandoning all accident for the profit of the diagram, or of a profile of the sweep of volumes and the internal dynamic of the forms.

It is in this sense that Kahnweiler's famous contrast between analytical and synthetic cubism takes its true meaning. Until then, in effect, the common work of Braque and Picasso had above all isolated the constituent elements as much of the pictorial representation of three dimensions as of the autonomous language of painting. What is put in concrete form at Sorgues by the invention of *papier collé* is their understanding that the composition of painting—which had taken on more importance in their eyes as they separated themselves from the imitation of nature—was not in itself the only bearer of the meaning and coherence of the canvas; that it acted only as an element of information, on an equal footing with color, relief, signs or guidelines of the presence of the objects. Therefore that which the painter presented only organized itself in the end by synthesis in the brain of the sum of information contained in the work. MacLuhan, for his part, was right to emphasize that cubism, in rejecting the illusion of perspective, provided "an instantaneous sensorial consciousness of the whole" of what it gave to see.

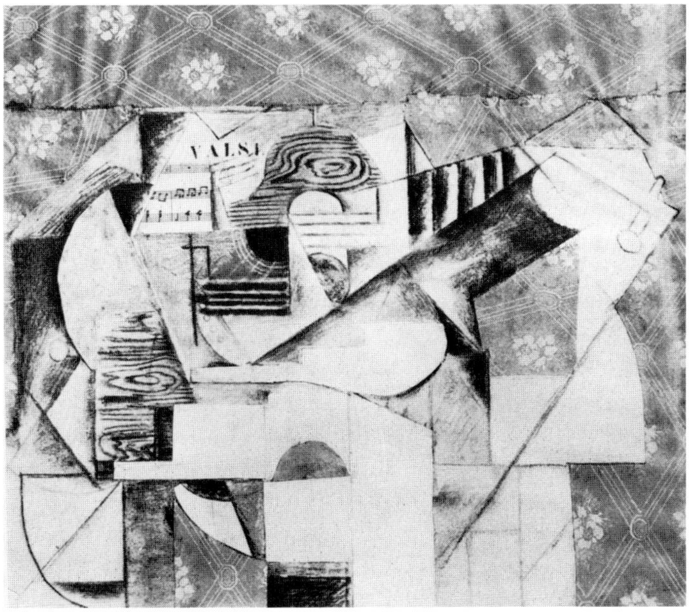

23. Pablo Picasso (Spanish, 1881-1973), *Guitare et feuille de musique,* 1912-1913, *papier collé,* pastel and charcoal. Collection of Pedro Vallenilla Echeverria, Caracas, Venezuela.

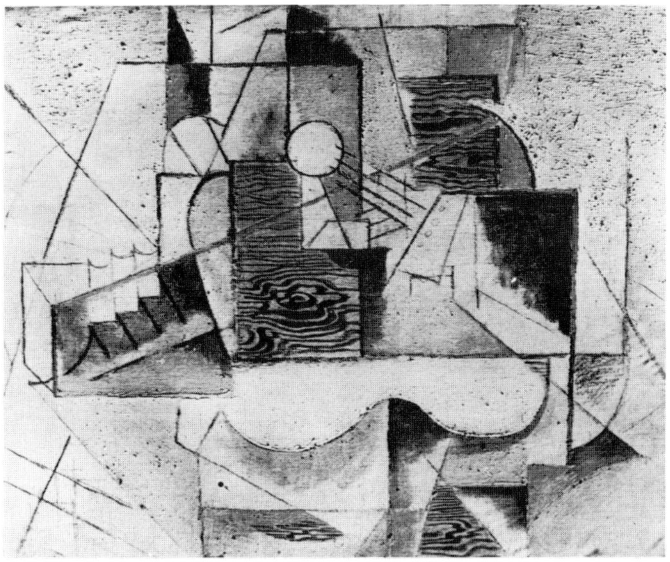

24. Pablo Picasso (Spanish, 1881-1973), *Guitare sur une table,* 1912-1913, oil, sand, and charcoal on canvas. Hood Museum of Art, Dartmouth College, Hanover, New Hampshire. Gift of Nelson A. Rockefeller, Class of 1930.

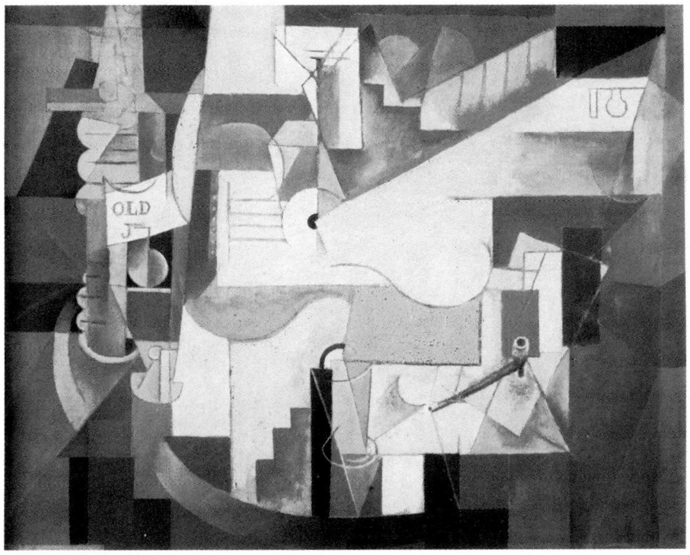

25. Pablo Picasso (Spanish, 1881-1973), *Bouteille, guitare, pipe,* 1912-1913, oil on canvas. Museum Folkwang, Essen.

It is this complete understanding that Picasso learned to master at the end of his stay in Sorgues through his guitars enclosed in triangular, abstract structures which would result in *Le violon (The Violin;* fig. 22*)* at the Kröller-Müller.[26] It is this stylistic evolution which has led me to place the sequence which resulted in *Guitare sur une table (Guitar on a Table;* fig. 24*)*,[27] which belonged originally to Gertrude Stein, at the very beginning of the stay in Paris. Proof of this comes from Picasso himself in a letter discovered in the Laurens archives and sent to Braque at Sorgues on 9 October: "I am using your latest paperistic and powdery processes. I am in the process of conceiving a guitar and I use a little dust against our horrible canvas."

The sequence includes a painting with collages of painted or colored papers, *Guitare et feuille de musique (Guitar and Sheet of Music;* fig. 23*)*, a synthetic drawing of the theme,

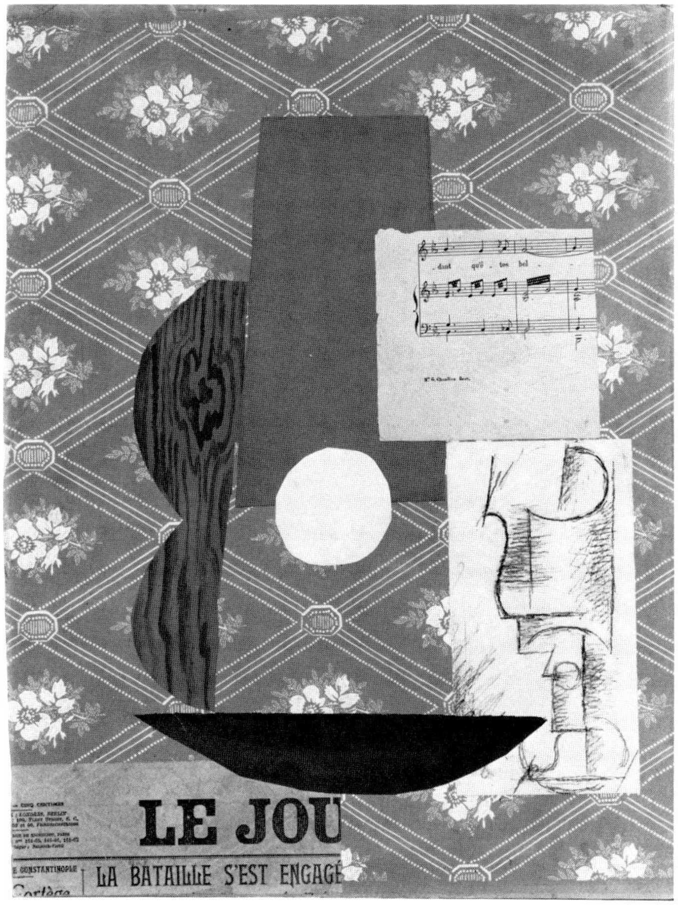

26. Pablo Picasso (Spanish, 1881-1973), *Guitare, partition et verre,* 1912, *papier collé* and charcoal on paper. McNay Art Institute, San Antonio.

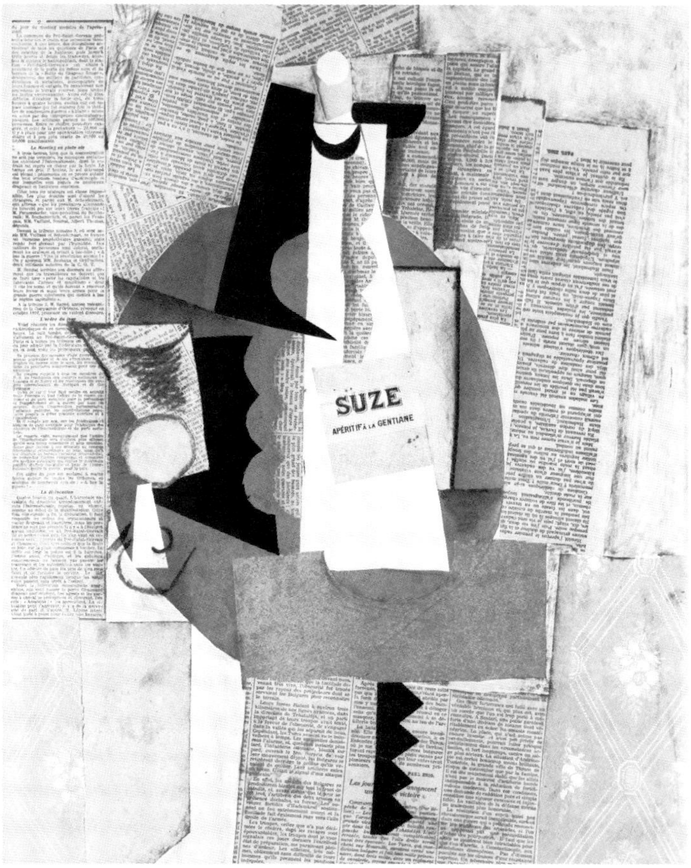

27. Pablo Picasso (Spanish, 1881-1973), *La bouteille de Suze,* 1912-1913, *papier collé* with charcoal. Collection, Washington University, St. Louis.

repeated in an oil on cardboard kept by the artist, and later completed, in a recently rediscovered version, by a minimum collage of painted paper. The final canvas evokes *La nature morte à la grappe de raisins,* wedding synthetic design with fields of sanded (with dust!) paint. Picasso introduced in it also the succinctly painted imitation wood of the *Compotier* and differentiated himself from Braque by contrasting the colored pigments which border the angles of the construction on one side and on the other tend to dilute themselves in the colorless spatial container.

This freedom of recomposition is quickly confirmed in a canvas of pure painting, *Bouteille, guitare, pipe (Bottle, Guitar, Pipe;* fig. 25*),*[28] in the Folkwang Museum and in some pastel drawings. The second step forward in *papier collé* by Picasso, *Guitare, partition et verre (Guitar, Musicbook and Glass;* fig. 26*)*[29] would also give rise to replica paintings, from which other *papiers collés* would be born. One has the impression that in Picasso's eyes, *papier collé* is an intermediary medium, a springboard. The novelty is the use of printed text as color, while emphasizing that it is a directed color, in the manner of imitation wood. Printed text serves as background in *La bouteille de Suze (The Bottle of Suze;* fig. 27*),* and, in *Le violon (The Violin;* fig. 28*)*[30] of the Donation Cuttoli, it fulfills exactly the function of the strip of imitation wood in Braque's first *papier collé.* Since the newspaper used there dates from the end of November, Picasso had taken a little

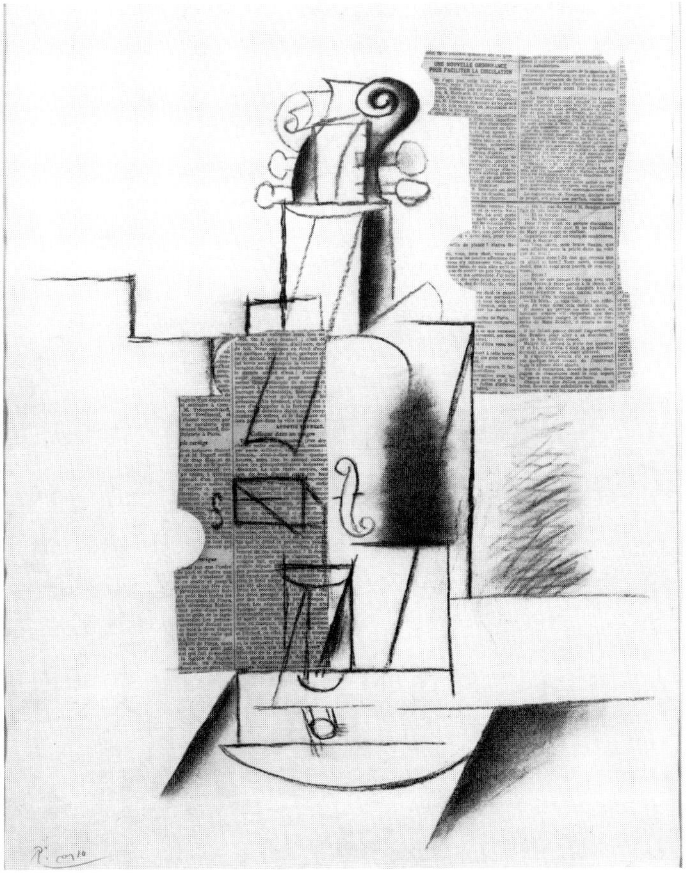

28. Pablo Picasso (Spanish, 1881-1973), *Le violon*, 1914, *papier collé* and charcoal on paper. Musée national d'art moderne, Centre Georges Pompidou, Paris.

over two months to take up on his own account Braque's problem.

A canvas by Picasso, known only through a black and white photograph until it reappeared at Sotheby's in 1981, *Paysage aux affiches (Landscape with Posters)*, which Zervos placed in Sorgues, brings us an interesting intermediary stage of Picasso's thinking. As in *Guitare sur une table*, the geometrical angles of the city forms are underlined, but by some white very lightly placed on the sizing of the canvas with gray contrasts which are also completely fluid. In return, the posters scream their flat tints: ochre yellow, Japan green, pink—and the color is entirely dissociated from the form of a cube, by the play on words of *bouillon Kub*, while it is enclosed in the form of a *Pernod fils* bottle. But each time one sees the contrast between the geometric angles on one side and the dilution in the colorless spatial container on the other. Let us add also that Picasso confronts here the stencil letters of *Kub*, the painted ones of *Pernod fils* and the cursive ones of the third poster. We have there what will characterize Picasso's creative activity until the war of 1914: the systematic confrontation of all the new means of pictorial language and the upsetting of all the contrasts of effects and syntax. Surely he thinks first of the work, the painting, and not of experimentation, but he never stops piercing the meaning of the successes he obtains.

After the discovery of *papier collé*, Braque appeared to create in the dazzle of a new mastery and of surprises of entire arrangments of color and form unknown till then; Picasso did so in a fever of impatience to extract from these novelties all the secrets of painting.

The difference between Braque and Picasso bursts out abruptly in this Parisian period where they find themselves separated after having worked closely together. It results not only from the opposition of their methods of work where Braque goes deeply and minutely into the same track, while Picasso multiplies the advances, the breakthroughs in all directions to measure or to remove resistances. It shows itself in the very handling of the painting.

Where Braque concentrates on optical expression and on the ways to vary, contrast, and refine it in his schemes, Picasso, in the final analysis, submits this pictorial work to his figurative solutions, to his shortcuts, to his graphic innovations. Braque concentrates on the painted or pasted matter, Picasso on the design which continues to bring about in his work catalysis and synthesis. And so much the better if, thanks to Braque, he can arrange a scale of optical modifications infinitely more rich with possibilities and better adapted to his objectives. In the end, their relations in that autumn of 1912 recommence their beginnings of 1908, when Picasso, confronting Cézanne, had revived the contrasts of rhythms and colors and the inversion of perspective but not the gradations of tones which created the dynamic, while Braque mastered these gradations of texture better than the graphic rhythms and the constructivism of the Aix master.

Everything leaves us to think, as Edward Fry is convinced, that the *Guitare en tôle (Guitar in Sheet-Iron),* which Picasso hung in his boulevard Raspail studio in the midst of his first *papiers collés,* does not date before the departure for Céret in the spring of 1912, but from the fall. And what we see in the photograph is probably the identical preliminary version in cardboard, given by Picasso to William Rubin and now restored in the Museum of Modern Art. That could even allow us to think that this guitar, which Kahnweiler said had been induced by the Wobé mask whose inversions of reliefs it translates, was one of a whole series of constructions by Picasso, contemporary with Braque's lost paper reliefs. Perhaps it had already been made during the last part of the stay at Sorgues.

Whatever the case, it is not a simple coincidence that the *Guitare* construction dominates the *papiers collés.* Its "superimposed" planes, its open form, its inversions of volumes served evidently as model for the "synthetic" transpositions which Picasso created in his *papiers collés* and painting. So that where Braque worked at pictorial writing, Picasso responded as it were: total understanding of form. Where Braque reflected on the color/form dialogue and industrial color/subjective form, Picasso discovered that collage allows within the container of the painting all imaginable figurative meetings. He discovered the heterogeneity of the space of synthetic cubism. If the synthesis can work with a décor of painted paper, a newspaper headline, a synthetic drawing of a glass, cut-outs of colored paper, a piece of imitation wood and a bit of a musical score—and I have just described his *papier collé Guitare, partition et verre,* which contains one of the oldest identifiable newspaper clippings, from 10 November 1912—then one can also include truly "pastable" objects such as a tobacco or cigarette package. But why not, then, pieces of illusionist drawing or painting? And why not make traditional figuration and synthetic figuration coexist in a painting, to wed cubism and portraiture? This is the key to the drawing *Portrait de Max Jacob (Portrait of Max Jacob)* of January 1915 which, when it was published at the end of 1916, would signify to the eyes of the uninformed a break with cubism. More generally, it is the key to the return to portraiture and classicism, apparent after 1917-1918, which would provoke misunderstandings and rupture with Braque.

In Picasso's hands the *papier collé* thus became a machine for exploring pictorial space. At the same time, he had a hand in three-dimensional assemblages—aren't they in fact like *papiers collés* in tinkering with and composing preexisting elements which owe little or nothing to the hand of the painter? And in plastic creation, as much traditional in the drawing, the painting, the imitative *trompe l'oeil* as "synthetic" in the sandings, the coats of sawdust, etc. Painting would be asked by Picasso to reproduce all the effects of *papiers collés,* effects of reliefs, and effects of contrasts of materials; to amplify them even to rearrangements of the composition by assemblage. It would borrow from this some degrees of unknown liberties in abstract recomposition as well as in the elaboration of plastic signs.

The End of the Climb

Picasso's installation on the boulevard Raspail upon his return from Sorgues thenceforth placed all the distance from Montmartre to Montparnasse between him and Braque. The move was due to the arrival of Eva in his life and to the desire to install himself far away from Fernande and the milieu which they had known together. But it surely played a role in the divergence between Braque's itinerary and his own starting in the fall of 1912.

The gathering of Braque's total output of *papiers collés* at the same time multiplies the number of them and underlines in them his remarkable continuity of inspiration as opposed to the three very diverse periods of Picasso's handling of the medium. Braque was totally cut off from Picasso's work during the latter's third stay at Céret from the beginning of March to the end of June 1913. Even if they could have met at the beginning of the summer, either in Paris or at Céret after Picasso's return there, the contact could only have been superficial and they could only have met again upon Braque's return from Sorgues in the fall of 1913 when Picasso was caught up with the *Femme en chemise dans un fauteuil (Woman Wearing a Blouse in an Armchair),* far from Braque's preoccupations. Thus, the association between the two oeuvres was becoming rare and besides, it is sometimes very difficult to specify the meaning.

If, as I believe, the painting *Compotier* served for Braque as a model for his first *papier collé,* verification through painting was an initiative of Picasso. As was his practice, he multiplied the approaches from the very beginning of his experimentation with the new medium. With Braque, on the contrary, the passage from *Compotier et verre (Fruit-dish and Glass),* the first *papier collé,* to *Nature morte au jeu de cartes (Still Life with Card Game)* from the spring of 1913, if it corresponds to a very precise translation of the theme in painting, even to the imitation of the lines of the drawing, marks a profound enrichment of it, not only in an increase of complexity with the introduction of playing cards and the spatial environment, but also by the utilization of modalities of composition which arose in the interval of work on the *papiers collés*—i.e., the contrasts of obliques in the imitation wood and the presence of the internal oval frame, evoking this time the roundness of a table. Braque, in reintroducing concrete elements, radically broke away from naturalistic appearances, creating a frontality without concession, while his desire to compete with the effects of collage led him to an extraordinary refinement of the painted matter.

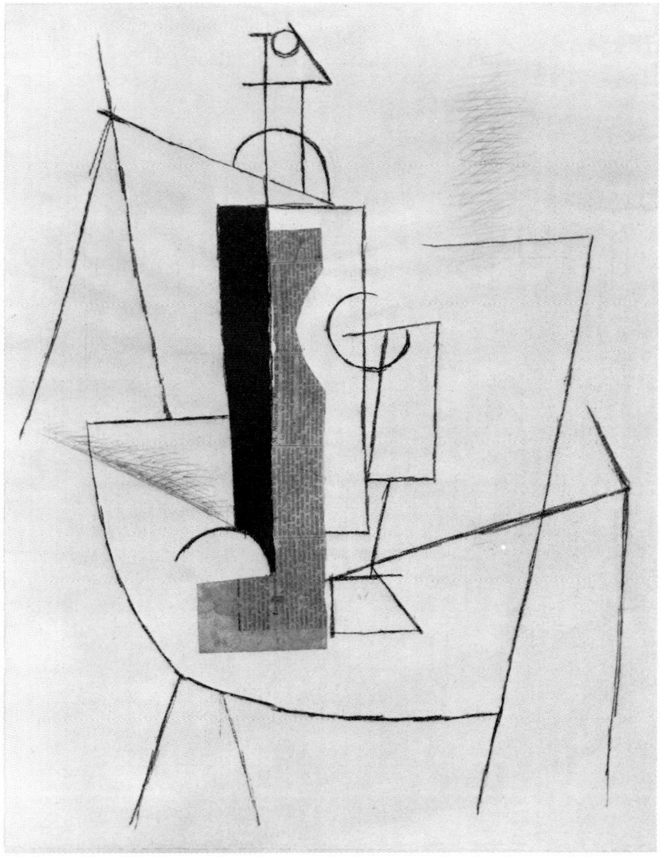

29. Pablo Picasso (Spanish, 1881-1973), *Bouteille et verre sur un gueridon,* 1912, *papier collé,* ink and charcoal on paper. The Metropolitan Museum of Art, Alfred Stieglitz Collection, New York.

It remains that the composition of the canvas is marked in depth by the vertical bands of the *papiers collés,* a means which one sees especially in Picasso who created a good fifty of them in the interval. This preeminence of verticals, which Picasso developed, finishing by organizing in 1913 the composition of a sequence of violins around a vertical axis, is in a certain number of *papiers collés* by Braque, notably the *Nature morte au violon (Still Life with Violin;* cat. no. 9*)* at Yale University Art Gallery, the *Nature morte BOC (Still Life BOC),* and the *Nature morte BACH; (Still Life BACH;* cat. no. 8*)* of the Kunstmuseum, Basel. The dates of these have not been established with enough precision to know who influenced whom. But experimentation is much more vast and varied in Picasso's work and seems to pursue its own logic.[31] Similarly, the *papier collé La bouteille de Marc (The Bottle of Marc;* cat. no. 12*),* with the notch of roundness, has every chance of having been influenced by Picasso's especially rich sequence on the theme (fig. 29),[32] a sequence begun at the very latest at the beginning of December 1912. Attempts to make figures in the new medium were parallel in the two artists, but Picasso developed a very different treatment of the face, which derived from his attempts to transpose the Wobé mask.

In return, the frontality of the oval of the table used as the frame for the *papier collé,* found only once in Picasso in *Verre et violon (Glass and Violin;* fig. 30) (in a figuration of autumn 1912),[33] is doubtless taken from Braque, for whom it was a preferred theme. Ditto, it seems, for the study of the violin's obliquity in the same sequence.

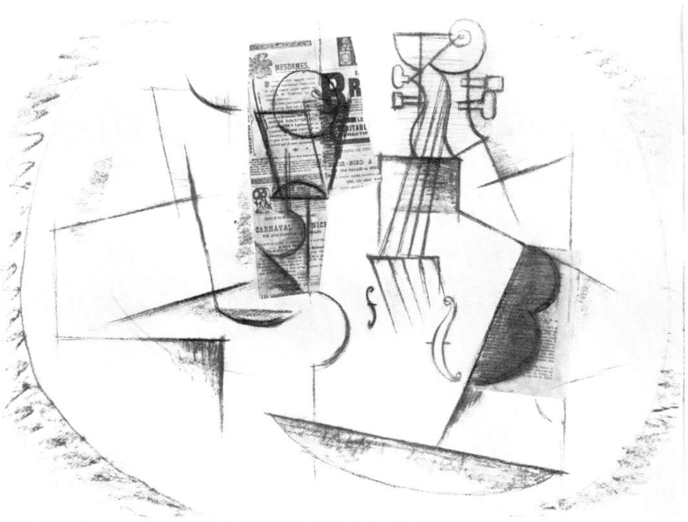

30. Pablo Picasso (Spanish, 1881-1973), *Verre et violon*, 1912, *papier collé* and charcoal on paper. Sara Hildén Art Museum, Tampere, Finland.

These are few of the total, and even though the Braque-Picasso team until then shared its innovations, it seemed to reduce the common features to secondary properties.

What continues to mark their relationship, as John Golding has shown,[34] derives from the very usage of the technique of *papier collé* and its influence on the technique of composition in painting. This influence goes beyond verification in painting of the effects of collage, because it deals with the practice of another mode of composition. Instead of making outlines and flat areas of color appear progressively, the cut-outs of the collages allow the artists a total grasp of the preexisting surfaces and of the possibilities of arranging and covering them.

This different view of painting in the process of being worked out would modify the works of Braque as well as those of Picasso, and also those of Juan Gris starting in 1913, conferring a particular air of cubist family which would be shared only by Severini, another skilled maker of *papiers collés.* Some of Picasso's *papiers collés* remained in a state of pinned papers, as this type of composition allowed, and at times Picasso continued to proceed in his painting while using this technique of pinning mobile colored surfaces in order to work out the whole structure of his composition and no longer only by the graphic balance of his sketchbooks.[35]

This new mode of composition, joined with the tendency to abstract recomposition, resulted from the very invention of *papier collé,* and developed through "synthetic" experimentation, could only give free rein to the decorative pleasure of painting. Since one composed by colored surfaces, why not use all possibilities to please the eye. Picasso here played his part independently of Braque, as much by the use of "rare'" collages (gorgeous paper in the *Guitare* of spring 1913, formerly in the collection of Nelson Rockefeller, and *Figaro* of 1883, that is to say a newspaper which was already old in a whole sequence of *papiers collés* from the same time, etc.) as by all imaginable contrasts of painted matter (use of encaustic painting in the *Homme à la guitare (Man with the Guitar)* formerly in the André Meyer collection, colored reliefs, pointillism). Moreover, he multiplied the reciprocal challenges between collage and painted imitation, reproducing in painting, for example, the first crumpled paper introduced in a canvas, the student's beret of *L'étudiant à la pipe (Student with a Pipe)* of the Gertrude Stein collection.

If no absolute proof exists that Picasso took the first step toward decorative pointillism at Céret, several convergent indications, notably stylistic ones, do exist. It seems that this time it was he who suggested a decorative possibility to Braque, since Braque's *papiers collés* (like the paintings) which employ it take us to the end of 1913 or the beginning of 1914.

Picasso became intoxicated with the lyricism of colors and of their sheen, to the point that one came to speak of "rococo cubism" in his work. In his *papiers collés* and canvases, the contrasts between painted fields of pointillism would end by taking on the value of collages in the course of the extraordinary exploration of the spring of 1914, when he seems to abolish all borders between *papier collé* and painting, as well as between cubism and perspective figuration.

It was, in the same way as Braque's rigor and orthodoxy in matters of *papier collé* or of cubism, the triumph of "synthetic" composition. Composition by assemblage proved indeed the autonomy of the art of painting. A new mode of perceiving the arrangement of forms, colors, and their optical contrasts, it brought about the qualitative leap of the practical existence of a new craft of painting, adapted to the space of cubism and of abstract painting, just as classic easel painting with its perspective and chiaroscuro was to the illusionism of the Renaissance. In this sense, as Clement Greenberg wrote, the discovery of *papier collé* was indeed a revolution, the realization of the modern revolution in painting.

NOTES

1. Cf. Pierre Daix, *Le cubisme de Picasso* (Neuchâtel, 1979), 111. Catalogue raisonné of paintings, *papiers collés*, and assemblages by Picasso, 1907-1916; text by Pierre Daix, catalogue by Daix and Joan Rosselet.

2. Daix 1979, 37, 38.

3. In *Cézanne: The Late Work* [exh. cat., The Museum of Modern Art] (New York, 1977), 151-202.

4. Daix 1979, 47, 48.

5. Christian Zervos, *Pablo Picasso* (Paris, 1932-1978), vol. 2, no. 66; and *Sammlung Justin Thannhauser*, Kunstmuseum Bern, 1978, no. 35.

6. Daniel-Henry Kahnweiler, *Confessions esthétiques* (Paris, 1963).

7. Daix 1979, 356.

8. Georges Isarlov, *Georges Braque* (Paris, 1932), 101.

9. Isarlov, 75.

10. Daix 1979, 413 and 414.

11. Daix 1979, respectively 368, 422, 423, 424.

12. Daix 1979, respectively 454, 457, 462.

13. Daix 1979, 458.

14. Daix 1979, 460.

15. Daix 1979, respectively 451, 466.

16. Daix 1979, 463-465.

17. Daix 1979, 476. If the first stay at Céret had already provoked a change in Picasso's palette, changing the monochromes to a remarkable blondness as one could see in the gathering of works at the Picasso retrospective at the Museum of Modern Art in 1980, the second sojourn there, in 1912, completed the liberation of color, as if Picasso's introverted cubism became extrovert.

18. Daix 1979, 485.

19. Daix 1979, 483.

20. Kahnweiler, *Confessions esthétiques*, from the essay "L'art nègre et le cubisme."

21. Edward Fry remarked to me that the drawings, Zervos 2: 741 and 744, notably could not be explained otherwise than by the presence of the Wobé mask. The trip to Marseilles is attested by the drawing Zervos 2: 754. But Marseilles, a large colonial port, was then the best place to find Negro objects to buy.

22. The drawings Zervos 2: 745 to 747, especially, with the sign of the eyes joined by an oblique diagonal and coming out of the face, characteristic of the *papier collé* heads and the canvas *Femme nue, j'aime Eva (Nude Woman, I Love Eva)* of the autumn, are related to the cylinder eyes of the Wobé mask.

23. When I was working on my cubism catalogue, the only accessible version of *La guitare* was the assemblage in sheet metal. Now that the cardboard version has been restored in the Museum of Modern Art, it appears more and more probable that it was the first and the one that appears in the photographs of the Boulevard Raspail studio.

24. Called also *Compotier, bouteille et verre (Fruit-dish, Bottle and Glass).*

25. *G. Braque de Draeger.* Text by Francis Ponge, Pierre Descargues, André Malraux (Paris, 1971), 112.

26. Daix 1979, 503.

27. From Daix 1979, 506 to 509—collages of painted paper, of pastel drawings of which some imitate wood, and of a piece of musical score.

28. Daix 1979, 510.

29. Daix 1979, 513.

30. Daix 1979, 523 and 524.

31. This can be seen in the series *Guitare, bec à gaz et flacon (Guitar, Gas Burner and Flagon)* from the beginning of 1913, from which derived the composition of *Violon, bouteille et verre (Violin, Bottle and Glass),* and finally that of *Violon au café (Violin in the Café),* where the vertical decomposition is the most complete (Daix 1979, 565, 569, and 571).

32. Daix 1979, 544, 546 to 552, 567.

33. Daix 1979, 529.

34. John Golding, *Cubism: A History and an Analysis, 1907-1914* (New York, 1959), 117 ff.

35. This is the case, for example, with the course of work on *La chute d'Icare (The Fall of Icarus)* for UNESCO in 1958. Cf. Gaétan Picon, *"La chute d'Icare" de Picasso* (Geneva, 1971).

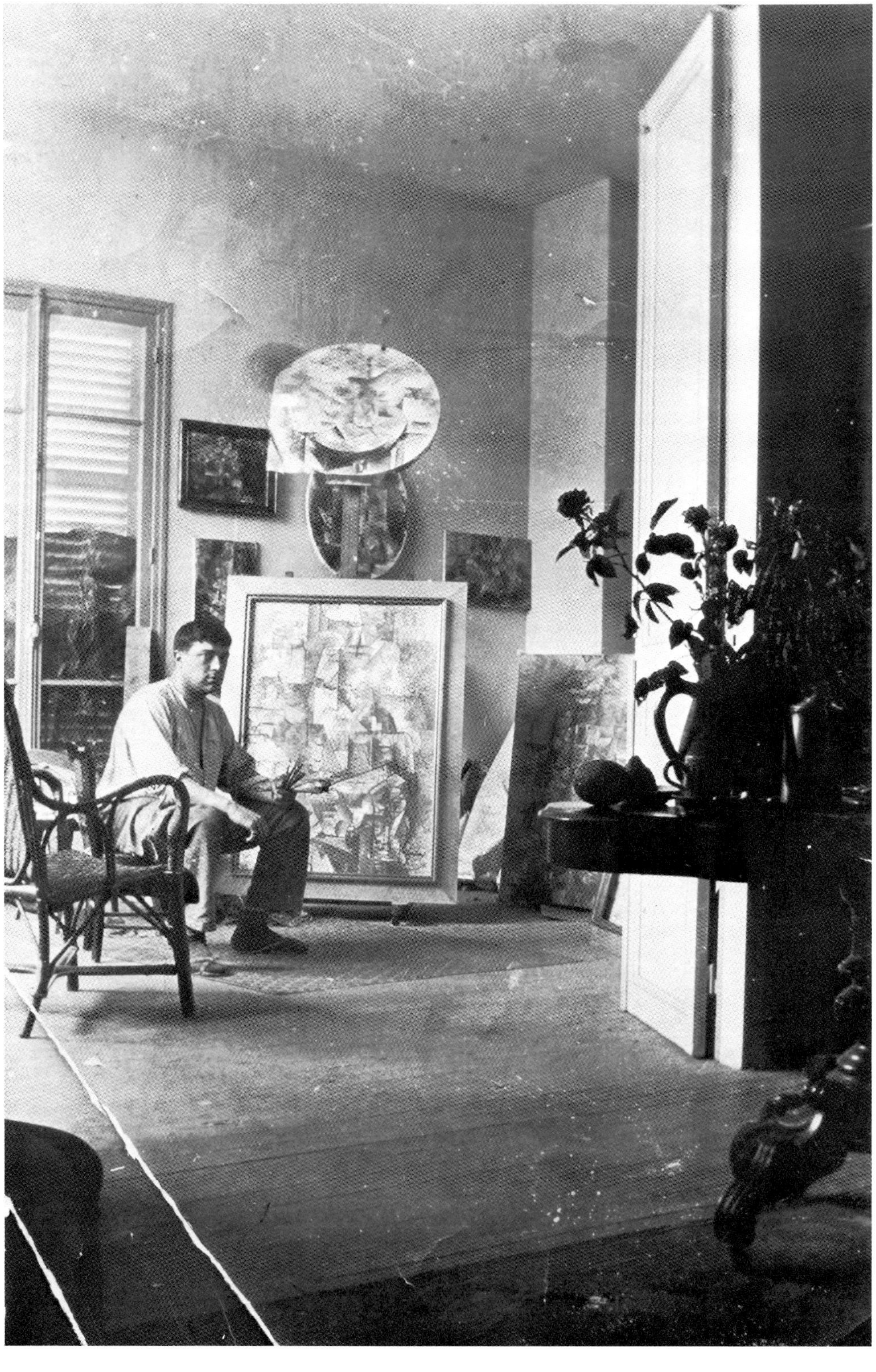

31. Georges Braque in his studio, 1911. Photo: Archives Laurens.

BRAQUE, CUBISM, AND THE FRENCH TRADITION

Edward F. Fry

THE MIND OF AN ARTIST such as Braque possesses certain immutable characteristics that, with minor variations, persist throughout life. But these same fundamental constants of personality and consciousness also undergo transient modifications in particular circumstances, just as a compass that indicates the north magnetic pole will also interact with another compass: the resulting directions indicated are the product both of the local or particular event and of the more general laws of magnetism.

It is in the sense of this metaphor that the general context of Braque's identity must be brought to bear upon the unique moment of his cubism and his *papiers collés.* The cubist moment witnessed many of his most perfectly realized works, but it also marks the point of contact between two distinct but historically related artistic traditions, each of which is revealed all the more clearly through the intensity of their confrontation and the instability of their ephemeral fusion.

If we not only review Braque's cubist production but also juxtapose it with his entire oeuvre, the major strands of his personality emerge with surprising clarity. These strands, or basic components of address to the world, are: *craftsmanship,* not virtuosity; *pictorialism,* including fidelity to the medium of painting, and hence a preoccupation with tonalities rather than with draftsmanship; *sensibility,* and the apprehension of experience by contemplative absorption, in the place of questing intellect; measured and *equilibrated responsiveness* rather than aggressive exploration; and an overwhelming preference for *experiential familiarity* in the choice of subject matter for art, in contrast to mental, verbal, poetic, or other intangible motivations.

These constants of Braque's artistic personality were as much present during the years of his cubist involvement, and specifically in his production of *papiers collés,* as they were in his début as a fauvist painter or in the still lifes and ateliers of his late years. The problem posed by Braque's cubism is therefore the interaction of his firmly rooted sensibility with the challenges posed successively by the achievements of Cézanne and by his ongoing confrontation with Picasso. It is to Braque's everlasting honor that he rose to these challenges, but the mystery of his ambition is overshadowed by its consequences. Braque's attempt to fathom, by means of absorptive emulation, Cézanne's unrepeatable and ultimately unassimilable art led to a provisional solution by 1909 that, in contrast to Picasso's struggle against, and rivalry with, Cézanne at the same moment, resulted in the partial recuperation of Cézanne for the artistic traditions of Paris and the Ile de France. But Braque's intuitive recuperation of Cézanne was a wholly different order of challenge from that posed by Picasso, whose mind and art stand at as much a polar antithesis to Braque as is possible within the broad limits of representational art in early twentieth-century France.

The interaction of Braque and Picasso that created cubism was far more complex than has ever been fully acknowledged; and it was precisely the antithetical, rather than complementary, qualities of their minds which generated the cubist achievement. The principal elements of this interchange may be summarized chronologically, as follows:

1907-1908. In the midst of his shift from a fauvist to a Cézannist style, Braque responds to the *Demoiselles d'Avignon* with the *Grand nu,* following which he returns to Cézanne-inspired landscapes.

1909-1910. In a series of still lifes with musical instruments during the winter and spring of 1910, Braque translates Picasso's experiments with a new, faceted and antiillusionistic draftsmanship, begun in mid- and later 1909, into a lyrical and surface-bound pictorial equivalent; Picasso, reciprocally, modifies his always implicitly sculptural bias in favor of a greater integration of figure and ground.

1910-1911. Following Picasso's radical extension of his anticlassical draftsmanship developed at Cadaquès in the summer of 1910, in which a grid of horizontal and vertical lines serves as a schematic means of representational notation, the two artists enter upon an ever more convergent path in a series of small, experimental still lifes during the winter and spring of 1910-1911. At Céret, in August 1911, the Picasso-Braque convergence reaches its first crescendo, in which Braque, following Picasso's lead, paints figural compositions incorporating many of Picasso's experiments with schematic representation through lines and planes. Conversely, Picasso intensifies his efforts to achieve a pictorial unity of figure and ground and, following Braque, introduces lettering into his paintings, without, however, accepting to the same degree as Braque the physical flatness of the pictorial medium as a *tableau-objet*. Probably also as a result of Braque's example, Picasso by the summer of 1911 achieves a greater degree of both visual harmony and tonal unity in his paintings than ever before.

1912. Braque, following his sense of craft and his respect for the primacy of pictorial surface, introduces false wood graining into his paintings during early 1912: a technique which Picasso quickly adopts in the spring of 1912 and integrates into his rapidly evolving language of nonillusionistic but representational signs and images. Braque's other experiments with texture, however, including his use of sand mixed with paint, are used only occasionally by Picasso.

1912, summer. Braque uses wallpaper with imitation wood graining—the beginning of all cubist *papier collé*—in September; this innovation marks both a continuation of Braque's previous comb-effected wood-grain illusions and a shift to a more physical, ever more surface-bound means of achieving the same end.

1912-1913. Braque begins to use colored papers, with or without patterned imprinting, as surface-bound image/signs for representation, in combination with drawn signs, profiles, and schematic images. Picasso, in October, responds initially to Braque's innovation in a tentative fashion but by early to mid-November he effects a radical transformation of *papier collé* into an entire new syntax of visual and intellectual representation.

1913, spring. Braque translates back into painting the results of his work with *papiers collés*, as does Picasso at the same time. By mid-1913 at the latest, however, the paths of Braque and Picasso begin to diverge: Braque's toward an increasingly pictorial and painterly elaboration of his prior cubist explorations, Picasso's toward an ever more intellectualized interrogation of both cubist and classical representation.

Thus in almost every single instance of this Braque-Picasso interchange during the development of cubism, the effect upon Picasso of Braque's presence was to provide the pictorial means necessary for Picasso's transformation of classical conventions. Conversely, the stimulus of Picasso made it possible for Braque to transcend the limits of symbolism and to become the first twentieth-century painter within the French tradition.

From this double perspective, both of Braque's artistic personality and of the specific character of his interactions with Picasso, the essential elements of Braque's achievement in *papiers collés* may now be clearly understood. In the earliest examples, from the autumn of 1912, wood-grained paper predominates and is used tentatively, as an adjunct to compositions which are otherwise cubist drawings on paper. But even in these first attempts, the wood-grained paper strips function at least tentatively as totally non-illusionistic yet fully pictorial invented signs for the color and location, but *not* form, of walls, tables, or drawers. Braque achieves this end in part through accompanying cubist draftsmanship, but far more important is the way in which he orients the direction of the wood-grain pattern of the paper strips themselves. Braque very soon also begins to use other types of colored paper, in conjunction with either drawing or wood-grained paper or both. In many examples from later 1912 and 1913 he does not hesitate to superimpose papers of different colors or textures, so that one paper appears to be closer to the observer than another, despite the network of cubist draftsmanship extending across both. This unifying cubist draftsmanship also has the effect of binding all planes to the pictorial surface, an end Braque also eventually achieves in his *papiers collés* by establishing the cognitive equivalent of "passage": in many examples of 1913, the paper strips indicate a given sequence of space relations at one point yet a contradictory sequence elsewhere. In earlier examples, however, Braque seems to have thought of *papier collé* overlays as a more straightforward indication of shallow space, since in other *papiers collés* of late 1912-early 1913 he juxtaposes differing paper elements so as deliberately to avoid any overlapping.

Braque's treatment of space, however, is notable for his essential disinterest in depicting it throughout his career,whether by illusionistic or cubist means. This avoidance of space is apparent not only in his fauve paintings but also in his Cézannian transcriptions of 1908-1909. His Symbolist instinct for the pictorial surface as the prime constituent of painting thus presents an extreme contrast to the classically formed mentality of Picasso, for whom space is *always* present. With Picasso space is a given, if neutral, element of experience; it is the field within which the mind operates. For Picasso, space can therefore be acknowledged illusionistically or, as at Horta in 1909, be both accepted as a general context but also be perturbed through localized inversions of perspectival conventions. In 1911-1914 space is apparently banished in many of Picasso's paintings and *papiers collés,* but in fact the continuity of space and of spatial extension remains implicit in even the most nonillusionistic of his compositions. Picasso's cubist reformulation of representation is always accompanied by the mental category of a latent spatial continuum.

Thus Braque, who contributed immeasurably to the cubist enterprise by encouraging Picasso to develop surface articulation rather than spatial extension, was himself uniquely well suited to the medium of *papier collé.* For just as in 1909-1910 he depicted illusionistic nails in walls to suggest the physical flatness of painting, and in 1911 used stenciled lettering as though the canvas were a printed page, so in *papier collé* his surface orientation led him to use this technique in a physical, nonillusionistic manner which emphasized the objectlike qualities of pictorial art. But it is the relation between surface and space in Braque which gives his works their characteristic lyricism and intimacy.

Braque's works, whether paintings, drawings, or *papiers collés,* resonate harmoniously between the extremes of object and illusion; but the resonance is from the flatness of pictorial surface *outward* into the illusionistic space of shallow relief. Unlike Picasso's acceptance of the category of spatial extension as a norm, Braque's space is both limited and circumstantial. It is a space that may best be understood as a thin, amorphous cushion which exists only nominally behind the picture plane, extending inward from the plane of physical surface to the plane of the nearmost limit of representational illusion: at which point lies the invisible barrier, like a proscenium arch, between the world of art and the world of the viewer. In the best of Braque's works, and above all in his *papiers collés,* the distance between the audience and the stage-world of art is diminished until the observer, even while remaining in the audience, is brought to the very plane of illusion, even as the plane of physical support collapses forward and dissolves the intervening spatial cushion of pictorial illusion. The result is a communion between observer and representation, in which elements of the world, transformed into art, offer themselves anew to the world as intermediaries between two realms. Braque's *papiers collés* thus function as secular descendants of the Catholic Mass, within a cultural tradition which, despite the secularized theology of Cartesianism, has its roots in the French High Middle Ages of the thirteenth and fourteenth centuries rather than in the Italian Renaissance. Thus the differences between Braque and Picasso in the cubist period may be understood in an historical perspective as those separating the *Adam* of c. 1200 from Notre-Dame, in the Musée Cluny, from Donatello's bronze *David,* or alternatively as the contrast between van Eyck and Masaccio: in the one, optical sensitivity, surface nuance, and texture rather than mass, and the primacy of exterior verisimilitude over intellectualized inner structure; in the other, an intellectual domination of the world and the structures within it, with the volumes as well as the surface appearances of things being the inevitable visual residues of invisible mental processes and relationships.

Questions of space and the picture surface inevitably lead to the fundamental issue in cubist art: the problem of nonillusionistic representation and the development of the cubist sign. Here also the role of Braque in relation to Picasso requires careful analysis and review. In 1907-1908, Picasso began a radical critique of the classical tradition, negating classical content by his exploration of primal sexual and psychic experience, and subverting classical style by seeking alternatives to normative conventions of draftsmanship, spatial illusion, and chiaroscuro. Simultaneously he sought alternatives to the classical/academic fidelity to the particularities of the visual world by exploring new modes of generalization. The first of these was the process of *reduction,* by which the many details of a human face, a tree, or a still-life object were reduced in detail and number to the point where a new, composite, shorthand image emerged to replace the old particularities. This new image was an image/sign, like an abbreviated word. Braque was particularly successful in making such abbreviated image/signs for houses and trees or for musical instruments in 1908-1909, when he was engaged in the study of Cézanne.

The second of these processes of generalization was mental *invention:* the creation of new signs, an act comparable to the coining of a new word. It was Picasso who took the lead in this instance, beginning with new micro-sign units, like letters of the alphabet, for the language of visual representation. These new units—lozenges, triangles, rectangles—were only partially arbitrary, since Picasso arrived at them usually through a process of inversion or negation, by which rounded, curved or otherwise organic forms were replaced by their nonorganic antitheses. This second kind of generalization was more radical than reduction, which was essentially a later nineteenth-century symbolist device through which all representational elements were reducible to a unified and mutely expressive pictorial surface. By later 1909 Picasso was well launched on the task of turning his newly invented, nonreductive micro-signs into the alphabet of a new visual language, the functioning of which would depend on context, as with the placement of letters in a word. This first phase was followed by a second step in which new macro-signs, generated by the assemblage of micro-signs, would in turn take on signification through their contextual relations to each other. The appropriate linguistic metaphor is the sequence from letters to words to sentences, the last of which function according to a certain grammatical structure. In the case of Picasso and cubism, this grammatical structure rested upon the preexisting representational norms of the classical tradition; these norms were preserved even as they were radically restated, including the most fundamental norm of all, namely the existence of objects in continuous and consistent space. For, to develop the grammatical analogy one step further, this fundamental classical postulate of volume in space is equivalent to the equally fundamental premise that words organized into sentences can convey meaning.But even with respect to this basic tenet of volumes in space, Picasso invented a means by which this classical principle would be honored but simultaneously destroyed through inversion and contradiction. In his organization of invented micro- and macro-signs after 1910, the continuity of space between planar elements is a fundamental assumption that Picasso nevertheless negates through deliberate inconsistencies in the spatial relations among micro- and macro-signs.

The very different approaches of reduction and invention are both present throughout Picasso's cubist endeavors, but what may be called the ratio of their relative importance shifts from an uneasy coexistence before 1909 to an overwhelming predominance of invention after 1911. Braque, by contrast, remains a primarily Symbolist/reductivist painter until 1912, and partially so afterward. The interaction of Braque and Picasso is in fact nothing less than the confrontation of the principles of reduction and invention. A clue to this confrontation lies in the challenge presented by Cézanne: where Picasso in late 1908 and 1909 makes intellectual constructs that rival Cézanne's experientially disjunctive cognition, Braque during the same period translates Cézanne into Symbolist pictorialism, using such reductivist devices as "passage" in order to give surface/depth unity to Cézanne's spatial discontinuities.

The confrontation of Braque's reduction and Picasso's invention has unexpected consequences, however, for the full development of cubist representation, because the building of a cubist language from letter to word to prose—from invented micro-sign to depicted object as composite macro-sign to entire theme or motif—reached an impasse in 1910-1911. It was at this moment that Picasso's deployment of invented signs had reached so high a degree of complexity that his paintings were no longer legible. Braque participated in this crisis of so-called hermetic cubism as well, but to a lesser extent; for Braque, as he responded to each stage of Picasso's invention of a new pictorial language, rapidly translated the elements of that new language into a more reductive and hence more apprehensible visual dialect.

The crisis of intelligibility in hermetic cubism is based on the dilemma that the whole, whether a word made up of letters or an image composed from visual signs, is not only greater than the sum of its parts but also differs from those constituent parts in kind rather than in degree. It is in the passage from pure invented signs to nonillusionistic yet representational sign/images during the course of 1912 that the interaction between Braque and Picasso reaches its climax: a true "force-field," in Adorno's sense of the term, is established between the two mental principles represented by these two artists, culminating by way of their *papiers collés* in the solution to the problem of cubist representation. The crux of the problem is in the relation between the human experience of the world and a sign or image that can represent that world. For such signs or images do not appear from nowhere, but must be either learned from the already existing stock of images, signs, words, or conventions; or, alternatively, a new sign or image must somehow be forged out of whatever mental materials are available, including if necessary the existing stock of such cultural materials. It is this second alternative that concerns cubism, for the first is the province of normative classicism and academism.

With a reductivist approach one can arrive at a composite image through the generalization of conventional academic/classical imagery, until a point of imageless abstraction has been reached and all signifying function has been lost. Similarly, invented micro-signs can be multiplied to the point where, even when assembled into a single macro-sign, the legibility of the depicted object also disappears. Thus neither the purely reductive nor purely inventive approach is capable of resolving the dilemma of postclassical signification. The solution lies instead in the combination of the two modes; and in the cubism of Braque and Picasso this combining of approaches occurs in two ways. The first is their sheer juxtaposition: reductive image/signs, "passage," and synecdoche—the use of part of something, such as the fragment of a newspaper title, to stand for the whole—are used in close proximity to purely invented signs and planar discontinuities. The second solution is more important, for it amounts to no less than the fusion of the reductive and inventive methods. This fusion, however, is more complex than it might seem and requires a recapitulation of the issues involved.

To the extent that a retinal-mental image is not only an image but also in part a learned sign, so also may the images in Renaissance classical art, generated by a process of "making and matching," be termed image/signs; this result is only part of the more general Renaissance amalgam of optical phenomena and invented mental conventions, notably in canons of figure proportions and in perspectival/atmospheric space, and as is also reflected in the iconographic fusion of the basic realities of the human condition—birth, love, and death—with the great invented mythic structures of classical and Christian culture. But late nineteenth-century Symbolism, which is ultimately descended from the classical/academic representational tradition, was accompanied by an emphasis on surface, including reductive image/signs that were subsequently intensified by Braque to the point of image/sign reduction to the second degree. By contrast, in the tradition of linear classical draftsmanship to which Picasso was heir, images generated by pure line are already more invented than they are the result of reduction; they are "sign/images," mental constructs, "lies which tell the truth." But in order to arrive at new, truly cubist signs, it would be necessary for Picasso, following the example of the reductivist tradition exemplified by his colleague Braque, to perform the intellectual equivalent of visual reduction upon his own sign/images. It was this process, which has, I believe correctly, been compared to the Husserlian eidetic reduction, that Picasso carried out between the summer of 1912 and the spring of 1913.

That Picasso was preoccupied by the problem of sign and image during the summer at Sorgues is evident in a note written in his sketchbook: "trouver le equilibre entre la nature et votre imagination" (Musée Picasso 1864-32 verso). The catalytic impetus that led to his establishing a new equilibrium, a new relation between sign and image, was his acquisition of a Wobé mask while he was at Sorgues and his consequent discovery of the representational yet nonmimetic signs evident in such masks. But it was Braque's development of *papiers collés* that provided the final impetus. For where Braque used pasted paper as an extension and confirmation of the image/signs of reductive flatness, Picasso saw the potential of these areas of flat color for use not only as pure arbitrary invented signs but also as new kinds of representational sign/images, arrived at through eidetic reduction. The new equilibrium between nature and the imagination would be achieved if the various mental sign/images of an object were subjected to the mental process of fusion, resulting in a new sign/image uniting all previous mental and visual details at the level of their highest, most generalized common denominator: a sign/image raised to the second degree of mental invention.

The entire short history of *papier collé* as practiced by Braque and Picasso reveals a beautiful interpenetration of these two distinct approaches. By mid-1913, the two are separated only by an invisible membrane, on one side of which is Picasso's movement from imagination toward nature on a newly classicized plane of intellect, and on the other side of which is Braque's movement from intuitive reduction toward ideated sign. At times, both artists employ as many as three different approaches to sign and image simultaneously, as in Picasso's great *papier collé* of 1912-1913, *Nature morte au violon et au compotier (Still Life with Violin and Compote of Fruit;* Daix 530; fig. 32). A somewhat later example among Braque's *papiers collés,* c.1913-1914 (the precise dating is problematic; see cat. no. 38), is the *Violon et pipe ("Le Quotidien") (Violin and Pipe;* fig. 33). Here Braque uses reductively illusionistic draftsmanship to depict a table in outline, but also seen from above so that the top is made to coincide with the pictorial surface. A large sheet of newsprint functions as a pure invented sign for

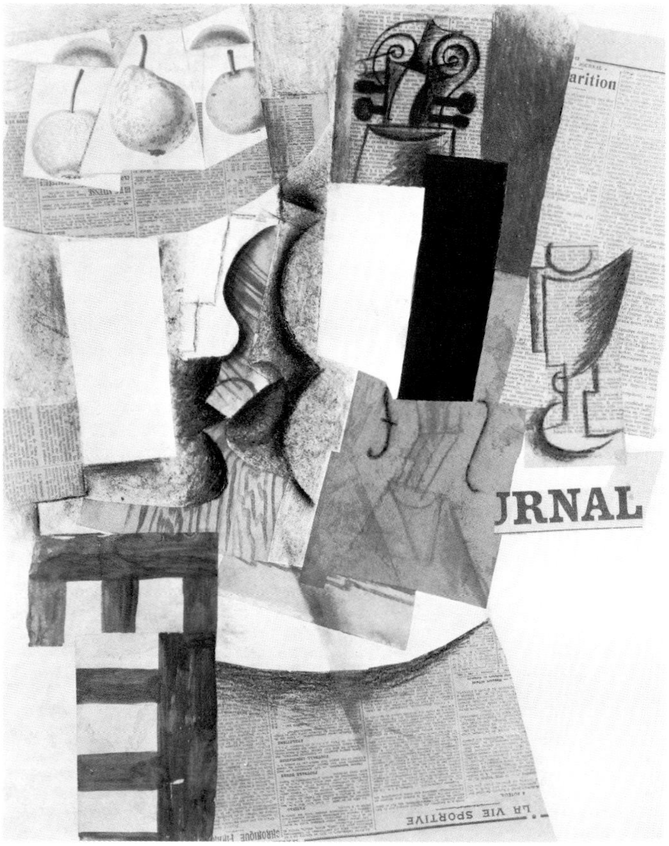

32. Pablo Picasso (Spanish, 1881-1973), *Nature morte au violon et au compotier,* 1912, *papier collé,* gouache and charcoal on cardboard. Philadelphia Museum of Art, The A. E. Gallatin Collection.

the table top itself; atop this newsprint, and therefore on the table, lies a sheet of black paper that is a reductive image/sign for the characteristic redoubled curve of the silhouette of a violin. Adjoining this reductive sign, however, is a vertical sheet of wood-grained paper that, unlike the black silhouette, gives an indication of the material of the violin, as well as its color. But the shape of this wood-grained paper, in combination with the lines drawn upon it, is an invented eidetic cubist sign/image for a violin. Above is a narrow vertical strip of patterned wallpaper that is an invented sign, with a faintly eidetic suggestiveness, which represents the stringed neck of the violin. To the left, a portion of an actual newspaper functions as a direct, surface-bound, reductive image/sign for the totality of a newspaper; and below, another fragment, cut in the shape of a pipe with superimposed illusionistic drawing, is an image/sign that is both illusionistic and reductive and is also surface-bound by virtue of being flat newsprint.

Throughout 1913 and 1914 Braque employs not only the new eidetic sign/images of cubist representation but also the method of contextual representation which Picasso began as early as 1909 but which achieved its full potentiality only with *papier collé.* In every instance, however, even as he and Picasso increasingly share a common goal of thought and method, Braque never abandons his instinctive commitment to Symbolism. Similarly, Picasso never disavows his own austere and highly intellectual linear classicism even as he responds to Braque's fidelity to surface, texture and pictorial unity. Their contrasting modes of composition at this time are in themselves highly revealing, for Braque's preference is for a centralized circular format, from which pictorial elements often radiate like spokes from the hub of a wheel. But even when he disperses his major compositional elements, he almost always seeks a balance of accents—left against right, top against bottom—across an invisible central fulcrum. Picasso's more intellectual approach can lead him to the one extreme of building a dense central structure of signs, which is the ideated cubist equivalent of sculptural mass. Or conversely he expands across the entire surface, where contextual signs, visual and verbal puns, or interplays between two or more systems of representation fuse the whole into an intellectual rather than visual unity in which the work is to be read—literally as well as figuratively—as much as it is to be seen.

The cubist enterprise, above all the achievements of these two artists between 1912 and World War I, revitalized the entire classical tradition of Western art and brought that tradition to its final, postacademic, posthumanist, and post-Christian endpoint; it remains the single greatest intellectual and visual achievement in modern art. It was the interpenetration, at the highest

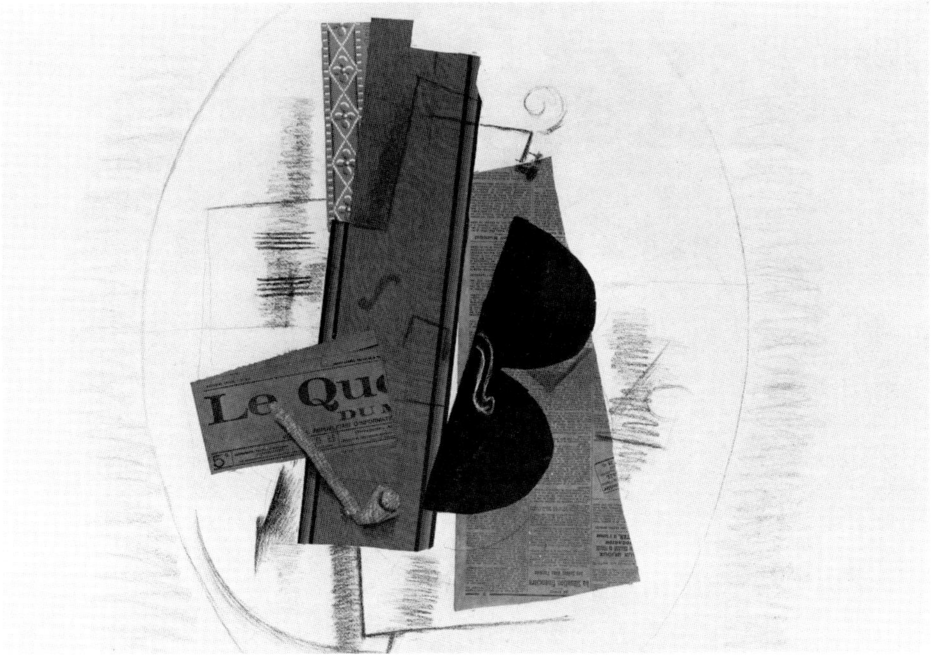

33. Braque, *Violon et pipe ("Le Quotidien")*, 1913-1914 (cat. no. 38).

possible level, of intellectual power and visual sensitivity that brought the cubism of Picasso and Braque into being. But there is more than one historical irony in the relations of these two artists to each other and to past artistic and cultural traditions. For just as Picasso's background, if not his innate gifts, was at best that of a provincial, austere, academic, and *retardataire* continuation of Mediterranean Renaissance and Baroque classicism, so was Braque's point of departure a French pictorial tradition that was at a far remove from authentically classical roots. Together they achieved that fusion of idea and experience—the equilibrium between nature and the imagination—which is the touchstone of the classical spirit.

Braque was thus doubly a mediator, who not only provided in large part the pictorial substructure for cubism but who also in turn translated this new, and final, version of classical art into the traditions and sensibility of the Ile de France. For French art, Braque's cubist achievement served as an equivalent to what Rome, from Poussin to Ingres, had provided in the past: a catalytic challenge and a point of reference for much of the subsequent twentieth-century School of Paris.

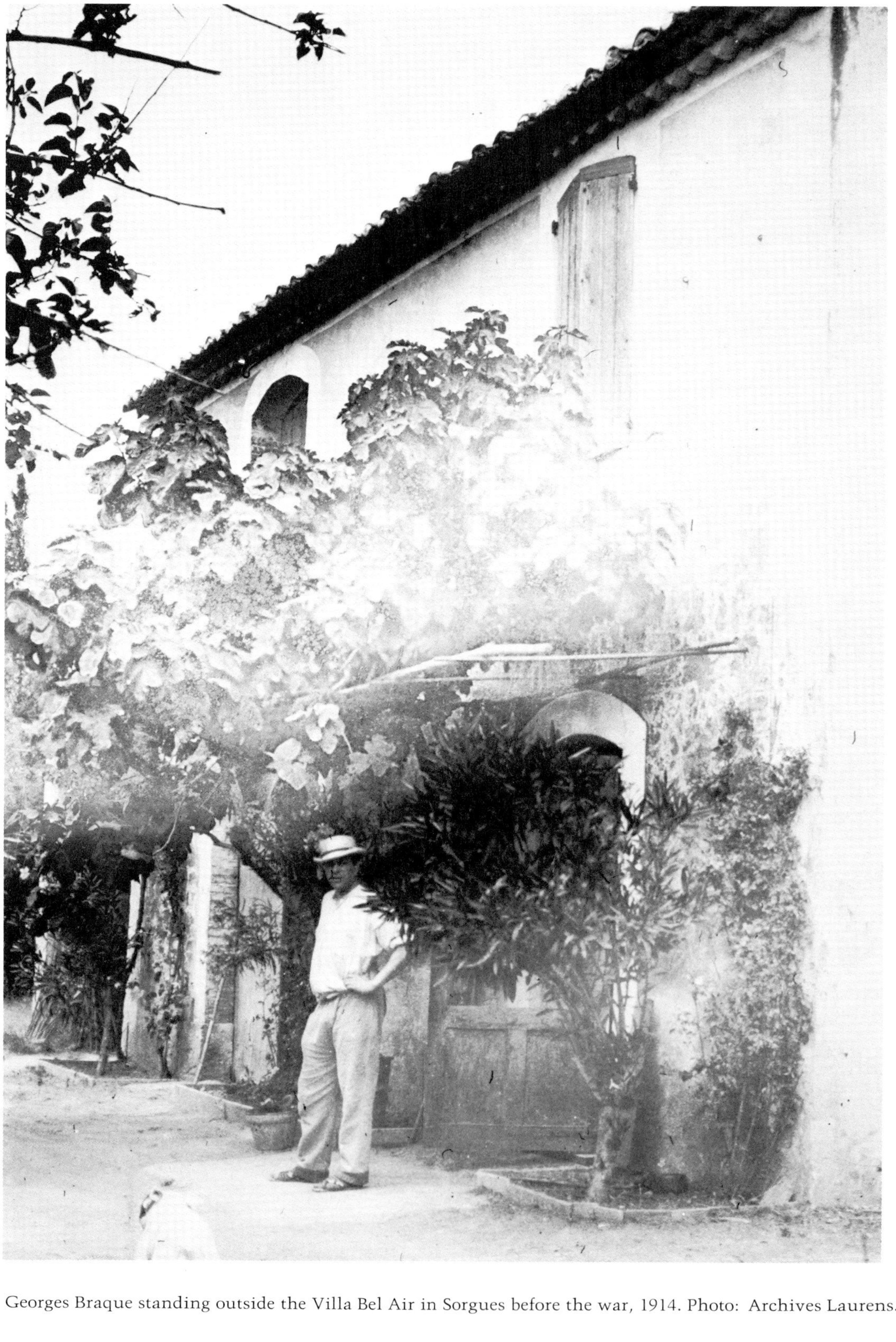

34. Georges Braque standing outside the Villa Bel Air in Sorgues before the war, 1914. Photo: Archives Laurens.

BRAQUE, THE SLOWNESS OF PAINTING

Isabelle Monod-Fontaine

ONE THINKS OF BRAQUE, both the man and the painter, as slow, as taking a long time. Did he not have behind him, as the foundation of his work, an accumulation of craftsmanly traditions, the remembrance of lovingly familiar relations with the materials, of layers placed with a careful hand, in a precisely calculated time? One of the first important critical texts devoted to him (by another painter, Roger Bissière, in 1920) strongly underlines—even goes so far as to offer in explanation—Braque's belonging to a line of artisans who knew how to make of time, which they had in quantity, a sure ally because it had been proven so.

Georges Braque is the son of a house-painting contractor. This is important, and those who would ignore it risk not understanding fully an art and an oeuvre which flow logically from their early formation.

Braque, in effect, inherited the recipes and formulae which after all are perhaps the essential part of painting or at least its most solid foundation. He passed his youth in contemplating the patient work of imitating wood or marble; he was initiated into the complicated art of 'thin layers' and 'thick layers'; he learned from his father's workers the science of exactly mixing a tone, and of placing it properly; he knew how to make the 'thread' and 'letter.' This education must have left a strong imprint on him and influenced considerably his works to come.

This essential text and others founded a vision of Braque to which he himself added several strokes. Thus in 1954, in his conversation with Dora Vallier, he made the magnificent and profound panegyric for slowness in painting, slowness to which the slowness of the gaze, which marks, recognizes, and takes possession of the road of the painter, would respond. "I find that one must work slowly," said Braque. "He who looks at the canvas retraces the same road as the artist and as it is the road which counts more than the thing, one is more interested by the road."

Along the same line of thinking, it was very quickly seen in Braque's painting, from the time that it appeared in greatest numbers as provocative and incomprehensible, that it was in continuity with a specifically French pictorial tradition. It seemed that from Chardin to Braque, in passing by Cézanne, a relationship imprinted with respect for the past, for the masters, for formulae, for experience, was not broken. In witness of this, one finds explicit reference to Chardin[1] from 1910, often repeated thereafter, like the comparison with Corot, with painters placed under the sign of slowness, of patience in the search for perfection, of modesty. Chardin's remark, reported by Charles-Nicolas Cochin,[2] "One uses colors, but one paints with feeling," could be an aphorism by Braque, especially given his reflections on emotion: "Emotion ought not to be translated by an affected trembling, it does not add to itself nor imitate itself. It is the germ, the work is the blossoming," or "Nobility comes from contained emotion," recapitulate exactly the ways of Chardin and spring from the same sensitive family.

This common vision of Braque, that one could justly develop, was naturally built on the constant comparison (rivalry?) with Picasso. Confrontation of the two oeuvres and above all of the two images of the artists, all the more exemplary than these two personalities had been as tied up as possible in the *risks* taken in common. Comparisons are also made between the "French temperament" and the "Spanish temperament," as Braque put it, between considered slowness and fire, between the patient tracks of one and the overwhelming and unpredictable advances of the other, between Braque's continual turning back upon himself (often seen as a retreat) and Picasso's giant curiosity. One might roll out even more of these antithetical portraits, but with this kind of convenient opposition one could quickly drift and move away from what one would, on the contrary, like to bring closest together: Braque's connection with time, not as simple as the one which the craftsman of his family maintained with it; and more precisely, Braque's connection with time at

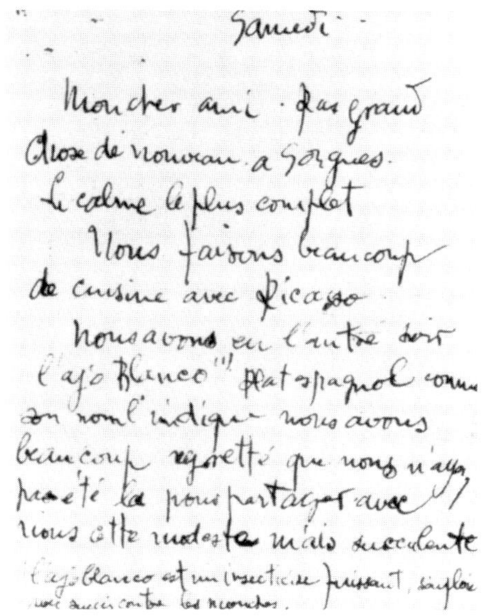
Samedi

Mon cher ami · Pas grand chose de nouveau à Sorgues. Le calme le plus complet. Nous faisons beaucoup de cuisine avec Picasso. Nous avons eu l'autre soir l'ajo blanco !!! plat espagnol comme son nom l'indique. Nous avons beaucoup regretté que vous n'ayez pas été là pour partager avec nous cette modeste mais succulente

(l'ajo blanco est un insecticide puissant, [illegible] contre les moustiques.)

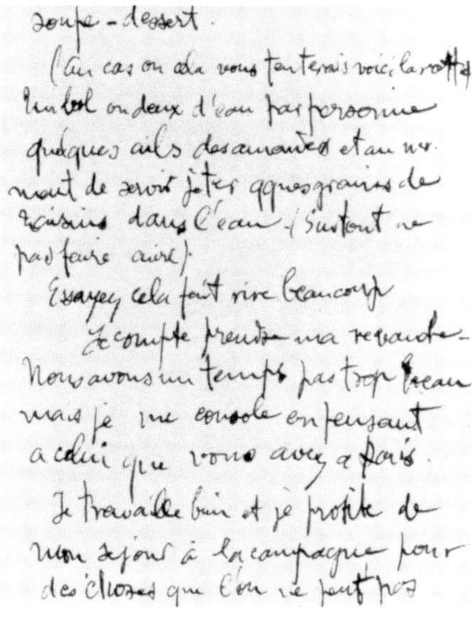
soupe-dessert. (Au cas où cela vous tenterais voici la recette) Un bol ou deux d'eau par personne quelques ails desamandes et au moment de servir jeter quelques grains de raisins dans l'eau (surtout ne pas faire cuire) Essayez cela fait rire beaucoup. Je compte prendre ma revanche. Nous avons un temps pas trop beau mais je me console en pensant à celui que vous avez à Paris. Je travaille bien et je profite de mon séjour à la campagne pour des choses que l'on ne peut pas

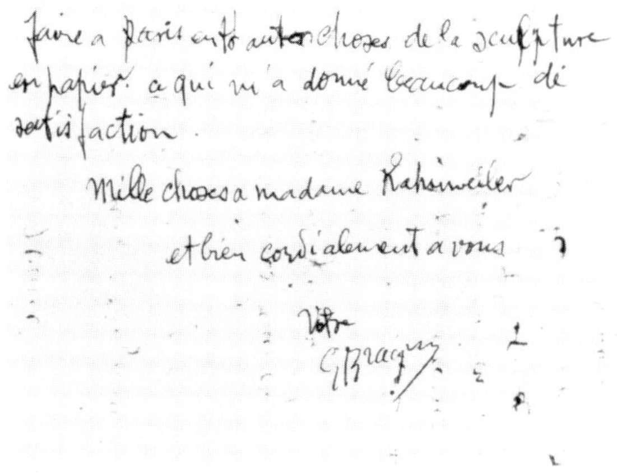
faire à Paris entre autres choses de la sculpture en papier ce qui m'a donné beaucoup de satisfaction.

Mille choses à madame Kahnweiler et bien cordialement à vous

Votre

G Braque

35.-36.-37. Letter from Braque in Sorgues to D.-H. Kahnweiler. See note 6.

the moment of the *invention* (in the plenary and Latin sense of the term, as one refers to the invention of a relic) of *papier collé.*

One begins, indeed, to catch a glimpse of the very short duration of cubism. More and more refined analyses reveal the extreme rapidity of the intuitions, the explorations, the actions, and the reactions. If the chronology of the months and even of the weeks is just about clarified as far as Picasso is concerned, thanks especially to the publication by Pierre Daix of a catalogue raisonné of the cubist works and to the important documentary material which finds itself garnered there, work remains to be done on Braque: the diffusion of his work was not as organized as it was for Picasso's, the documentary archives are less abundant, more difficult to reconstitute and use to advantage. Thus the too summary research conducted for this catalogue has permitted us to cull from the press of the period some allusions in 1913 and 1914 to *papiers collés*—by Picasso. As an example, we can cite these few sentences by Tabarant from *L'Action* of 1 March 1914:

> Because Picasso, that enormous and so uneven creator is thinking of painting no more, of simply pasting pieces of paper, colored or not, that he cuts haphazardly out of store catalogues, advertising posters, or from calendars, because this genial madman amuses himself that way—distraction of the colossus—so in their turn his poor followers cut and paste! What good is it to paint if Picasso paints no more!

Braque's role thus found itself being constantly minimized, if not completely hidden, until very recently. We would like here, in examining what happened during the short summer of 1912 from the point of view of Braque alone, to show the powerful rapidity of conception and execution of which he then showed himself capable, rapidity which does not contradict what he said about slowness, but which adds to it its true dimension: Braque wanted "to work slowly"; it was a choice, not a destiny. In the Braque-Picasso link, at the time when it was functioning, there was not a leader and a follower; there was alternation, dialogue, generous exchange of strengths.

Braque arrived in Sorgues sur l'Ouvèze toward the end of July 1912. With his young wife Marcelle, he lived in the Villa Bel Air on the Entraigues road ("a Japanese farm with nice old walls painted with lime as in France"). Picasso, with Eva, lived in the Villa Les Clochettes.

In the beginning of August came the trip to Marseilles.[3] We can situate it around 8-9 August by the postcard sent by Braque from Marseilles to his friend, the dealer D. H. Kahnweiler, which arrived on 11 August in Switzerland where the latter was then living. Braque declared, "After having bought all the African sculpture and shown the city to Picasso, I return to Sorgues where I am installed. I am anxious to work." From the beginning, then, there is this shock, the African sculpture goes to the Villa Bel Air (as well as to the Villa Les Clochettes) to accompany the summer's work.

In the course of the month of August (before September in any case), Braque wrote—again to Kahnweiler—that he was doing some amusing cooking with Picasso (see figs. 35, 36, and 37), but also "things that one cannot do in Paris, among other things some sculpture out of paper, which has given me a lot of satisfaction." Nothing remains of these ephemeral construction games, in which Picasso surely participated. Of Braque's reliefs in paper only this sentence remains, an archival photograph (fig. 38) which belongs to a later time since the newspapers used date respectively from 1914 (for the construction, *Le Matin* of 18 February 1914) and 1913 (for the *papier collé, Havre-Eclair* of 11 January 1913), and the affectionately ironic name of "Vilbure" (Wilbur) given to Braque at that time by Picasso. A valuable notice by Christian Zervos which appeared in 1932 in number 1-2 of *Cahiers d'Art* (certainly based on conversations with Braque and on his archives) mentions these trials and the nickname which is connected to them: "From 1911 dates also the first paper sculptures conceived by Braque and soon abandoned by him because he saw them only as an experiment to enrich and organize his painting. All this time Braque was making multifarious inventions, which earned for him from Picasso the nickname Wilbur, public attention being then monopolized by the inventions of Wilbur Wright."

Multifarious inventions? Among them, certainly, was *"papier collé."* Here also the collection of some documentary data[4] available to us allows us to fix almost the moment that Braque's gaze encountered in the window of an Avignon color merchant a paper printed with a woodgrain motif (*faux-bois* paper), to the end of August or the very beginning of September, before Picasso's departure for Paris (3 September). Encounter, instantaneous *revelation*—this was the word used by Braque—followed by a pause, since Braque decided to wait for Picasso's departure before going to buy the paper and to use it.

Upon Picasso's return on 12 Sep-

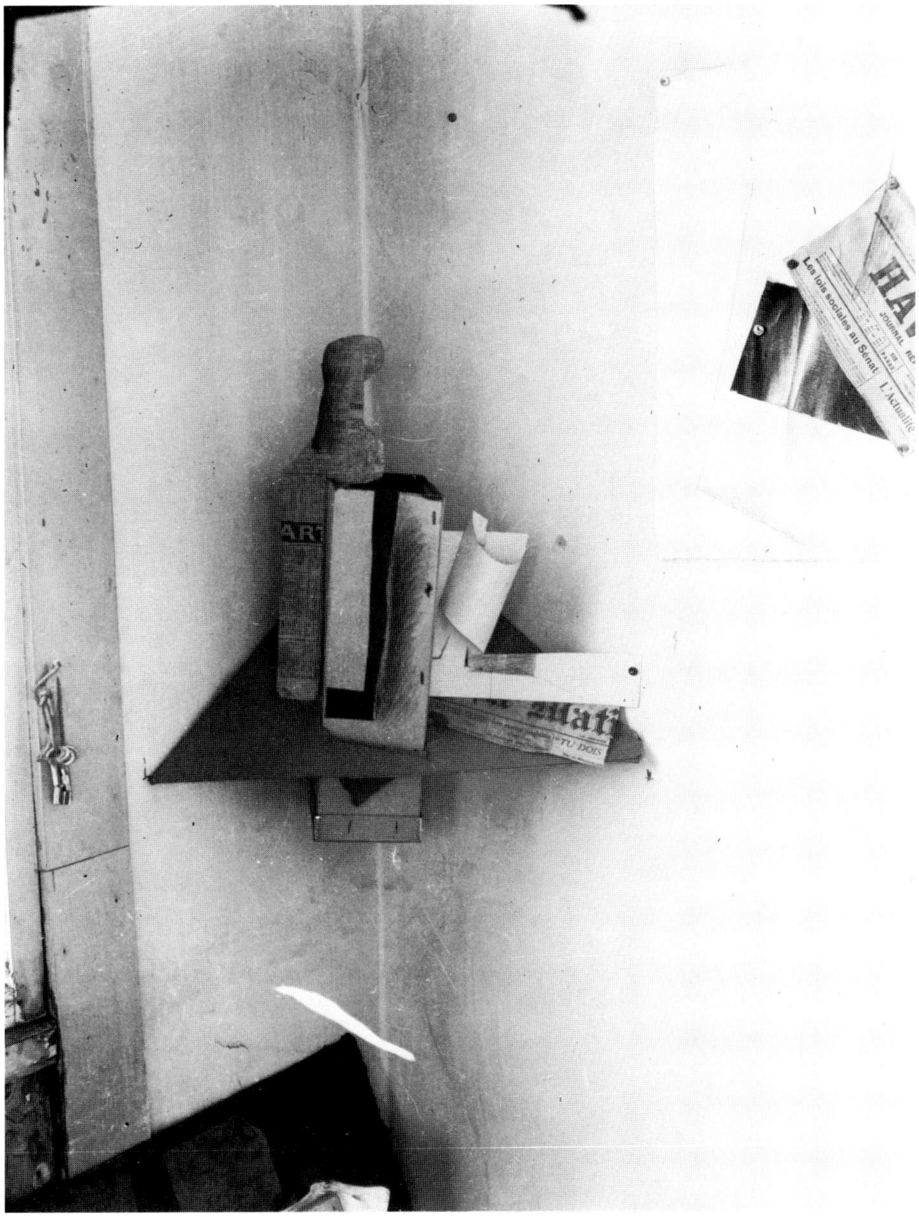

38. Braque, cardboard and paper construction, 1914. Photo: Archives Laurens.

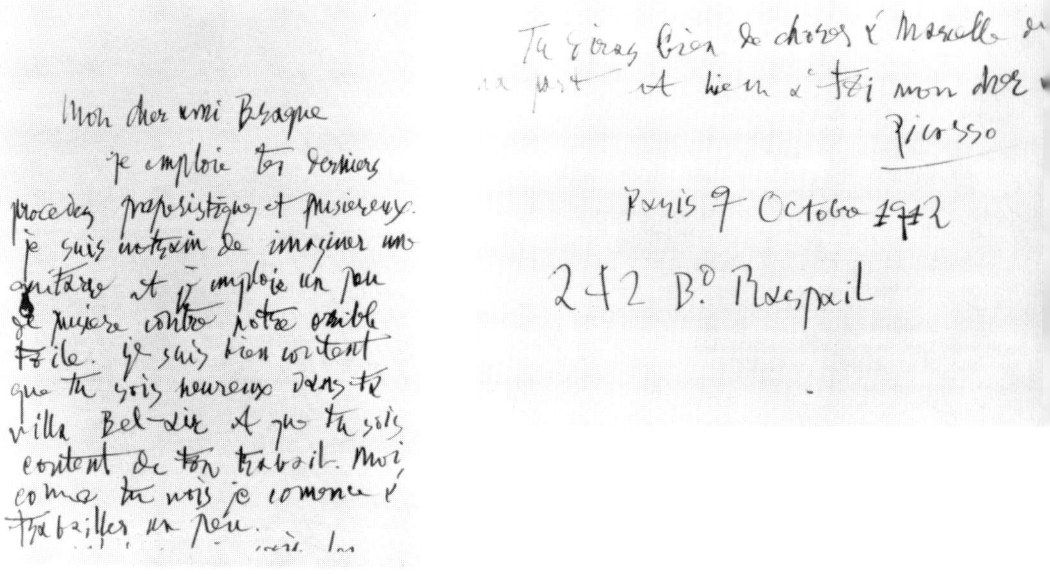
Mon cher ami Braque
je emploie tes derniers
procedes paperistiques et pusiereux.
je suis entrain de imaginer une
guitare et je emploie un peu
de pusiere contre notre horrible
toile. je suis bien content
que tu sois heureux dans ta
villa Bel-Air et que tu sois
content de ton travail. Moi
comme tu vois je comence à
travailler un peu.

Tu diras bien des choses à Marcelle de
ma part et bien à toi mon cher
Picasso

Paris 9 Octobre 1912

242 Bd Raspail

39.-40. Letter from Picasso in Paris to Braque in Sorgues, 9 October 1912. See note 7.

tember, Braque could show him one, or more probably several, "pasted papers" (see cat. nos. 1 and 2), which we customarily call *papiers collés* and which did not yet have a name: charcoal drawings punctuated with a cut-out and pasted color-texture. The very gesture of découpage is rapid, a decision which forms itself in a short time, more irreversible than the time of drawing. Collage, also, in a single gesture brings to life a whole plane of color. To continue in terms of time, pasting a piece of *faux bois* paper goes more quickly than painting a given surface in imitation of the grain or color of wood. There is in this procedure, besides all its considerable formal and spatial implications, a manner of saving time, which if we follow Braque's lesson, and if "the road counts more than the thing" should be taken into consideration for the *papiers collés,* ought to help us to perceive them fully in all their dimensions.

At the end of the month of September, Braque again wrote to D. H. Kahnweiler: "... Complete calm: I try to profit from it as much as possible. I am working a lot. Since my arrival, I have been working on a fairly large canvas (1.60 meters) of a woman in which I have innovated painting with sand. I have also made a violin and another woman with a violin, some small still lifes and begun some others ... in short, I am very happy to be here. Picasso told me about his trip to Paris...." Another innovation then, the addition of sand to colored pigments. We know that these experiments are contemporary with the first *papiers collés* and are to be viewed with them. The proof of this lies, it seems to us, in the repetition of motifs (table, fruit dish, pears, bunch of grapes, match box) with two *papiers collés, Compotier et verre (Fruit-dish and Glass;* cat. no. 1) and *Le compotier (The Fruit-dish;* cat. no. 2), and three canvases, *Compotier et cartes (Fruit-dish and Cards;* oil on canvas, 41 x 33 cm., with painting zones imitating wood), *Compotier, bouteille et verre (Fruit-dish, Bottle and Glass;* oil and sand on canvas, 41 x 33 cm.), and *Compotier, verre et raisin (Fruit-dish, Glass, and Grape;* oil and sand on canvas, 50 x 64 cm.), these last two having areas where sand and powder add a granular quality to the color, thereby modifying it.

Always during this chopped up, rapid, full time, Picasso—who is indeed a "climbing companion"—reacted immediately. He adopted Braque's "procedures" to the extent that these inventions were immediately shared, discussed, and exploited together. After his return to the boulevard Raspail, Paris, he wrote on 9 October to Braque, who had remained in Sorgues (see figs. 39 and 40): "My dear friend Braque, I am using your latest paperistic and powdery procedures. I am in the process of conceiving a guitar and I use a little dust against our horrible canvas. I am very glad that you are happy in your Villa Bel Air and that you are pleased with your work. As you see I begin to work a little."[5] This letter, marvelously important, had been mentioned by Zervos in the notice cited above (in 1932). As far as we know, it is published here for the first time. Minimal fragment of one of the most important dialogues of the twentieth century, it incites one to both reflection and reverie.

Braque still delayed some weeks at Sorgues, not returning to Paris until about 15 November. The contract-letter which defines his commercial relations with Kahnweiler was sent from Paris on 30 November (see figs. 41 and 42).

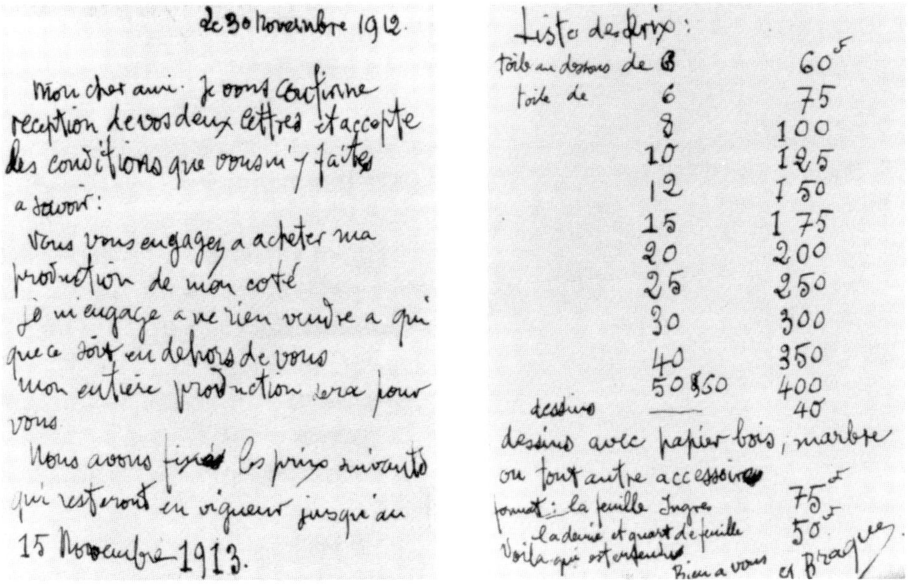

le 30 Novembre 1912.

Mon cher ami. Je vous confirme reception de vos deux lettres et accepte les conditions que vous m'y faites a savoir:
Vous vous engagez a acheter ma production de mon coté
je m'engage a ne rien vendre a qui que ce soit en dehors de vous
mon entière production sera pour vous
Nous avons fixés les prix suivants qui resteront en vigueur jusqu'au 15 Novembre 1913.

Liste de prix:
toile au dessous de 6 — 60 F
toile de 6 — 75
8 — 100
10 — 125
12 — 150
15 — 175
20 — 200
25 — 250
30 — 300
40 — 350
50 — 400
dessins — 40
dessins avec papier bois, marbre ou tout autre accessoire
format: la feuille Ingres — 75 F
la demie et quart de feuille — 50
Voila qui est entendu
Bien a vous G Braque.

41.-42. Letter from Braque in Sorgues to D.-H. Kahnweiler, 30 November 1912. See note 8.

Work on the *papiers collés* had advanced sufficiently: there existed, either finished or projected, a large enough number of them for Braque to feel the need to give them a separate category in the list of prices agreed upon with the dealer. "Drawings" were to sell for 40 francs; the "drawings with wood paper, marble or any other accessory" would be valued according to their sizes, either 75 or 50 francs.

Picasso's contract-letter is also known, dating from 18 December 1912. Must one see there an indication of the directions which were still hardly different, but which starting in 1913 would move farther away from each other, in what the two companions contracted for separately? Nowhere does Picasso mention drawings heightened with paper. Instead the word "sculptures" appears twice in this letter: "I promise to sell you at a fixed price my entire production of paintings and *escultures* (the word is underlined by Picasso), of drawings, prints while keeping at most only five paintings per year." And in the list of prices, drawings are worth 100 francs and the "price of *escultures* and prints is to be discussed."

One can also suppose that in December 1912, Picasso was only beginning his exploration of *papier collé*—which in any case he would conduct very differently from Braque—and that in consequence he did not judge it useful to mention this special category of works in his contract.

To return to Braque and the summer of 1912, the experiments which he conducted simultaneously with extraordinary exploratory energy had been of three kinds, starting with space in the paintings of 1911 and the first half of 1912: experiments with relief and the third dimension (folding in space of paper constructions); perfecting color in space, dissociated from form (with the cut and pasted *faux bois* paper); and exploration of the very substance of color and research on the interior of color (with powder and sand). All of these are conveniently dissociated, yet in reality completely linked since the pieces of cut paper or grains of sand both deal with color, relief, shadow, light—with the entire body of painting.

In the accelerated time of the summer at Sorgues, all the directions which would engage Braque's work in 1913 and 1914 before the cut-off of the summer of 1914, had been put in place. At first, drawings "heightened with paper," the *papiers collés* would be progressively reinvested with painting and would play a transitional role in the return to a more synthetic color and figuration.

On 5 October 1912, Braque sent a postcard to D. H. Kahnweiler: "Impossible to work outdoors. The trees already have no more leaves. This is a summer that has passed quickly."

NOTES

1. Jean Metzinger, in *Pan,* October-November 1910: "Braque who fashions new signs with joy, does not commit errors of taste. The new word does not deceive us! I can, without diminishing the innovative audacity of this painter, compare him to Chardin and to Lancret."

2. Cited by Pierre Rosenberg, in the preface to the exhibition catalogue, *Chardin* (Paris: Galerie Nationale du Grand Palais, January-April 1979).

3. See also the chronology in this volume. All the citations of letters to D. H. Kahnweiler which follow come from the archives of the Galerie Louise Leiris. We extend our keen thanks to Mme. Louise Leiris who generously gave us access to them.

4. See also, on the first *papier collé,* evidence given by Douglas Cooper in his introductory essay, "Braque as Innovator : The First *Papier Collé.*"

5. This letter was kindly brought to our attention by M. and Mme. Claude Laurens, whom we thank heartily.

6. Figs. 35-37:
My dear friend, Not much new at Sorgues. Complete calm. We are doing a lot of cooking with Picasso. The other evening we had l'ajo Blanco, a Spanish dish as its name indicates. We were very sorry that you were not here to share with us this modest but succulent (l'ajo blanco is a powerful insecticide, used with success against flies) soup-dessert.
(In case this tempts you, here is the recipe. One or two bowls of water per person, some garlic, some almonds, and just before serving throw some grapeseeds in the water (above all do not cook it).
Try it, it will make you laugh alot.
I am counting on having my revenge. Our weather is not very beautiful, but I console myself in thinking about yours in Paris.
I am working alot and am profiting from my stay in the country to do things that one cannot do in Paris, among other things some sculpture out of paper, which has given me a lot of satisfaction.
A thousand messages to Madame Kahnweiler and very cordially yours,
Yours,
G Braque

7. Figs. 39-40:
My dear friend Braque
I am using your latest paperistic and powdery procedures. I am in the process of conceiving a guitar and I use a little dust against our horrible canvas. I am very glad that you are happy in your Villa Bel-air and that you are pleased with your work. As you see I begin to work a little.
Give all sorts of good wishes to Marcelle from me and the best to you my dear friend
Picasso
Paris 9 October 1912/242 Bd. Raspail

8. Figs. 41-42:
30 November 1912
My dear friend, I confirm receipt of your two letters and accept the conditions that you have made, to wit:
you engage to buy my output on my side I engage to sell nothing to anybody else but you.
My entire production will be for you.
We have fixed the following prices, which will remain in effect until 15 November 1913.
List of Prices:

canvas under 6	60F (French francs)
canvas of 6	75
8	100
10	125
12	150
15	175
20	200
25	250
30	300
40	350
50 & 60	400
drawings— —	40

drawings with wood paper, marble or any other accessory

format: "Ingres" sheet	75F
half or quarter sheet	50F

This is what is understood.
Best wishes,
G Braque

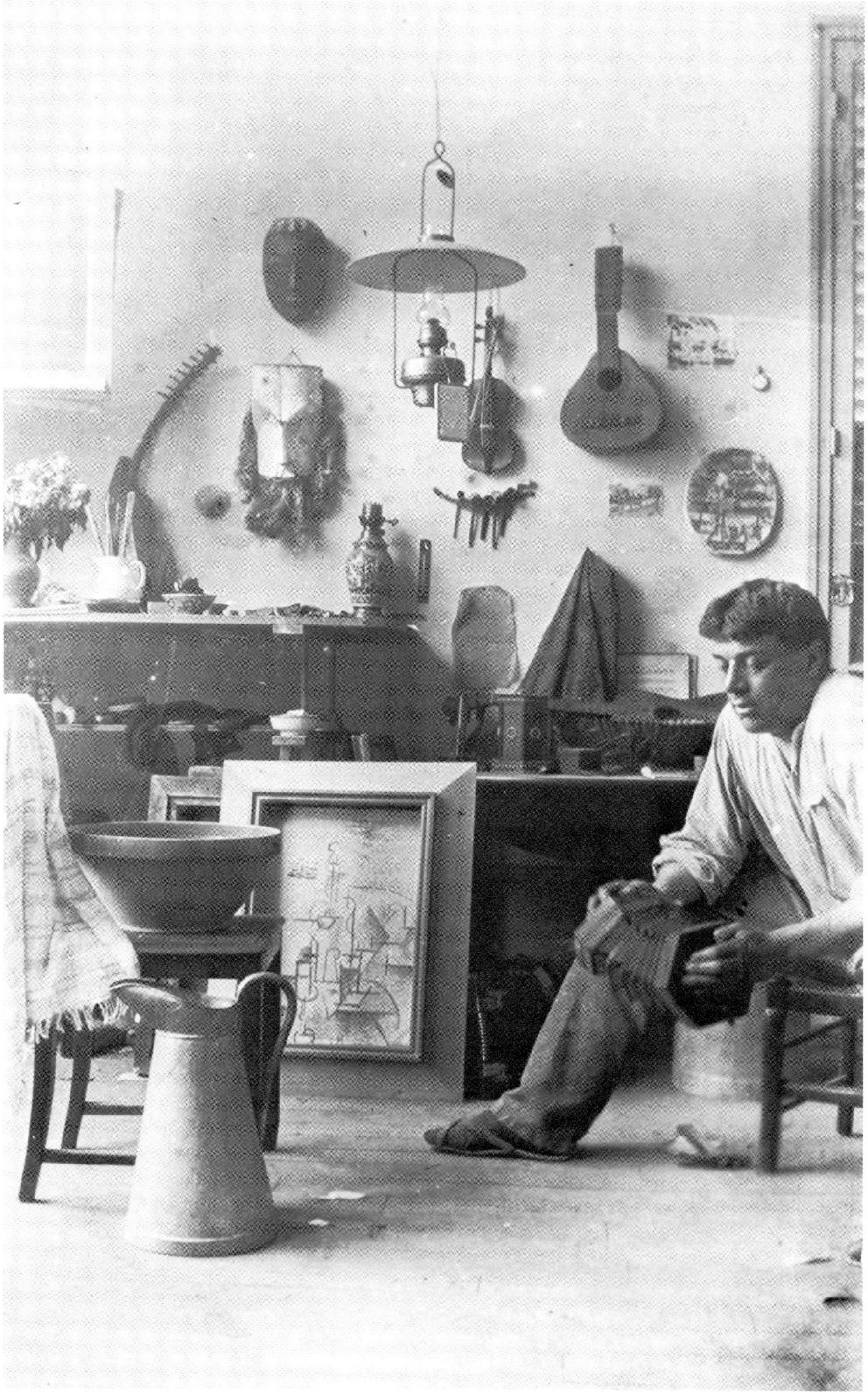

43. Georges Braque in his studio, 1910-1911. Photo: Archives Laurens.

GEORGES BRAQUE AND THE ORIGINS OF THE LANGUAGE OF SYNTHETIC CUBISM

Alvin Martin

ONE OF THE MOST intriguing characteristics of the work of Georges Braque and Pablo Picasso during the "synthetic" period (1912-1914) of their collaboration is their inclusion of signs and letters in paintings, *papiers collés,* and collages to create witty visual and verbal plays on words and forms.[1] The impulsive wit of Picasso is legendary. Braque, however, is often seen in the role of straight man to his Spanish colleague. Indeed, until recently, Braque's contribution to the development of cubism has been somewhat obscured by the genius and personality of Picasso. Leo Steinberg's critiques notwithstanding, William Rubin, in his essays, "Cézannisme and the Beginnings of Cubism" and "Pablo and Georges and Leo and Bill," demonstrates that Braque led the way in the development of "early cubism" (1904-1909) in his synthesis and abstraction of the structural implications of the late Cézanne. Ultimately, however, Rubin confers on Picasso the mantle of life-giver to Braque's discoveries.[2]

It is not my point here in any way to downgrade Picasso's achievements, but rather to illuminate some of Braque's. To overlook the poetic lyricism, wry humor, and subtle inventiveness of his genius is to miss in large measure the richness of his art. By an analysis of his seminal painting, *Nature morte, violon et cruche* of 1909 *(Still Life, Violin and Pitcher;* fig. 44), in relation to several other works by himself, Picasso, and Gris, it will be shown that Braque's own inventive humor provides an essential and delightful contribution to later cubist innovations.

One of the barriers to comprehending this aspect of Braque's art has been the contrast between his and Picasso's public personalities. Picasso actively enjoyed being the center of attention. Braque, however, a more private person, was often shy, even reticent, in formal situations, particularly when interviewed by critics.[3] Thus he is frequently characterized as being too shy to engage in artistic high-jinks.[4]

This perception of Braque has two faults. First, it developed in comparison to the gregarious Picasso. Second, it emerges in the literature largely after World War I, in which Braque received a serious head wound, suffered a long convalescence, and, ironically, achieved his first official government recognition— two decorations for valor in combat. Before 1914, however, he appears as a different personality in private life and among his friends. He is recalled as a tall, handsome young athlete who loved boxing and cycling, singing and dancing, and who played the accordion well.[5] After 1907 he was a member of a group that included some of the wittiest and zaniest personalities in the Parisian world of art and letters. The poet Guillaume Apollinaire, an intimate friend, often referred to him in articles in ironic terms, such as a sickly and delicate young man who has "ruined his health by excessive spitting while he smokes his pipe."[6] Maurice de Vlaminck (who wore a wooden necktie) was a frequent companion. Daniel Henry Kahnweiler, his first art dealer, described Braque as "a complete dandy," who had specially cut suits, square-toed shoes and a black string tie, which he wore with "great chic." Together with Picasso, Max Jacob, André Salmon, André Derain, Apollinaire, Kahnweiler, and others, Braque was an habitué of such *boits de nuit* as *Le Rat Mort* and the *Lapin Agile,* as well as the *Cirque Médrano.*[8] He was a guest at Picasso's banquet for Douanier Rousseau in 1908.[9] No one could long associate with this group, much less develop a close rapport with Picasso, without a well-developed sense of humor and ready wit.

Although they met in 1907, the friendship between Braque and Picasso did not mature until 1909. Meanwhile, in the public's eye, Braque assumed the leadership of the emerging cubist movement. He exhibited the first cubist painting at the Salon des Indépendants in the spring of 1908.[10] Apollinaire praised him, recognizing his "will to construct."[11] During this exhibit, an American journalist, Gelett Burgess, interviewed Braque, calling him "the originator of nudes with feet as square as boxes."[12] In November 1908, Braque exhibited a series of landscapes and still lifes done in his new geometric style and completed during the summer of 1908 at L'Estaque. Louis Vauxcelles, the critic for *Gil Blas,* a prominent newspaper, called Braque "very audacious" and published the word "cube" in regard to modern painting for the first time.[13] A few weeks later in *Mercure de France,* Charles Morice again noted the "geometric a priori" of Braque's art.[14] In December, Braque exhibited six cubist works in a group exhibit at the Galerie Notre-Dame des Champs in Paris. On 9 January 1909, Karl Max reviewed Braque's work in *Le Télégramme* of Toulouse, and quoted Apollinaire's introduction to the Kahnweiler exhibition catalogue in its entirety.[15] In February 1909, four of Braque's cubist paintings appeared at the prestigious Russian *Toison d'Or* exhibition in Moscow. Two of these were reproduced in the magazine *Toison d'Or,* which served as the catalogue for the show.[16] That same month, Braque showed for the first time at the Galerie Berthe Weill.[17] He then entered two more cubist paintings in the Salon des Indépendants. Morice and Vauxcelles, previously dubious of Braque's work and the attention it was receiving from other artists, became his detractors. Vauxcelles called his pictures *"bizarreries cubique."*[18] Morice referred to Braque as the "leader of the audacious" and used the word "cubism" in print, thus affirming the term's currency.[19]

Braque spent the summer of 1909 working and traveling. In June he participated in the fourth annual exhibit of the *Cercle d'Art Moderne du Havre,* an event of which he was cofounder.[20] The critic for *La Cloche Illustrée du Havre,* Claude Lantier, was perplexed by the exhibit, particularly by the works by Braque, Othon Friesz, and Kees Van Dongen. On 12 June 1909 he wrote that their works demonstrated "painfully readable studies, inexplicable deformities which approach ugliness; that is too much."[21] However, he was also somewhat impressed by the exhibit and the notoriety and mysteriousness of the artists and their works. He warned his readers against provincialism and blind laughter. Similar warnings are implied in all critiques of Braque at this time. Picasso was not then exhibiting; therefore Braque bore the brunt of public and critical astonishment at the new style.

The rest of the summer of 1909 Braque passed at La Roche Guyon, and later painted at Carrières-Saint-Denis with Derain. Picasso, with Fernande Olivier, was at Horta in Spain, where he spent what William Rubin believes to have been the most valuable vacation of his life.[22] Here he completed his own assimilation of "Cézannisme" and extended this into abstractions of forms and vantage points paralleling those which Braque had explored for the past year and a half.[23]

By late August, Braque was back in Paris and was again exhibiting at the Galerie Kahnweiler with Derain and Van Dongen. On 1 September 1909 a perceptive review by Emile Zavié appeared in *Le Feu,* which lends further insight into general and critical response to Braque's work and personality at this time. Zavié found Van Dongen "very uneven" and Derain "one might say a colorless Cézanne." But of Braque he stated:

> I like Braque very much. He is trying to express an idea, not yet fully formed, but done so well that one feels compelled to praise his efforts. What a pleasant music hall performance he would make were he to present his own works in person. Some self-styled art lovers can do nothing but laugh at his works. Perhaps they would be surprised to discover such an eccentric humorist lost in the paintings.[24]

Zavié once again noted the critical consternation and public amusement caused by Braque's work. The artist himself soon responded. Shortly afterward, late in 1909 or early in 1910, Braque painted his *Nature morte, violon et cruche* (fig. 44), which is a milestone not only in Braque's work but also in the history of cubism. Braque and Picasso, by this time, were fast friends, and the two of them were beginning a period of cooperation that would last until 1914. In Braque's work, this painting marks a transition from his previous concern with the formal extensions of the structural and spatial implications of Cézanne into that period known as "analytic" or "high analytic" cubism.[25]

The images of Braque, and then Picasso, as John Golding observed, "had become further removed from ordinary visual appearances than ever before. . . ."[26] Observers both sympathetic and hostile to cubism had difficulty in interpreting the subject matter of the paintings. The artists themselves were also very much aware of the abstract implications of their creations. Therefore, for many years the main thrust of the critical explanations of cubism was directed toward its formal or philosophical aspects rather than its iconography. Alfred Barr summed up this approach: "The Cubists seem to have had little conscious interest in subject matter. They used traditional subjects for the most part, figures, portraits, landscapes, still life, all serving as material for Cubist Analysis."[27] Barr, however, also noted Meyer Schapiro's concurrent theory "that consciously or unconsciously the Cubists through their subject matter reveal a significant preoccupation with the bohemian artistic life."[28] John Golding pointed out, somewhat later, the fallacy of purely formalistic interpretations:

> The fact that Cubism gave birth to so much abstract art may be one of the reasons why it has been so consistently misunderstood by the public, and even occasionally by serious critics and historians. Cubism, it must be stressed again, was an art of realism. . . . All the true Cubists had at one time or another come near to complete abstraction but each of them had almost immediately retracted and reasserted the representational element of their art.[29]

Golding's observations are certainly confirmed by the major eyewitnesses to the development of cubism. Daniel-Henry Kahnweiler, then dealer for both Braque and Picasso, has repeatedly confirmed the importance of titles in cubist paintings to establish references to the subject matter and the necessity for "reading" the pictures to reconstruct their meaning.[30] Picasso aptly stated: "When we invented Cubism we had no intention of inventing Cubism. We simply wanted to express what was in us."[31] He also said: "in our subjects we keep the joy of discovery, the pleasure of the unexpected; our subject itself must be the source of interest."[32]

In more recent scholarship, Rudi Blesh and Harriet Janis, Robert Rosenblum, Leo Steinberg, and William Rubin among many others have changed the focus of cubist studies from form to content.[33] All

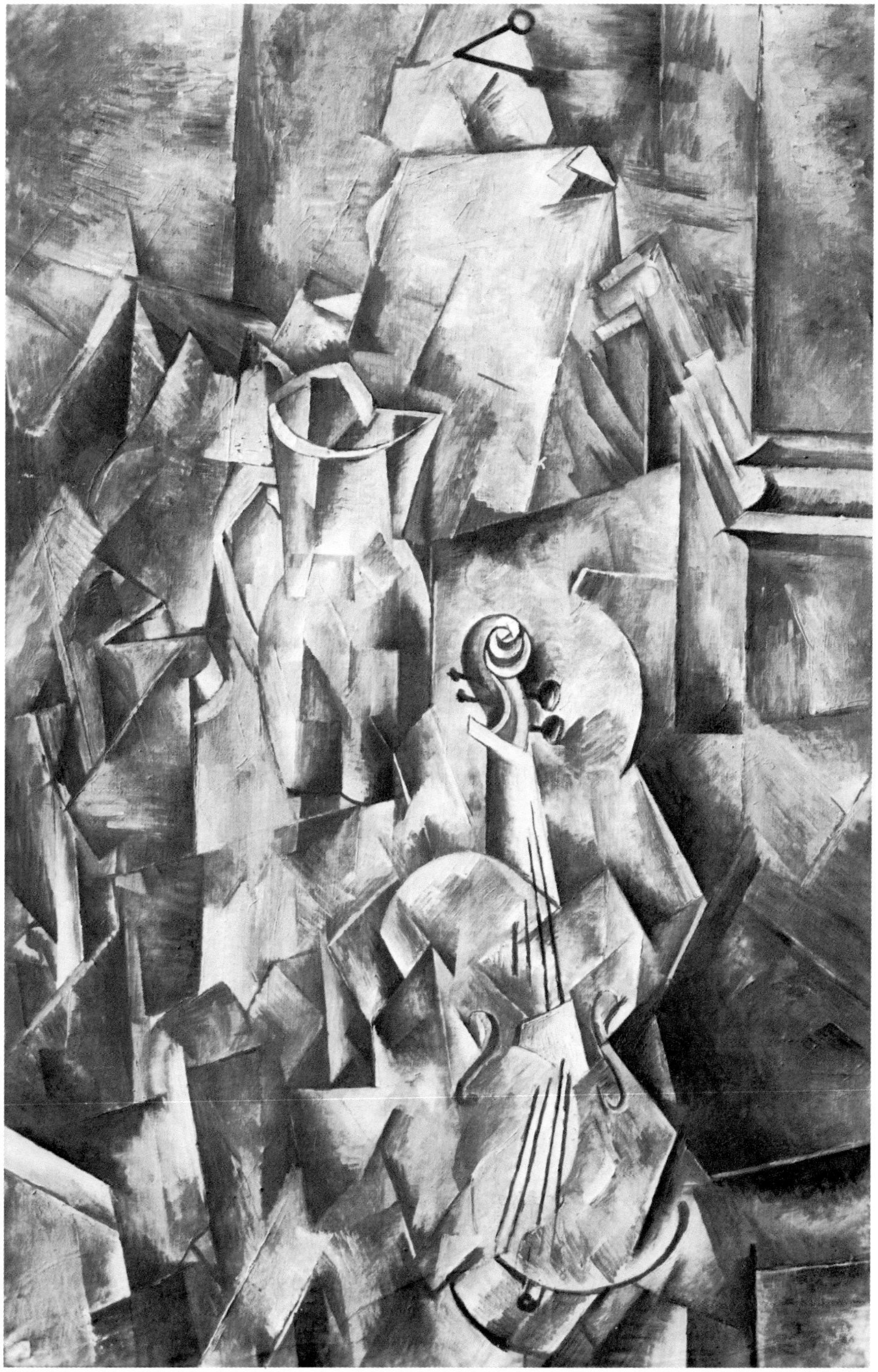

44. Braque, *Nature morte, violon et cruche,* 1909-1910, oil on canvas. Offentliche Kunstsammlung-Kunstmuseum, Basel.

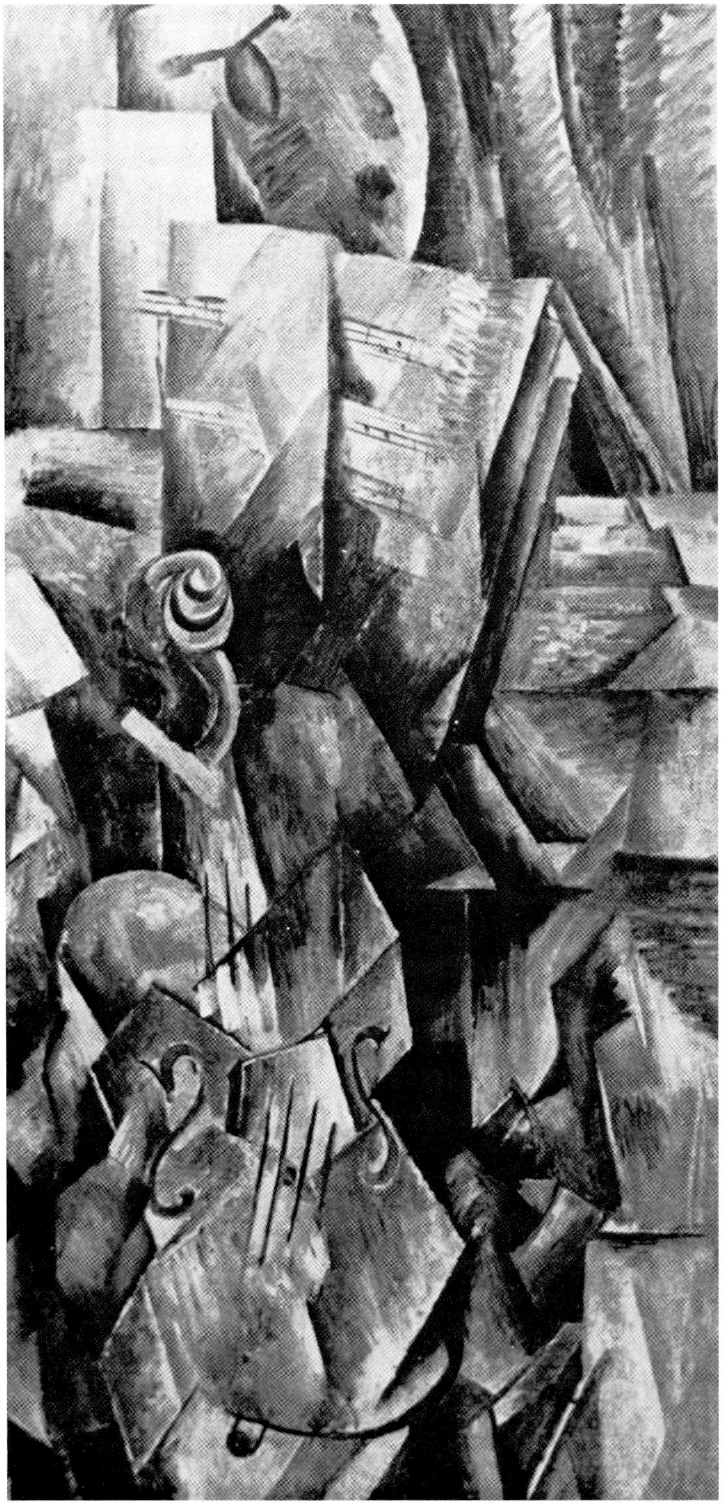

45. Braque, *Nature morte, violon et palette,* 1909-1910, oil on canvas. The Solomon R. Guggenheim Museum, New York.

have demonstrated that the inclusion of wit and humor in the form of visual or verbal puns is an integral part of "synthetic cubism." The basis for many of these puns may be found in Braque's *Violon et cruche,* which is a landmark in the development of not only cubism's form, but also its iconography.

A useful means of understanding this painting is supplied by a photograph of Braque in his studio, taken about 1910 (fig. 43). The objects displayed provide a catalogue of Braque's still-life subject matter. Bowls, musical instruments, pipes, masks, drapery, jugs, and pitchers appear repeatedly in his compositions throughout his career.

Nature morte, violon et cruche was developed from another still life painted about the same time (winter 1909-1910), *Nature morte, violon et palette (Still Life, Violin and Palette;* fig. 45) This is indicated by the more sophisticated and complex fragmentation of form and interaction of space and volume in *Violon et cruche.* The composition of the two works, however, is similar, and the subject matter of both comprises objects visible in the photograph.

Violon et palette is a relatively straightforward cubist still life. The violin rests upon a table amid a geometric interpretation of drapery, which cascades from the table to the left, and moves back along the table's surface to the configuration that depicts sheets of music on a music stand. Directly behind and to the left of the sheets of music are two less easily decipherable geometric shapes. Formally, these serve to repeat and complement the shapes of the music sheets, and establish a rhythmic progression through the shallow space between the music stand and the wall. These shapes probably represent such objects as pictures, or possibly other sheets of paper, such as those shown in the photograph on the lower table against the wall. The wall, the palette, and the drapery to its right define the narrow limits of the space occupied by the still life. Although painted in the geometric and faceted idiom of analytic cubism, the objects comprising the still life are readily ascertained, and all of these can be seen in the 1910 photograph.

Without doubt, the selection and portrayal of such objects was in large part to do with their suitability to the formal inquiries which Braque was pursuing.

Braque himself explained his reasons in formal and metaphorical terms:

> At that time I painted a lot of musical instruments, firstly because I was surrounded by them and then because their form, their volume, came into the realm of the still life exactly as I wanted. I was seeking a tactile, palpable space as I like to call it, and musical instruments, as objects, also have this characteristic, you can bring them to life by touching them.[34]

Thus to the artist the selection of these objects was more than incidental. The photograph certainly indicates the degree to which he was surrounded by these objects, indeed he is shown "bringing one to life." The palette, the violin, and the sheet music are the personally collected and carefully maintained possessions of a painter who loved music and the instruments which make it. In the painting, these objects become allegorical symbols of both the arts of painting and music. More important, they are the personal attributes of a particular painter-musician, Georges Braque, composed by him in a mode, cubism, which he was deeply involved in perfecting. To overlook this subjective content is to miss an essential element of this painting.

In both composition and content, *Violon et palette* and *Violon et cruche* are closely related, but significantly different. The most perplexing and often noted feature that they share is the depiction of a nail and its cast shadow, painted in *trompe l'oeil,* near the top of each canvas. In *Violon et palette* the nail serves both a formal and a practical function. It suspends the palette from the wall, and at the same time, its illusionistic appearance and cast shadow provide a contrast to the cubist abstraction of the composition as a whole. In *Violon et cruche,* however, the use of the illusionistic nail is less comprehensible, almost arbitrary. The jerky rhythms, the fragmentation of the objects into irregular geometric forms, and the more ambitious use of changing vantage points render the identity of the forms and spaces more obscure.

Braque's reason for using the realistic nail has been widely interpreted. Kahnweiler, writing as early as 1915, emphasized the importance of this invention in the development of cubism. He saw the nail as a space-defining element of reality, which induced memory images so that "physical representation comes into being in the spectator's mind."[35] Clement Greenberg saw it as an assertion of the picture surface creating a picture within a picture.[36] Robert Rosenblum has suggested that the nail forms a visual paradox indicating a complex interchange between artifice and reality.[37] John Golding has called the nail "an element of contradiction, almost perversity," and has written that "Braque was intensely concerned with maintaining contact with external reality" in the face of ever more abstract implications of his work at this time.[38] Each of these interpretations provides valuable insight into the rich vocabulary of the developing language of cubism. Each author has noted the importance of the juxtaposition of illusionism and abstraction in *Violon et cruche* as providing the foundation for the later addition of words and letters that culminates in the use of real materials in the collages and *papiers collés* of synthetic cubism. None, however, has explored the work from the point of view of its specific meaning.

In order to comprehend the subject matter of *Violon et cruche,* a comparison of it to Picasso's contemporaneous *Portrait de Braque (Portrait of Braque;* fig. 46) is instructive. Formally, Picasso exhibits the same interest in complex design and distance from natural appearance that appears in Braque's painting. Furthermore, both John Russell and Jean Leymarie have observed that *Portrait de Braque* provides insight into Braque's psychological attitudes at this time. Russell, however, interprets the portrait as being indicative of a mood of sober seriousness on Braque's part.[39] This conclusion does not stand well under close analysis of the painting.

In fact, once the baffling image is reconstructed, it emerges as a sympathetic portrait done in a clever spirit of caricature. The geometric shapes in the lower left of the composition create an almost whimsical representation of the shoulder, descending upper arm, and rising forearm of the sitter.

The forearm, composed of willfully drawn trapezoidal shapes, indicating the sitter's coat sleeve, leads to the bent wrist and the amusingly

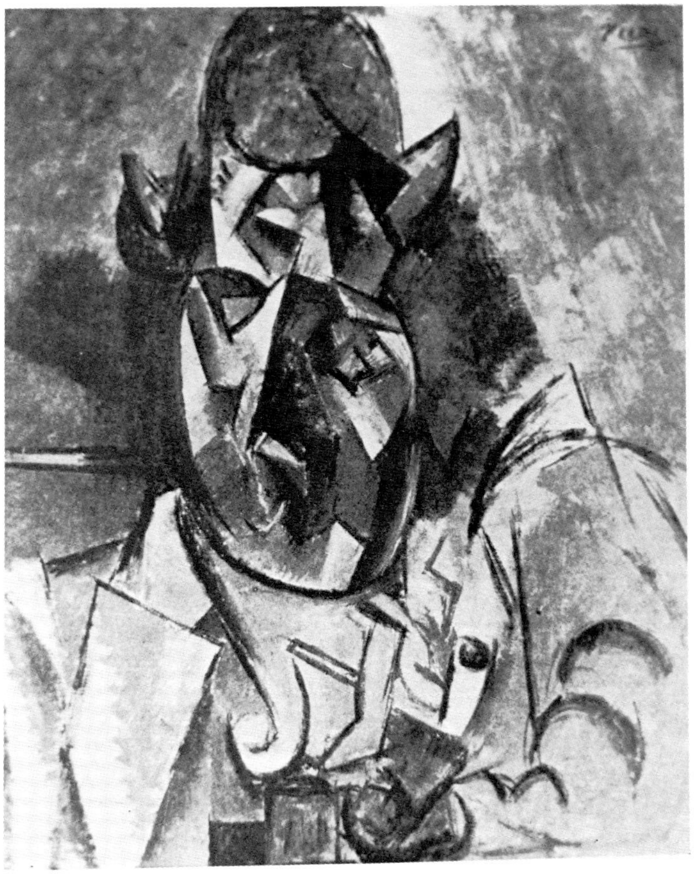

46. Pablo Picasso (Spanish, 1881-1973), *Portrait de Braque*, 1909, oil on canvas. Collection of E. Brageline, New York.

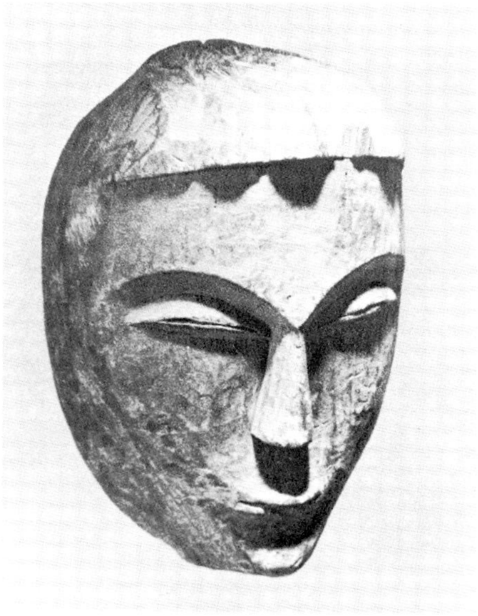

47. African mask (Gabon), former collection of Braque. Private collection. Photo from *Arts primitifs dans les ateliers d'artistes*, Musée de l'Homme, Paris, 1967.

drawn hand, upon which the subject rests his chin. The upper part of the hand descends, giving way to an intertwining dangle of fingers and thumb, which grasps a pipe. The pipe itself is of interest, because it is not any pipe, but one of Braque's own, which can be seen lying on the table in the photograph (fig. 43), just to the left of Braque's right arm.

The most interesting characteristic of the portrait, however, is that the face is comprised of not one set of features, but two. These features are composed as if made from two masks, rather like the theatrical symbols of comedy and tragedy, one being placed lower and overlapping the other. The lower masklike set of features, with its curved chin, faces slightly to the left, while the upper, with only eyes, bridge of nose, and forehead appearing, looks slightly to the right (fig. 46).

Once this double mask configuration is understood, both Picasso's wit and his sources become evident. Once again, the studio photograph (fig. 43) is useful. Picasso has used the two African masks visible on the wall as structural and iconographic sources for his *Portrait de Braque.* The lower rounded features derive from a cubist breakdown of the simple rounded planes of the upper African mask hanging from Braque's studio wall (fig. 47). The upper, more angular features, with inverted V-shaped eyebrows and semi-elliptical eyelids, develop from the other, more fierce and angular mask (fig. 48). The circular form at the top of the head is a cubist improvisation on both the curve of the forehead of this second mask and the roundness of Braque's own, bowllike haircut. The derivations from the masks are infused with exaggerations of the more prominent elements of Braque's own face, such as the flare of the nostrils and the pronounced shape of the mouth. Picasso, by combining his perceptions of Braque, his artifacts, and

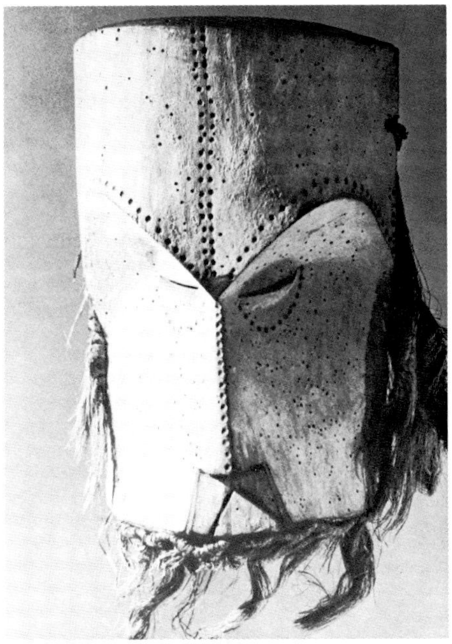

48. African mask (Gabon), former collection of Braque. Private collection. Photo from *Arts primitifs dans les ateliers d'artistes,* Musée de l'Homme, Paris, 1967.

his possessions, renders a playfully intimate composite portrait of his friend and colleague.

Picasso's *Portrait* gives us an indication of the relationship between the artist and his subject at this time. As Braque recalled:

> We were living in Montmartre, we saw each other every day. Picasso and I said things then that no one will say again, things that no one could say and no one would understand . . . things that were incomprehensible and that gave us enormous happiness. . . .

Braque also used his own objects, as shown in the photograph, in an intimate and subjective fashion. However, Braque's meaning is more complex and his humor more subtle. Apart from the obvious nail, violin, and pitcher, the rest of the subject matter is hidden in the fragmented, geometric volumes and voids that preoccupied the artist at this time.

In *Nature morte, violon et cruche* (fig. 44), the violin and pitcher rest on a table top, adjacent to an architectural molding (perhaps a wainscot) to the right of the composition. To the left of the violin is a mass of interacting planes derived from such objects as frames or pictures, as seen in the photograph. Behind the pitcher rises a series of geometric shapes, which, once understood, become the essential elements of the painting's subject matter. These forms reveal a visual pun on a human figure, which is related to both *Violon et palette* and Picasso's *Portrait de Braque.*

Behind the pitcher is a large, dog-eared piece of paper, compositionally analogous to the music in *Violon et palette.* The music, however, is supported by a stand. An illusion to this is retained in *Violon et cruche,* in the form of a right-angled shape which provides a formal complement to the molding behind which it disappears. The folds here, however, clearly indicate that the angled form does not support, but rather grasps, the piece of paper. A metamorphosis takes place. The paper, probably a newspaper, is held by a cubist rendering of a hand.

Behind the newspaper, the form across which the nail casts its shadow is revealed as the figure's head. This head is a simplification of that same angular mask that Picasso used as the upper element of the face in his *Portrait de Braque,* and which hangs on Braque's studio wall in the photograph. As have the other objects in the painting, this mask has been fragmented and dissolved into its surroundings. It is recognizable from its general shape, the angular relationship of the bridge of the nose and eyebrow and the suggestion of the eye below. Just above the pitcher, all but obscured by the left edge of the paper, are three small shapes that represent what can be seen of the figure's sleeve, wrist, and right hand, upon which the mask head rests its cheek. The body is hidden behind the paper. Like so many of Braque's works of this period, this amusing metamorphosis has its ultimate source in a painting by Cézanne. The placement of hands and head and the obscuring of the body behind a dog-eared newspaper in Braque's painting clearly correspond to the composition of the upper portion of the figure in Cézanne's *Le père de l'artiste* of 1866 *(The Artist's Father;* fig. 49), a work to which Braque referred again at this time (fig. 50).

The dominance of the pitcher's representation and location explains the pun. The present title of the painting is not that by which it was originally called. Its earlier and correct title was *Broc et violon* and is recorded as such by both Kahnweiler and Georges Isarlov in the first catalogue of Braque's oeuvre.[41] "Broc" is the phonetic homonym for the artist's name, and thus identifies the painting's subject, a hermetic self-portrait composed of the artist's cherished possessions.

The pun is further verified by the fact that just such a play on words regarding the artist's name was current at the time. Braque had exhibited at the Galerie Berthe Weill in February 1909, and, in her diary, later published as *Pan dans l'oeil!,* Mme. Weill recorded this event with the notation "Braque en Broc."[42] The pun is enriched by the

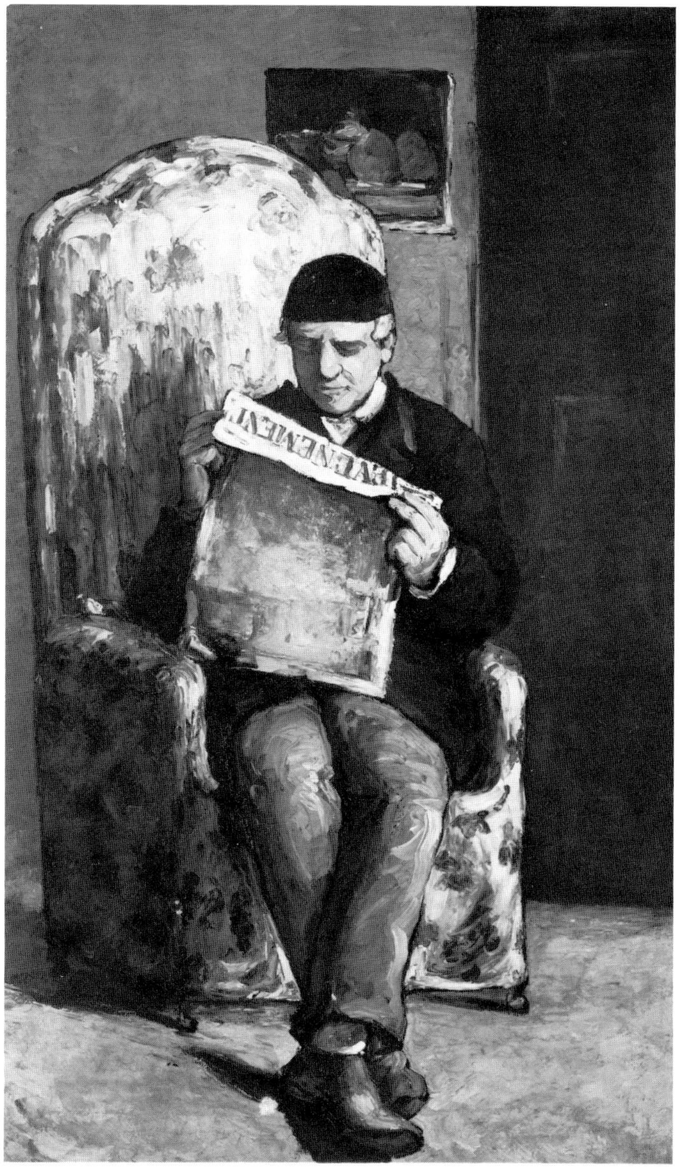

49. Paul Cézanne (French, 1839-1906), *Le père de l'artiste*, c. 1866, oil on canvas. National Gallery of Art, Washington, Collection of Mr. and Mrs. Paul Mellon, 1970.

fact that Braque's very name in context of the public's response to cubism made a delightful joke, particularly in light of Zavié's description of him as an "eccentric humorist." This, no doubt, amused Braque as much as it did his detractors. The French adjective *braque* means a hair-brained fellow or madcap—it also means to be of daft appearance.

In the context of Braque's pun, the *trompe l'oeil* nail becomes explicable. It is inspired by the fact that the mask on the studio wall hung from just such a nail. The small line running from the left of the mask to the top of the canvas represents the string from which the mask was suspended. Logically, the nail would be just above the top of the painting's edge. Braque has purposely placed it just above the mask/head to serve a double function. It establishes the ambiguous formal dialogue upon which critics have so often remarked. Simultaneously, the nail takes on a special meaning within Braque's elaborate play on words and forms. The verb *braquer* is also brought into the game. *Braquer* means to point, to direct, or to fix one's glance. Thus the nail "braque vers la tête braque de Braque."

François Ponge, Pierre Reverdy, and Stanislas Fumet have also noted the susceptibility of Braque's name to this kind of play on words.[43] John Russell offers another tantalizing proposition—that Braque included the nail in response to a favorite saying of his.[44] In a note in his journals Braque wrote: "One cannot always hold one's hat in one's hand: the hatrack was invented for this purpose. I discovered painting so as to hang my ideas from a nail."[45] Certainly this would be consistent with the "hermetic" punning so enjoyed by Picasso, Braque, and their friends at this time.

Braque, and then Picasso and Gris, became increasingly interested in paradoxically compounding relatively naturalistic and relatively abstract forms and words, creating those mysterious metamorphoses which characterize analytic cubism, from which the language of synthetic cubism later evolved. About the same time as *Broc et violon,*

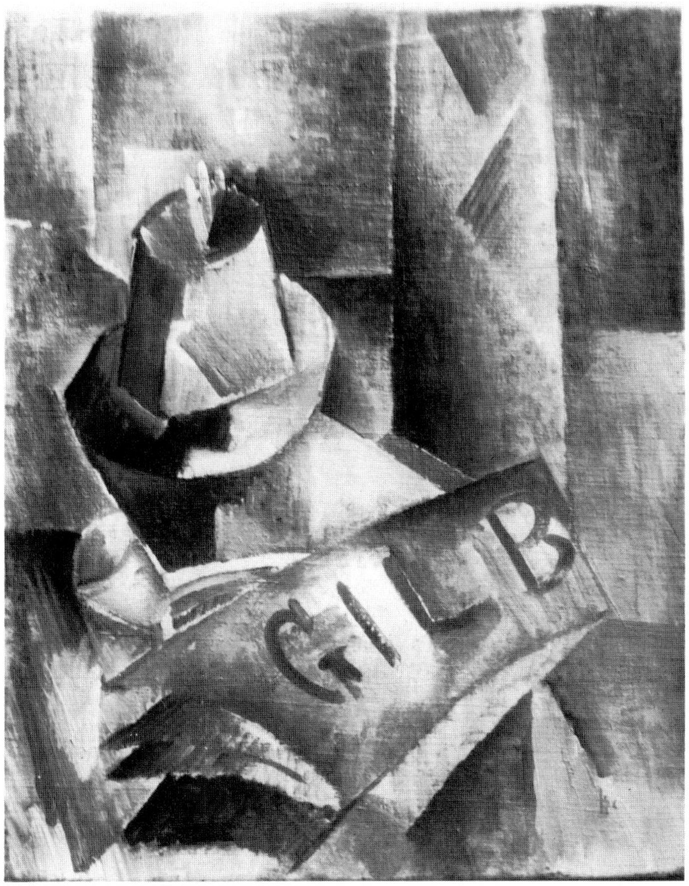

50. Braque, *Le pyrogène,* 1910, oil on canvas. Location unknown. Photo: Archives Leiris.

Braque painted the letters *GIL B* onto forms representing a folded newspaper in a painting called *Le pyrogène* (fig. 50). Behind this paper appears his pipe, again a personal artifact which had become his attribute. (Picasso had used it as the identifying feature in his *Portrait de Braque,* and Apollinaire had referred to Braque's "excessive spitting while smoking his pipe" in his review of the 1907 Salon d'Automne.[46]) Above the pipe is an object that appears to be a candle or match holder.[47]

The letters refer to the newspaper *Gil Blas.* Here Braque refers again to Cézanne's portrait of his father. In *Le père de l'artiste,* Cézanne included the title of the journal *L'Evénement,* in which his father is supposedly reading an article by Emile Zola. Braque's inclusion of letters also refers to a critic, Louis Vauxcelles, who, in *Gil Blas,* had become cubism's principal enemy. Braque's choice of title and his subject matter again create a multi-leveled meaning. A *pyrogène* is something that starts a fire or which, by extension , is inflammatory. The subject matter of Braque's painting—a rolled newspaper, a pipe, and a candle or match holder—comprises objects which both ignite and inflame. They are painted in the cubist style which was inflammatory in both the eyes of public and critical taste, particularly to the critic of *Gil Blas.* Metaphorically, the picture remarks on the inflamed relationship between the artist represented by his pipe and the critic symbolized by his paper. Finally, the paper itself is rolled in the form of an *allume feu,* itself a *pyrogène.* The artist, therefore, disdainfully says that the best use for this source of criticism is to warm his hearth.[48]

The use of witty juxtapositions of visual metamorphosis and verbal metaphor proliferate in Braque and Picasso's analytic cubist abstractions. For example, in Braque's painting *L'homme à la guitare* (fig. 51), he includes a recognizable nail holding a sash cord in the upper left of the composition. At the right is a shape derived from the string bridge of a violin or fiddle, which alludes to the musical nature of the title. These clues contrast to the central mass of overlapping, interpenetrating transparent planes which mingle the forms and spaces that make the figure, the guitar, the chair, and the background into this cubist *jeu de forme.* Carefully read, however, these forms reveal a comic element. The head of the figure is a caricatural rendition of a man wearing a large beret at a rakish angle, clasping in his mouth an outsized cigar.

Words, letters, and objects from reality used in reference to hidden forms and figures or to intimate places, ideas, friends, or possessions become essential to Braque and Picasso's work in 1911-1914. Picasso used the words *Ma Jolie* (from a popular song) and *Jolie Eva* in two paintings of 1911-1912 to celebrate

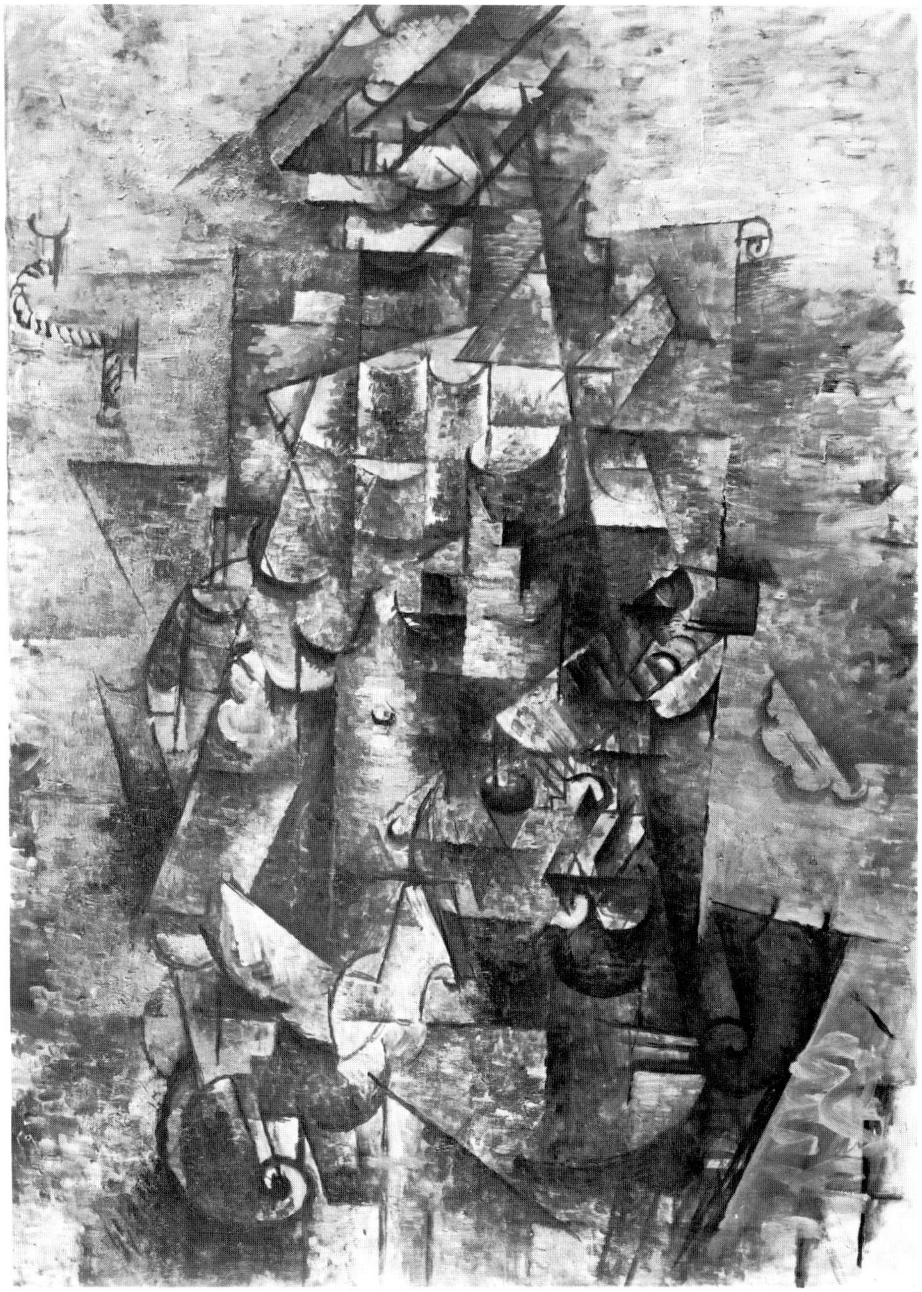

51. Braque, *L'homme à la guitare,* 1911, oil on canvas. The Museum of Modern Art, New York. Acquired through the Lillie P. Bliss Bequest.

his new-found love, Marcelle Humbert, who was also called Eva.

By 1912, these inclusions gave rise to the use of unconventional methods and materials drawn from the world of everyday life in the creation of works of art. First Braque, then Picasso and Gris, entered the "synthetic" stage of their cubism. Braque referred to his early training as a painter-decorator by employing the commonplace *trompe l'oeil* techniques of *faux bois* and *faux marbre* to create paradoxical illusions of and allusions to reality. With the development of *papier collé* and collage, the formal synthesis was complete, and the intimate language of cubism flowered.

Robert Rosenblum, in "Picasso and the Typography of Cubism," has eloquently enumerated Picasso's use of selected advertisements, images, stories, and headlines from newspapers to create wonderfully witty, often naughty visual and verbal puns. For example, his *Nature morte (Au bon marché)* of 1912-1913, Rosenblum points out, is a "clandestine and witty . . . lascivious joke" made up of

> a collection of pastings that advertise two famous Department stores, LA SAMARITAINE and AU BON MARCHE. Above, we see a commercial drawing of a properly dressed lady cut off at the waist; below, the label of the *lingerie* and *broderie* department at the Bon Marché, and below that, in much smaller letters, that point directly up to the word "lingerie" and that, in turn, partly fill a pictorial hole in the jig-saw puzzle compactness of the collage, we read the fragmented words TROU ICI.[49]

He has also shown Braque's own poetic use of carefully chosen words or fragments, such as "sonate, étude, duo, aria, rondo or even the names

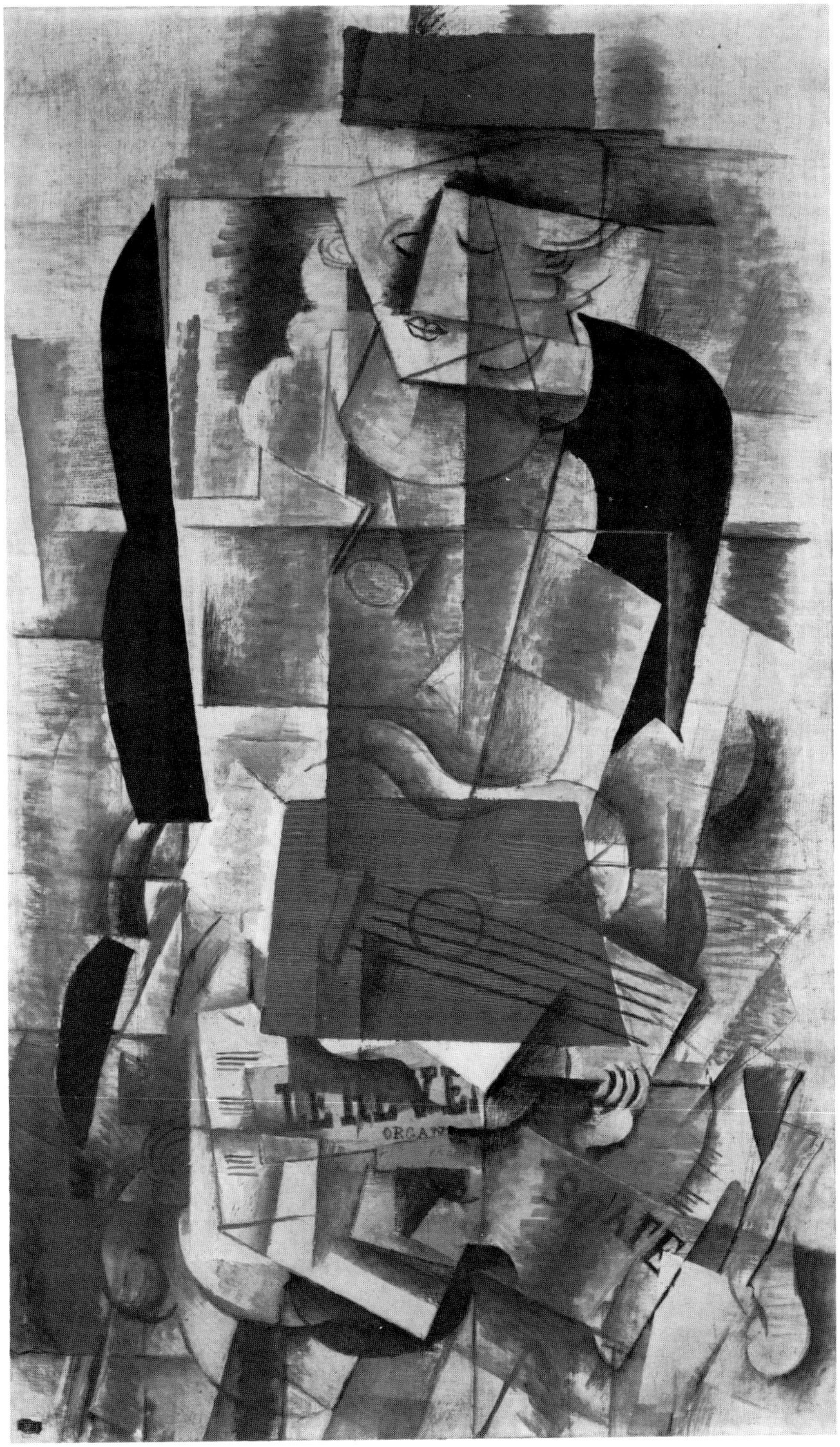

52. Braque, *La femme à la guitare,* 1913-1914, oil on canvas. Musée national d'art moderne, Centre Georges Pompidou, Paris.

Bach, Mozart, Kubelick,"[50] to allude to the musical themes of many of his still lifes.

Braque's own playful sense of humor, however, tends to be overlooked. Douglas Cooper, for example, says of Braque's work: "one never finds in it deliberately selected news items, topical references, or punning witticisms that Gris as well as Picasso delighted in."[51] Rosenblum, writing in *Cubism and Twentieth Century Art,* states of Braque's *La femme à la guitare* (fig. 52) that

> Although the visual pun on navel and sound hole in the five-stringed guitar and the intrusion of a realistically drawn mouth in an abstract environment produce an element of whimsy that might have been excluded from, say, a 1911 study of the same subject, the humor is more prosaic than Picasso's and without Picasso's disturbing overtones.[52]

Both statements miss the point. In fact, Braque's *Femme à la guitare* is a superb example of his sophisticated and subtle wit. The elegant composition of line and transparent planes juxtaposed with sensuous, curved shapes with imitation wood grain and written words is a perfect example of what Rosenblum himself calls "punning between the animate and the inanimate."[53] While Rosenblum cites the puns and contrasts involving the navel and mouth of the figure, he does not mention the painting's most subtle humorous *jeu de forme.* The sensuous curves of the guitar which the figure is playing blend into the soft breast just above it. This form, in turn, acts with the curves that make up the figure's upper torso to create a parallel repetition of the guitar's shape. The bridge and sound hole of this "torso-guitar" are placed just below the curve that simultaneously indicates the base of the figure's neck and the indentation of the upper part of this echoed guitar's body. The sound hole of this second guitar becomes an anatomical pun on the nipple of the woman's left breast. The most amusing aspect of this painting is, however, made by the writing just below the wood-grain surface of the first guitar. The writing is hand-painted, and is therefore quite intentional. It alludes to a newspaper title, *Le Reveil,* but, once again, this allusion obscures the meaning of the letters. These letters clearly form the words *Le Reve . . . organ* or "the dream organ," followed by the fragment *so—ate,* which Rosenblum believes refers to the musical term *sonate.* Perhaps, but when pronounced aloud, the letters approximate the word *souhait,* which means desire. The proximity of the words to the anatomical location of the woman's genital organs makes the sexual overtones of the painting unmistakable and adds a bawdy touch to the sensuous composition.

The very name of the painting is in this case a pun. *La femme à la guitare* certainly signifies a woman with a guitar, but may also mean a woman as, or like a guitar. This perfectly describes Braque's blending of the instrument and the woman's torso and gives meaning to Juan Gris' observation that Braque made of the guitar a new Madonna.[54]

The combinations of form and word, fact and illusion, culminate in the *papiers collés.* In this technique, discovered by Braque in mid-September of 1912, many of the most poetic, intimate, and amusing jokes in the secret language of cubism are told.[55] Picasso was delighted with the possibilities of this form of expression, and he became by far its most prolific exponent. Braque also continued to make both witty and poetic statements in this medium. In his *Le Courrier* (cat. no. 43), he uses a fragment from the journal *Le Courrier,* which reads *le Courr.* Below this are the words and the fragment *organ de mad. . . .* Below these letters is a tiny heart. When verbally reassembled in the mind, the implication is read as "le coeur [the heart], organ de madame." Through the amalgamation of sounds, words, and symbols, Braque again creates anatomical association in this poetic Valentine.

Juan Gris, another initiate in the sign language of cubism, created a work which, it is tempting to believe, was done in homage to Braque's hidden self-portrait. In his *Le Matin* (fig. 53) of 1912, he hides a mysterious figure behind the morning paper in a way very similar to Braque's. In the middle ground of the painting he places a glass of *Boc* in a position very close to that of Braque's *Broc.*

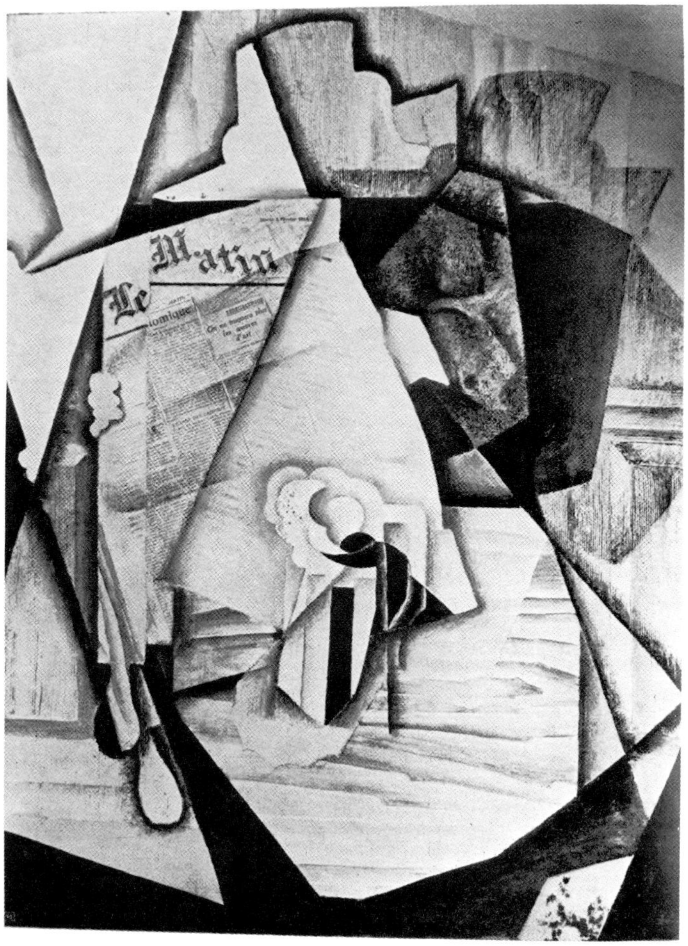

53. Juan Gris (Spanish, 1887-1927), *Le Matin,* 1914, oil on *papier collé* on canvas. Collection of Mr. and Mrs. William Acquavella.

With his *Broc et violon,* Braque opened not one avenue but two in the development of cubism. He established the possibility of combining illusions of reality with the concrete reality of the painting as an abstract object, which led to the formal evolution of both "analytic" and "synthetic" cubism. Simultaneously, his metamorphic metaphor of himself cached in the obscure visual vocabulary of cubism, but revealed by the verbal identity of the still-life objects that create it, set in motion the evolution of cubism's witty and intimate secret language, which was known only to its adepts. As André Salmon recalls: "We made continual fun of everything.... We invented an artificial world with countless jokes that were quite unintelligible to others."[56]

Access to this world has been hidden by tacit vows of silence on the part of the participants. In Braque's own words, these intimate and incomprehensible jokes "will die with us."[57]

NOTES

1. Robert Rosenblum, "Picasso and the Typography of Cubism" in *Picasso in Retrospect,* ed. Roland Penrose and John Golding (New York and Washington, 1973), 49-75.

2. Leo Steinberg, "Resisting Cézanne: Picasso's Three Women," *Art in America* 66 (November 1978), 114-133, and "The Polemical Part,"*Art in America* 67 (March 1979), 114-127. William Rubin, "Cézannisme and the Beginnings of Cubism" in *Cézanne: The Late Work,* ed. William Rubin [exh. cat., The Museum of Modern Art] (New York, 1977) 151-203, and "Pablo and Georges and Leo and Bill,"*Art in America* 67 (March 1979), 128-147. Rubin's conclusion is supported by my own independent research contained in "Georges Braque: Formation and Transition 1900-1909" (Ph.D. diss., Harvard University, 1979). A copy of this document is on file in the archives of the Musée Picasso, Paris, and at Harvard University.

3. The earliest account of Braque's shyness in such circumstances appears in Gelett Burgess, "The Wild Men of Paris," *The Architectural Record* (May 1910), 400-407. Braque himself recalls his timidity at the opening of his exhibition at the Galerie Kahnweiler in November 1908 in Dora Vallier's "Braque la peinture et nous," *Cahiers d'art* 1 (1954), 17.

4. Douglas Cooper, *The Cubist Epoch* [exh. cat., Los Angeles County Museum of Art and The Metropolitan Museum of Art] (London, 1970), 189.

5. Henry Hope, *Georges Braque* [exh. cat., Cleveland Museum of Art and The Museum of Modern Art] (New York, 1949), 6. François Crémieux and Daniel-Henry Kahnweiler, *My Galleries and Painters,* trans. Helen Weaver (New York, 1971), 43-45, 81.

6. Guillaume Apollinaire, "The Salon d'Automne, " *Je dis tous,* 12 October 1907, from L. C. Breunig, ed. *Apollinaire on Art: Essays and Reviews 1902-1918,* trans. Susan Suleiman (New York, 1972), 34.

7. Kahnweiler and Crémieux, *My Galleries and Painters,* 81.

8. Kahnweiler and Crémieux, *My Galleries and Painters,* 81.

9. Accounts of this affair appear in Roger Shattock, *The Banquet Years: The Arts in France 1885-1918* (London, 1959), 53-57; Gertrude Stein, *The Autobiography of Alice B. Toklas* (New York, 1933), 103-107; André Salmon, "The Testimony against Gertrude Stein," *Transition* 23 (1935), 14-15.

10. Apollinaire, "Cubisme," *Intermediare des Chercheurs et des Curieux* 66 (10 October 1912), 475, 476, in Breunig, *Apollinaire on Art,* 257.

11. Apollinaire, "Le Salon des Indépendants," *La Revue des Lettres et des Arts* (1 May 1908), in Breunig, *Apollinaire on Art,* 46.

12. Burgess, "The Wild Men of Paris," 405.

13. Louis Vauxcelles, "Exposition Braque," *Gil Blas* (14 November 1908), in Edward Fry, *Cubism,* trans. Jonathan Griffin (London, 1966), 50.

14. Charles Morice, "L'art moderne," *Mercure de France* (16 December 1908), in Fry, *Cubism,* 52.

15. Karl Max, *Le Télégramme* (9 January 1909) (press clipping in Kahnweiler's archive, Galerie Louise Leiris, Paris) Apollinaire, *Exposition Georges Braque* [exh. cat., Galerie Kahnweiler] (Paris, 1908).

16. *Toison d'Or* (February 1909).

17. Berthe Weill, *Pan dans l'oeil! ou trente ans dans les coulisses de la peinture* contemporaine 1900-1930 (Paris, 1933), 153.

18. Vauxcelles, *Gil Blas,* 25 [March] 1909, n.p., in John Golding, *Cubism: A History and an Analysis 1907-1914* (Boston, 1968), 20, 143.

19. Morice, *Mercure de France,* 15 April 1909, 729.

20. This exhibition was founded by Braque, Othon Friesz, and Raoul Dufy in 1906 and took place annually in June. The previous year, 1908, Apollinaire wrote the introduction to the exhibition catalogue, which was his essay "Three Plastic Virtues." See Breunig, *Apollinaire on Art,* 47-49.

21. Claude Lantier, "Cercle d'Art Moderne," *La Cloche Ilustrée du Havre,* 12 June 1909, n.p.

22. See Rubin, "Pablo and Georges and Leo and Bill" and "Cézannisme."

23. Braque had been struck by the constructive aspect of Cézanne's oil paintings during the Cézanne retrospective exhibit at the Salon d'Automne of 1907. It was this encounter with Cézanne that put the evolution of cubism in motion. See Rubin, "Cézannisme" and "Pablo and Georges and Leo and Bill," and my own dissertation noted above.

24. Emile Zavié, *Le Feu,* 1 September 1909. This review was included among the clippings Kahnweiler kept in his scrapbook. Undoubtedly Braque read it. These documents remain in the Kahnweiler archive.

25. Cubism has traditionally been seen as having three essential stages of development: "early" or "Cézannesque" (1908), "analytic" (1909-1911), and "synthetic" (1912-1914). Douglas Cooper used the term "high analytic" to refer to those near abstractions of Braque and Picasso of 1910-1911. See Cooper, *The Cubist Epoch.* These works were also called "hermetic" by early critics, a reference to their arcane or mysterious character.

26. Golding, *Cubism,* 184.

27. Alfred Barr, *Cubism and Abstract Art* [exh. cat., The Museum of Modern Art] (New York, 1936), 15.

28. Barr, *Cubism and Abstract Art,* note, 15.

29. Golding, *Cubism,* 184.

30. Kahnweiler and Crémieux, *My Galleries and Painters,* 59. See also Daniel-Henry Kahnweiler, *Der Weg zum Kubismus* (Munich, 1920), and *Juan Gris,* trans. D. Cooper (London, 1947).

31. Alfred Barr, *Picasso, Fifty Years of His Art* [exh. cat., The Museum of Modern Art] (New York, 1946), 273.

32. Marius de Zayas, "Picasso Speaks," *The Arts* (May 1923), 315-326.

33. Rudi Blesh and Harriet Janis, *Collage: Personalities, Concepts & Techniques* (Philadelphia, New York, London, 1967). Rosenblum, "Picasso and the Typography of Cubism"; *Cubism and Twentieth Century Art,* 2d rev. ed. (New York, 1962); and "The Demoiselles Revisited," *Art News* 72 (April 1973), 45-48. Leo Steinberg, "The Philosophical Brothel," *Art News* 71 (September/October 1972), 20-29, 38-47. Rubin, *Picasso in the Collection of the Museum of Modern Art* (Greenwich, Connecticut, 1972).

34. Vallier, "Braque la peinture et nous," 15.

35. Kahnweiler, *Der Weg zum Kubismus,* translation from Herschel Chipp, *Theories of Modern Art* (Berkeley, 1968), 257.

36. Clement Greenberg, "Collage," *Art and Culture* (Boston, 1972), 72.

37. Rosenblum, *Cubism and Twentieth Century Art,* 64.

38. Golding, *Cubism,* 92.

39. John Russell, *G. Braque* (London, 1959), 13. Jean Leymarie, *Georges Braque,* trans. James Emmons (Geneva, 1961), 44.

40. Vallier, "Braque la peinture et nous," 15.

41. Georges Isarlov, "Georges Braque," *Orbes* 3 (Spring 1932), 82.

42. Weill, *Pan dans l'oeil!,* 153.

43. François Ponge, "Braque or the Meditation of the Work" in Pierre Descarges and François Ponge, *G. Braque,* trans. Richard Howard (New York, 1971), 29. Pierre Reverdy, letter to Georges Braque, c.1950, from the files of Nicole Mangin (Nicole de Romilly). Stanislas Fumet, *Georges Braque* (Paris, 1965), 19.

44. Russell, *Braque,* 15.

45. L. V. Masini, *Braque* (New York, 1971), 44.

46. Apollinaire, see note 6 above.

47. It is called *The Matchholder* by Blesh and Janis, *Collage,* 9.

48. Blesh and Janis also refer to this work as a response to Vauxcelles, "The gesture said to this critic: 'Since you don't or won't understand cubism, here I give you the name of your newspaper. Can you read that?'" (12).

49. Rosenblum, "Picasso and the Typography of Cubism," 53.

50. Rosenblum, "Picasso and the Typography of Cubism," 57

51. See note 4 above.

52. Rosenblum, *Cubism and Twentieth Century Art,* 96.

53. Rosenblum, *Cubism and Twentieth Century Art,* 64.

54. Blesh and Janis, *Collage,* 21.

55. This is generally conceded in the literature of cubism. Braque and Picasso had been working together during the summer of 1912 at Sorgues near Avignon. Picasso had returned to Paris in September to move from Clichy to boulevard Raspail. In a letter in the possession of Claude Laurens, Picasso wrote to Braque that he intended to try Braque's new discovery.

56. André Salmon, "The Testimony against Gertrude Stein," 14.

57. Vallier, "Braque la peinture et nous," 14.

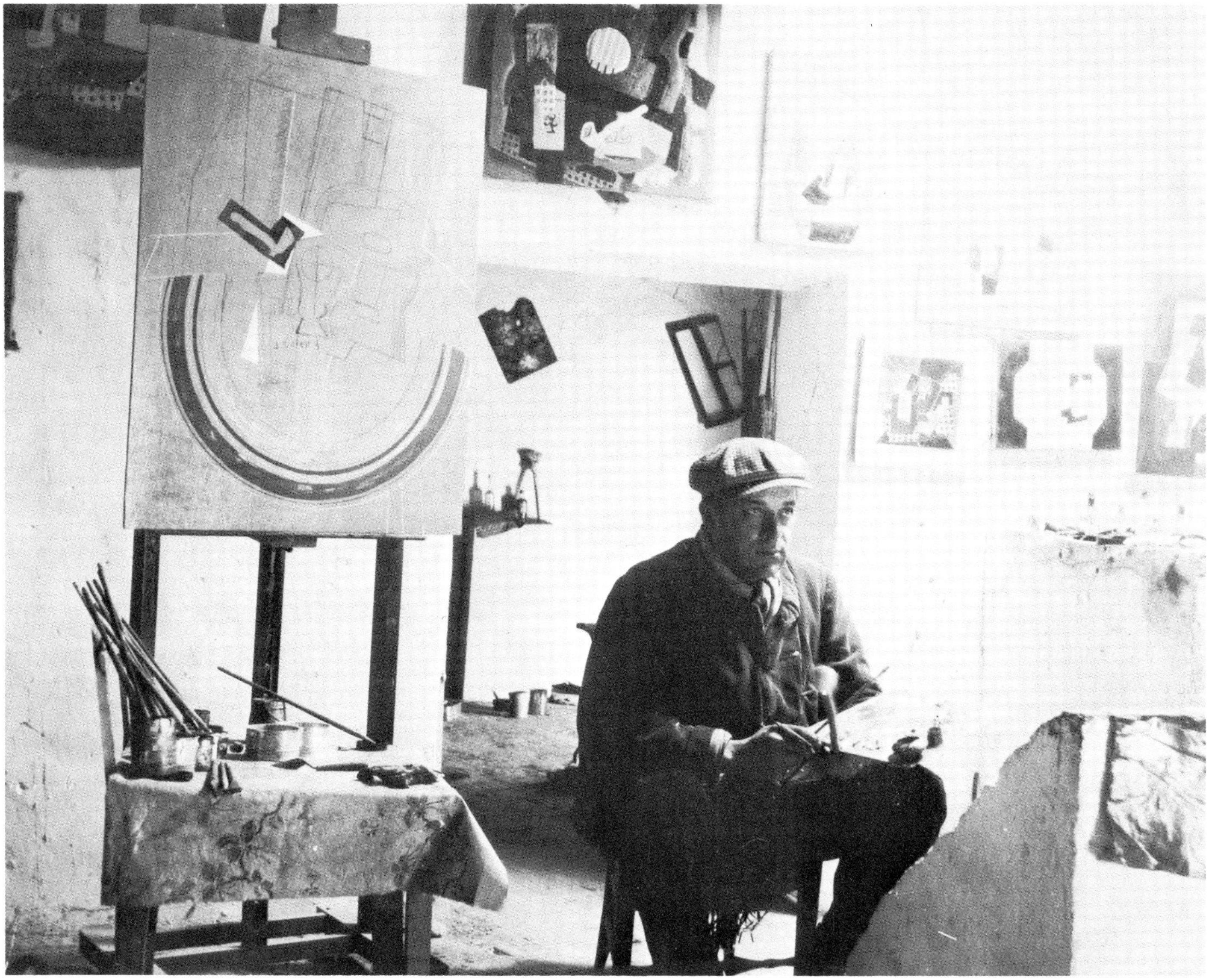

54. Georges Braque in 1917. Photo: Archives Laurens.

BRAQUE, COLLAGE, AND LATER CUBISM

E. A. Carmean, Jr.

IN THE SUMMER OF 1914 Georges Braque left Paris for Sorgues in the south of France, the town where he had invented *papier collé* two years earlier. Pablo Picasso and André Derain had already arrived in Avignon, ten kilometers away, but the promise of a productive period with these cubist friends was interrupted by the start of World War I. Both Braque and Derain, aged thirty-two and thirty-four respectively, were called up for duty in the army. Picasso, exempted as a Spanish national, saw them off to Paris from the train station at Avignon. He later said that he "never found them again."[1]

Of course Picasso did see Braque after the war, but the changes in each artist's life precluded a resumption of their friendship. This break, and the intervention of the war, marked the end of cubism's synthetic phase—but not the end of cubism itself. By 1918 its later style was beginning to emerge. Braque's last collages play an important role in its development.

In August Braque joined his regiment at Amiens. By September he was given the rank of sergeant, advancing to lieutenant within three months. On 11 May 1915, while engaged in action in Carency in the Artois section, he was seriously wounded in the head by an exploding shell and underwent a trepanning operation at a field hospital. Three weeks later he was returned to Paris (fig. 64).

Braque had been on the danger list while at Carency, and his recovery was slow. For a brief period he lost his eyesight, surely the most traumatic experience for a painter. By April 1916 he had returned to his regiment as a convalescent, but in the autumn he was back in Paris again, where his progress toward health continued to be gradual. Braque was well enough to attend a banquet in his honor on 15 January 1917, which Juan Gris described as "charming, spiritual and full of good humor."[2] By the summer of 1917, Braque had returned to Sorgues and resumed painting.

Braque's first postwar paintings are tentative in character, and they show a strong dependence on pictorial ideas then current in the work of Henri Laurens and Gris. His *Jeune fille à la mandoline (Young Girl with a Mandolin),* with its sharply defined geometric patterns and juxtapositions of solidly colored planes, is very close in theme and style to the Gris' *Femme à la mandoline (Woman with a Mandolin)* of the previous year (itself based on a Corot painting of the subject).[3] In this same work, Braque's boxlike rendering of both the mandolin and the girl's hands also suggests musical instruments seen in contemporary collages by Laurens (fig. 55).

Braque would have turned to these two artists partially out of freindship. He had been close to Laurens before the war—their wives had known each other from childhood—and his friendship with Gris had grown deeper during his hospitalization in Paris.[4] Beyond personal regard, however, the works of these two companions also provided Braque access to the changes in cubism since 1914.

This connection was especially important, because the articulation of the later cubist style in the intervening war years had largely been charted by Gris. To some degree the shift was due to the absence of Braque and to Picasso's interest in other things. But it also derived from Gris' devotion to cubism—he very rarely worked in any other style after 1911—and to certain elements already in his own version of the synthetic cubist style. In late 1915 Gris radically altered his work. While earlier paintings and collages had a rigid geometric organization as their understructure, during the war Gris began to emphasize this factor by making it a dominant pictorial characteristic. As we can see in *Fantômas* (fig. 56), the emphasis was accomplished by introducing broad areas of dense black shading around clearly stated planes, creating the effect that these elements were raised into relief. The disparate portion of the pictorial scene which the individuated plane contains reads as if that section of the composition had been produced onto the plane and thus stands apart

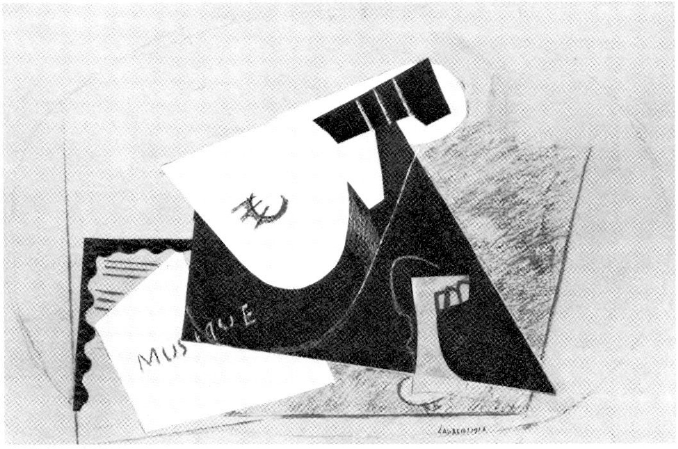

55. Henri Laurens (French, 1885-1954), *L'instrument de musique,* 1916, charcoal and *papier collé* on paper. National Gallery of Art, Washington, Ailsa Mellon Bruce Fund, 1981.

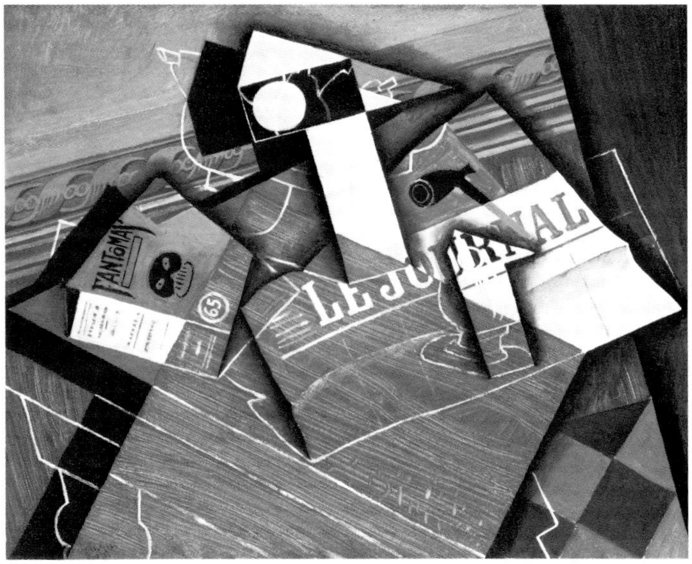

56. Juan Gris (Spanish, 1887-1927), *Fantômas,* 1915, oil on canvas. National Gallery of Art, Washington, Chester Dale Fund, 1976.

spatially from the other areas. It is an effect visually akin to that achieved when a film is projected onto solid surfaces set at different levels.

These two features, of projection and of a relieflike surface, are the central characteristics which distinguish the later, "third" style of cubism from its preceding two formulations. Already by *Fantômas,* this quasi-bas-relief style creates a sense of solidity that is almost palpable, a quality radically different from that of the thin, linear scaffolding of analytical pictures and far more intense than that of the planar construction of synthetic works.

This characteristic had become so strong by late 1917 that Gris began a series of pictures which either simulate painted relief sculpture or illusionistically place the image in a *trompe l'oeil* sculptural frame.[6] Other cubists quickly picked up these presentations. Jacques Lipchitz, who worked with Gris in Beaulieu in the spring of 1918, not only made paintings in this style, but also executed two related polychrome low-relief still lifes following Gris' new convention (fig. 57). Picasso, who returned to Paris in the spring, also made "bas-relief" paintings based on Gris' work, while Laurens followed (probably) Lipchitz in creating similar carved reliefs. Minor cubists, such as Marie Blanchard and Albert Gleizes, worked in this format too, though slightly later.

As noted above, Gris' pictures carry the evolution of later cubism up to 1917. This new, widespread sharing and development of his thematic material, its formal vocabulary, and its means of presentation in 1917-1918 shows how broadly based was the foundation for the subsequent, further articulation of the cubist style. Although Braque's postwar work has traditionally been seen as his partial resumption of earlier ideas, followed by their transformation into a personal idiom, it is argued here that his collages and paintings demand rather to be understood as a direct part of the later cubist style.

Indeed, Braque's participation in this first stage of later cubism was not only complete, it was early. Already in late 1917 he had understood Gris' format and begun his own "bas-relief" paintings, fully six months before Picasso and Lipchitz started to work in this vein. Braque's still lifes are enclosed in distinctively shaped illusionistic and non-illusionistic painted "frames," including diamond, oval, and walnut- or lemon-shaped formats. Although paintings predominate, he also made his first postwar collage, *La Guitare (The Guitar)* in this style (fig. 58), as

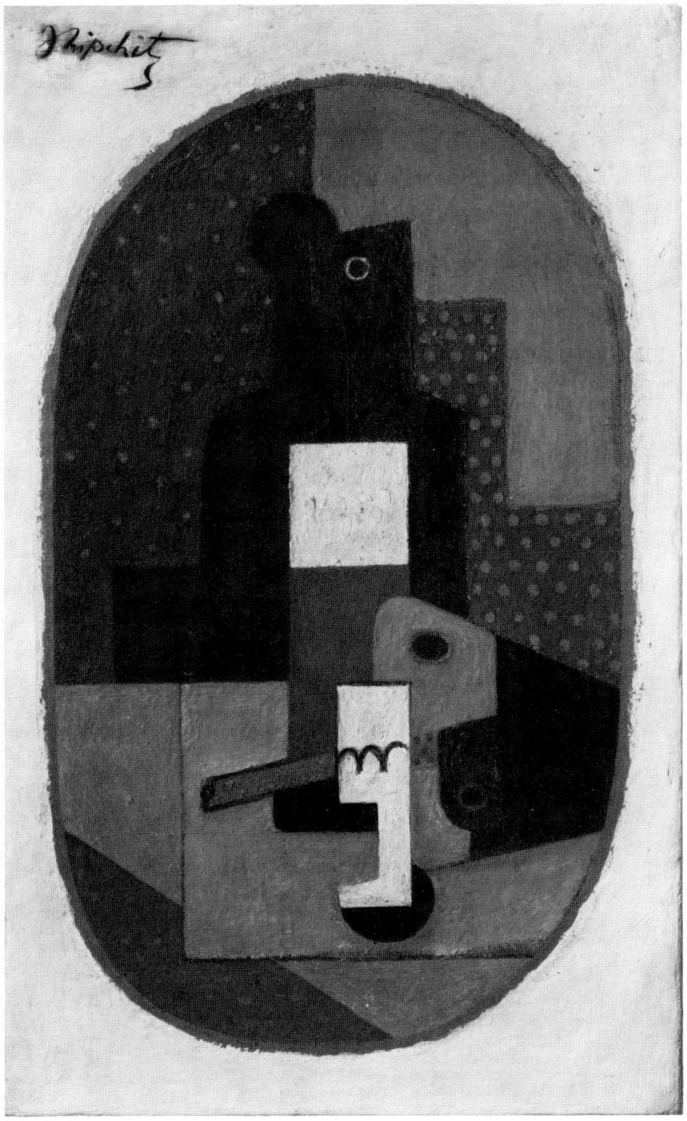

57. Jacques Lipchitz (Russian/American, 1891-1973), *Still Life*, 1918, oil on canvas. National Gallery of Art, Washington, Gift of Mr. and Mrs. Burton Tremaine, 1973.

well as a directly related drawing with gouache.

In this collage, the still life almost floats in the center of a strong geometric field, which is broken into patterns of alternating tones. Braque centered the image by drawing diagonal lines from opposing corners, and by using horizontal and vertical divisions in the middle. Between these lines other, wider diagonals are drawn, creating the spiderweblike pattern which organizes the composition. This arrangement, in turn, is set upon a larger rectangle, which is shaded at the right and lower edges so as to be illusionistically projected forward into relief.

The collage still life at the center contains a sheet of music, a glass, and a guitar, set on a tabletop. The guitar is cut from a sheet of newspaper, painted over with gouache. Its strings are drawn in charcoal on pasted white paper. However, these elements are more freely painted and drawn than the geometric background and thus give the work a kind of looseness which makes it different from Braque's earlier collages and from his and Gris' contemporary works; in this regard it curiously predicts the more fluid handling of forms found in Braque's 1920 pictures.

Formes musicales

The preceding comments provide a summary context for understanding the last and one of the greatest of Braque's *papiers collés*, the *Formes musicales (Musical Forms)* now in Philadelphia (fig. 60). This work, also known as *Guitare et clarinette (Guitar and Clarinet)*, has such clarity and authority that questions of its style being transitional or of its author being tentative do not occur. This resolution is even more amazing when we realize that it is in this collage more than any other work of its period that Braque both reviews his earlier collage inventions and introduces the basis for his work for the next decade.

Although it dates from March 1918,[8] *Formes musicales* has often appeared in the Braque literature as a synthetic cubist collage of 1913-1914. Other publications, even when correctly citing it as 1918, join *Formes musicales* with Braque's earlier works. This curious history is

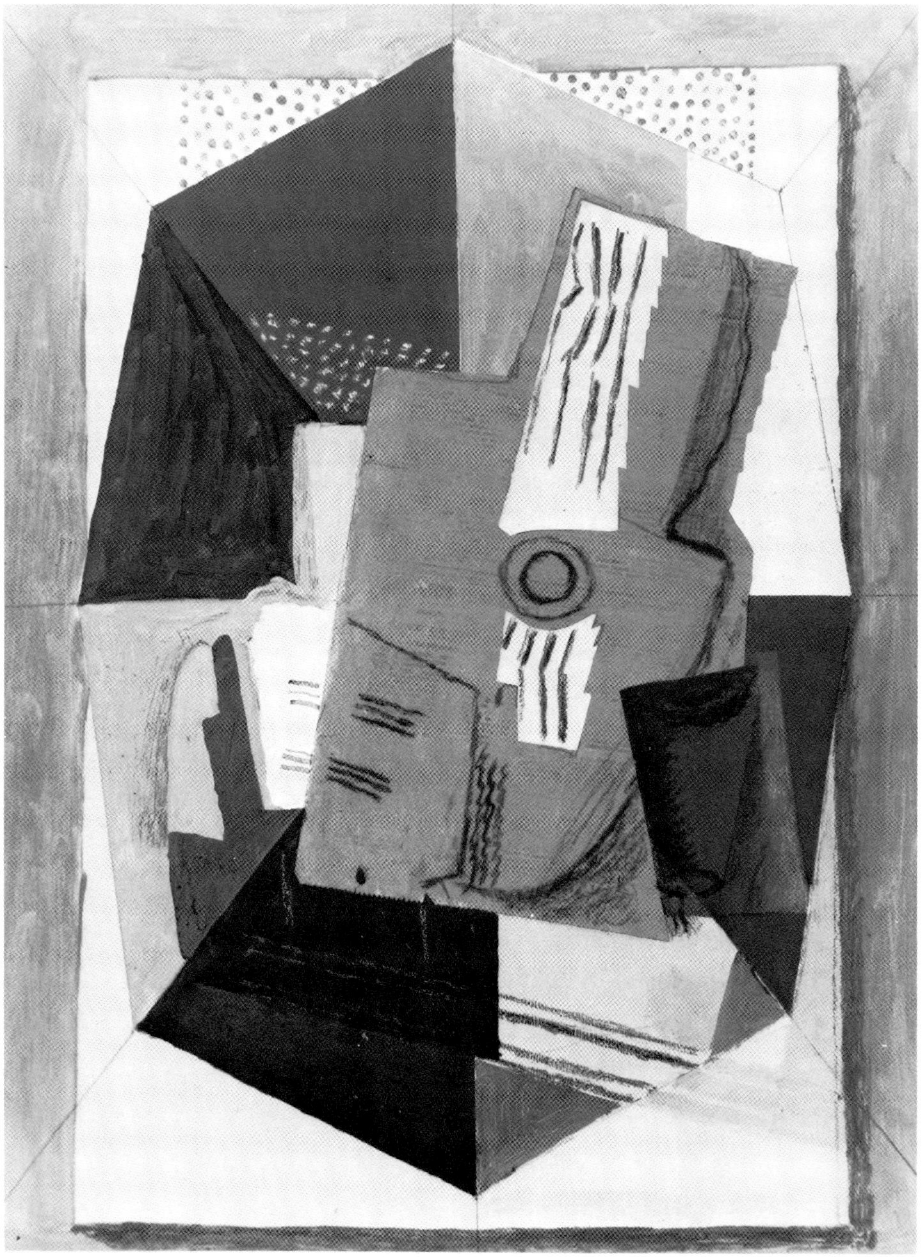

58. Braque, *Guitare,* 1918 (cat. no. 54).

due in part to the fact that it is a collage, and as such was thought to belong with the synthetic works, since it was assumed Braque had stopped making collages in 1914. (The two other later collages, *Guitare* [fig. 58] and *Bouteille et instruments de musique* [*Bottle and Musical Instruments;* cat. no. 55] have largely remained obscure.) And, *Formes musicales* does partially derive from the vocabulary of synthetic works in its large planes of pasted paper, its use of *faux bois* paper, and its palette of tans, black, and white.

Other features, however, mark it as clearly later in conception. Chief among these is the amplitude of its subject. Braque's earlier collages had primarily been intimate in scale; even when composed of several still-life objects, the attention was closely focused and the angle of view down onto the table. But in *Formes musicales,* we see the still life at a greater distance and from the side, so much so that an alternative title could be "Guitar and Clarinet on a Table" or "Musical Forms on a Buffet." Of the other *papiers collés,* only *Duo pour flûte (Duet for Flute;* fig. 59), traditionally dated 1914, is comparable, in its side view of the table and its overlaying of large planes. The wind instruments in each work, a flute in the Fogg collage and a clarinet in the later picture, are also similar in their shapes and in the manner in which their midsections are placed behind other objects. But, again, their relative pictorial scales are greatly different; in the Fogg collage the flute almost fills the entire diagonal of the format, while the clarinet in *Formes musicales* occupies only a fraction of the pictorial surface. Nevertheless, these two works are similar enough—and both so

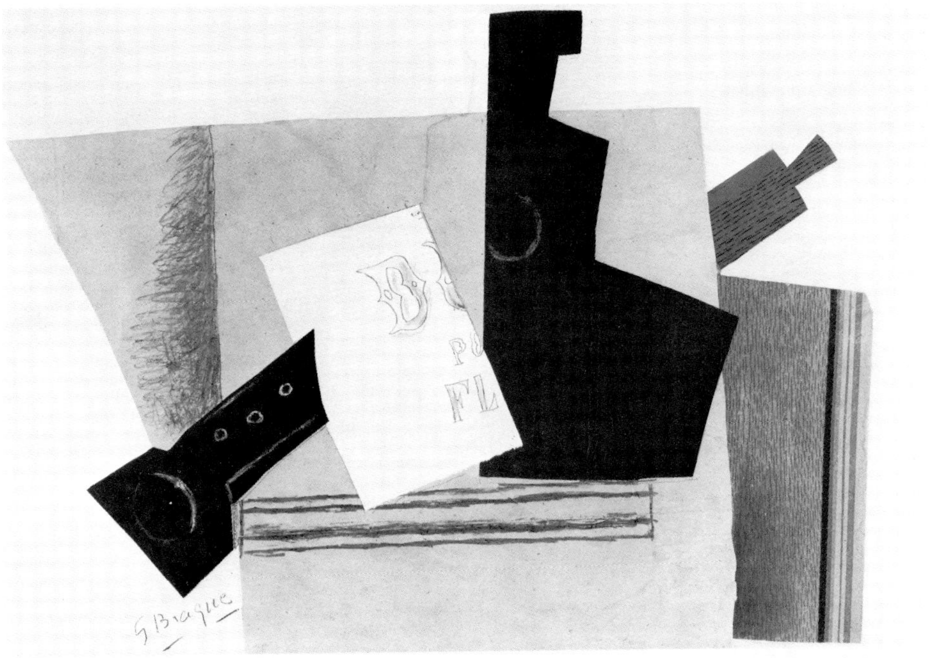

59. Braque, *Nature morte à la flûte (Duo pour flûte)*, 1912-1913?/1914?/1917-1918? (cat. no. 56).

distinct from the other collages—as to raise the question of the date of *Duo pour flûte* (see cat. no. 56).

Formes musicales is also distinguished by its use of dense black shadows cast by the still-life objects, a device recalling the lighting in *Fantômas.* In Braque's collage, the shadow to the lower right of the clarinet is even bigger than the instrument itself, and it is matched by the curvilinear black band which profiles the guitar's lower edge. The third black plane, at the top, remains unidentified, possibly the cast shadow of the white plane to its immediate right— although this reading would reverse the direction of light and shadow in the picture. This upper white plane itself is mysterious, possibly being a sheet of music, similar to the one below, known by its black staff lines.

The third white sheet, placed at an angle, is presumably a section of tablecloth, its curvilinear edge suggesting the undulating side of the tabletop.[9] Beneath it lies another fragment of tablecloth, stated by a checkered paper, the same as that used in *Bouteille et instruments de musique.* At the lower left, *faux bois* paper marks a table leg, echoing the same paper used above for the top half of the guitar. The top of the table and the bottom section of the guitar are stated by the large piece of tan paper. On the right, another sheet of patterned paper falls over the edge of the table, its curvilinear design here drawn onto the pasted element. Finally, to return to the clarinet, it is formed of three separate pieces of corrugated cardboard.

Beyond the sheer number of paper elements in *Formes musicales,* what is amazing is the complex manner in which they have been assembled. We can gain some idea of this process through a series of diagrams (A-E) which illustrate the sequential steps Braque used in making this collage. Derived from studying the work in a laboratory, these illustration are based on the clearly visible separations between the collage elements and show how they were applied.[10]

Braque began *Formes musicales* by painting the large supporting sheet of paper a deep blue-gray, a step which already sets this collage apart from earlier works. Diagram A shows the initial three papers applied to this field: first the small *faux bois* sheet, then the large checkered paper, which in turn is partially covered by the diagonally placed white sheet.

Diagram B illustrates the next additions to the work. A longer rectangle of white paper touches the first white sheet, but more than a third of this is then covered by the large sheet of *faux bois* paper, cut for the guitar's upper profile, and also placed at an angle. Much of this wood-grained paper is itself covered in the next step, as in diagram C, which shows the placement of the large sheet of tan paper for the tabletop. Interestingly, laboratory study shows that this tabletop sheet was originally cut so as to contain the curvilinear profile discussed above (shown in diagram C with the dotted line). This was then covered by the second sheet of checkered paper, and its original edge drawn in charcoal.

Diagram D shows two of the black shapes being added. The wide shadow of the guitar is placed in position to echo the profile above the *faux bois* paper; it also covers

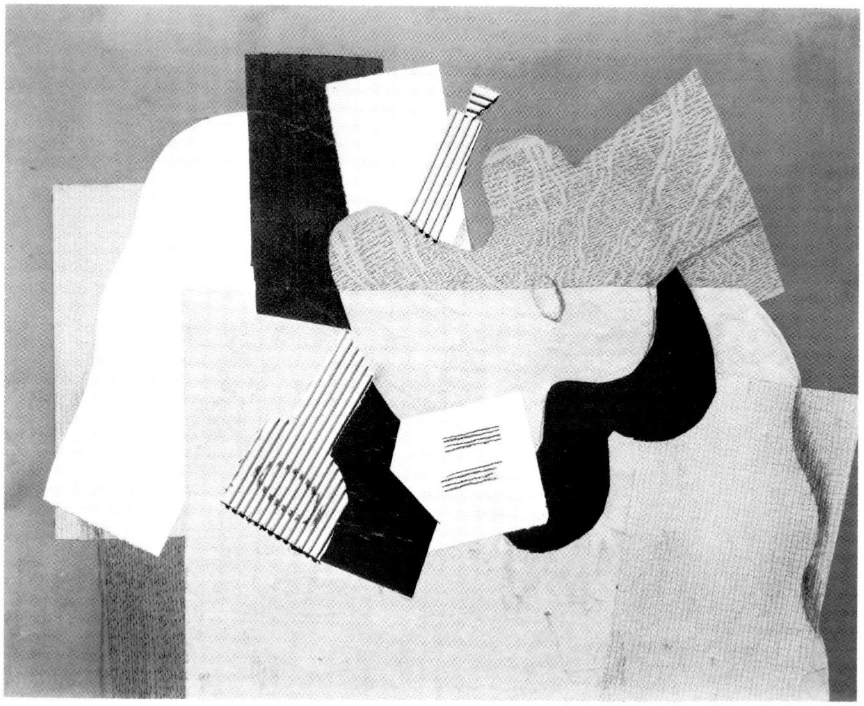

60. Braque, *Formes musicales (Guitare et clarinette),* 1918 (cat. no. 57).

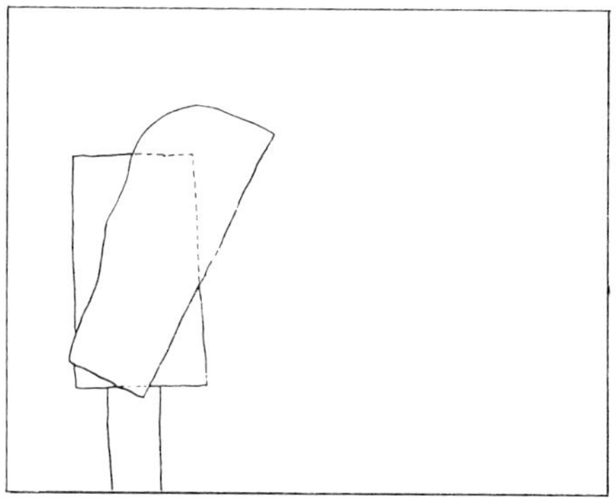

diagram A

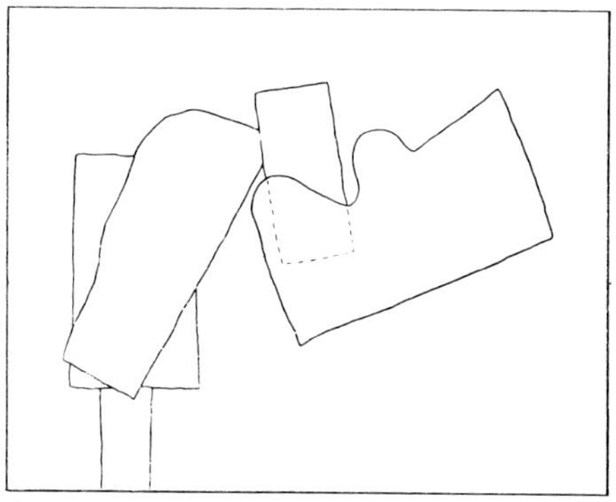

diagram B

the upper left corner of the checkered paper. At the top of the work, a more complicated addition takes place. Here a piece of black paper is attached over the angular white sheet but slipped under the right rectangle and the *faux boix* guitar. But when it reaches the tan table top, Braque slits the paper vertically, slipping the right section under the tan paper, and pulling the left section over the edge of the tabletop.

The last major steps are represented in diagram E. First a long rectangular piece from the white sheet covers the left corner of the guitar's shadow. This piece is in turn covered by the black shadow of the clarinet. Finally, the left edge of this black paper is covered by the cardboard of the clarinet, which continues with the two pieces above to complete the instrument.

This reconstruction should not be taken as implying that Braque created *Formes musicales* in a manner as direct as the steps from the abstract diagram A to the complicated diagram E might suggest. Clearly the composition was worked out with loose sheets of paper, Braque rearranging them, cutting adjustments, sliding elements underneath each other, etc. Whether Braque worked flat on a table or attached the elements to a wall is

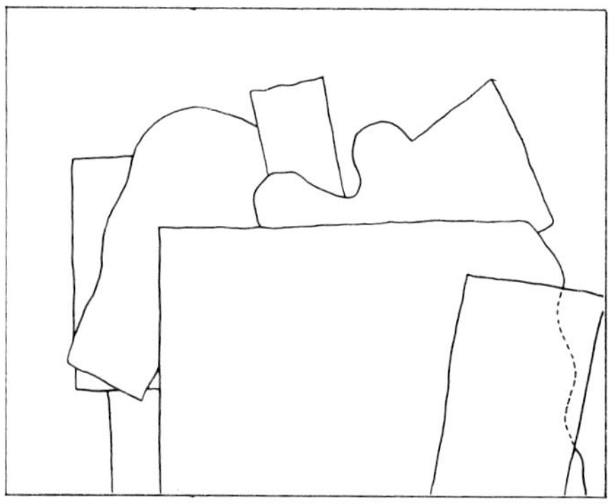

diagram C

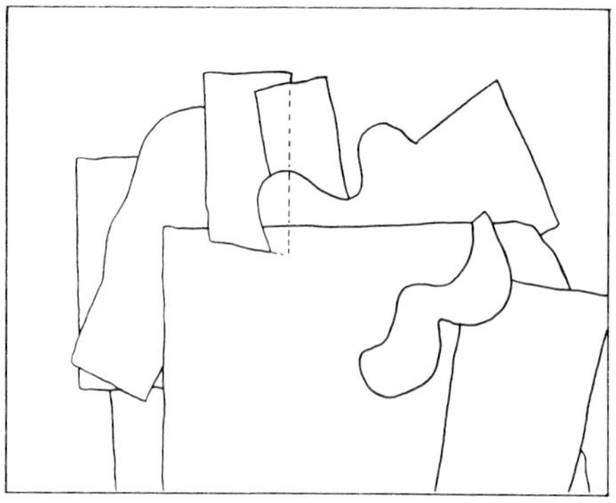

diagram D

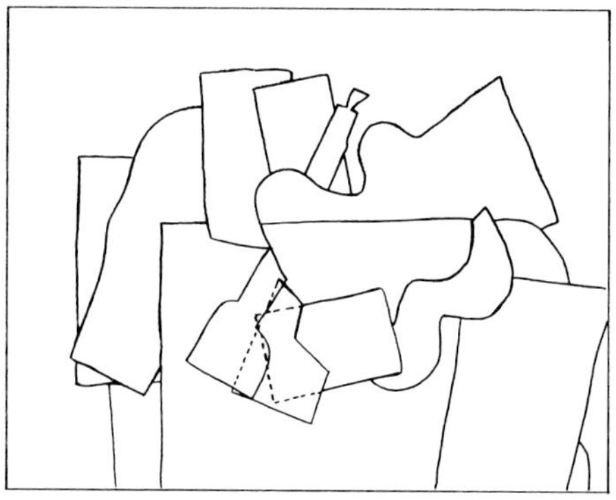

diagram E

61. Braque, *Le buffet,* 1919, oil on canvas. The Solomon R. Guggenheim Museum, New York.

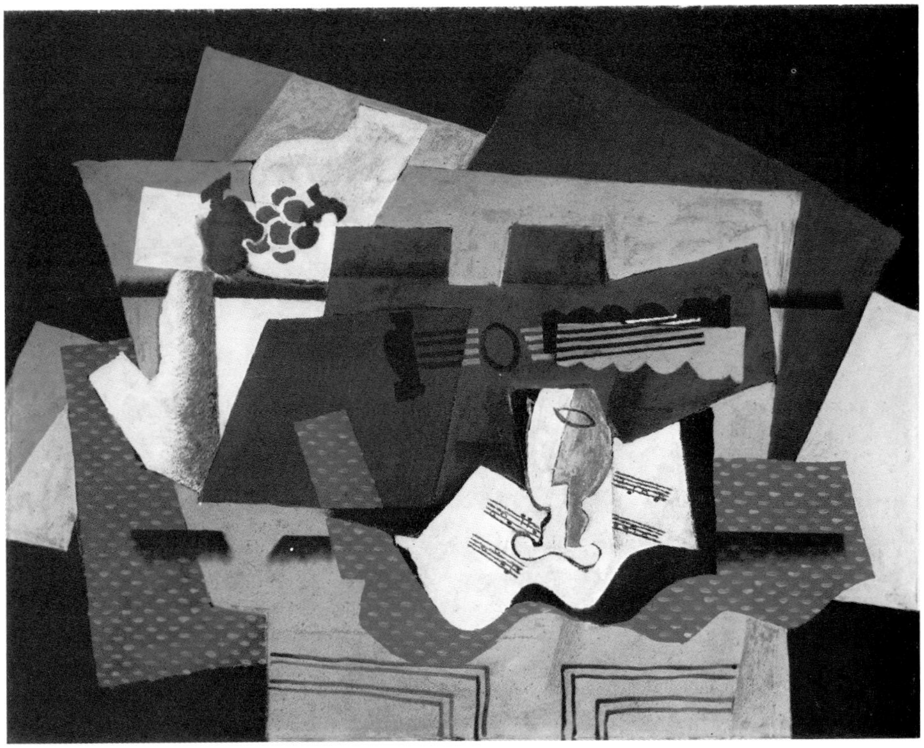

unclear—although the latter method is suggested in certain pieces which have tiny pin holes in their upper corners.

After completing these first steps, Braque followed the same order in gluing the collage. As we see the composition emerge we realize that Braque increasingly covered the blue-gray field until it appeared only as a background to the still-life assembly. This unified density sets the still life apart from the earlier works. Furthermore, within this assembly, the individual elements themselves are many and interconnected, again giving *Formes musicales* a formal complexity which corresponds to its thematic amplitude.

The diagrams also show that Braque followed a consistent pattern in making this collage. Beginning at the lower left with the small piece of *faux bois* paper, Braque moved around the center in a clear spiral motion; up, then across the top, down the right side, across the lower center, then upward through the middle. Were *Formes musicales* a painting, this spiral procedure would merely be an interesting feature; but in a collage it has meaning, for as layer is placed upon layer, the center of the work is raised upward, culminating with the pronounced texture of the corrugated cardboard clarinet.[11]

However subtle the differences between levels are, this layering gives *Formes musicales* a sculptural quality. Earlier collages also had this character, witness Braque's references to them as "tableaux objets." But there the pasted sheets are like individual planes standing in a

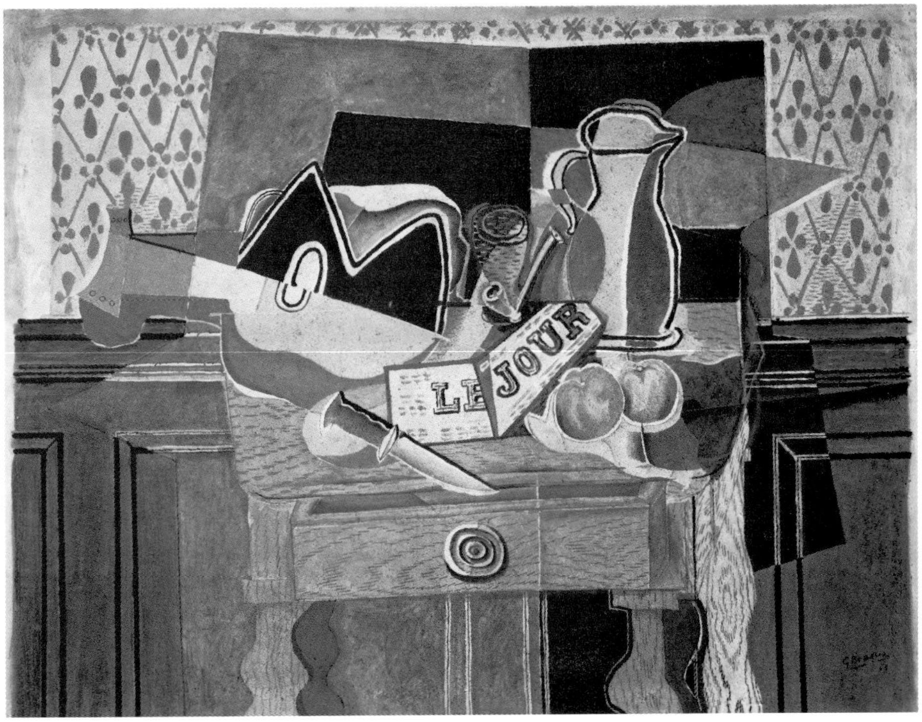

62. Braque, *Le Jour,* 1929, oil on canvas. National Gallery of Art, Washington, Chester Dale Collection, 1962.

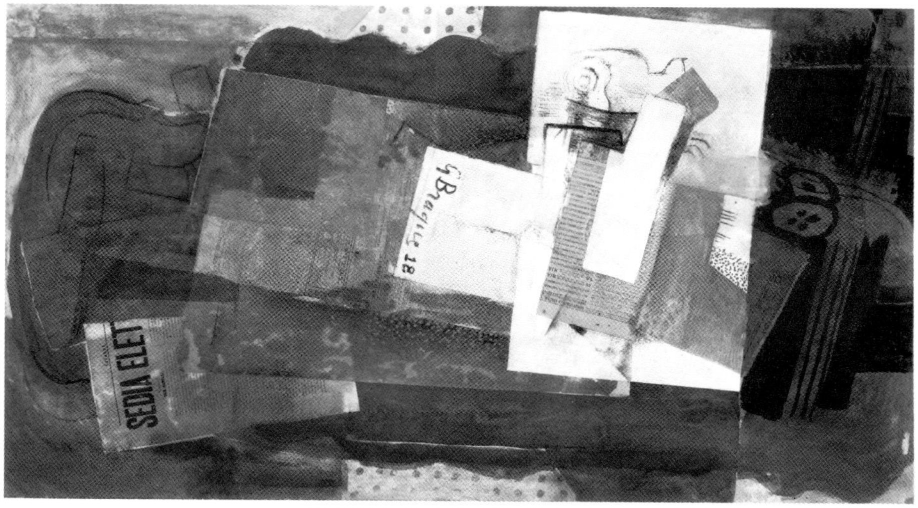

63. Braque, *Still Life,* 1914?/1917-1918 (cat. no. 54 bis).

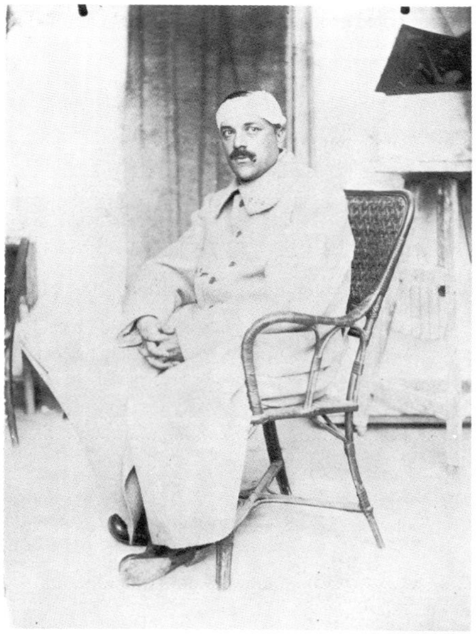

64. Georges Braque in the studio of sculptor Henri Laurens, 1915. Photo: Archives Laurens.

world of constructed space, partially reflective of *papier collé*'s origin in Braque's paper sculpture.

By contrast, in *Formes musicales,* the dense spiral of pasted elements fuses the assemblage together, and even the background of the blue-gray has a pictorial force. The closest parallel for this structure is not earlier collage, but bas-relief sculpture, which projects forward in shallow levels, and where we are always aware of the background plane. Seeing *Formes musicales* in this way allows us to place it within the context of the illusionistic bas-relief paintings begun earlier in 1917 by Gris and Braque. Furthermore, it precedes the actual bas-relief sculpture of Laurens and Lipchitz. This work alone shows how much Braque's postwar work directly plays a part in the evolution of later cubism.[12]

Formes musicales was Braque's last collage. Despite the brilliance of its assemblage, he wasted no time in further developing his work. Within a year he had moved to a new style whose curvilinear vocabularly and loose, painterly facture led Gris to call it "Impressionist."[13] It was clearly not compatible with the more rigid elements of *papier collé;*[14] nevertheless, the inventions of the great *Formes musicales* do continue to inform Braque's work for the next decade, from *Le buffet (The Buffet)* of 1919, one of the first "Impressionist" pictures, through *Le Jour* of ten years later, perhaps the last work in the style of later cubism (figs. 61 and 62). Whether set on a buffet, *gueridon,* or mantlepiece, all of these works share the theme of the great still life, as established in *Formes musicales.* It is a distantly viewed, integrated gathering of objects whose amplitude matches the complexities of the later cubist style. And in these paintings we find the centralized massing of clear, overlapping planes. Despite the openness of their structures, they still have the focused density of the bas-relief. Indeed *Le Jour* has a mixture of sand and paint so thick that certain areas virtually stand out from the surface. This too is a later reflection of the new ideas begun in Braque's last collage.

NOTES

1. Picasso's comment has a double edge, suggesting that Braque was not a major artist after the war. The two had argued early in 1914, and thus their prewar relationship had already grown cold.

2. Gris, in a letter to Maurice Raynal, 18 January 1917, letter LVI in *Letters of Juan Gris (1913-1927)*, trans. and ed. Douglas Cooper (London, 1956), 45.

3. Braque's painting, *La joueuse de mandoline (The Mandolin Player)*, 1917, is in the Donation Masurel at Le musée d'art moderne du Nord, Lille. Gris' painting, *Femme à la mandoline (Woman with a Mandolin)*, 1916, is in the Kunstmuseum, Basel. The Corot, *Reveuse à la mandoline (Dreamer with a Mandolin)*, 1860-1865, is in the St. Louis Art Museum.

4. Already in 1914 Gris had written, "I have no news of Braque, the one person who interests me most," in letter XIX (*Letters*, ed. Cooper, 14-15). It was through Gris that word of Braque's injury was given to other artists in Paris, through his letters and his visits to Braque in the hospital.

5. For a detailed discussion of this work, see the author's *"Fantômas," Arts* 51 (January 1977), 116-119.

6. See especially Gris' *Nature morte à la plaque*, 1917, in Kunstmuseum, Basel. For a discussion of this point, and its relationship to the work of Piet Mondrian, see the author's *Mondrian: The Diamond Compositions* [exh. cat., National Gallery of Art] (Washington, 1979).

7. See for example the two still lifes of 1917-1918 now at Kröller-Müller Museum in Otterlo. The gouache is in the Gallatin Collection at the Philadelphia Museum of Art.

8. According to a Léonce Rosenberg label on the verso.

9. It is possible—but not likely—that the diagonal white paper and the two vertical planes of black and white make up a sculptural bust placed on the table. The forms do bear a resemblance to formulation later used by Laurens for this purpose, in his *Femme de profil (Woman in Profile)*, 1919, Donation Masurel (no. 61), and the *Femme à l'eventail (Woman with a Fan)*, 1921 (see catalogue of the Donation Laurens, [Paris, 1967], no. 4).

10. My appreciation to Anne d'Harnoncourt and Ann Percy of the Philadelphia Museum of Art, who arranged for me to study *Formes musicales* in their paper conservation laboratory and shared their insights into the collage.

11. The corrugated paper is the most emphatic of the bas-relief elements. Braque had used this material as early as 1914, in his *Nature morte à la guitare* (cat. no. 49). Laurens made several collages in 1916 and 1917 using corrugated paper, and employed a small piece (as guitar strings over the sound hole) in a three-dimensional guitar constructed of tin, sheet metal, and painted wood (present location unknown: illustrated in *L'Esprit Nouveau*, no. 10). Made in October 1918, this work with its deeply folded planes seems to reflect Braque's *Formes musicales*.

12. *Formes musicales* contains another formal aspect which appears in later work by Braque, Gris, and Picasso. This is the way in which the lower portion of the guitar is stated by means of an outline, established by the lower black shadow, the upper edge of the clarinet and its shadow, and the right edge of the overlapping plane. These elements create a profile of the guitar. But when we recognize the surface of the guitar defined by this outlining, at the same time we realize that we are looking through it to the surface of the table below: the guitar is there in outlined surface and not in actual surface. Picasso was especially taken with this idea, exploring it not only in paintings and drawings, but also making three-dimensional models to further study its implication. (See for example the two 1919 constructions at the Musée Picasso, M. P. 257 and M. P. 258.) Interestingly, Picasso also returned to collage to study this concept in a work which parallels these constructions (M. P. 382).

13. In a letter to D. H. Kahnweiler, 17 February 1920: "I have seen some new things by Braque which I find soft and lacking in precision. It's a turn toward Impressionism. I'm quite pleased to discover I don't like them because it takes a great weight off my back. For I was such an admirer of his painting that I was being crushed by it" (letter XCIII, *Letters*, ed. Cooper, 77-78).

14. The Philadelphia Museum of Art has another, unfinished collage by Braque which remains a mystery (fig. 63). It is located on the verso of a finished painting, the large *Gueridon* of 1918. Given this location, and a large inscription "G. Braque 18," this collage is generally thought to belong to this postwar period. However, this inscription clearly relates to the vertical painting on the other side, as the collage still life is a horizontal composition; the wine bottle (with a pasted newspaper clipping of "VIN") and the fruit above make this orientation clear. Even more curious, the pasted page from *Lacerba* at the lower left (proper) can be dated to January 1914, suggesting an earlier making of the collage. However, this unfinished collage does follow *Formes musicales* in the massing of overlapping planes and the more distant perspective of the larger still-life grouping. Its long format and more painterly passages atop the paper find a parallel with the 1919 *Le buffet*. This suggests that it served as a transitional work between the 1918 *Formes musicales* and this later painting and was rejected when Braque's evolving style made collage an alien format.

DÉSIGNATION

A. - DESSINS, GOUACHES, AQUARELLES

BRAQUE (Georges)

1 — Nature morte. Ovale — Haut. : 0m25 ; Larg. : 0m20
Dessin, papier collé — (Signé au dos).

2 — L'As de Pique. Ovale — Haut : 0m30 ; Larg. : 0m25
Dessin, papier collé — (Non signé)

3 — La bouteille de Marc. Ovale — Haut. : 0m35 ; Larg. : 0m29
Dessin, papier collé — (Non signé).

4 — La Guitare. Ovale — Haut. : 0m35 ; Larg. : 0m29
Dessin, papier collé — (Non signé).

5 — L'Arlequin. Haut. : 0m62 ; Larg. : 0m48
Dessin, papier collé — (Non signé).

6 — Nature morte. Haut. : 0m53 ; Larg. : 0m60
Dessin, papier collé — (Non signé).

7 — Nature morte. Haut. : 0m32 ; Larg. : 0m47
Dessin — (Non signé).

8 — L'As de Trèfle. Haut. : 0m45 ; Larg. : 0m81
Dessin — (Signé au dos au crayon bleu).

9 — Le Damier. Haut. : 0m65 ; Larg. : 0m92
Dessin, papier collé — (Signé au dos au crayon bleu).

10 — Le Violon. Haut. : 0m92 ; Larg. : 0m60
Dessin, papier collé — (Non signé).

11 — La Guitare. Haut. : 1m ; Larg. : 0m65
Dessin, papier collé — (Signé au dos au crayon bleu).

12 — Nature morte. Haut. : 0m73 ; Larg. : 1m02
Dessin, papier collé — (Non signé).

13 — Violon et Pipe. Haut. : 0m76 ; Larg. : 1m08
Dessin, papier collé — (Signé au dos).

14 — Flûte et Verre. Haut. : 0m95 ; Larg. : 1m21
Dessin, papier collé — (Signé au dos au crayon bleu)

15 — Figure. Haut. 0m62 ; Larg. : 0m47
Dessin — (Non signé)

16 — Nature morte. Haut. : 0m47 ; Larg. : 0m62
Dessin — (Non signé).

17 — Nature morte. Haut. : 0m70 ; Larg. : 0m51
Dessin — (Non signé).

18 — Le Compotier. Haut. : 0m48 ; Larg. : 0m62
Dessin, papier collé (Non signé).

19 — L'As de Pique. Haut. : 0m32 ; Larg. : 0m50
Dessin, papier collé — (Non signé).

20 — La Guitare. Haut. : 0m37 ; Larg. : 0m46
Dessin — (Non signé).

21 — Le Bock. Haut. : 0m33 ; Larg. : 0m25
Dessin, papier collé — (Non signé).

22 à 40 — Dix-neuf dessins, crayon et fusain, quelques-uns avec papier collé.
Sujets divers — (Quelques-uns signés).

41 à 46 — Six dessins, crayon et fusain, quelques-uns avec papier collé.
Sujets divers — (Quelques-uns signés).

See figs. 94-96

CATALOGUE

The following is a complete catalogue of Braque's *papiers collés.* It results from the combined research of the Musée national d'art moderne, at the Centre Georges Pompidou, and the National Gallery of Art. The version published here is a variation from the *catalogue raisonné* organized by Isabelle Monod-Fontaine for the French exhibition. Additional elements have been contributed by Trinkett Clark, who coorganized the preliminary Washington catalogue. Douglas Cooper has also provided notes about provenance on certain works. The general chronological arrangement of the collages also differs from Mme. Monod-Fontaine's initial sequence, but in doing this I had the advantage of having seen them gathered together in Paris. The CGP number in each entry refers to the Centre Georges Pompidou's catalogue. The works are listed by their traditional titles, with the exception of nos. 41, 46, and 49, where I have given new ones in light of studying what they contain. Each is followed by its title in French. For these works, and for others where different titles are also known, the alternative appellations are listed below in parentheses. Dimensions are given in centimeters followed parenthetically in inches. Accompanying texts are signed.

E. A. Carmean, Jr.

A ✓ indicates the work is in the exhibition.

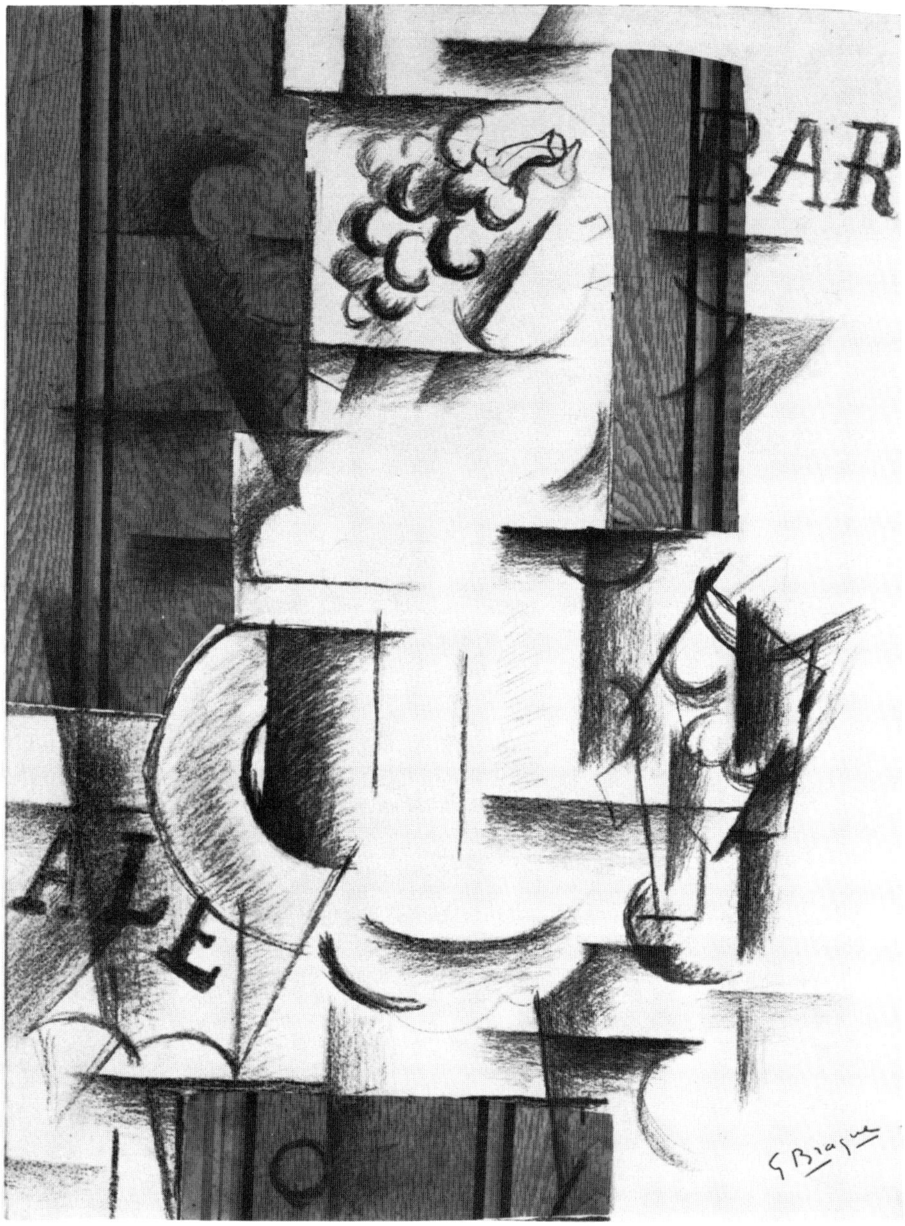

See plate 9

1.

Fruit-dish and Glass
(Compotier et verre)
(The Grapes, The Fruit-dish)

1912
Charcoal, *faux bois* paper, on paper
62 x 44.5 (24 3/8 x 17 1/2)
Signed, later, at lower right: *G Braque*
(the signature does not appear on the Kahnweiler photo, taken around 1913)
(On the back of a photograph, in Braque's handwriting: "Premier papier collé [first papier collé]. Sorgues, Septembre 1912")
CGP 1

Provenance
Galerie Kahnweiler, Paris (no. 1083)
Collection Wilhelm Uhde (until 30 May 1921)
Collection Léonce Rosenberg
André Breton
Collection Simone Breton (by 1933, until 1946)

Literature
Raynal 1921, reproduced on cover
Raynal 1924, reproduced
Einstein 1931, reproduced pl. 347
Isarlov 1932, no. 144, p. 18
Einstein 1934, reproduced pl. XVIII
Hope 1949, p. 64, reproduced p. 54
Paulhan 1952, p. 76
Raynal 1953, reproduced color p. 177
Wescher 1953, p. 33, reproduced p. 34
Gieure 1956, p. 32
Greenberg 1958, p. 48, reproduced p. 46
Golding 1959, p. 103
Leymarie 1961, p. 56, reproduced color p. 54
Richardson 1961, p. 14, reproduced p. 15
Cabanne 1963, p. 182
Fry 1966, p. 27, reproduced. p. 158
Rosenblum 1966, p. 69, reproduced pl. 37
Mathey 1968, reproduced p. 158
Mullins 1968, p. 74, reproduced p. 74
Cooper 1970, p. 185
Cogniat 1970, p. 72
Carrà 1971, reproduced no. 87
Schwartz 1971, p. 98, reproduced p. 99
Wolfram 1975, p. 16, reproduced p. 17
Judkins 1976, reproduced p. 443
Daix 1979, pp. 111-114
Wescher 1979, p. 22, reproduced pl. 14
Mangin (Worms de Romilly) 1982, no. 150, reproduced

Exhibitions
Basel 1933, no. 60, reproduced
Edinburgh 1956, no. 33, reproduced pl. 21a
Cincinnati 1962, unnumbered, reproduced
Munich 1963, no. 37, reproduced pl. 33

Paris 1963, no. 7, reproduced
Paris 1973, no. 46, reproduced
Paris 1974, reproduced pl. 3 (not in exhibition)
Paris 1982, no. 1, reproduced color p. 67

Private collection

Fruit-dish and Glass is traditionally given as the first *papier collé,* even by Braque himself (as a manuscript note on the back of an archive photograph proves). As such it has been abundantly reproduced and discussed since 1921. It can be dated, currently, to the first half of September 1912 and more precisely to the days which preceded Picasso's return to Sorgues (13 September) after a brief stay in Paris (see Douglas Cooper's essay in this volume). It was during Picasso's absence that Braque would have bought in an Avignon shop the famous roll of *faux bois* paper, simulating oak paneling and consisting of two kinds of printed motifs on a dark beige background: wood grain (which Braque knew how to imitate anyway with a housepainter's comb) and the rectilinear relief of the moldings in *trompe l'oeil,* indicated through lines of different thickness (lines exactly reproduced in the painted translation of the first *papier collé*—in spring 1913— the *Nature morte à l'as de trèfle* [*Still Life with the Ace of Clubs*] in the Musée national d'art moderne, Paris). Braque would use these three constituent elements of the *faux bois* paper—color, grain, and parallel lines—in a first series of *papiers collés* putting them in relation with structure drawn in charcoal.

The second (?) collage (cat. no. 2) which also has a fruit dish as its subject, is closely related to *Fruit-dish and Glass* and to all of Braque's work at the time: if one compares the three canvases[1] which, to our mind, are immediate contemporaries of the first *papiers collés* (and in which, as Pierre Daix has rightly emphasized,[2] the light additions of sand to the pigments are another kind of experimentation with space and color, and are equivalent to the pieces of paper) one notes the extreme overlapping from one work to the other of formal signs designating the table, the compote, the fruit (pears and grapes), the glass, and eventually the drawn letters. The overlapping is such that it is just about impossible to determine which is the very first version, and whether it was a *papier collé* or painted version.

Let us note finally that the first *papier collé* belonged (until 1921) to Wilhelm Uhde, one of the first collectors of Braque (from 1907). I.M.-F.

1. *Le compotier (The Fruit-dish),* 1912 (41 x 33 cm); *Nature morte à la grappe (Still Life with a Bunch of Grapes),* 1912 (60 x 73 cm); *Compotier, verre et raisin (Fruit-dish, Glass and Grapes),* 1912 (50 x 65 cm).
2. Daix 1979.

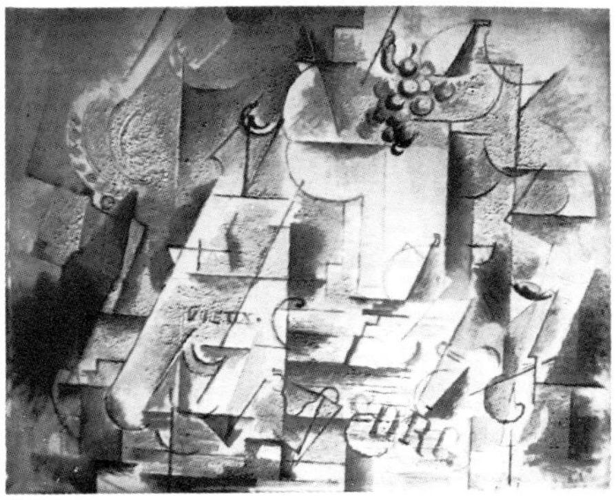

65. Braque, *Compotier, bouteille et verre,* 1912, oil on canvas. Private collection.

66. Braque, *Le compotier,* 1912, oil on canvas. Private collection.

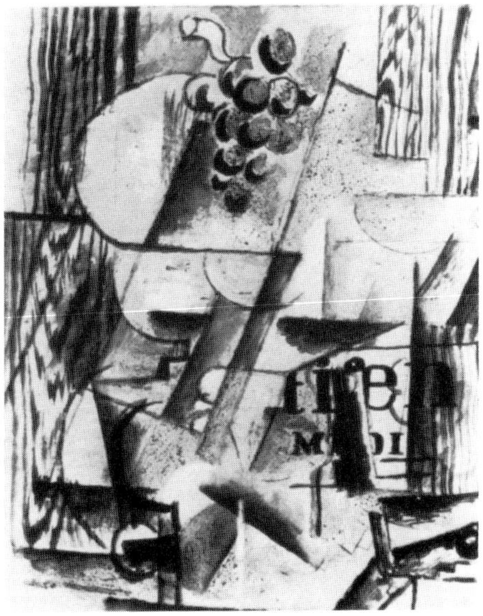

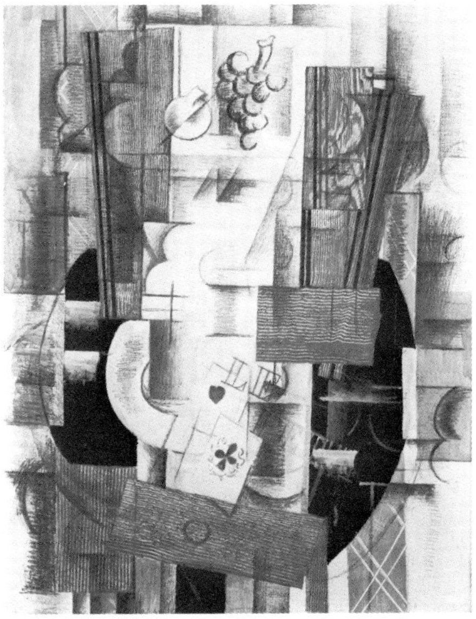

67. Braque, *Compotier et cartes,* 1913, oil, heightened by pencil and charcoal, on canvas. Musée national d'art moderne, Centre Georges Pompidou, Paris.

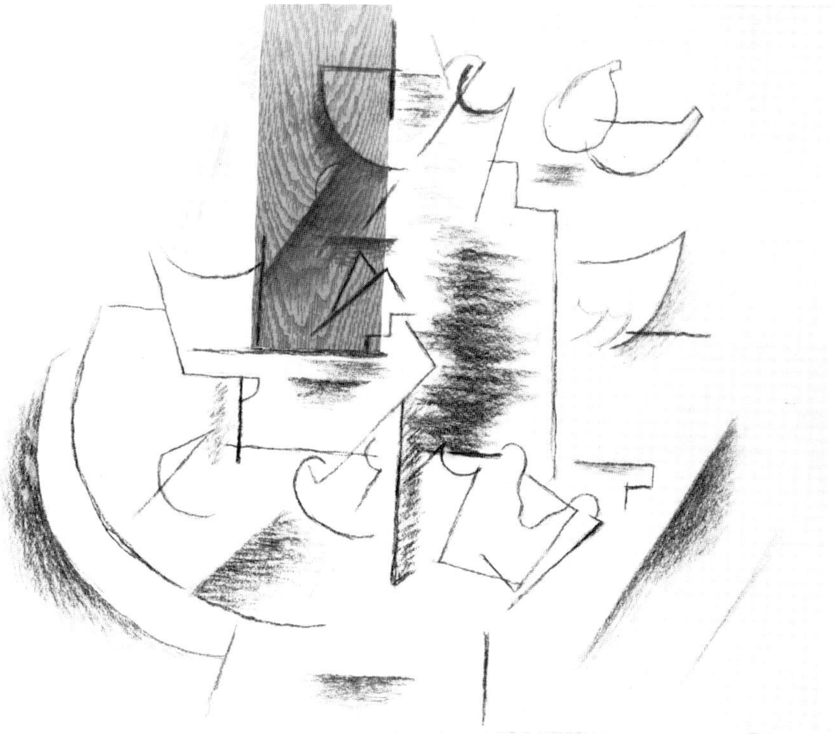

2.

The Fruit-dish (Le compotier)
(Still Life)

Charcoal, *faux bois* paper, on paper
48 x 62 (18 15/16 x 24 3/8)
Signed on back ?
CGP 2

Provenance
Galerie Kahnweiler, Paris
4th Kahnweiler sale, 1923, no. 18, *Le compotier* (48 x 62 cm), for 35F
Collection Jacques Zoubaloff (sale of 27-28 November 1935, no. 25, *Le compotier* [47 x 62 cm], signed on back)
Collection Lee Miller Penrose

Exhibitions
Berne 1953, no. 39
Zurich 1953, no. 44
Paris 1982, no. 2, reproduced color p. 69

Private collection

Like *Fruit-dish and Glass* (cat. no. 1), *The Fruit-dish* is closely tied to painting; a canvas is known *(Compotier, verre et raisin,* 1912, Kahnweiler photo no. 1076) whose dimensions are about exactly the same as those of the *papier collé* (48 x 62 cm for the *papier collé,* 50 x 65 cm for the painting). The drawing of the structure seems to have been carried over exactly onto the canvas (or vice versa from the canvas to the page?), making even more instructive the comparsion, square inch by square inch, of the shadowed, sanded, white-heightened areas . . . or those covered with *faux bois* paper.

This *papier collé* seems to be the one which belonged to Jacques Zoubaloff, collector of the impressionists, then of the cubists (and generous patron of the national museums of France), whose collection of modern art was dispersed in 1935. I.M.-F.

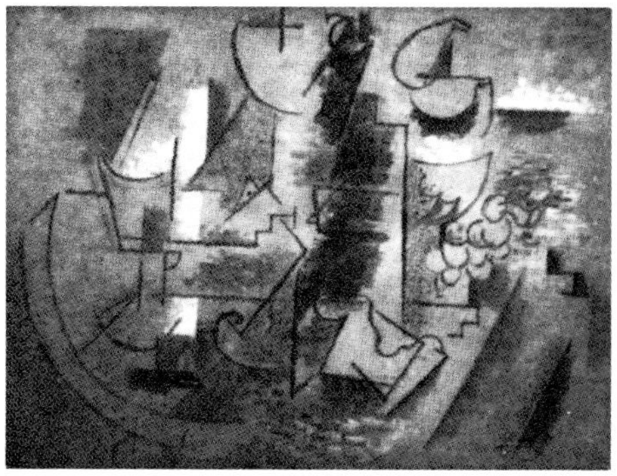

68. Braque, *Compotier, verre et raisin,* n.d. Location unknown.

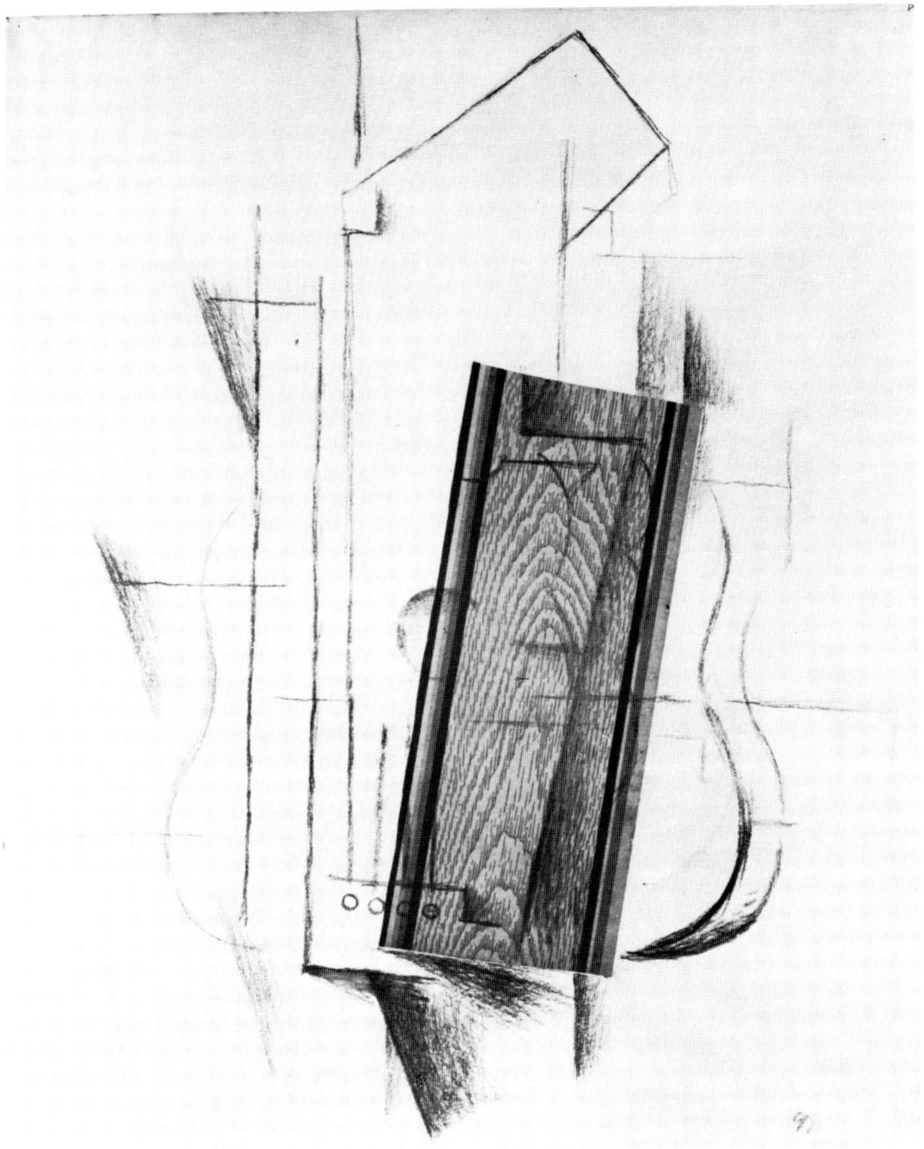

3.

Still Life with Guitar
(Nature morte à la guitare)
(Still Life with Mandolin)

1912
charcoal, *faux bois* paper, on paper
62.1 x 48.2 (24 7/16 x 19)
Initialed at lower right: *G.B.*
(On the back of a photograph of this work, in Braque's writing: "J'ai exécuté ce papier collé en 1911 G. Braque" [I made this *papier collé* in 1911])
CGP 3

Provenance
Collection Flechtheim, Berlin ?
Collection G. David Thompson, Pittsburgh
Collection Rosengart, Lucerne

Literature
Wescher 1979, p. 22, reproduced pl. 15
Mangin (Worms de Romilly) 1982, no. 170, reproduced

Exhibitions
London 1957, no. 8, reproduced p. 27
Zurich 1960, no. 14, reproduced
The Hague 1962, no. 13, reproduced
Bielefeld 1979, no. 142, reproduced
Paris 1982, no. 3, reproduced color p. 71

Collection of Riccardo Jucker

The *faux bois* paper in *Still Life with Guitar* apparently has the same characteristics as that used in the two preceding works. We have compared it to a whole group of works—which seem to us to be among the first, although we have no certain proof, consisting of only one band of *faux bois* paper in a simple metaphorical relation with a drawn structure representing a stringed instrument.

On the back of a photograph, Braque himself noted a date (1911), which is certainly incorrect but which tends to classify this *papier collé* among the earliest. I.M.-F.

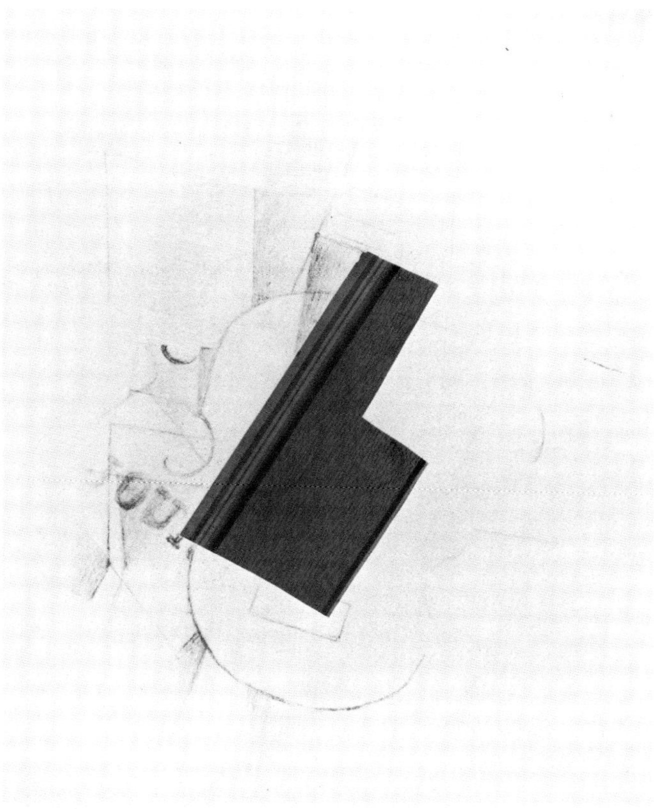

4.

The Guitar (La Guitare)

1912
charcoal, *faux bois* paper, on paper
70.2 x 60.7 (28 1/16 x 23 15/16)
CGP 4

Provenance
Studio of the artist

Literature
Draeger 1971, reproduced color p. 115
Jouffroy 1980, reproduced
Mangin (Worms de Romilly) 1982, no. 191, reproduced

Exhibitions
Paris 1974, no. 458
Saint-Paul 1980, no. 49
Paris 1982, no. 4, reproduced color p. 73

Private collection

See plate 3

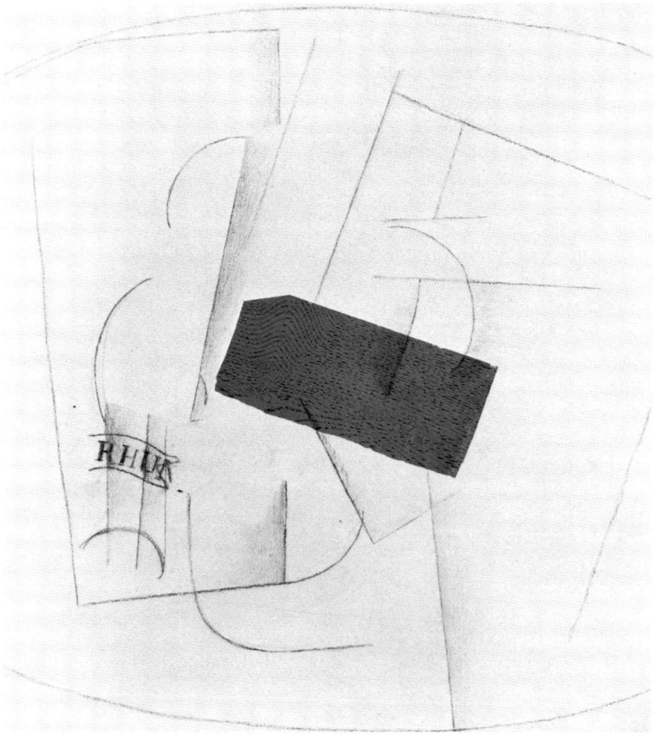

4 bis.

Rhum

1912
charcoal, *faux bois* paper, on paper
70 x 63 (27 1/2 x 24 3/4)
CGP 57

Provenance
Studio of the artist

Exhibitions
Paris 1982, no. 57, reproduced p. 178
(not in exhibition)

Private collection

This large still life, comprising a bottle of rum and a guitar, was not finished, and it remained in Braque's studio until his death in 1963. Even in this early stage we see that the collaged element, a piece of *faux bois* paper indicating the guitar's wooden surface, has been fixed at the center of the composition and the preliminary drawing of it and other objects is also in place. Study of the work shows that Braque has very lightly added touches of shading around several lines, evenly distributed over the entire surface. Judging from finished works of this period, he would have next gone on to strengthen this modeling in certain passages. The relative simplicity and openness of the composition, the scale of the work, and its focal subject matter of a large musical instrument placed at an angle, relate this collage directly to cat. no. 4, *The Guitar.* E.A.C.jr.

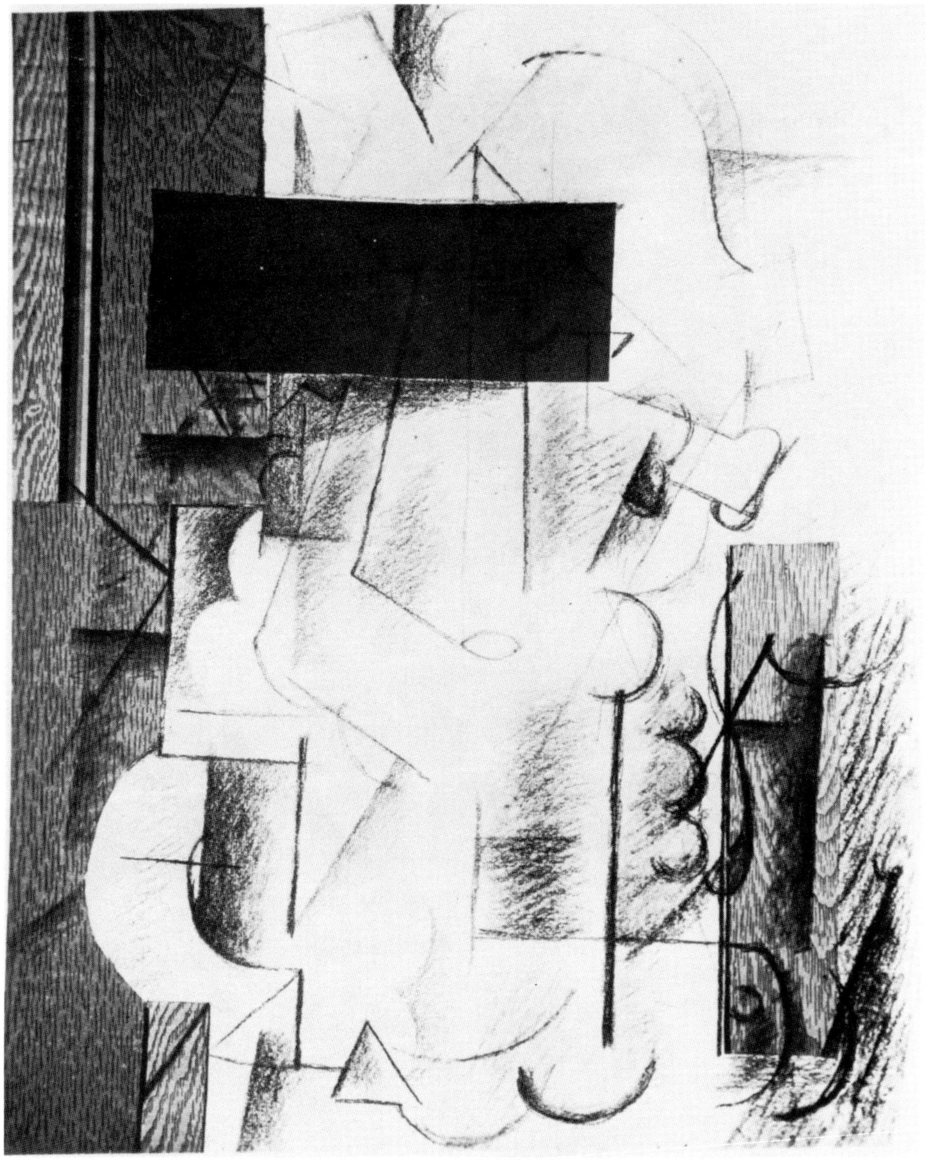

5.
Harlequin (L'Arlequin)

1912
charcoal, *faux bois* paper, and colored paper, on paper
62 x 48 (24 3/8 x 18 15/16)
CGP 8

Provenance
Galerie Kahnweiler, Paris
4th Kahnweiler sale, 1923, no. 5, *L'Arlequin* (62 x 48 cm), for 55F
Dr. F. J. Bossard, Paris and Zurich (in 1963)

Literature
Ashbury 1963, reproduced p. 78
Mangin (Worms de Romilly) 1982, no. 163, reproduced

Exhibitions
Basel 1962, no. 20 ?
Paris 1963, no. 20, reproduced
Paris 1982, no.·8, reproduced p. 81 (not in exhibition)

Location unknown

This is the only known representation of Harlequin in the whole of Braque's oeuvre.
D.C.

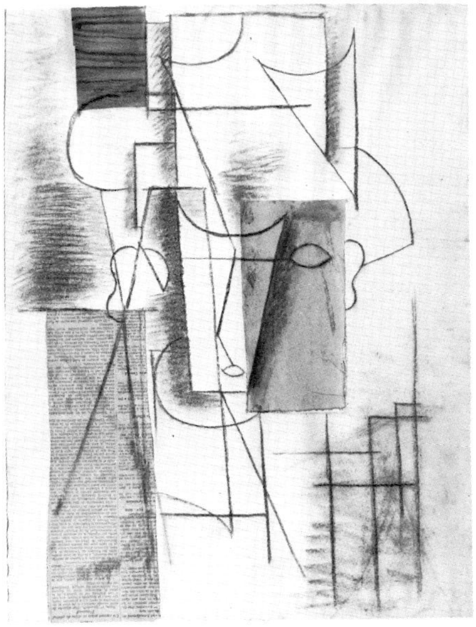

69. Pablo Picasso (Spanish, 1881-1973), *Tête d'homme,* 1912, *papier collé,* watercolor, charcoal, on paper. Private collection.

Cat. nos. 5, 6, and 7

These three collages *(Harlequin* [cat. no. 5], *Man with a Pipe* [cat. no. 6], and *Head of a Woman* [cat. no. 7]) form a small separate series, the only one among Braque's *papiers collés* which have the human figure as subject (unlike Picasso who often treated this theme, head or figure, in a way which was at first somewhat analogous to Braque's—see Daix 1979, nos. 532, 533, etc.; then later in a completely different direction—see Daix 1979, nos. 594, 595).

This series is constructed formally like the preceding *papiers collés* on a very dense, drawn grid, punctuated by the color of the *faux bois*: but it is evident here that the metaphor of the wood color cannot be taken at face value as before, when it was used for tables or musical instruments.

In all three cases, the bands of *faux bois* paper are set on a vertical axis, framing the system of elements which signify an eye, a nose or a mouth; the "face" thus produced is placed askew: it is not the same with Picasso. His comparable *papiers collés* are constructed on a single central vertical axis. I.M.-F.

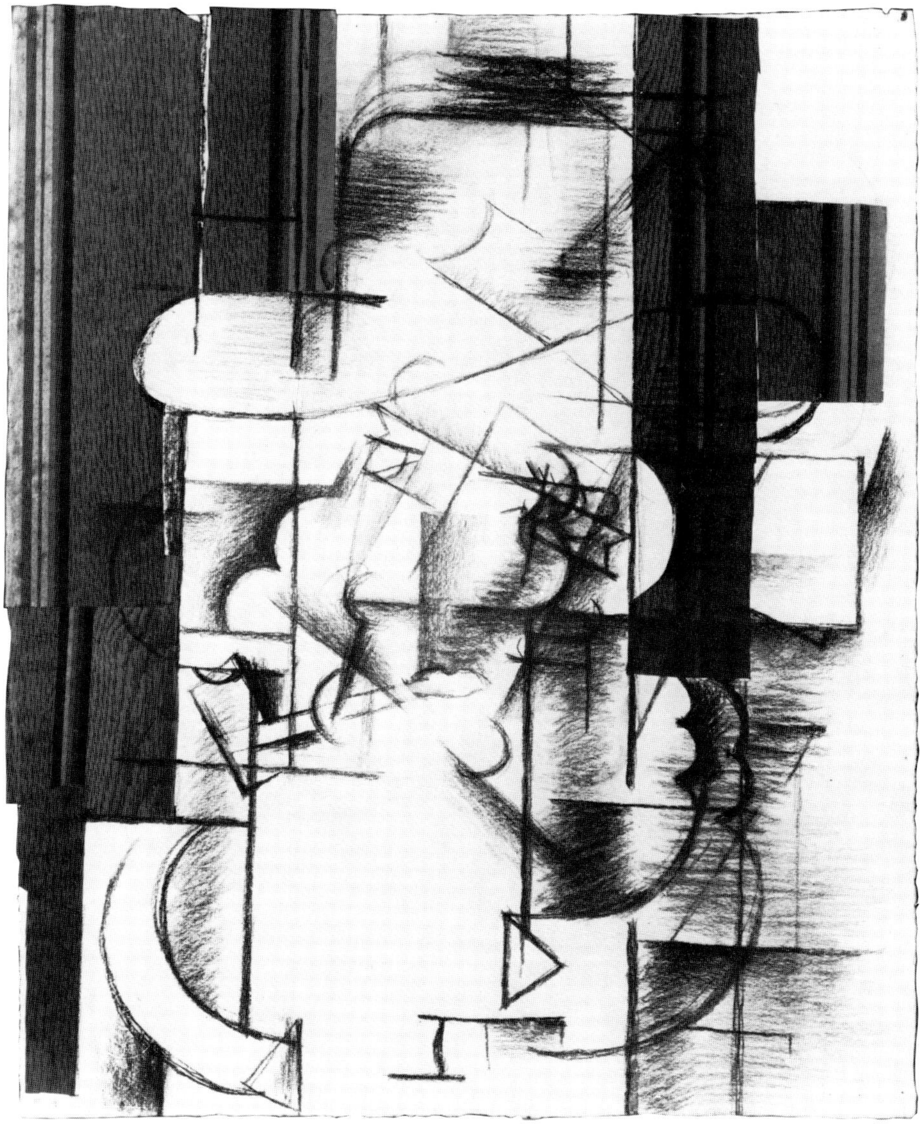

6.

Man with a Pipe (L'homme à la pipe)

1912
charcoal, *faux bois* paper, on paper
61.9 x 49 (24 3/8 x19 1/4)
Signed in the back with pencil, lower left: *G. Braque*
CGP 9

Provenance
Galerie Kahnwieler, Paris (no. 1126)
4th Kahnweiler sale, 1923, no. 46, auctioned in a lot of 6 drawings (nos. 41-46) for 210F*
Collection Raoul La Roche
Gift of Raoul La Roche to the Kunstmuseum, Basel, 1963 (inventory number 1963-24)

Literature
Koepplin 1969, no. 30, reproduced on cover
Cooper 1970, reproduced p. 183, pl. 198
Carrà 1971, no. 94, reproduced
Mangin (Worms de Romilly) 1982, no. 159, reproduced

Exhibitions
Basel 1963, p. 21, reproduced
Paris 1963, no. 19, reproduced
Zurich 1968, unnumbered, reproduced p. 59
Los Angeles 1970, no. 37, reproduced
Bielefeld 1979, no. 140, reproduced
Saint-Paul 1980, no. 50, reproduced
Paris 1982, no. 9, reproduced color p. 83

Kunstmuseum Basel, Kupferstichkabinett
Donation Dr. h. c. Raoul La Roche

*Information kindly provided by Douglas Cooper, 25 June 1982.

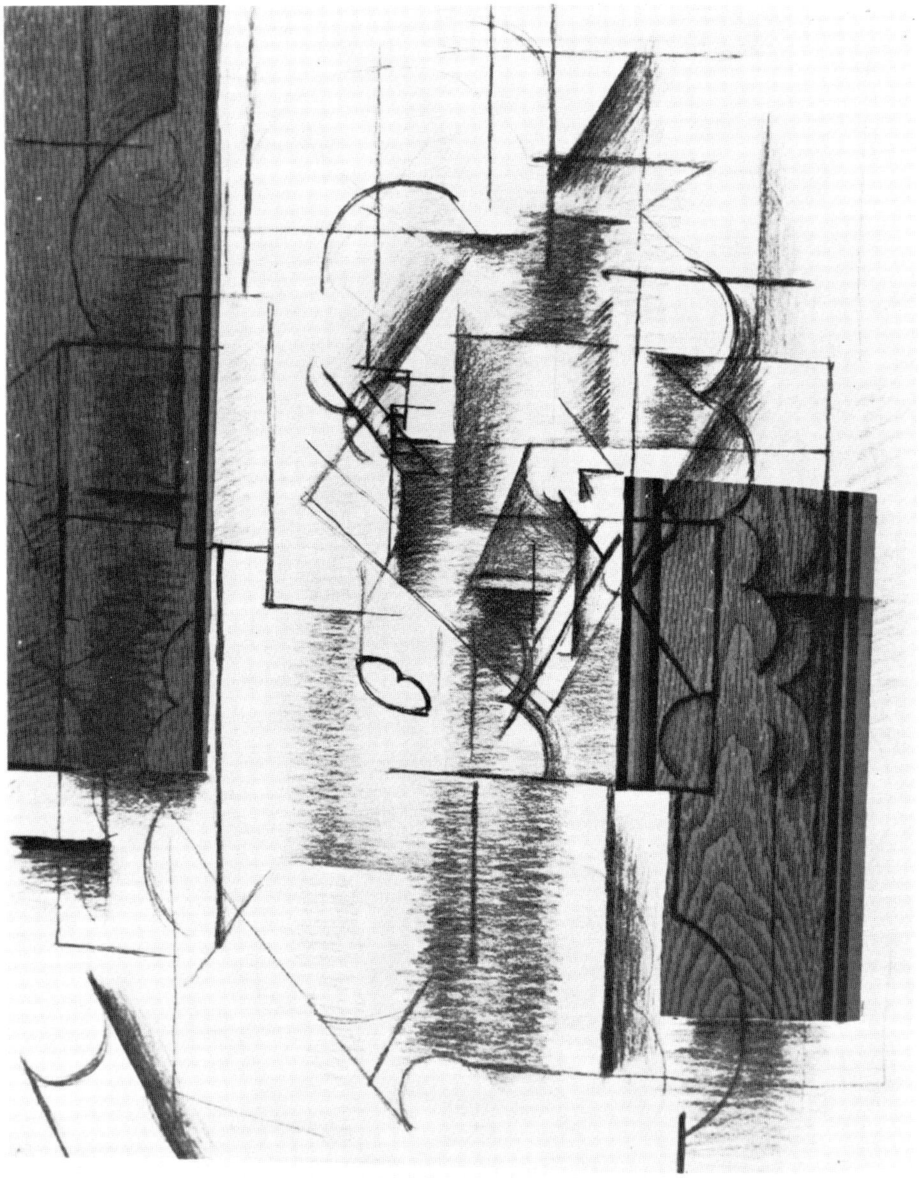

7.

Head of a Woman (Tête de femme)

charcoal, *faux bois* paper, on paper
61 x 47 (24 x 18 1/2)
Signed on back, in pencil: *G. Braque*
CGP 10

Provenance
Galerie Kahnweiler, Paris (no. 1134)
Collection Henriette Gomès
Collection Berggruen
Collection Jean-Claude Bellier (in 1967)

Literature
Mangin (Worms de Romilly) 1982, no. 163 B, reproduced

Exhibitions
Paris 1967, no. 2
Bielefeld 1979, no. 139, reproduced (not in exhibition)
Paris 1982, no. 10, reproduced color p. 85

Private collection, Geneva

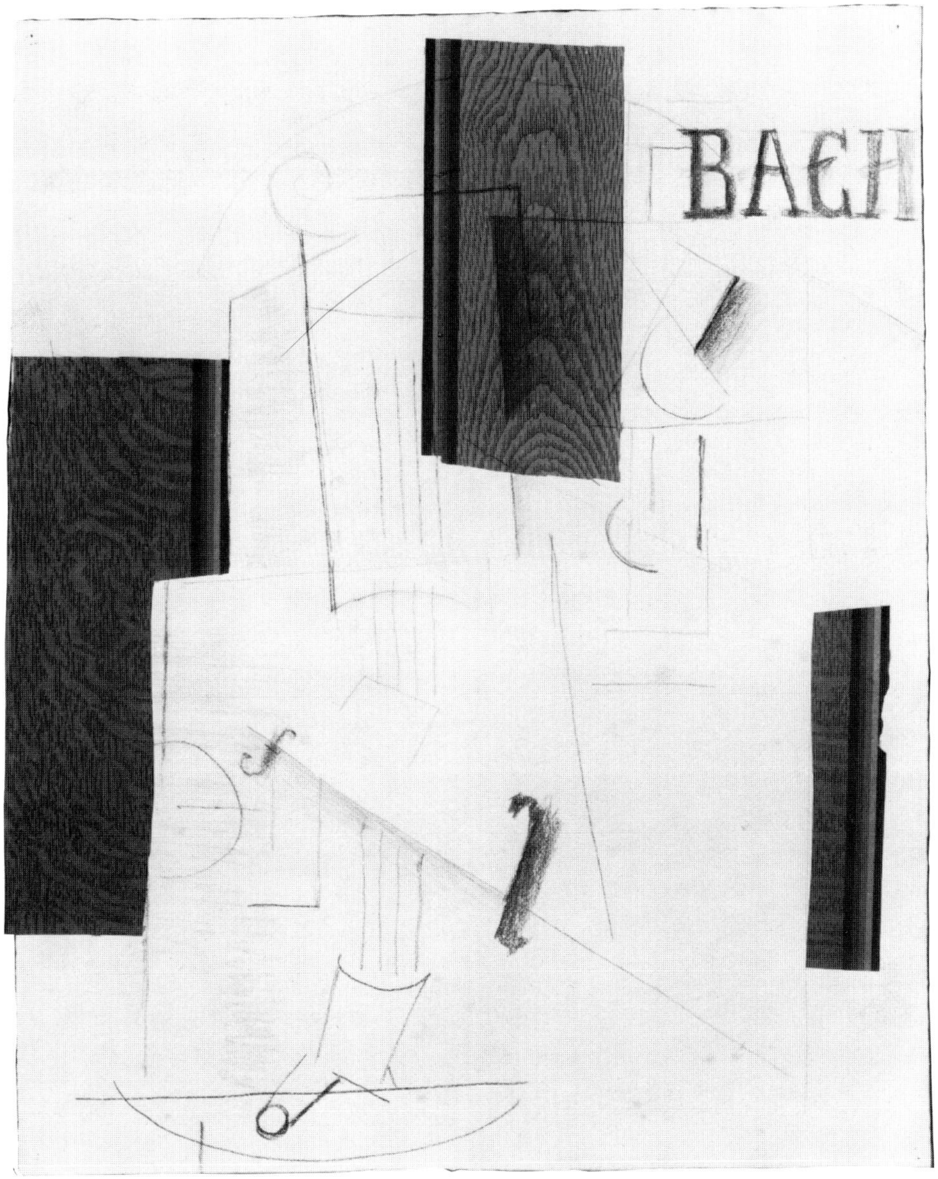

8.

Still Life BACH
(Nature morte BACH)

1912
charcoal, *faux bois* paper, on paper with drawing
63 x 48.3 (24 13/16 x 19)
CGP 11

Provenance
Galerie Kahnweiler, Paris (no. 1191)
4th Kahnweiler sale, 1923, no. 37, auctioned in a lot of 19 drawings (nos. 22-40) for 780F*
Collection Raoul La Roche
Gift of Raoul La Roche to the Kunstmuseum, Basel, in 1963 (inventory number 1963-22)

Literature
Koepplin 1969, no. 33, reproduced
Schwartz 1971, pp. 100-102, reproduced p. 103
Mangin (Worms de Romilly) 1982, no. 165, reproduced

Exhibitions
Basel 1963, reproduced
Paris 1963, no. 13, reproduced
Zurich 1968, unnumbered, reproduced p. 56
Amsterdam 1971, no. 33, reproduced
Bielefeld 1979, no. 157, reproduced
Saint-Paul 1980, no. 52, reproduced
Paris 1982, no. 11, reproduced color p. 87

Kunstmuseum Basel, Kupferstichkabinett
Donation Dr. h. c. Raoul La Roche

*Information kindly provided by Douglas Cooper, 25 June 1982.

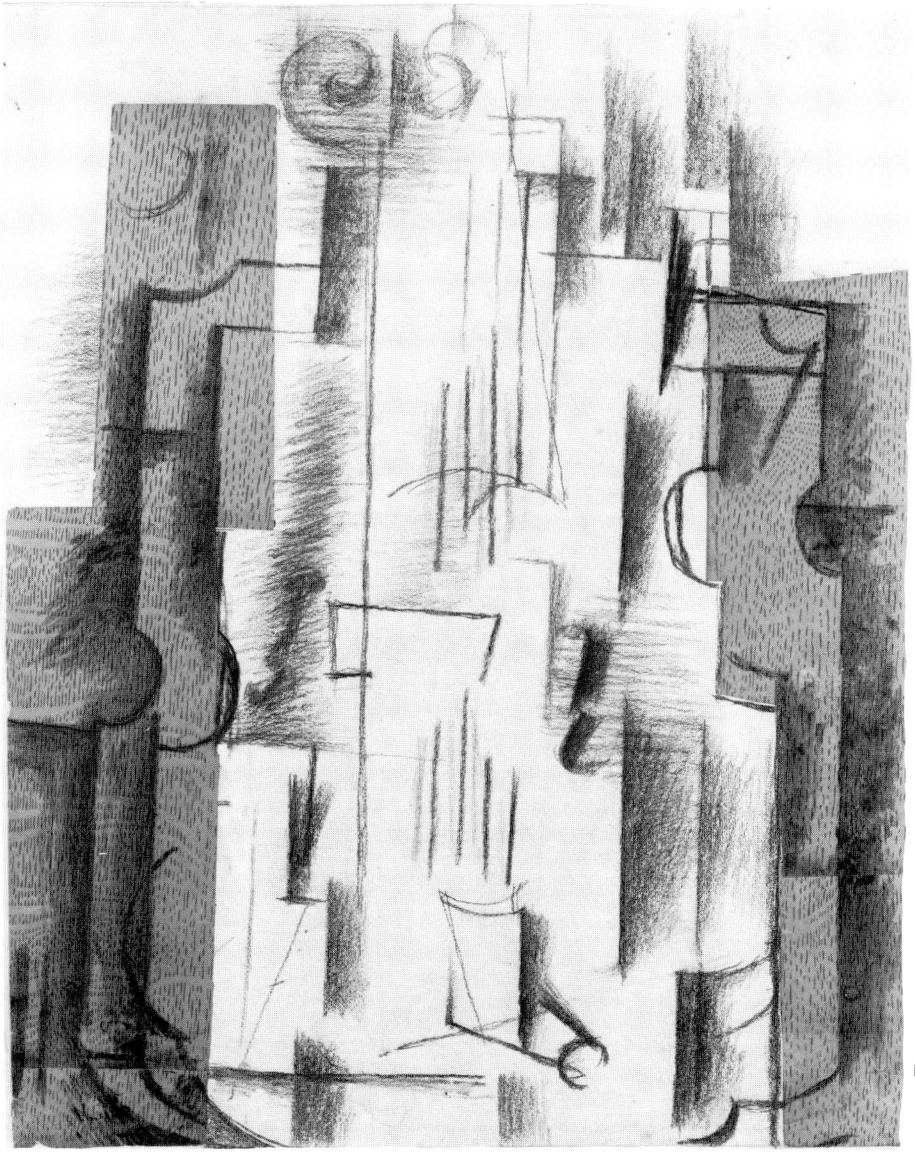

9.

Still Life with Violin
(Nature morte au violon)
(Still Life with Violincello)

1912
charcoal, *faux bois* paper, on paper
62 x 48 (24 7/16 x 18 7/8)
Signed on verso, lower left: *G. Braque*
CGP 12

Provenance
Galerie Kahnweiler, Paris
Collection Carlo Frua di'Angeli
Collection Berggruen, Paris (in 1974)
Collection Artémis (in 1976-1977)
Present collection, 1978

Literature
Carrà 1971, no. 117, reproduced
Mangin (Worms de Romilly) 1982, no. 171, reproduced

Exhibitions
Paris 1973-2, no. 10, reproduced color
Paris 1974, no. 457
Bielefeld 1979, no. 137, reproduced (not in exhibition)
Paris 1982, no. 12, reproduced color p. 89

Yale University Art Gallery, New Haven, Connecticut. The Leonard C. Hanna, Jr., B.A. 1913, Susan Vanderpoel Clark, and Edith M. K. Wetmore Funds

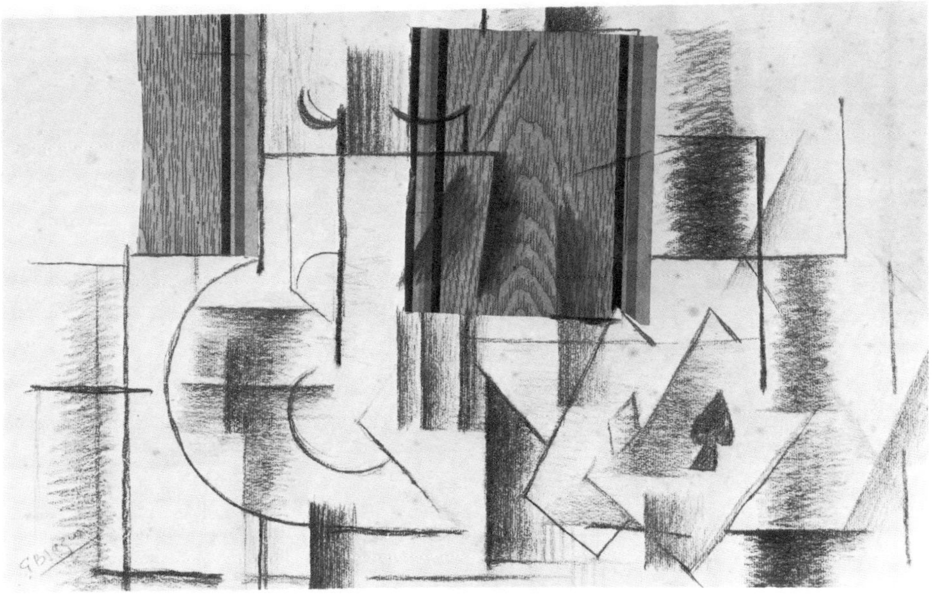

10.

Glass and Playing Cards (Verre et cartes à jouer)

1912
charcoal, *faux bois* paper, on paper
29 x 46 (11 7/16 x 18 1/8)
Signed, lower left: *G. Braque*
CGP 5

Provenance
4th Kahnweiler sale, 1923, no. 19, *L'as de pique*, for 30F
Collection André Lhote, Paris
Galerie Pierre, Paris
Collection of Mr. and Mrs. William Preston Harrison, 1926
Present collection, 1931

Literature
Flanner 1957, p. 148
Hope 1949, pp. 62-64
Leymarie 1961
Janis and Blesh 1962, p. 15
Cooper 1970, no. 36, pl. 199, p. 184
Carrà 1971, no. 95, reproduced
Mangin (Worms de Romilly) 1982, no. 166, reproduced

Exhibitions
Brussels 1931
Los Angeles 1970, no. 36, reproduced
Paris 1982, no. 5, reproduced color p. 75

Los Angeles County Museum of Art, Mr. and Mrs. William Preston Harrison Collection

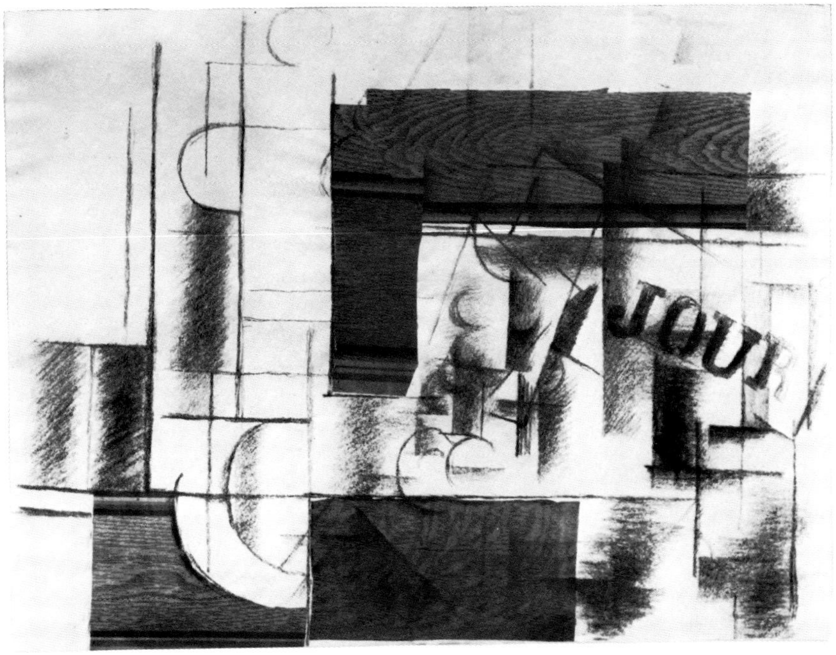

11.

Composition (Composition)

1912
charcoal, *faux bois* paper, on paper
48 x 62 (18 15/16 x 24 3/8)
Signed on back
CGP6

Provenance
Galerie Kahnweiler, Paris
4th Kahnweiler sale, 1923, no. 43, auctioned in a lot of 6 drawings (nos. 41-46) for 210F*
Collection Raoul La Roche, Basel
Collection Thomas Speiser, Basel
Galerie Beyeler, Basel

Literature
Mangin (Worms de Romilly) 1982, no. 162, reproduced

Exhibitions
Paris 1961, no. 15, reproduced

Basel 1962, no. 19
Paris 1963, no. 11, reproduced
Saint-Paul 1980, no. 56, reproduced
Basel 1980, no. 11
Paris 1982, no. 6, reproduced color p. 77

Collection of Ernst Beyeler, Basel

*Information kindly provided by Douglas Cooper, 25 June 1982.

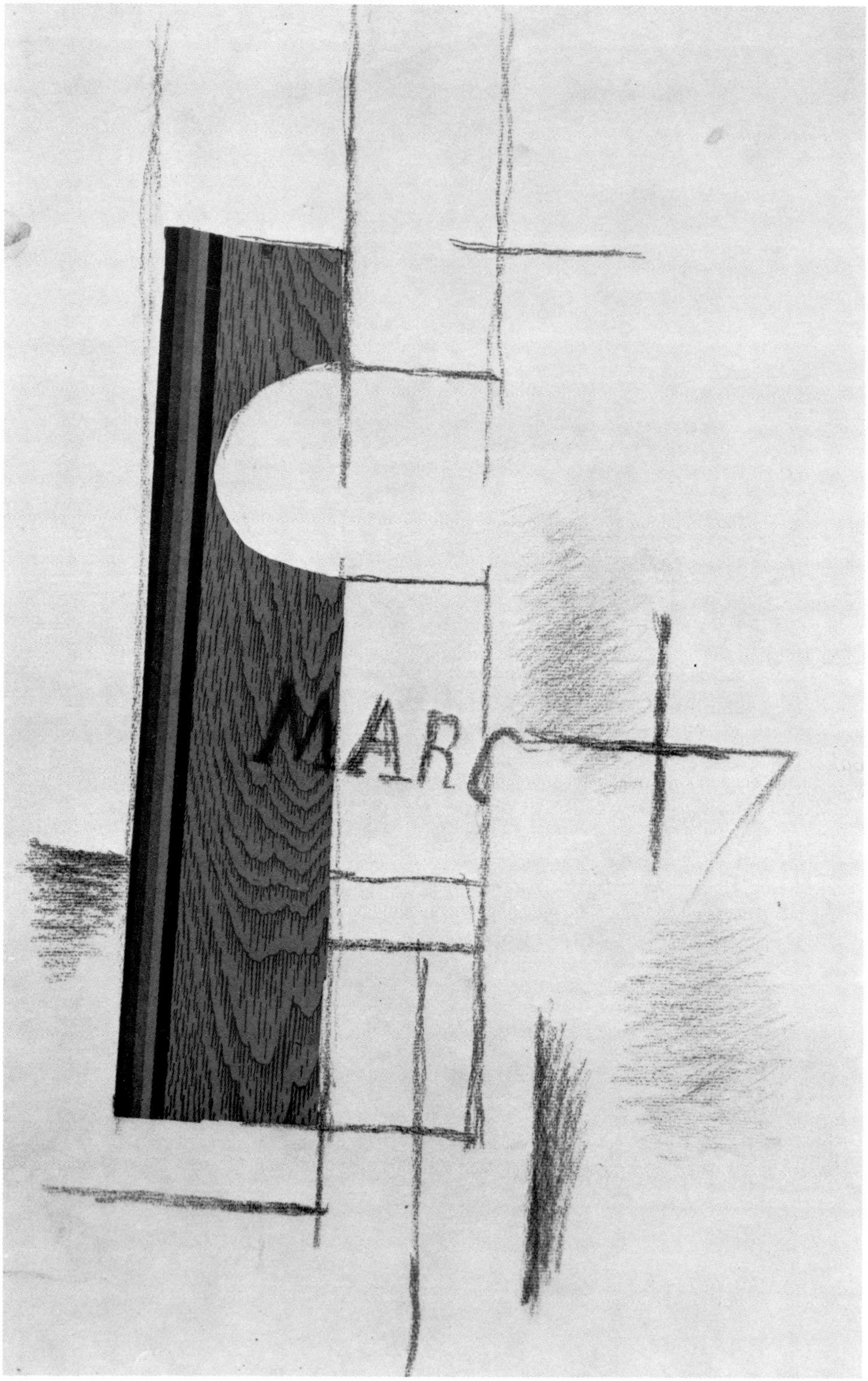

12.
The Bottle of Marc
(La bouteille de Marc)

1912
charcoal, *faux bois* paper, on paper
48 x 30 (18 15/16 x 11 13/16)
CGP 7

Provenance
Galerie Berggruen, Paris

Literature
XXme Siècle, January 1956, no. 6, reproduced p. 4
Mangin (Worms de Romilly) 1982, no. 164, reproduced

Exhibitions
Bielefeld 1979, no. 159, reproduced (not in exhibition)
Paris 1982, no. 7, reproduced (not in exhibition)

Location unknown

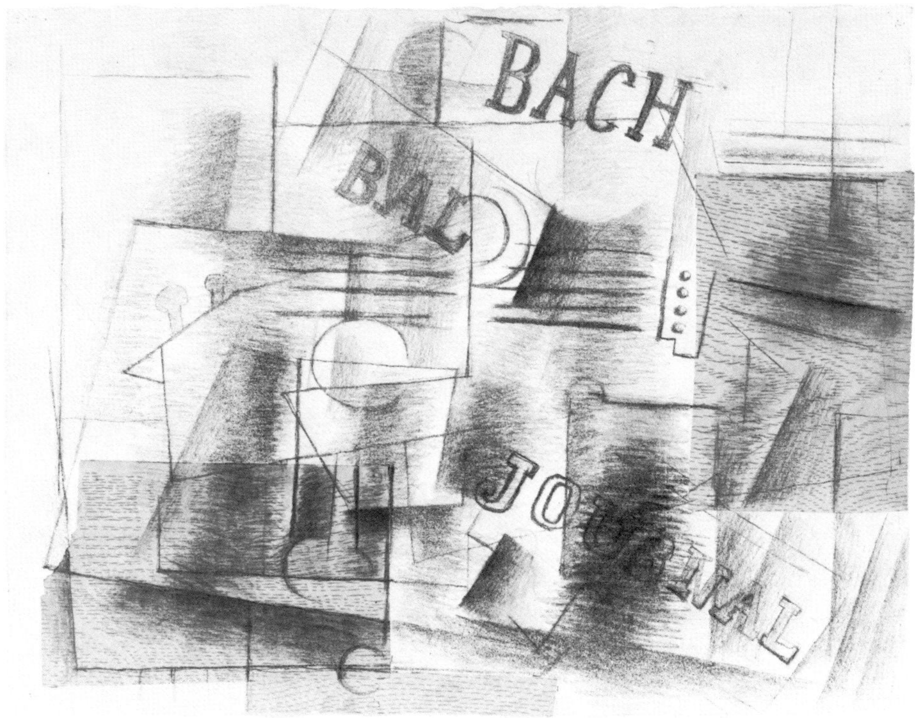

13.
Bal

1912
charcoal, *faux bois* paper, on paper
47.5 x 61.8 (18 11/16 x 24 3/8)
Signed on verso, lower left
CGP 16

Provenance
Galerie Kahnweiler, Paris (no. 1133)
Collection Henriette Gomès
Galerie Louise Leiris, Paris
Collection Mr. and Mrs. Daniel Saidenberg, New York

Literature
Kachur 1980, p. 13, reproduced
Mangin (Worms de Romilly) 1982, no. 166 B, reproduced

Exhibitions
New York 1980, unnumbered, reproduced
Paris 1982, no. 16, reproduced color p. 97

Saidenberg Gallery, New York

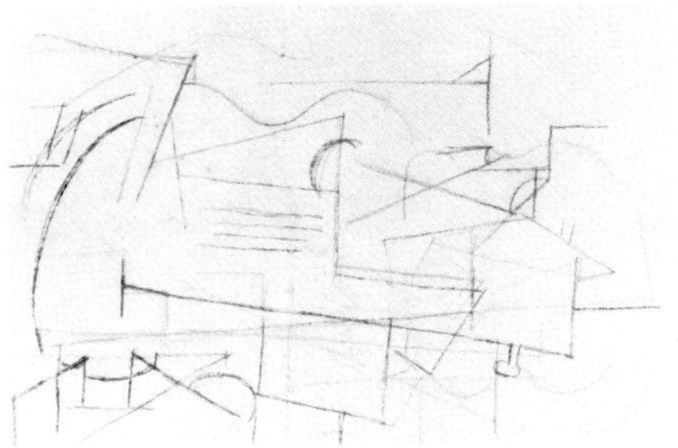

70. Braque, verso of *Bal.*

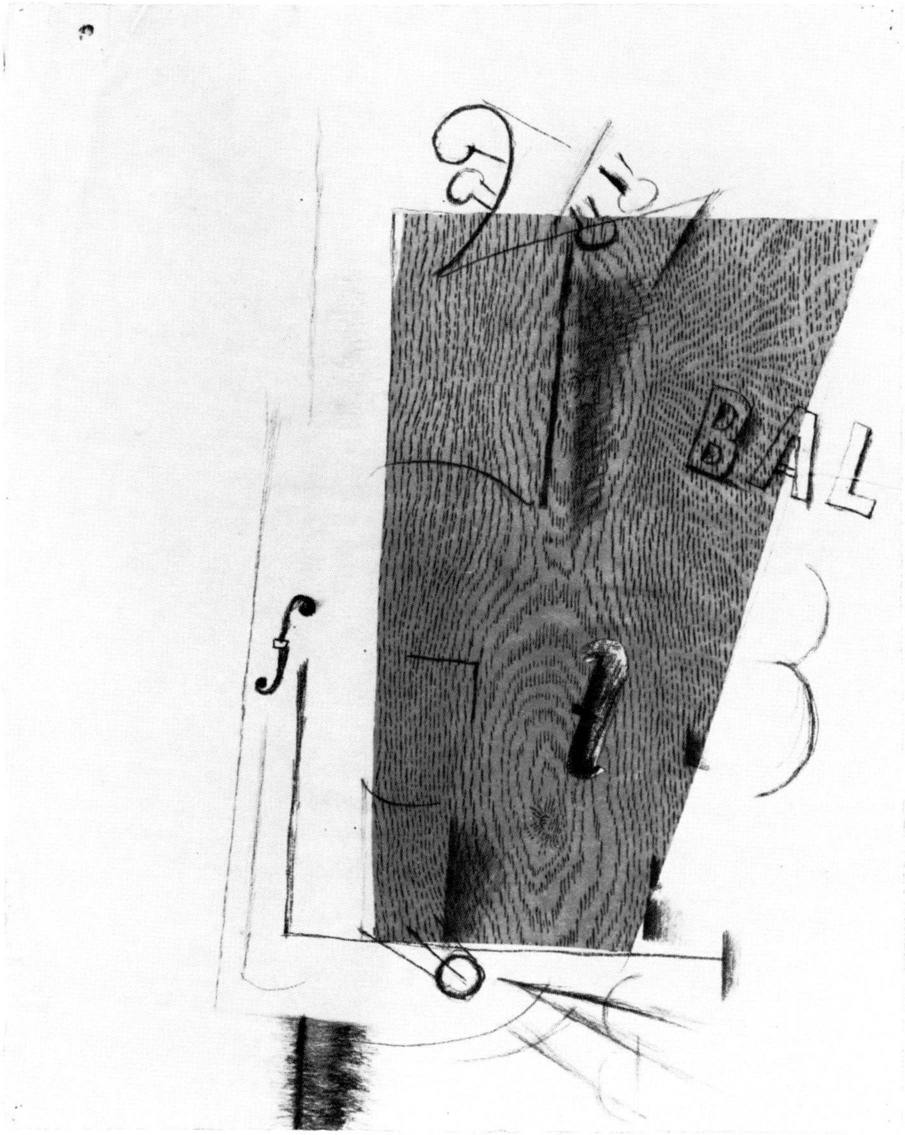

14.
Still Life with Violin BAL
(Nature morte au violon BAL)

1912
charcoal, *faux bois* paper, on paper
62.1 x 47.7 (24 7/16 x 18 13/16)
Not signed
CGP 13

Provenance
Galerie Kahnweiler, Paris (no. 1192)
4th Kahnweiler sale, 1923, no. 39, auctioned in a lot of 19 drawings (nos. 22-40) for 780F
Collection Raoul La Roche
Gift of Raoul La Roche to the Kunstmuseum, Basel, in 1963 (inventory number 1963-21)

Literature
Koepplin 1969, no. 34, reproduced
Mangin (Worms de Romilly) 1982, no. 167, reproduced

Exhibitions
Basel 1963, unnumbered, reproduced p. 20
Paris 1963, no. 14, reproduced
Amsterdam 1971, no. 34
Paris 1973, no. 137
Bielefeld 1979, no. 160, reproduced
Saint-Paul 1980, no. 51, reproduced
Paris 1982, no. 13, reproduced color p. 91

Kunstmuseum Basel, Kupferstichkabinett
Donation Dr. h. c. Raoul La Roche

The paper used here also simulates wood, but its appearance is different; it seems thinner, the lines reproducing the wood grain are on a smaller scale and of a decidedly orange color. This paper does not seem to have had vertical lines indicating the moldings or the wainscoting. Braque consequently did not use it in the same fashion: the other paper was always cut out in bands of unequal length, including most often the black or brown lines imitating relief. Here, and in the other compositions where the paper with orangy motifs seems to have been used (see cat. nos. 9, 15, 16), the cut-out forms are freer, and the drawing which supports or heightens them plays in a different way.

The hole of the violin is cut out, allowing the black of the charcoal, the shadow in the hollow, to appear (this practice reappears on numerous

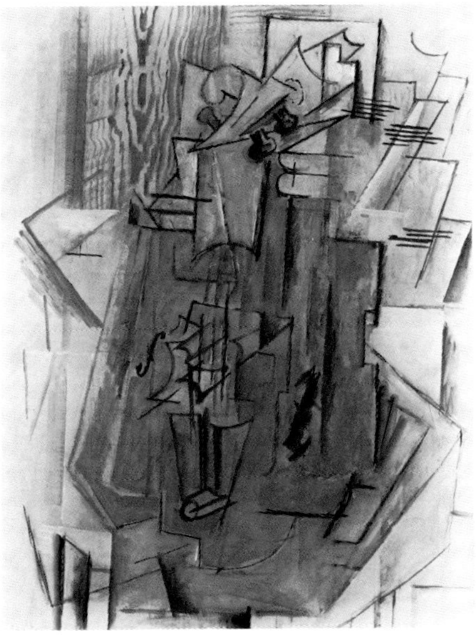

71. Braque, *Le violoncelle,* 1912, oil on canvas. Staatsgalerie Stuttgart.

occasions in the *papiers collés*). This hole, strongly marked in black, is found again in a painting, *Le violoncelle (The Violincello),* 1912 (80 x 60 cm), in which the drawn structure is practically identical to that of the *papier collé.* I.M.-F.

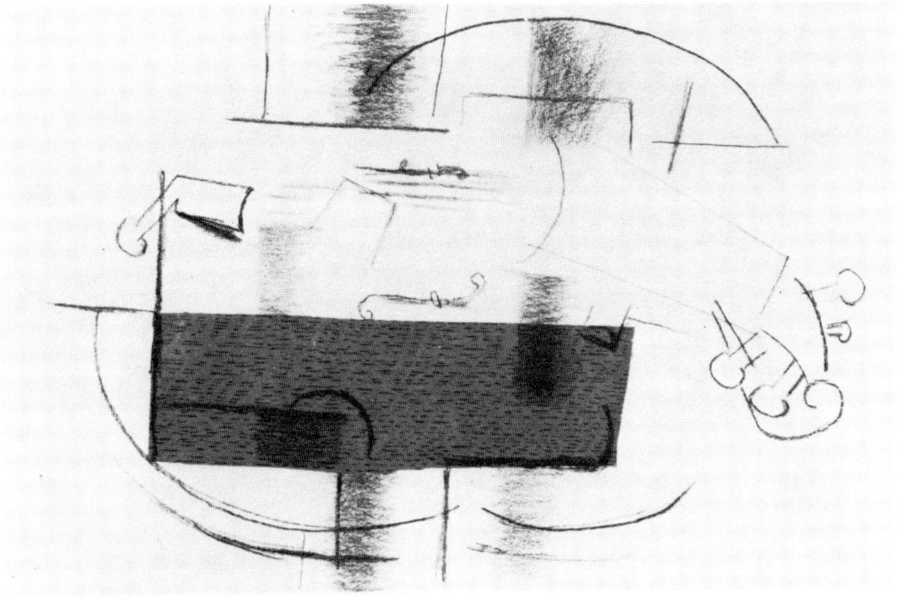

15.
Papier collé

1912
charcoal, *faux bois* paper, on paper
31 x 48 (12 3/16 x 18 15/16)
CGP 14

Provenance
Private collection, Zurich (in 1963)

Literature
Mangin (Worms de Romilly) 1982, no. 168, reproduced

Exhibitions
Paris 1963, no. 15, reproduced
Paris 1982, no. 14, reproduced (not in exhibition)

Location unknown

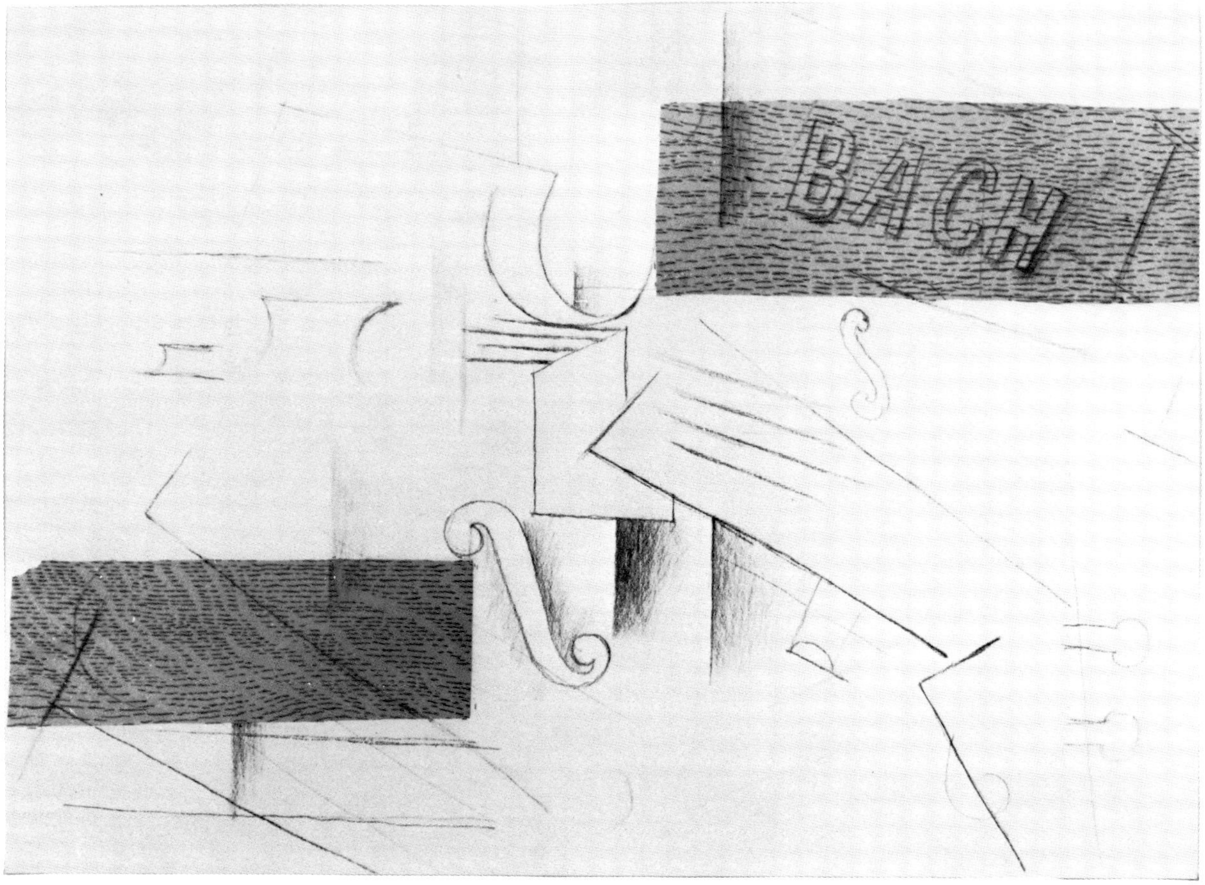

16.

Papier collé

(Still Life Bach)

1912
charcoal, *faux bois* paper, on paper
47 x 62 (18 1/2 x 24 7/16)
Signed on back
CGP 15

Provenance
Collection Raoul La Roche
Private collection, Basel

Literature
Mathey 1968, reproduced p. 158
Mangin (Worms de Romilly) 1982,
no. 161, reproduced

Exhibitions
Paris 1963, no. 10, reproduced
Paris 1982, no. 15, reproduced color p. 95

Galerie Rosengart, Lucerne

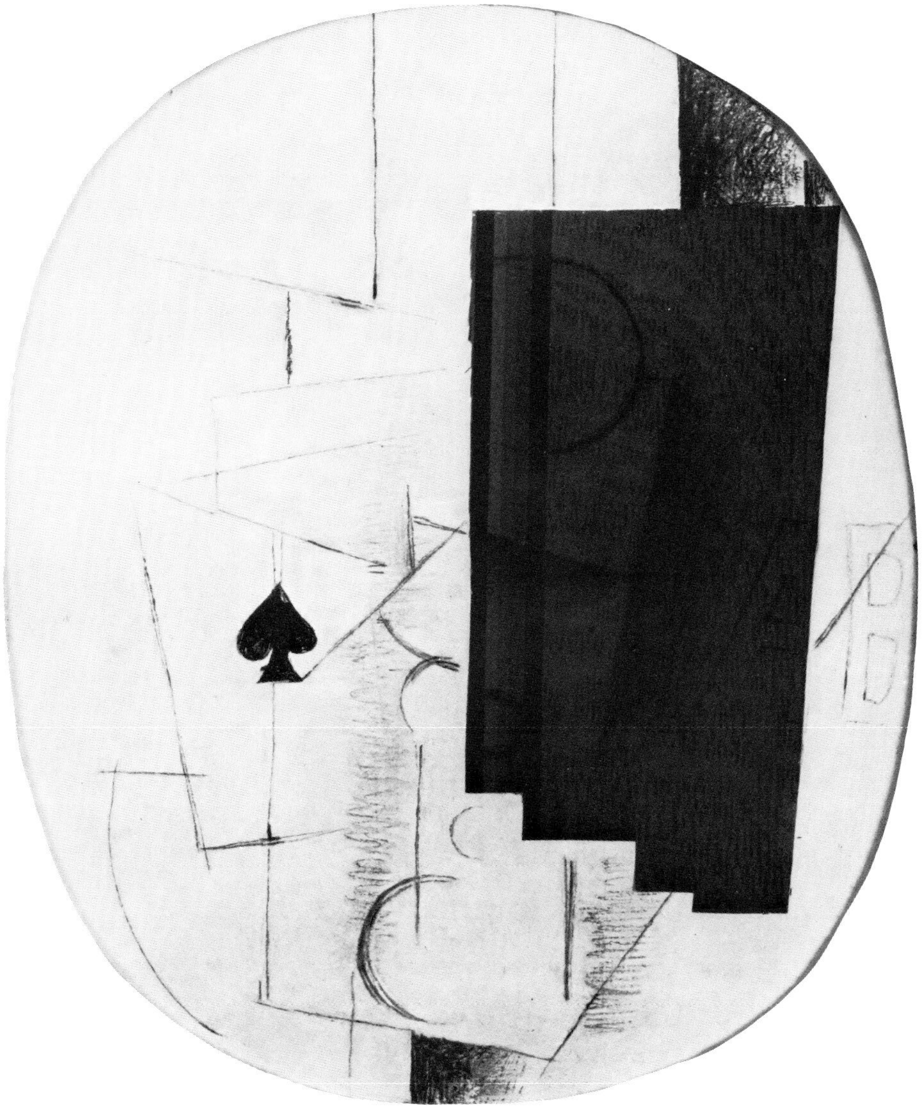

18.

The Ace of Spades (L'as de pique)

(Ace of Spades and Glass)

1913
charcoal, watercolor, *faux bois* paper, on paper
30 x 25 (11 13/16 x 9 7/8)
CGP 21

Provenance
Galerie Kahnweiler, Paris (no. 1189)
4th Kahnweiler sale, 1923, no. 2,
L'as de pique oval (30 x 25 cm), for 45F
Galerie Berggruen, Paris

Literature
Mangin (Worms de Romilly) 1982, no. 209, reproduced

Exhibitions
Bielefeld 1979, no. 154, reproduced (not in exhibition)
Paris 1982, no. 21, reproduced color p. 107

Private collection

75. Braque, verso of *L'as de pique.*

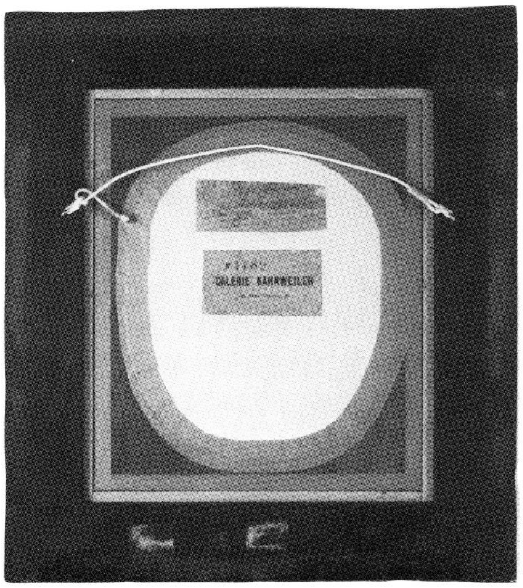

19.
Still Life (Nature morte)

drawing, *papier collé*
oval composition, 25 x 20 (9 7/8 x 7 7/8)
signed on back
not in CGP

Provenance
4th Kahnweiler sale, 1923, no. 1, for 55F

Location unknown

As we have not been able to uncover any more information about this *papier* collé, and no reproduction has yet been found, we are unable to provide an exact date. The Kahnweiler sales catalogue entry lists the work as an oval, and it is directly followed by three more such ovals, which are our cat. nos. 18, 21, and 22. For this reason, we have included the work here in our sequence. However, its smaller size sets this *Still Life* apart from the others, and also eliminates it from being any of the other known works. T.C., E.A.C.jr.

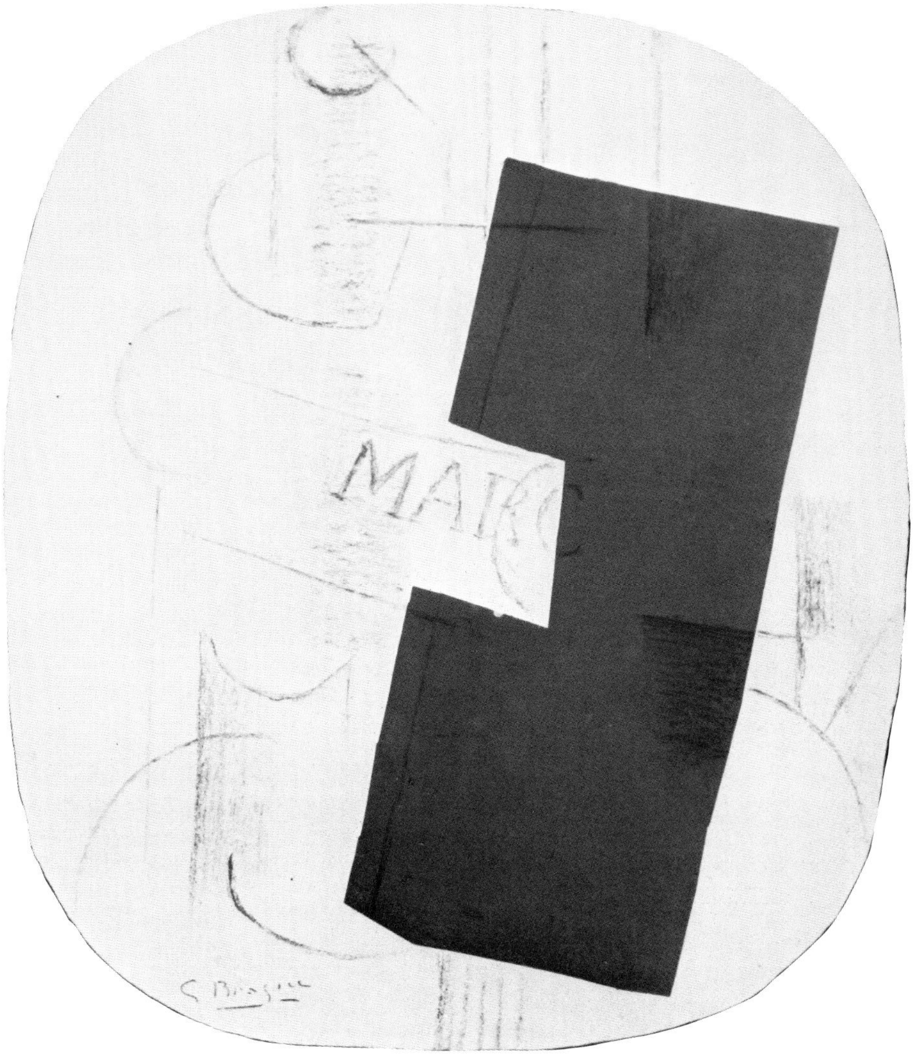

20.
The Bottle of Marc
(La bouteille de Marc)

1913
charcoal, colored paper, on paper
36 x 29 (14 3/16 x 11 3/8)
Signed, lower left: *G. Braque*
CGP 19

Literature
Mangin (Worms de Romilly) 1982, no. 208 B, reproduced

Exhibitions
Paris 1982, no. 19, reproduced p. 103

Monsieur and Madame Jean Riboud

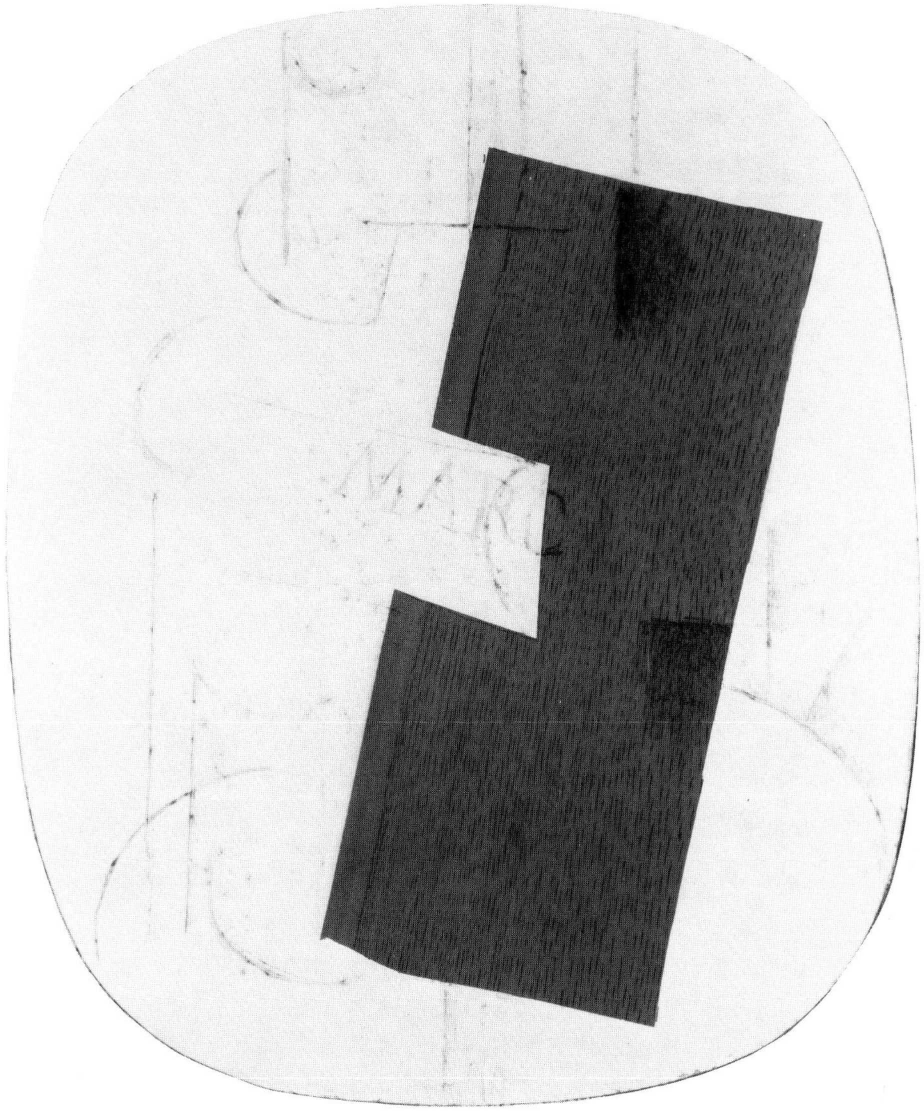

21.
The Bottle of Marc
(La bouteille de Marc)
(Marc)
1913
charcoal, *faux bois* paper, on wood
35 x 38.6 (13 13/16 x 11 1/4)
CGP 20

Provenance
Galerie Kahnweiler, Paris
Galerie Simon, Paris
4th Kahnweiler sale, 1923, no. 3,
La bouteille de Marc oval (35 x 29 cm),
for 35F
Mr. Schottlander, New York
Hugo Gallery (Iolas), New York
Sold 17 May 1950,* Parke Bernet Galleries,
Inc., New York, lot no. 140, for $350

Literature
Mangin (Worms de Romilly) 1982,
no. 208 A, reproduced

Exhibitions
Galerie Kahnweiler, Paris 1914?*
Houston 1958
Houston 1968, no. 3, reproduced p. 13
Rouen 1970, no. 3, reproduced
Paris 1982, no. 20, reproduced color p. 105

Menil Collections, Houston

*Previous catalogues all cite the auction date as 10 May 1950; however, it has been discovered that the sale actually took place on 17 May 1950, entitled "Modern Paintings, Drawings and Prints."

According to the entry in the Parke Bernet 17 May 1950 catalogue, this work was exhibited at the Galerie Simon 1914. (The actual note is: "Executed in 1912/Exhibited at the Galerie Simon, Paris, 1914/ From the Galerie Kahnweiler, Paris 1921," p. 29.) However, the Galerie Simon did not exist until 1920 (it was Kahnweiler's postwar gallery). Based on this information, one must assume that the 1950 entry really meant the following: "Exhibited at the Galerie Kahnweiler, Paris 1914/ From the Galerie Simon, Paris 1921." No 1914 Galerie Kahnweiler catalogue had been found to confirm this; as the 1912 date is incorrect, it is possible that the 1914 exhibition is also unreliable. T.C.

Cat. nos. 20 and 21

These two collages (see cat. no. 21) are at the same time identical (in format, composition, and design), and different (in the color of the paper used). Would this be sufficient perhaps to suggest another space?

Braque adopted for them, as for others in the series, an oval format of very small dimensions, giving to these *papiers collés* the quality of a precious object without excluding a sense of monumentality. I.M.-F.

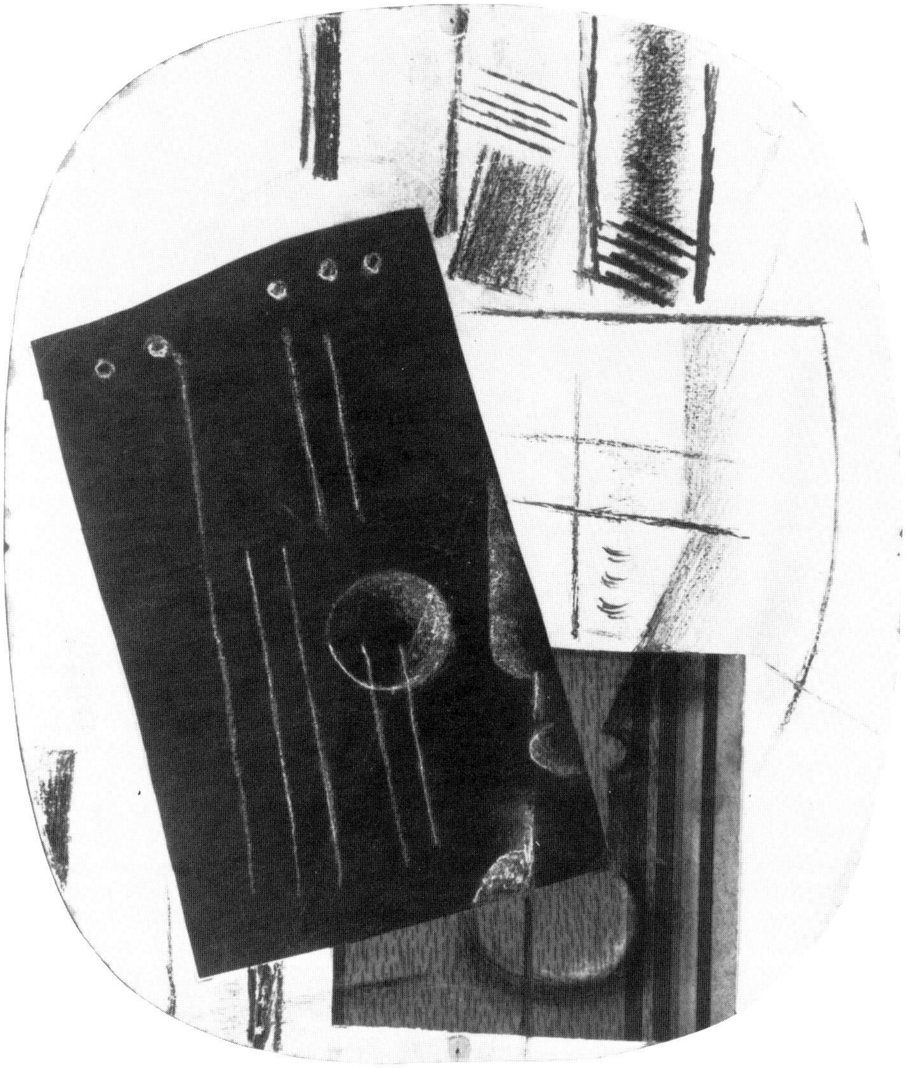

22.

The Guitar (La guitare)

(Guitar and Glass)

1913
charcoal, *faux bois* paper, brown paper, chalk, on paper, on painted wooden panel
35 x 28.9 (13 13/16 x 11 3/8)
CGP 22

Provenance
Galerie Kahnweiler, Paris
4th Kahnweiler sale, 1923, no. 4, *La guitare* (35 x 29 cm), for 80F
Collection Mrs. Charles H. Russell, New York, from 1930 (?) onward
Collection Eugene V. Thaw, New York
Collection Artémis, 1975-1976

Literature
Gallatin 1943, reproduced color, frontispiece (upside down)
Mangin (Worms de Romilly) 1982, no. 211, reproduced

Exhibitions
New York 1964, no. 29, reproduced
Paris 1982, no. 22, reproduced color p. 109

Collection of Mrs. Thomas J. Hardman

This is one in a series of five small oval collages, two of which, cat. nos. 20 and 21, are close variants of each other. Here the initial paper surface has been covered with white paint, and the original tan of the ground shows through at the top and bottom where thumbtacks have been removed. Cat. nos. 20 and 21 are also on painted paper. The brown paper with white chalk drawing here leads to the subsequent set of three collages (cat. nos. 24-26) where white chalk is used on solid black paper.

E.A.C. jr.

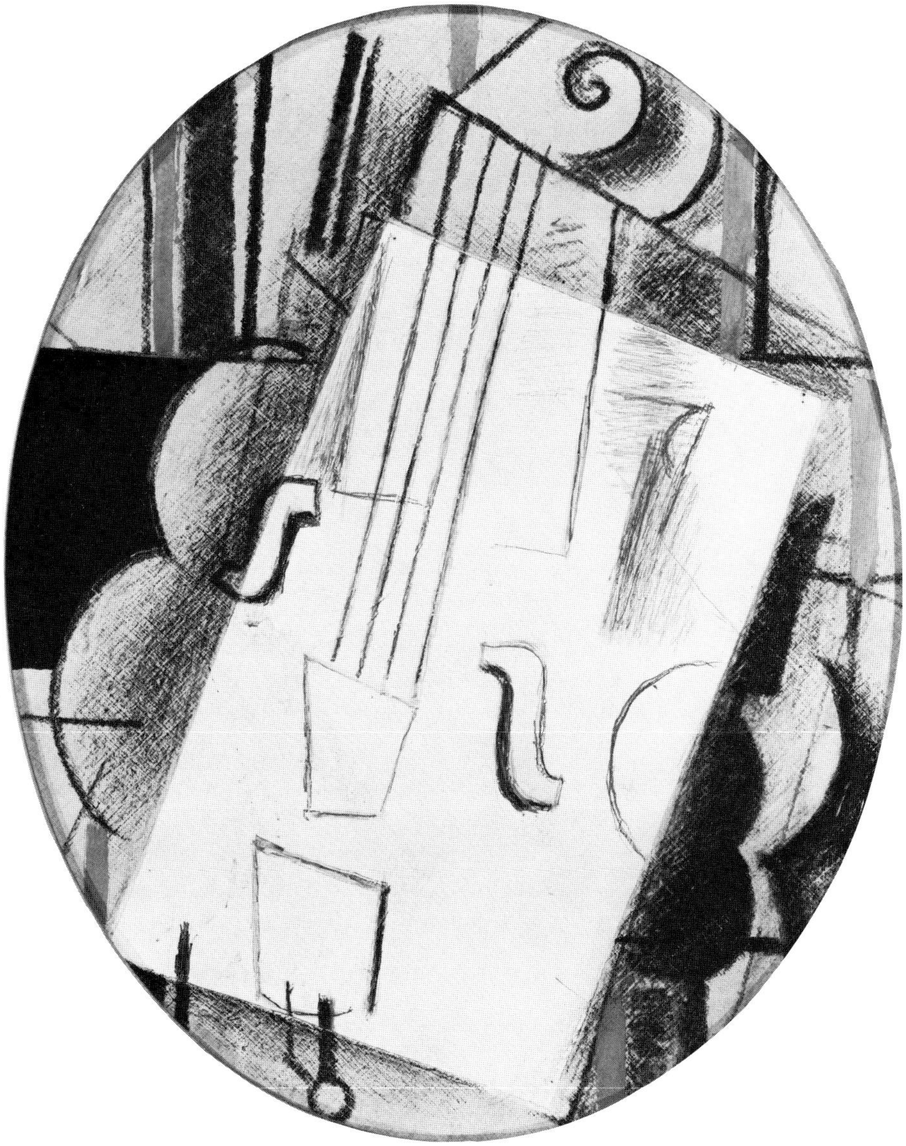

22 bis.
The Violin (Le violon)
(Guitar)

1913
charcoal, paper painted white, on canvas
35.2 x 26.9 (13 7/8 x 10 9/16)
Signed on back: *G. Braque*
CGP 18

Provenance
Galerie Kahnweiler, Paris (no. 1097)
Collection Louise and Walter Arensberg, Hollywood
Present collection, 1954

Literature
Isarlov 1932, no. 152 (not referred to as a *papier collé*)
Arensberg Collection 1954, no. 25, reproduced
Mathey 1968, reproduced color p. 124
Carrà 1971, reproduced color pl. XXVI, reproduced no. 104

Exhibitions
Chicago 1939?
Bielefeld 1979, no. 161, reproduced (not in exhibition)
Paris 1982, no. 18, reproduced color p. 101 (not in exhibition)

Philadelphia Museum of Art, The Louise and Walter Arensberg Collection

Although *The Violin* appears in the literature as a collage, there was some doubt about calling this work a *papier collé.* It seems in fact that the central white rectangle is not a piece of painted paper glued to the canvas, but is rather a highly visible relief created with the help of a stencil, or a rectangular form. It acts with the very means of collage. This technique was used numerous times by Braque, notably in an important painting in the Kunstmuseum, Basel, *Verre et violon (Glass and Violin),* 1913/1914. However, in *The Violin* Braque simulated pinholes in the corners of this painted area, creating in effect a *trompe l'oeil* collage.

I.M.-F., E.A.C. jr.

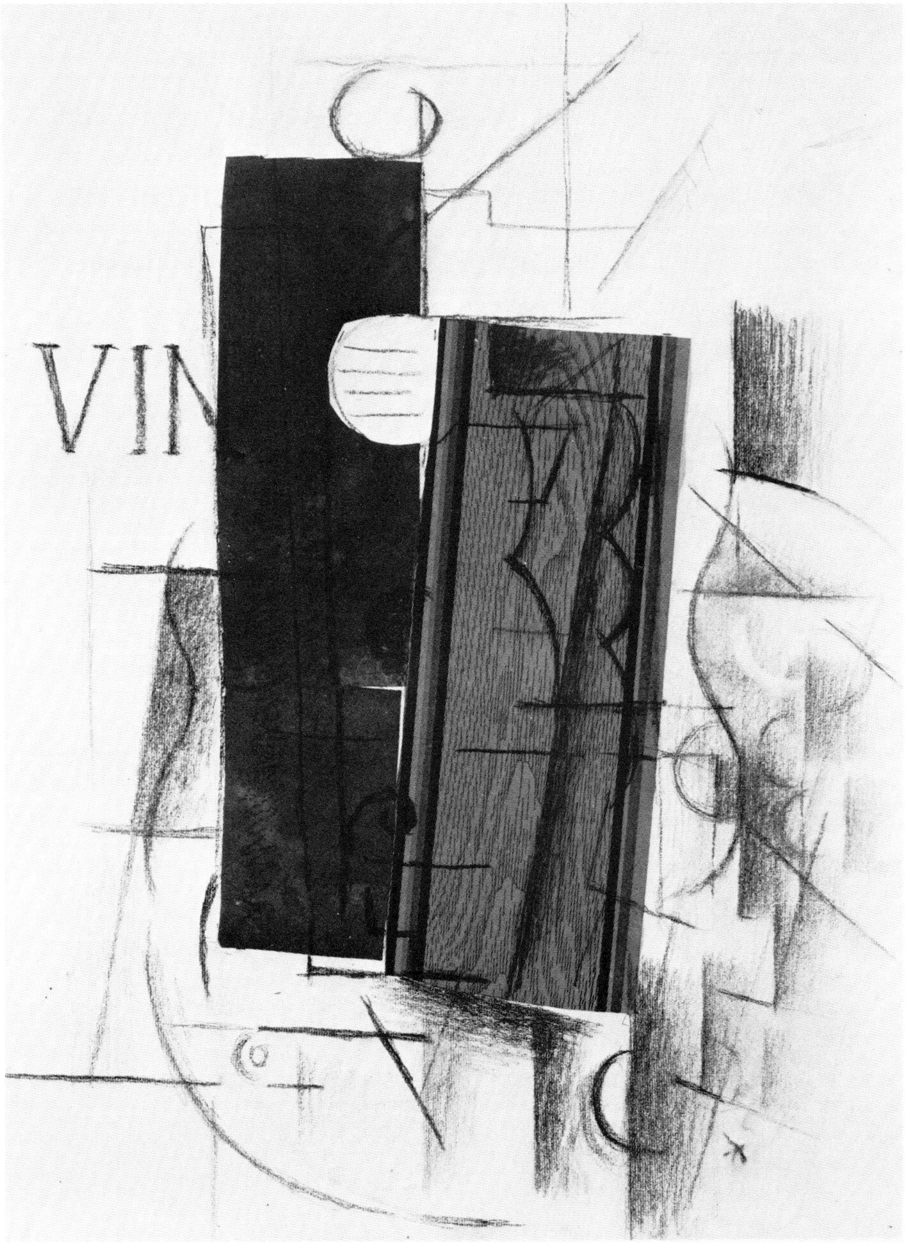

23.
Still Life with Guitar
(Nature morte á la guitare)
(Still Life with VIN)

1912
charcoal, cut printed paper, cut blue wove paper on off-white laid paper, adhered to wood-pulp board
62.2 x 48 (24 1/2 x 18 7/8)
CGP 26

Provenance
Collection Louise and Walter Arensberg, Hollywood
Present collection 1954

Literature
Arensberg Collection 1954, reproduced pl. 23
Golding 1959, p. 106, reproduced pl. 35
Carrà 1971, reproduced no. 100
Mangin (Worms de Romilly) 1982, no. 192, reproduced

Exhibitions
Chicago 1939, no. 21
The Art Institute of Chicago 1949, no. 26, reproduced p. 46
Philadelphia 1981
Paris 1982, no. 26, reproduced color p. 117 (not in exhibition)

Philadelphia Museum of Art, The Louise and Walter Arensberg Collection

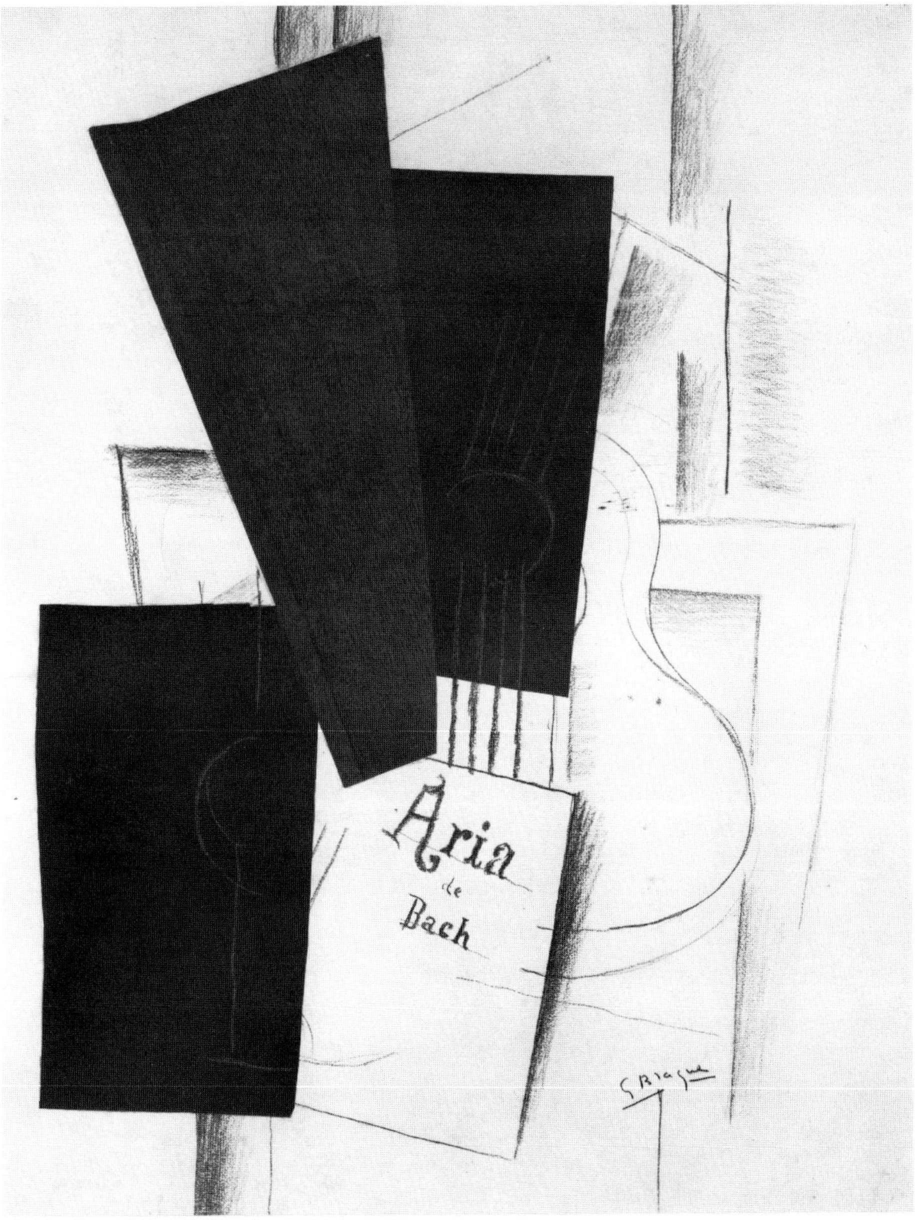

See plate 2

24.
Aria de Bach

1913
charcoal, *faux bois* paper, black paper, on handmade paper
61 x 45.7 (24 x 18)
Signed, lower right: *G Braque*
CGP 25

Provenance
Collection Mme. Marie Cuttoli, Paris, until 1970
Galerie Beyeler, Basel
Collection Mr. and Mrs. Paul Mellon, Upperville, Virginia
Present collection, 1982

Literature
Lejard 1949, reproduced color pl. 5
Gieure 1956, p. 31, reproduced pl. 33
Habasque 1959, reproduced color p. 83
Leymarie 1961, p. 57, reproduced color p. 58
Mathey 1968, reproduced color p. 141
Mullins 1968, p. 76, 79, reproduced p. 77
Masini 1969, reproduced p. 1
Paulhan 1970, reproduced fig. IVa
Draeger 1971, reproduced color p. 117
Carrà 1971, reproduced color pl. XXX, reproduced no. 128
Cogniat 1976, reproduced fig. 14a
Fortunescu 1976, reproduced pl. 21
Creer 1977, reproduced
Wescher 1979, p. 22
Mangin (Worms de Romilly) 1982, no. 199, reproduced color

Exhibitions
Paris 1952, no. 8
Paris 1953
Edinburgh 1956, no. 35, reproduced pl. 21b
Paris 1958, no. 4, reproduced
Rome 1958, no. 7, reproduced
Basel 1960, no. 29, reproduced
Paris 1960, no. 68
Paris 1963, no. 8, reproduced
Munich 1963, no. 38, reproduced pl. 34
Saint-Etienne 1964, no. 12, reproduced fig. 5
Oslo 1964, no. 9
Honfleur 1964, no. 14
Le Havre 1967, no. 11
Basel 1970, no. 5, reproduced color (date is 1917 in this catalogue)
Washington 1978, no. 18, reproduced p. 31
Paris 1982, no. 25, reproduced color p. 115

National Gallery of Art, Washington. Collection of Mr. and Mrs. Paul Mellon, Upperville, Virginia, 1982

25.
Black and White Collage
(Collage noir et blanc)

1913
charcoal, black paper heightened with white chalk, on paper
62 x 46 (24 3/8 x 18 1/8)
Signed, lower left: *G. Braque*
CGP 23

Provenance
Collection Pierre Loeb, Paris*
Collection Katherine S. Dreier, 1926
Gift of Katherine S. Dreier to the Société Anonyme, 1949
Present collection, 1949

Literature
Der Querschnitt 1924, reproduced p. 2 (upside down)
Hope 1949, p. 64, reproduced p. 56
Judkins 1976, reproduced p. 444
Mangin (Worms de Romilly) 1982, no. 210, reproduced

Exhibitions
Brooklyn 1926, no. 30 or 31 (30 is "Charcoal Drawing," 31 is "Music")
New York 1949-2, no. 19, reproduced
Paris 1982, no. 23, reproduced color p. 111

Yale University Art Gallery, Gift of Collection Société Anonyme

*The Paris catalogue cites the provenance as "Collection Gertrude Stein?." However, as far as can be determined, Stein owned only two works by Braque, both of them small still lifes. There is a letter on file at the Yale University Art Gallery from Marcel Duchamp to Katherine S. Dreier (27 April 1926) which discusses the acquisition of *Black and White Collage,* stating that the work was available through Pierre Loeb, Paris. T.C.

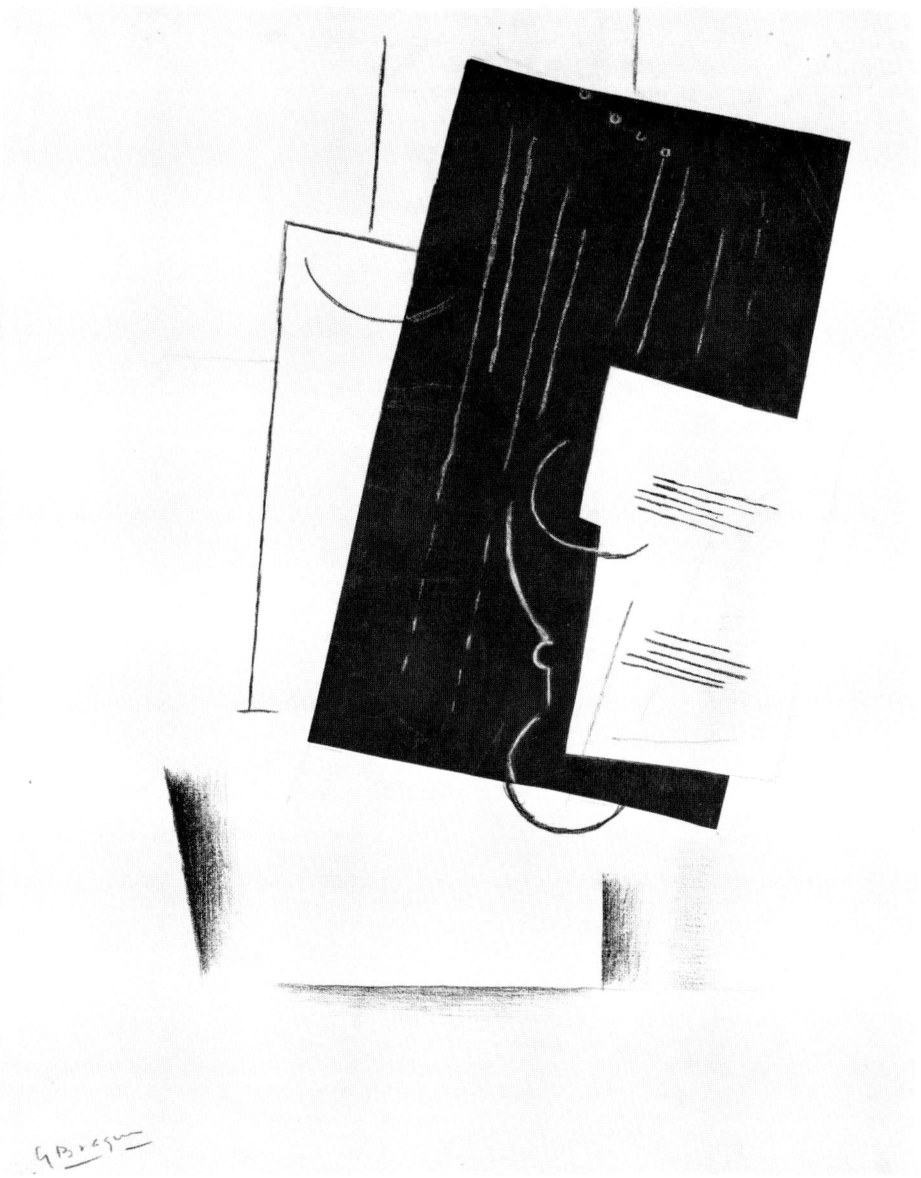

Other materials were rapidly substituted for or added to the *faux bois* paper, the visual shock and starting point for the fabrication of the "seeing machine" which was, according to Paulhan, the collage. Thus this black paper with brown highlights which Braque preferred to use as often alone, as in this example, as together with other types of papers (see *The Guitar,* cat. no. 29, *Aria de Bach,* cat. no. 24, *Le Quotidien,* cat. no. 38). The black paper allowed him to inscribe the drawing, as a negative, with white chalk, thus inverting the values of opacity and transparency, while at the same time modulating the effects of relief and superimposition.

The drawn structure, less dense than in the preceding examples, reinforces the impression of the proper minimum the *papiers collés* of this series give.

I.M.-F.

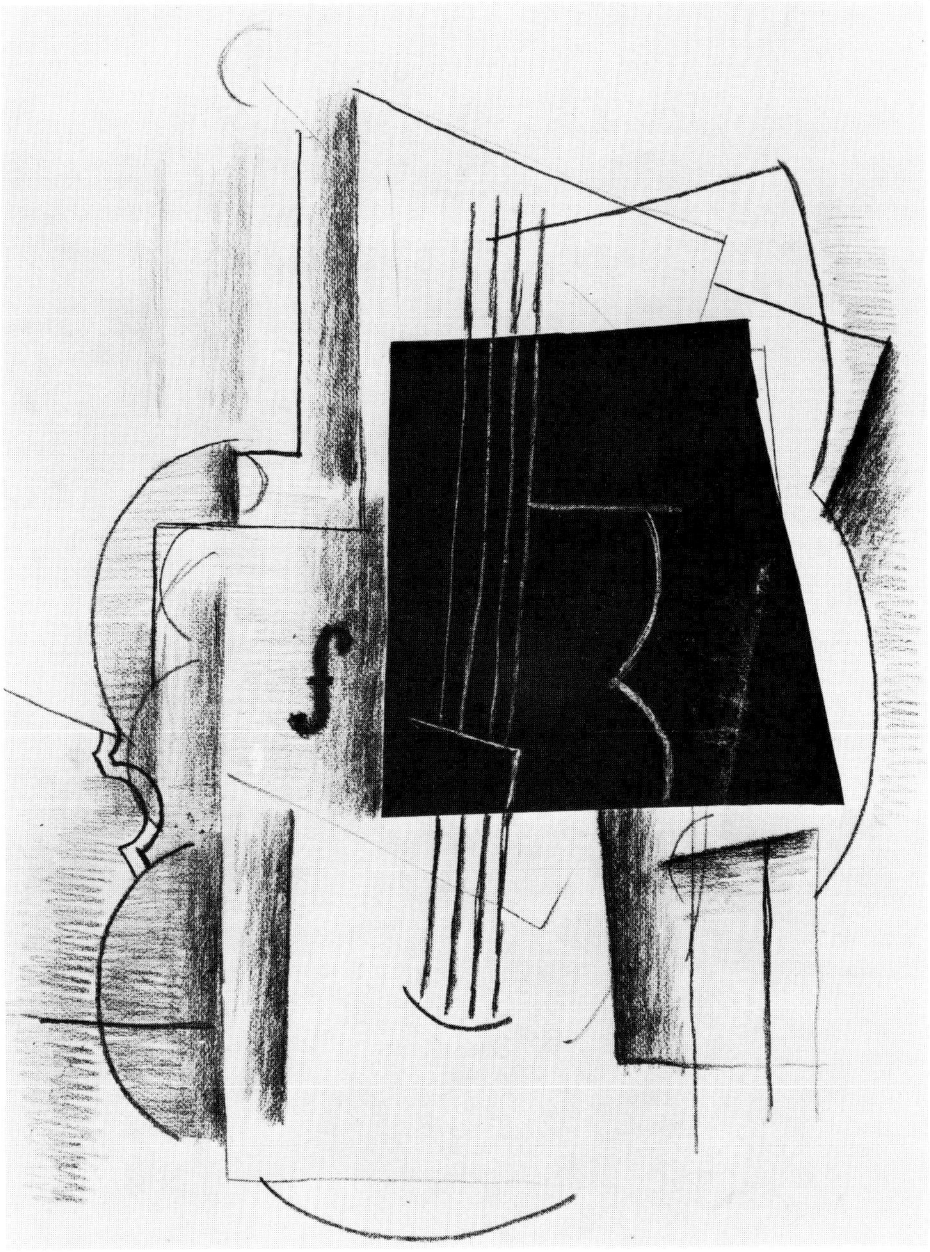

26.
Still Life (Nature morte)

1913
charcoal, brownish-black paper heightened with white chalk, traces of graphite on off-white laid paper, on cardboard
63.5 x 48.3 (25 x 19)
CGP 24

Provenance
Collection Louise and Walter Arensberg, Hollywood
Present collection, 1954

Literature
Arensberg Collection 1954, reproduced no. 22
Carrà 1971, reproduced no. 113
Mangin (Worms de Romilly) 1982, no. 205, reproduced

Exhibitions
Chicago 1939, no. 23 or 24
Bielefeld 1979, no. 153, reproduced (not in exhibition)
Philadelphia 1981
Paris 1982, no. 24, reproduced color p. 113 (not in exhibition)

Philadelphia Museum of Art, The Louise and Walter Arensberg Collection

27.

Guitar (Guitare)

(Mandolin, Violin and Newspaper; Violin and Newspaper; Le Petit Eclaireur)

1913
charcoal, newspaper, *faux bois* paper, blue paper, and black paper, on canvas
92 x 65 (36 3/16 x 25 5/8)
Signed on back: *Braque*
CGP 27

Provenance
Galerie Kahnweiler, Paris (no. 1087)
Possibly 4th Kahnweiler sale, 1923, no. 10, *"Le violon"* (92 x 60 cm), for 200F
Collection Cuttoli, 1934
Galerie Kleinmann, 1945 (?)
Collection Dutilleul
Collection Masurel
Gift of Geneviève and Jean Masurel to the city of Lille, 1979

Literature
George 1921, reproduced p. 648
Isarlov 1932, no. 149, p. 18
Einstein 1934, reproduced pl. XXXIV
Wescher 1953, reproduced p. 34
Fry 1966, p. 29, reproduced fig. 42
Carrà 1971, reproduced no. 101
Wescher 1979, p. 22
Mangin (Worms de Romilly) 1982, no. 200, reproduced color

Exhibitions
Basel 1933, no. 64, reproduced
Paris 1945, no. 4 (?)
Paris 1953, no. 114
Lille 1965, no. 18, reproduced
Bielefeld 1979, no. 158, reproduced (not in exhibition)
Paris 1980, no. 16, reproduced p. 60, reproduced color p. 30
Paris 1982, no. 27, reproduced color p. 119

Musée d'art moderne du Nord, Villeneuve d'Asq. Donation Geneviève et Jean Masurel à la Communauté urbaine de Lille.

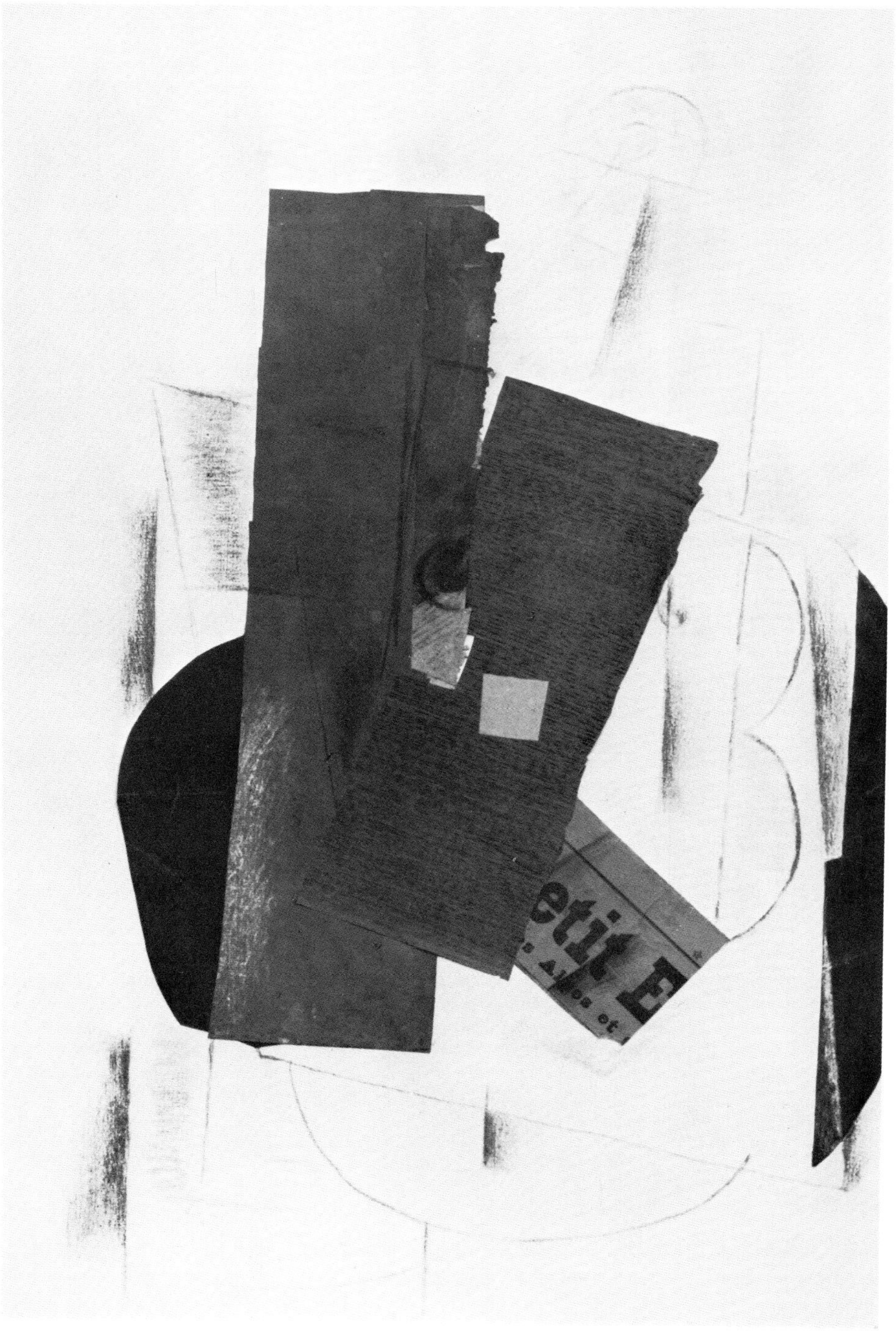

Cat. nos. 27, 28, and 29

In these three monumental *papiers collés* —not only so because of their exceptional dimensions—the rapport (or rivalry?) between *papier collé* and painting appears still more evident (two of them are adhered onto canvas). The increasing diversity of the materials being used engenders a space which is more and more com-

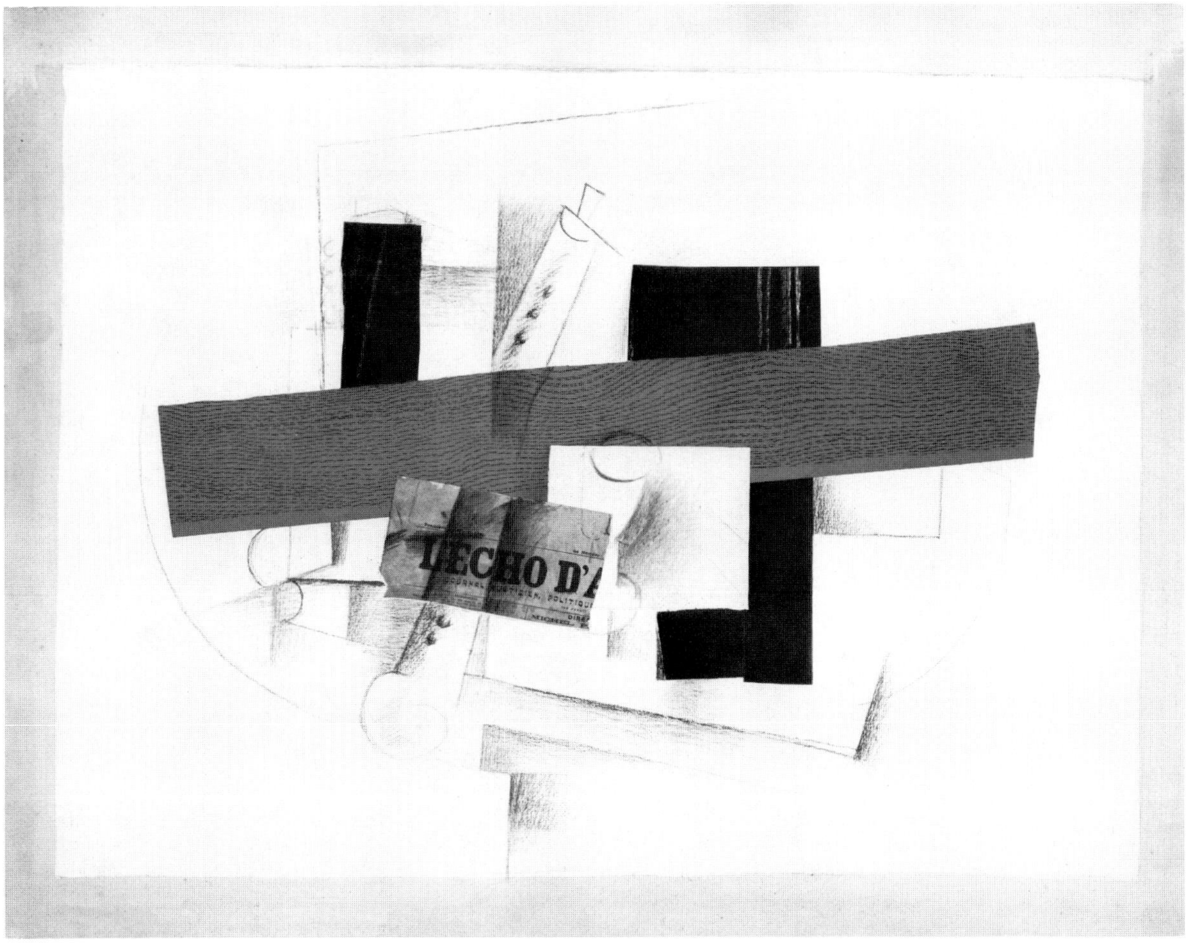

plex, deep and pictorial, with superimpositions of colored planes and subtle passages. Priority is given to color (in relation to the drawn structure), which is charged also with expressing depth.

One can note also the appearance of newspaper as an element of collage—which we believe Braque began to use after Picasso, and in a different way; in his first *papiers collés,* Picasso used pieces— rectangles—of newspaper, a little like Braque used *faux bois* paper, as texture and color, metaphorical or not. Here Braque retains the newspaper titles, particular typographical arrangements, to which are assigned precise roles in the distribution of space. I.M.-F.

28.
Glass, Clarinet and Newspaper
(Verre, clarinette et journal)
(The Clarinet; Flute and Glass; L'Echo)

1913
charcoal, newspaper, black paper, *faux bois* paper, on paper
95 x 120 (37 3/8 x 47 1/4)
Signed on back in blue pencil
CGP 29

Provenance
Galerie Kahnweiler, Paris (no. 1171)
4th Kahnweiler sale, 1923, no. 14, *Flûte et verre* (95 x 121 cm), for 430F
Collection Léonce Rosenberg, Paris
Collection Amédée J. Ozenfant, New York, by 1949
Collection Nelson Rockefeller, New York
Present collection, 1979

Literature
Raynal 1924, reproduced
Tzara 1931, reproduced p. 67
Isarlov 1932, no. 174, p. 19
Zervos 1933, reproduced p. 29
Hope 1949, p. 64, reproduced p. 59
Gieure 1956, p. 32
Golding 1959, p. 109, reproduced pl. 36a
Cassou 1959, reproduced color pl. 16
Leymarie 1961, p. 57, reproduced color p. 59
Seitz 1961, reproduced p. 18
Fumet 1965, reproduced color p. 42
Rosenblum 1966, p. 94, reproduced color pl. XIII
Mullins 1968, reproduced color p. 46
Cogniat 1970, reproduced color p. 14
Carrà 1971, reproduced, no. 120
Schwartz 1971, p. 102, reproduced color p. 105

Berne-Joffroy 1973, reproduced
Marcus 1973, pp. 25-27, reproduced p. 25
Cogniat 1976, reproduced color pl. 14
Judkins 1976, p. 446
Mangin (Worms de Romilly) 1982, no. 204, reproduced

Exhibitions
New York 1949, no. 20, reproduced
Tokyo 1952, no. 4, reproduced
Zurich 1953, no. 36
Edinburgh 1956, no. 41, reproduced pl. 21f
New York 1961, no. 21, reproduced p. 19
New York 1969-1, unnumbered, reproduced color p. 49
Paris 1982, no. 29, reproduced color p. 123

The Museum of Modern Art, New York. Nelson A. Rockefeller Bequest

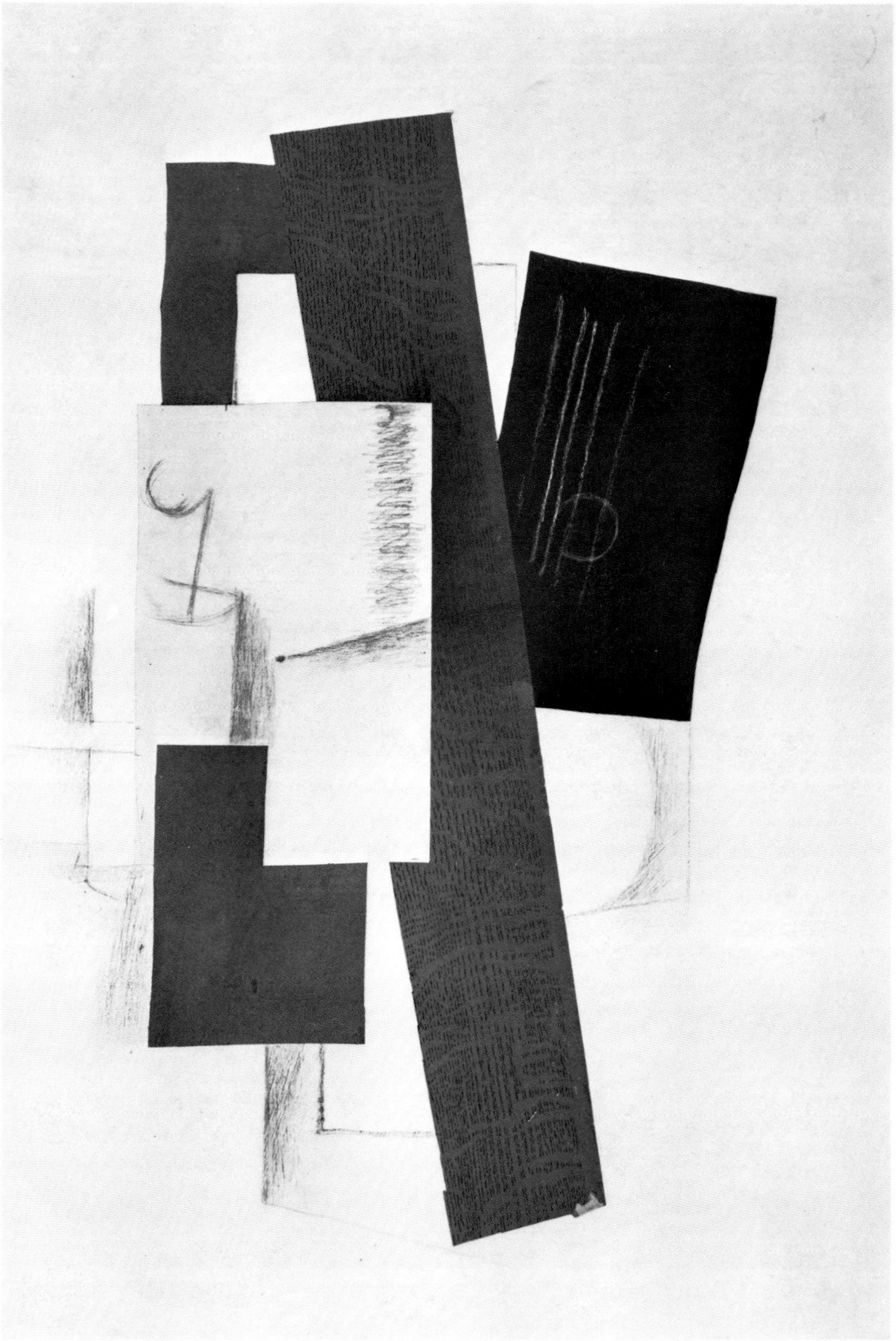

29.
Guitar and Bottle
(Guitare et bouteille)
(The Guitar)

1913 (1913-1914?)
gouache, pencil, charcoal, *faux bois* paper, black paper, brown paper, on canvas
99.7 x 65.1 (39 1/4 x 25 5/8)
Signed on back in pencil: *G. Braque*
CGP 28

Provenance
Galerie Kahnweiler, Paris (no. 1173)
4th Kahnweiler sale, 1923, no. 11, *La guitare* (100 x 65 cm), for 280F
Collection of Dr. André Cournand
Present collection, 1947

Literature
Einstein 1931, reproduced p. 348
Tzara 1931, reproduced p. 70
Isarlov 1932, no. 170
Zervos 1933, reproduced p. 26
Zervos 1938, reproduced p. 234
Hope 1949, p. 64, reproduced p. 61
Aragon 1965, reproduced p. 45 (upside down)
Carrà 1971, reproduced no. 124
Judkins 1976, reproduced p. 448
Wescher 1979, p. 22
Mangin (Worms de Romilly) 1982, no. 203, reproduced

Exhibitions
New York 1949-1, no. 24, reproduced
Basel 1960, no. 34
Bielefeld 1979, no. 169, reproduced (not in exhibition)
Paris 1982, no. 28, reproduced color p. 121 (upside down)

The Museum of Modern Art, New York. Acquired through the Lillie P. Bliss Bequest

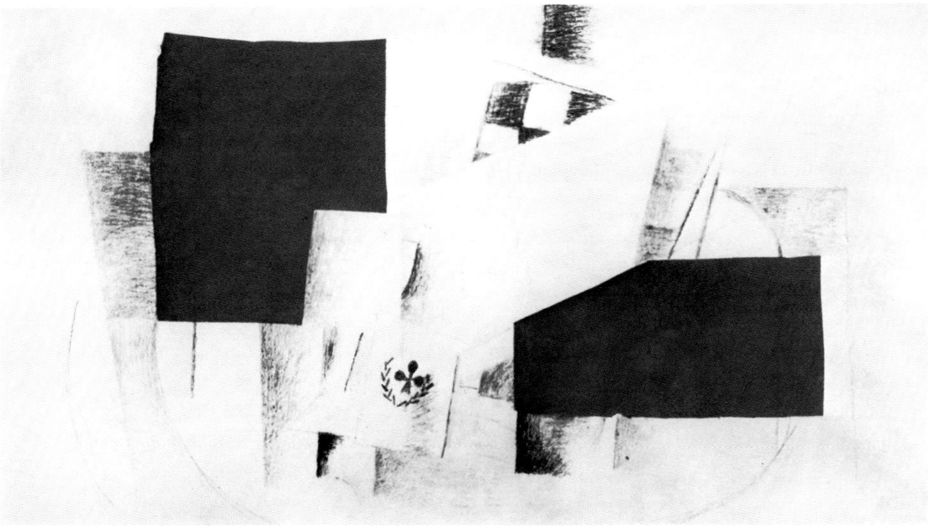

30.

The Checkerboard (Le damier)

(The Game of Checkers; The Ace of Clubs)

1913
charcoal, brown paper, on paper
45 x 81 (17 3/4 x 31 7/8)
Signed on back, in blue pencil: *G Braque*
CGP 31

Provenance
Galerie Kahnweiler, Paris (no. 1175)
4th Kahnweiler sale, 1923, no. 8, *L'as de trèfle* (45 x 81 cm), for 128F

Literature
Les Soirées de Paris 1914, reproduced p. 207
Isarlov 1932, no. 172, p. 19
Zervos 1933, reproduced p. 29
Einstein 1934, reproduced pl. XXVII
Elgar 1958, reproduced color pl. 12
Cassou 1959, reproduced color pl. 19
Mangin (Worms de Romilly) 1982, no. 197, reproduced

Exhibitions
Paris 1953, no. 113
Paris 1961, no. 14, reproduced
Paris 1963, no. 22, reproduced
Paris 1973, no. 49, reproduced
Paris, Bordeaux 1973, no. 41
Saint-Paul 1980, no. 55, reproduced
Bielefeld 1979, no. 167, reproduced
Paris 1982, no. 31, reproduced color p. 127

Private collection, Paris

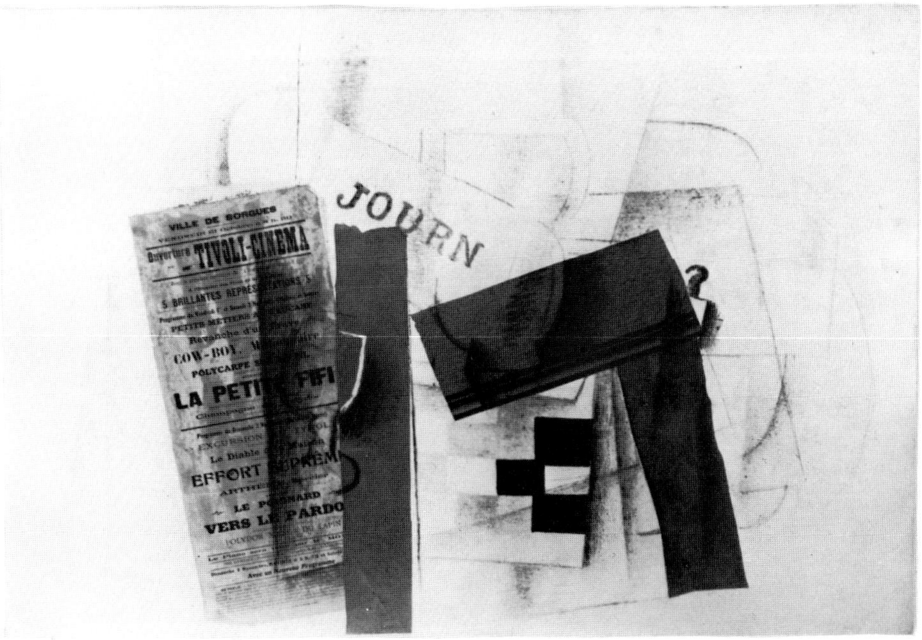

31.

The Checkerboard (Le damier)

(The Program; The Cinema Program)

1913
charcoal, oil, various papers, on paper (adhered to canvas)
On verso, sketch in watercolor
65.5 x 92 (25 13/16 x 36 3/16)
Signed on back, lower left: *G. Braque*
(On the back of a photograph, "le damier 1912" in Braque's handwriting.)
CGP 30

Provenance
Galerie Kahnweiler, Paris (no. 1174)
4th Kahnweiler sale, 1923, no. 9, *Le damier* (65 x 92 cm), for 170F
Collection Jeanne Bucher, Paris, 1956
Collection Bernard Reis
Collection Barbara Reis Poe, Los Angeles, 1970

Literature
Janneau 1924, p. 56
Isarlov 1932, no. 178, p. 19
Zervos 1933, reproduced p. 29
Einstein 1934, reproduced pl. XIX
Kahnweiler 1950, reproduced pl. 38
Wescher 1953, reproduced p. 34
Cartier 1956, reproduced p. 89
Gieure 1956, p. 32, reproduced pl. 32
Seitz 1961, reproduced p. 18
Art News 1966, reproduced p. 33
Mullins 1968, pp. 76-78, reproduced p. 77
Cooper 1970, reproduced p. 184, pl. 201
Carrà 1971, no. 116, reproduced
Mangin (Worms de Romilly) 1982, no. 194, reproduced color

Exhibitions
New York 1961, no. 20, reproduced p. 18
New York 1964, no. 28, reproduced
Los Angeles 1970, no. 40, reproduced
Bielefeld 1979, no. 163, reproduced (not in exhibition)
Paris 1982, no. 30, reproduced color p. 125

Galerie Rosengart, Lucerne

Like cat. nos. 27, 28, and 29 *The Checkerboard* (cat. no. 31) and *Guitar and Program* (cat. no. 34) describe a complex space. The letters play a particular role: Braque used two posters—"life-size" elements like the tobacco packets—listing the programs of a movie theater in Sorgues, the Tivoli Cinema. The poster in *The Checkerboard* announces the opening of the theater, with a special schedule, Friday, 31 October, Saturday, the first, and Sunday, the second of November (these days and dates correspond to the year 1913). The effect of the typography is not here the same as that of the newspaper—which Braque later used as he would a color or texture. The poster is composed only of titles of varying sizes and thicknesses, separated by white spaces, but constituting a homogenous and meaningful visual sequence in relation not only to the drawn letters *(JOURN)*, but also to the other elements of the composition (the bands of black paper and the gameboard where there plays a double contrast of black/white, collage/drawing.)
I.M.-F.

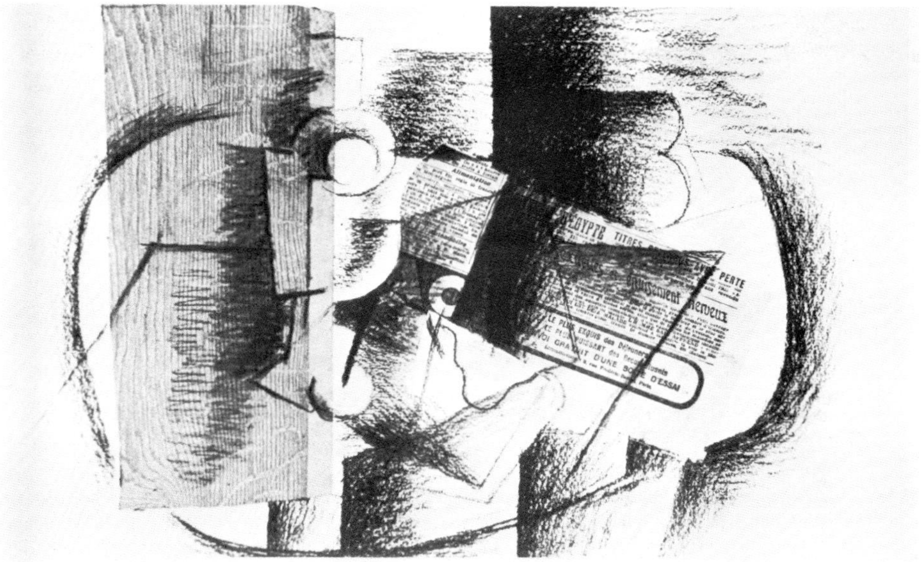

32.
Papier collé

1913
charcoal, *faux bois* paper, newspaper, on paper
29 x 45.5 (11 3/8 x 17 15/16)
CGP 33

Provenance
Galerie Kahnweiler, Paris
Private collection, Zurich (in 1963)

Literature
Mangin (Worms de Romilly) 1982, no. 169, reproduced

Exhibitions
Paris 1963, no. 17
Paris 1982, no. 33, reproduced p. 131 (not in exhibition)

Present location unknown

Cut newspaper is used here in full as color and textures: the close, finely printed lines act like the grain imprinted on *faux bois* paper. Braque positions the pieces of paper according to their directions: the newspaper placed on the horizontal on a "surface" which also supports a glass; the *faux bois* on the vertical signifies the surface of a table. The direction of the motifs therefore implies information about the differentiation of the planes. I.M.-F.

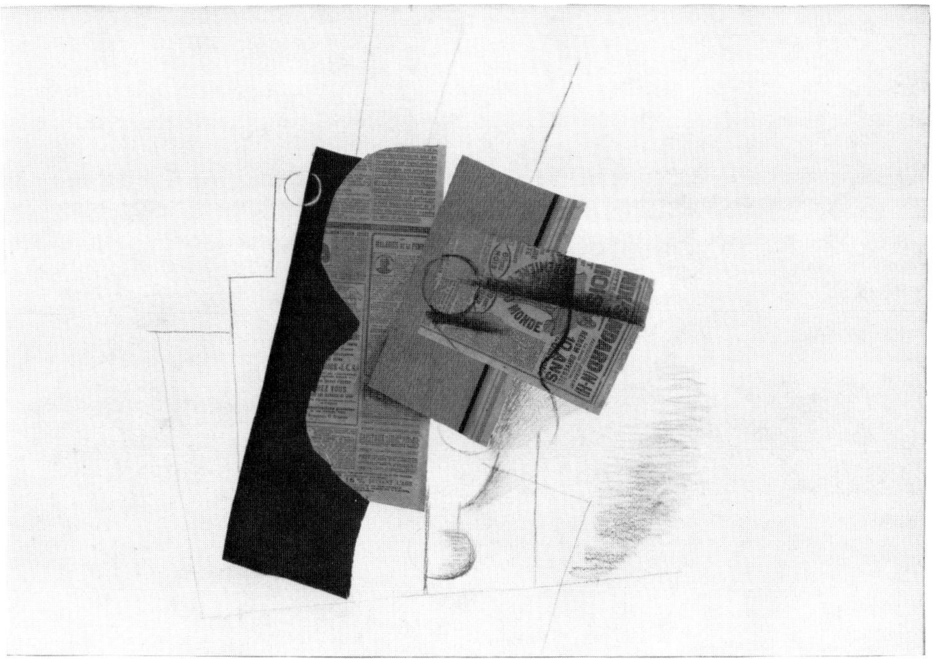

See plate 5

33.

Guitar and Glass (Guitare et verre)

(Still Life with Newspaper)

1913 or 1914
charcoal, newspaper, *faux bois* paper, black paper, on paper
71.8 x 100.9 (28 1/4 x 39 3/4)
CGP 34

Provenance
Galerie Kahnweiler, Paris (no. 1190)
Probably 4th Kahnweiler sale, 1923, no. 12, *Nature morte* (73 x 102 cm), for 100F
Collection of Douglas Cooper, London, 1937
Curt Valentin, 1946 or 1947*
Buchholz Gallery, New York
Collection of Mies van der Rohe, Chicago, by 1953

Literature
Hope 1949, p. 64, reproduced p. 57
Life 2 November 1949, reproduced p. 82
Life 6 June 1949, p. 36
Time 1949, reproduced p. 82
Cassou 1956, reproduced pl. 4
Cassou 1959, reproduced pl. 4
Dorival 1966, reproduced p. 115
Judkins 1976, reproduced p. 445
Mangin (Worms de Romilly) 1982, no. 206, reproduced

Exhibitions
Chicago 1939, no. 18
New York 1949, no. 14, reproduced
Zurich 1953, no. 34
Paris 1982, no. 34, reproduced p. 133 (not in exhibition)

Private collection

*Date kindly provided by Douglas Cooper, 25 June 1982

34.

Guitar and Program
(Guitare et programme)
(Guitar; Guitar and Cinema Program; Tivoli Cinema; La statue d' épouvante)

1913
charcoal, various papers, on paper
73 x 100 (28 3/4 x 39 3/8)
CGP 32

Provenance
Galerie Kahnweiler, Paris (no. 1172)
Collection Pablo Picasso, since 1914

Literature
Janneau 1924, p. 56
Breton 1928, reproduced pl. 16
Isarlov 1932, no. 180, p. 19
Zervos 1932, reproduced p. 23
Zervos 1938, reproduced p. 230
Hope 1949, p. 64, reproduced p. 62
Gieure 1956, p. 32
Russell 1959, p. 121, reproduced pl. 18
Carrà 1971, reproduced no. 108
Draeger 1971, reproduced p. 120
Wolfram 1975, p. 18
Judkins 1976, reproduced p. 449
Wescher 1979, p. 24, reproduced pl. 11
Cabanne 1980, reproduced
Granville 1980, reproduced
Huser 1980, reproduced
Mangin (Worms de Romilly) 1982, no. 189, reproduced color

Exhibitions
Bielefeld 1979, no. 164, reproduced (not in exhibition)
Saint-Paul 1980, no. 54, reproduced color
Paris 1982, no. 32, reproduced color p. 129

Private collection

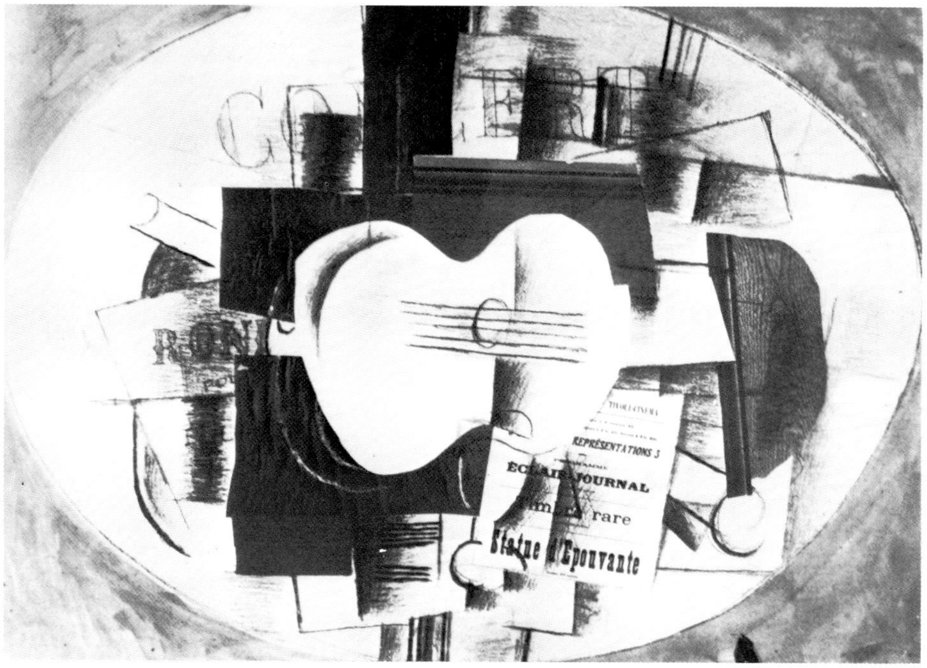

The oval space set horizontally resembles that of several paintings of the same time and leads us to view it as a table covered with various objects (see, for example, *La table du musicien* [*The Musician's Table*], Kunstmuseum, Basel, which has comparable dimensions). The painted "frame" isolates the composition and sets it back, as though seen from above, or from a distance.

This *papier collé* belonged to Picasso (it does not seem to have appeared in the Kahnweiler sales, and doubtless Picasso received it or acquired it directly from Braque), and as far as we know it is the only Braque *papier collé* which Picasso owned, one that is in a certain way atypical, executed at a moment—either at the end of 1913 or the beginning of 1914, since the Tivoli Cinema of Sorgues opened at the beginning of November 1913 and this program is necessarily later—when the trajectories of the two friends began to move apart from each other. Did Picasso appreciate the flavor, anticipating surrealism, of the title *La statue d'épouvante (The Dreadful Statue),* acting as a tear in the fabric of a composition which is so perfectly controlled, conscious, and classical? It is in any case the work which André Breton chose to illustrate in *Le surréalisme et la peinture,* which appeared in 1928.

I.M.-F.

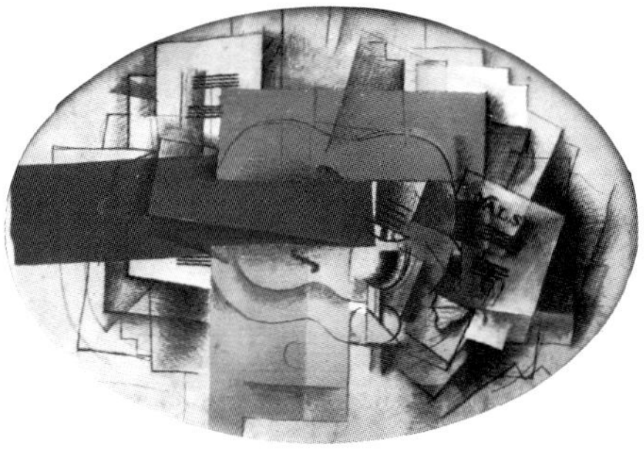

76. Braque, *La table du musicien,* 1913, oil on canvas. Kunstmuseum, Basel.

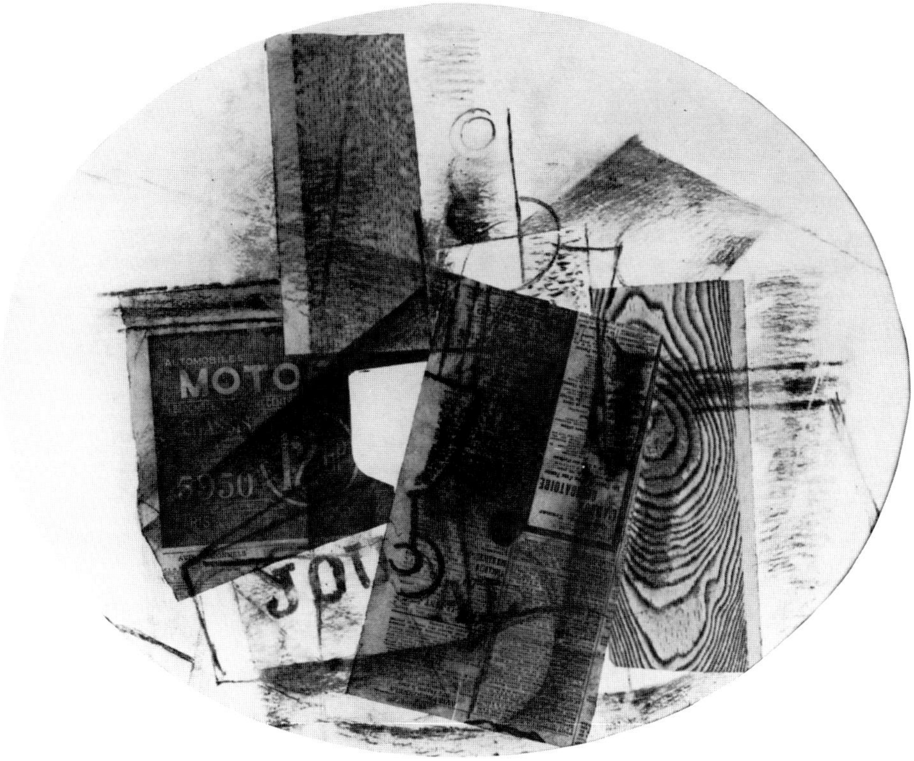

35.
Bottle, Glass and Newspaper (Bouteille, verre et journal)
(Bottle)

1913/1914
charcoal, *faux bois* paper, newspaper, on paper
48 x 60 (18 7/8 x 23 5/8)
CGP 35

Provenance
Galerie Kahnweiler, Paris (no. 1180)
Collection Dr. G. T. Reber, Lausanne
Collection Eichmann, around 1933
Private collection, on deposit to the Kunstmuseum, Zurich, since 1953 (inventory number 1953/13)

Literature
Tzara 1931, reproduced p. 65
Isarlov 1932, no. 191, p. 19
Zervos 1933, reproduced p. 30
Wescher 1953, reproduced p. 34
Richardson 1959, p. 13, reproduced pl. 10b
Mangin (Worms de Romilly) 1982, no. 225, reproduced

Exhibitions
Zurich 1953, no. 45
Bielefeld 1979, no. 148, reproduced color
Paris 1982, no. 35, reproduced color p. 135

Private collection

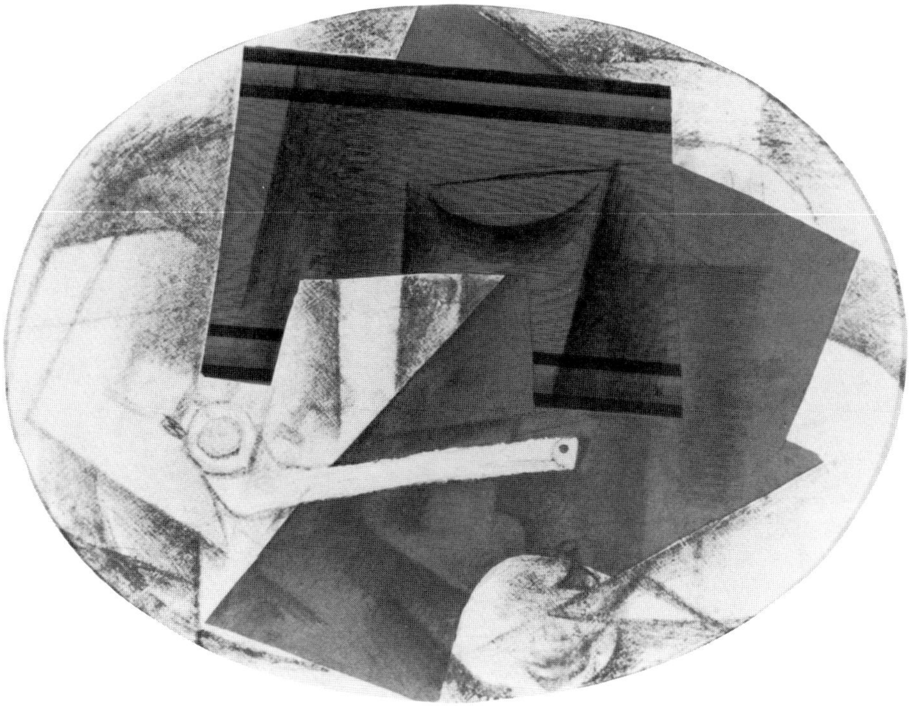

36.
Still Life with Pipe and Glass (Nature morte avec pipe et verre)

1913?
charcoal, *faux bois* paper, brown paper, on canvas
27 x 33 (10 5/8 x 13)
CGP 36

Provenance
Galerie Kahnweiler, Paris (no. 1194)
2nd Kahnweiler sale, 1921, no. 33
Collection Dr. F. J. Bossard?
Collection Helena Rubenstein, in 1964

Literature
Mangin (Worms de Romilly) 1982, no. 213, reproduced

Exhibitions
New York 1964, no. 26, reproduced
Paris 1982, no. 36, reproduced color p. 137

Collection of Mr. and Mrs. Sidney E. Cohn

37.
Glass and Bottle
(Verre et bouteille)

1913-1914
charcoal, *faux bois* paper, newspaper
48 x 62 (18 15/16 x 24 3/8)
CGP 38

Provenance
Galerie Kahnweiler, Paris
Collection Raoul La Roche

Literature
Fumet 1965, reproduced color p. 39
Carrà 1971, reproduced no. 121
Mangin (Worms de Romilly) 1982, no. 193, reproduced color

Exhibitions
Paris 1961, no. 16, reproduced
Paris 1963, reproduced color pp. 4-5
Paris 1982, no. 38, reproduced color p. 141

Private collection, Basel

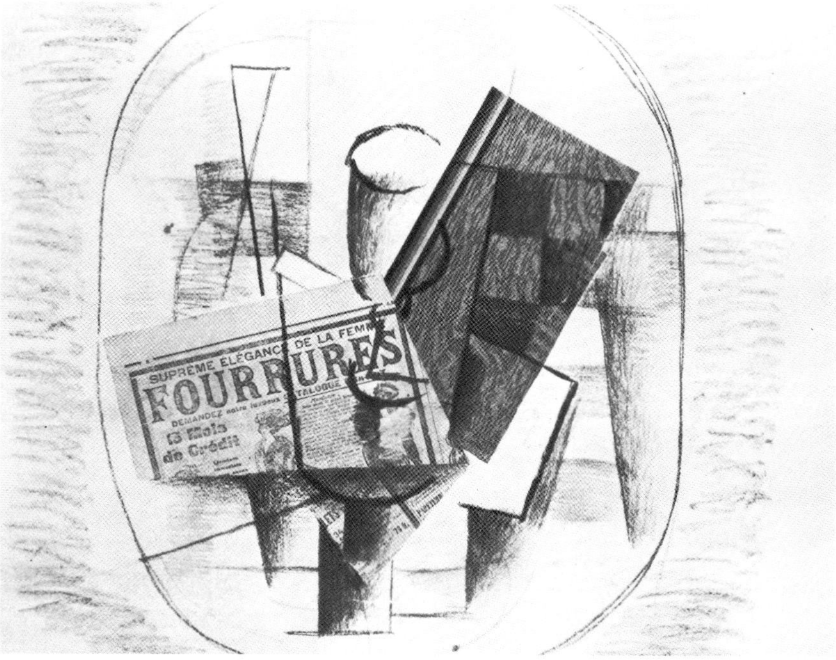

See plate 6

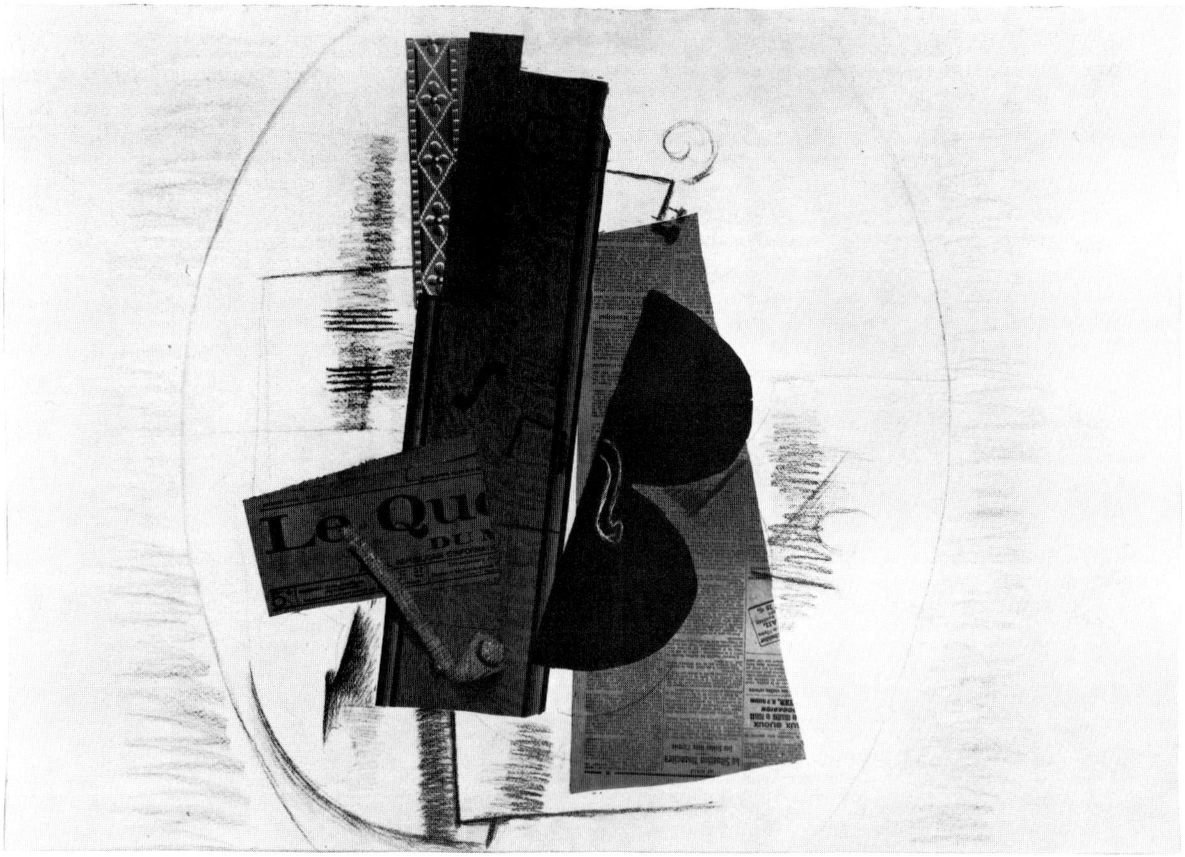

38.

Violin and Pipe (Violon et pipe)

(Le Quotidien)

1913-1914
charcoal, *faux bois* paper, painted paper lace, black paper, newspaper, on paper (adhered to cardboard)
74 x 106 (29 1/8 x 41 3/4)
Signed on verso in pencil: *G. Braque*
CGP 37

Provenance
Galerie Kahnweiler, Paris (no. 1212)
4th Kahnweiler sale, 1923, no. 13, *Violon et pipe* (76 x 108 cm), for 200F
Collection of l'Oeil clair (included in the sale of 5 November 1937, no. 4 reproduced, sold for 4000F)
Collection André Lefèvre (purchased at the sale on 5 November 1937)
Present collection, 1965 (purchased from the French state)

Literature
Einstein 1934, reproduced pl. XXVIII
Buffet-Picabia 1938, reproduced p. 33
Paulhan 1946, reproduced p. 71
Wescher 1954, reproduced p. 5
Vingtième siècle 1956, p. 8
Richardson 1961, reproduced pl. 15
Dorival 1966, pp. 111-115, reproduced p. 112
Masini 1969, reproduced color pl. 10
Paulhan 1970, reproduced color cover and illustrated in publication
Carrà 1971, reproduced color pl. XXII and reproduced no. 96
Guiney 1972, p. 17
Fermigier 1973, reproduced
Teyssedre 1973, reproduced
Cogniat 1976, reproduced fig. 15a
Saucet 1976, reproduced color p. 17
Mangin (Worms de Romilly) 1982, no. 196, reproduced color

Exhibitions
Fribourg 1948, no. 7
New York 1949, no. 28
Berne 1953, no. 38
Zurich 1953, no. 43
Edinburgh 1956, no. 34, reproduced pl. 21e
Paris 1960, no. 66
Paris 1961, no. 19, reproduced
Cincinnati 1962, reproduced
Paris 1964, no. 86
Paris 1973, no. 47, reproduced
Paris 1974, no. 13, reproduced
Bielefeld 1979, no. 151, reproduced (not in exhibition)
Rome 1980, no. 24, reproduced
Paris 1982, no. 37, reproduced color p. 139

Musée national d'art moderne, Centre Georges Pompidou, Paris

As Bernard Dorival demonstrated (Dorival 1966, 111-115) the *papier collé Violin and Pipe* comprises two elements of cut newspaper, an extract from *Le Quotidien du Midi,* dated Friday, 15 November 1912, and one from *Le Journal,* of Sunday, 28 December 1913. One can therefore date the collage, at least in its finished state, to the extreme end of 1913 or the first days of 1914. Dorival supposed that this piece was worked on twice, first in the autumn of 1912 (because of the usage of a contemporary newspaper and of the *faux bois* paper from the first collages), then finished in 1913-1914 (black paper, date of the second newspaper). In fact, one finds this *faux bois* paper, recognizable by its color and motifs, in *papiers collés* of a different time. And it is not unlikely that Braque, if he had this paper in "stock," also used newspapers which were completely out of date. Whatever the case, a certain number of other elements relate this collage to series from the end of 1913/beginning of 1914: the oval frame drawn with charcoal is similar to that which encircles *Glass and Bottle* (cat. no. 37) and the band of beige and gray painted paper appears also in the *Violin* that belonged to Jean Paulhan (see cat. no. 39). Finally one can compare *Violin and Pipe* very precisely to a small painting entitled *Le Quotidien du Midi* (33 x 41 cm, The Norton Simon Museum, Pasadena, California) dated in the archival photographs of the Galerie Kahnweiler to 1914. Braque there reused the motif composed of a piece of newspaper drawn from *Le Quotidien du Midi* (the form of the clipping is reproduced exactly in the painting, including the effect of the lightly deckled fold, like a miniature newspaper) and of the pipe (handled in the painting with a granular material, in relief). The motif is combined with others (tobacco packet, *eau-de-vie* label) and inscribed in a horizontal oval. It seems evident that in this case, as in some others, the *papier collé* preceded the painting. I.M.-F.

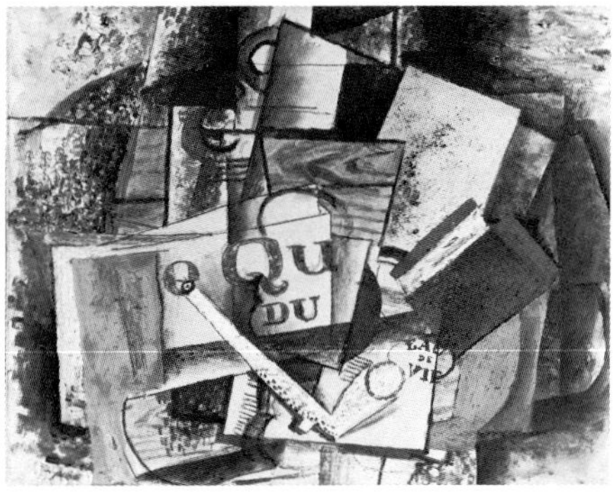

77. Braque, *Le Quotidien du Midi,* 1914, oil on canvas. Norton Simon Museum, Pasadena, California.

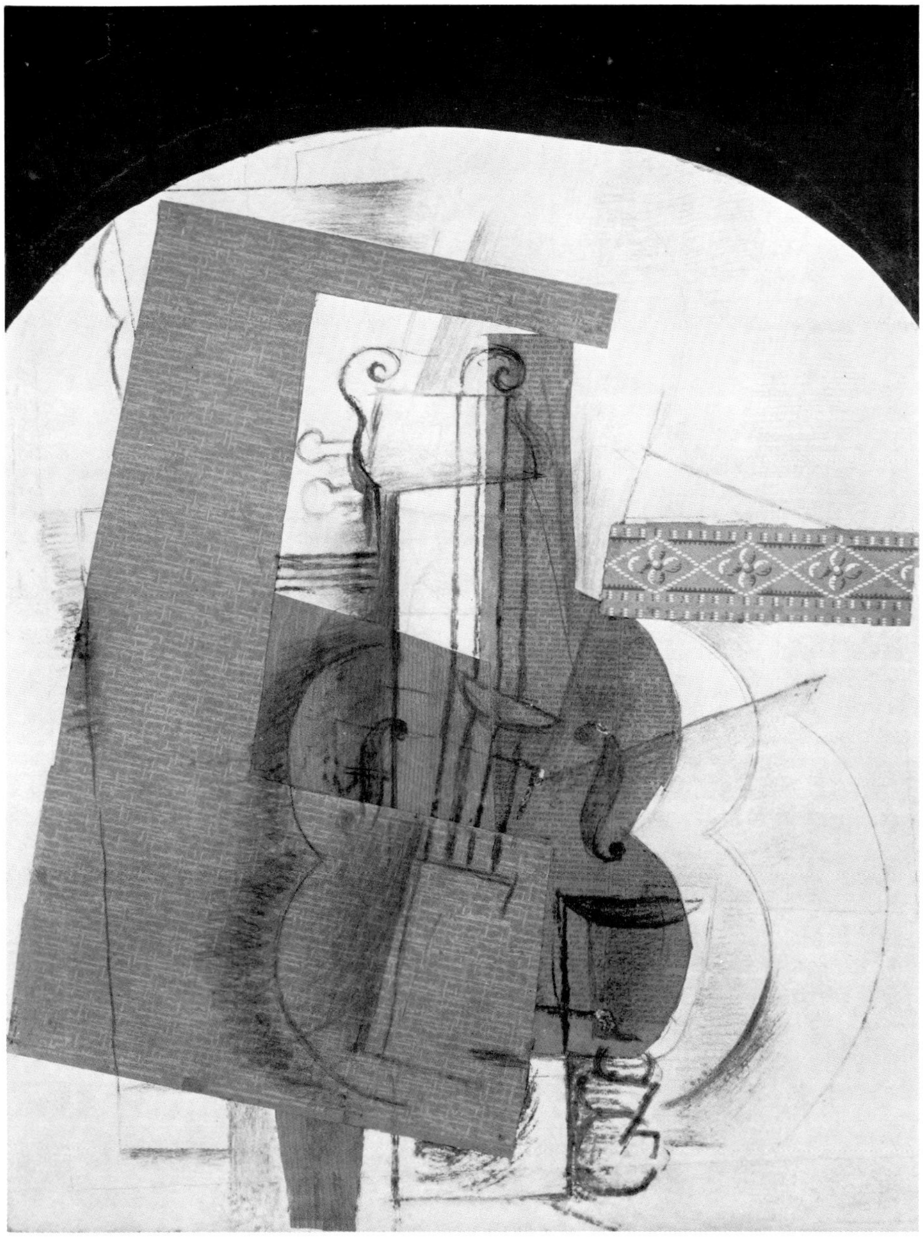

39.

Violin (Violon)

(The Guitar)

1914
charcoal, painted paper, painted paper lace, newspaper, on paper
71.8 x 52 (28 1/4 x 20 1/2)
CGP 42

Provenance
Galerie Kahnweiler, Paris (no. 1183)
Collection Jean Paulhan, at least by 1923
Collection Albert Loeb Krugier, in 1967
Present collection, 1968

Literature
Tzara 1931, reproduced p. 73
Isarlov 1932, no. 184
Zervos 1933, reproduced p. 27
Einstein 1934, reproduced pl. XXII
Ponge 1946, reproduced color pl. I
Dorival 1966, reproduced p. 113
Henning 1977, reproduced p. 56
Mangin (Worms de Romilly) 1982, no. 216, reproduced color

Exhibitions
Paris 1961, no. 17, reproduced
Geneva 1967, no. 4, reproduced
Paris 1974, no. 456, reproduced pl. 6
Paris 1982, no. 42, reproduced color p. 149

The Cleveland Museum of Art,
Purchase, Leonard C. Hanna, Jr., Bequest

Reappearing here are the violin and glass, the combination of a paper whose motif recalls woven materials (one will note that Braque does not use paper with figurative motifs as did Picasso and Gris, but uniquely uses papers referring to materials, grained or woven) with painted lace paper. On top of the composition the dark segment of an oval enframement supports (balances) the importance given to the violin, presented full-face.

This *papier collé* belonged to Jean Paulhan, friend and perspicacious commentator on Braque's work and above all one of the first (after Aragon in 1930 and Tzara in 1931) who did not underestimate the decisive contribution of *papier collé* in the evolution of cubism, and who tried to state precisely and define this contribution. For the record, we cite here an exchange of letters[1] between Paulhan and Braque at the time when the former was working out what would become *La peinture cubiste.*

Letter from Paulhan to Braque (Sunday, 24 May 1953):

Here is the gist of the theme of the article that I have proposed (at their invitation) to *Nouveau Fémina:*

Modern painting is given life by cubism. It is from that that it takes its *raison d'être;* it is on it that modern painting rebuilds support, if it begins to doubt itself.

Cubism consists of the substitution of an immediate and rough space for the planned space of the Renaissance and classical artists.

This substitution was permitted by the play of a device analagous to Brunelleschi's perspective machine and to Dürer's squared panes: *papier collé.*

Papier collé, anticipated from 1905 by several young painters, was brought into being on 13 September 1912 by Braque and was immediately used by Picasso.

Papier collé has tended over the last fifty years to be substituted for drawing in the presentation of the painting. Of a sensual and holy allure among Braque and his disciples, it is spiritual and playful among Picasso and his followers.

The title would be, I think "Braque ou le cubisme" (Braque or Cubism). All this is right, isn't it? What bothers me a little is the role, in *papier collé,* of printed letters. But the role of the band of tapestry, for example, seems to me very explainable: it makes classical perspective submit to the new space. But the lettering bears in itself, it seems to me, no combined perspective.

First response of Georges Braque (undated):

Here are brief responses to your questions. Our conversation will help you, I think, to complete them.

1. Indeed my first so called cubist preoccupations were to find a new mode of representation. Classical space was something that had been previously determined. Perspective—for the painter it was a question of reducing everything to its law.

For me it was to submit the object to a need of representation which created its space.

2. Cubism began with the investigation of space. *Papiers collés.* Integrating color. Evidence that color and form do not blend. These are two sensations which act simultaneously.

3. Space toward us until touching.

Second response of Georges Braque (8 June 1953):

I have read and reread your letter. What you have written about perspective seems to me very pertinent and will help a lot in putting certain people on the track. However, there is confusion where squaring is concerned. For the draftsman it serves as a very definite thing: it is the means used to enlarge or reduce a design. Perspective does not come into it.

I.M.-F.

1. Reproduced (and translated) from the exhibition catalogue *Jean Paulhan à travers ses peintres* (Paris: Grand Palais, 1979).

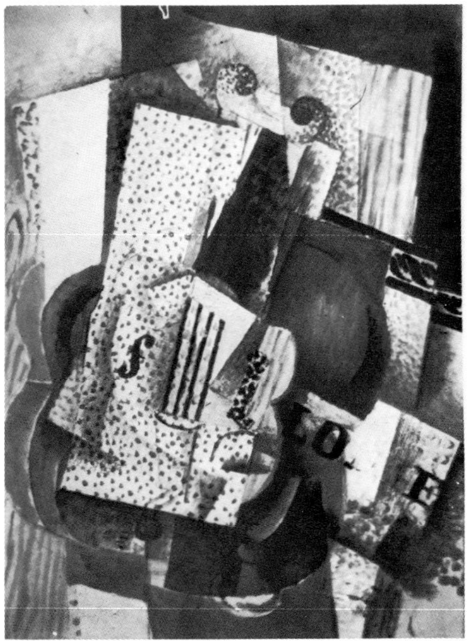

78. Braque, *Le violon,* 1914, oil on canvas. Private collection. Photo: Archives Leiris.

40.

Still Life with Packet of Cigarettes (Nature morte au paquet de cigarettes)

(Checkerboard, Cup and Packet of Cigarettes; Checkerboard)

1914
charcoal, *faux bois* paper, painted paper, wrapper from packet of cigarettes, on paper
28 x 44 (11 x 17 5/16)
Signed, lower left: *G Braque*
CGP 39

Provenance
Studio of the artist
Collection Pierre Gaut, Paris
Collection Berggruen, Paris
Collection Eugene V. Thaw, New York
Present collection, 1981

Literature
Le Point 1953, reproduced p. 9
XX siècle 1973, p. 5 (included in a photograph of Braque by Brassaï)
Mangin (Worms de Romilly) 1982, no. 195, reproduced color

Exhibitions
Edinburgh 1956, no. 38, reproduced pl. 21
Basel 1960, no. 37
Munich 1963, no. 40, reproduced pl. 36
Paris 1963, no. 24, reproduced
Bielefeld 1979, no. 168, reproduced (not in exhibition)
Paris 1982, no. 39, reproduced color p. 143

Collection of John R. Gaines, Lexington, Kentucky

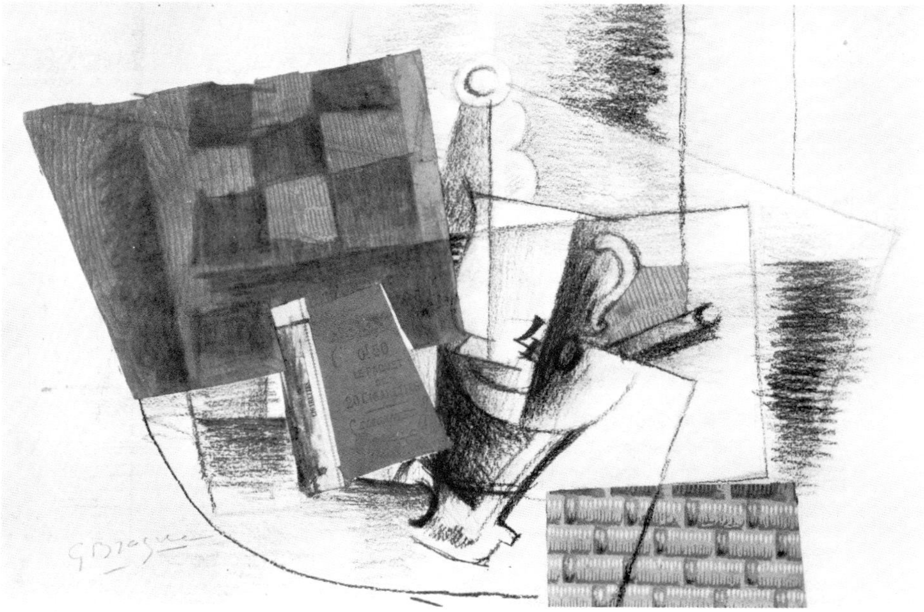

See plate 7

This handsome collage is one of several works from 1914 in which Braque not only employed *papier faux bois,* but began to use decorative papers as well, such as the simulated weave-patterned paper *(papier peint)* at the lower right. In other works of this set Braque employed long strips of wallpaper with decorative patterns, designed for use as borders or as simulated moldings *(galon de papier peint).* Picasso also used a wide variety of decorative wallpapers from the very beginning of making his paper collages (see fig. 26 for example).

E.A.C. jr.

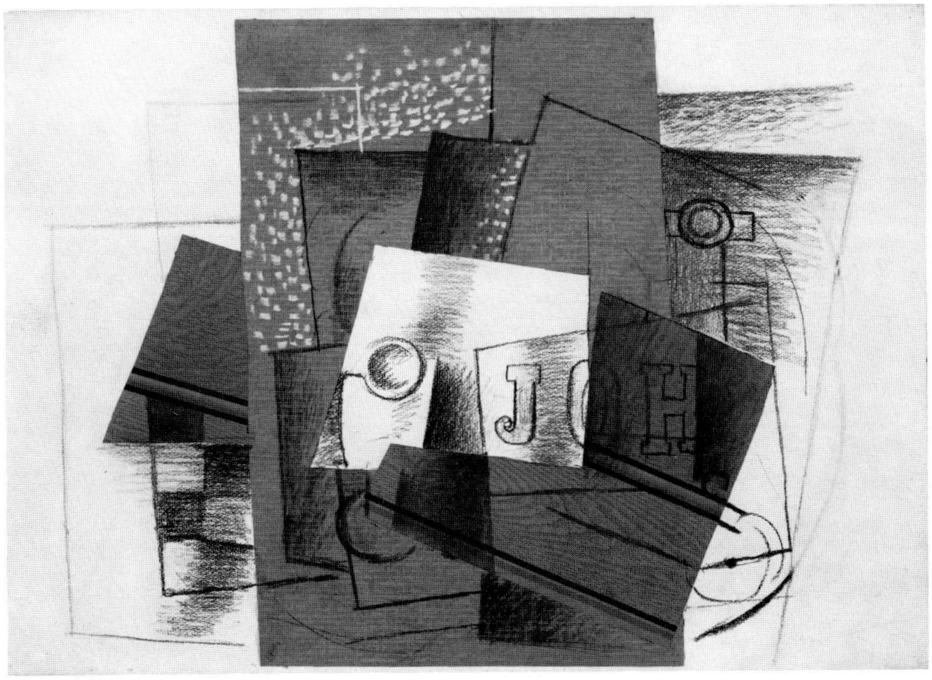

41.

Still Life with Glass and Letters (Verre et journal)

(Still Life with Letters; The Glass)

1914
faux bois paper, painted paper, charcoal, white paper, on paper
51.7 x 73 (20 5/16 x 28 3/4)
CGP 43

Provenance
Galerie Kahnweiler, Paris (no. 1181)
André Lhote, Paris
Galerie Louise Leiris, Paris
Collection Marius de Zayas
Mrs. Marius de Zayas, Connecticut*
Collection Joan and Lester Avnet, New York
Present collection, 1978

Literature
Isarlov 1932, no. 189, p. 19
Zervos 1933, reproduced p. 26
Zervos 1938, reproduced p. 234
Einstein 1934, reproduced pl. XXXIII
Hope 1949, reproduced p. 68
Gieure 1956, p. 31
Carrà 1971, reproduced no. 142
Mangin (Worms de Romilly) 1982, no. 222, reproduced

Exhibitions
New York 1948, no. 15, listed as "*Still Life,* Lent by Marius de Zayas"
New York 1969-2, no. 12, reproduced
New York 1978, no. 21, reproduced p. 58
Bielefeld 1979, no. 171, reproduced (not in exhibition)
Paris 1982, no. 43, reproduced color p. 151 (not in exhibition)

The Museum of Modern Art, New York. The Joan and Lester Avnet Collection

*Sold at "Impressionist and Modern Paintings, Drawings and Sculpture," New York: Parke-Bernet Galleries, 8 and 9 December 1965, lot. 59 (listed as *Le Verre: Collage,* with date of 1912).

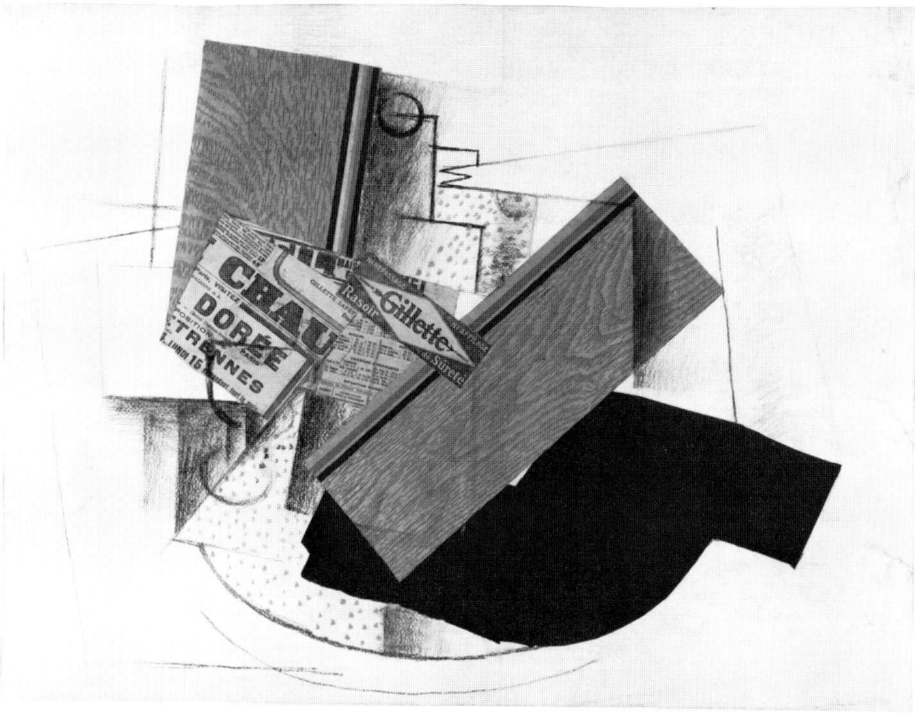

42.

Still Life on a Table
(Nature morte sur une table)
(Gillette)

1914
charcoal, *faux bois* paper, black paper, newspaper, heightened with gouache, on paper
48 x 62 (18 7/8 x 24 3/8)
CGP 44

Provenance
Studio of the artist

Literature
Cooper 1970, reproduced p. 184, pl. 200
Carrà 1971, no. 115, reproduced
Draeger 1971, reproduced color, p. 114
Mangin (Worms de Romilly) 1982, no. 240, reproduced color

Exhibitions
Humlebaeck 1969, no. 208
Los Angeles 1970, no. 39, reproduced
Bordeaux 1973, no. 40, reproduced color pl. 2
Paris 1973-1, no. 40, reproduced
Rome 1974, no. 11, reproduced
Marcq en Baroeul 1978, no. 11, reproduced
Saint Paul 1980, no. 57, reproduced
Paris 1982, no. 44, reproduced color p. 153

Private collection, Paris

43.

Newspaper, Bottle, Packet of Tobacco (Journal, bouteille, paquet de tabac)

(Le Courrier; Newspaper and Packet of Tobacco; Packet of Tobacco)

1914
charcoal, pencil, *faux bois* paper, newspaper, black ink, painted paper, wrapper from a packet of tobacco, on gray wood-pulp cardboard with two layers of white paint on the top and bottom edges
58.6 x 52.4 (23 1/16 x 20 5/8)
Signed, lower right: *G Braque* (signed later)
CGP 40

Provenance
Galerie Kahnweiler, Paris (no. 1182)
Collection The Gallery of Living Art, New York University
Collection A. E. Gallatin, New York, by 1936
Present collection, 1952

Literature
Raynal 1921, reproduced
Raynal 1924, reproduced
Tzara 1931, reproduced p. 62
Isarlov 1932, no. 187, p. 19
Barr 1936, reproduced fig. 64
Gallatin Collection 1933, reproduced
Gallatin Collection 1936, reproduced pl. 11
Gallatin 1943, reproduced pl. 5
Hope 1949, p. 64, reproduced p. 58
Gallatin Collection 1954, no. 19, reproduced p. 71
Gieure 1956, p. 32
Habasque 1959, reproduced color p. 69
Carrà 1971, reproduced no. 119
Draeger 1971, reproduced p. 119
Cogniat 1976, reproduced fig. 15b
Print, vol. 9, no. 5, May-June 1955
Mangin (Worms de Romilly) 1982, no. 226, reproduced

Exhibitions
Paris 1930, reproduced pl. IV
New York 1936, no. 24, reproduced
New York 1949, no. 18, reproduced
New York 1964, no. 27, reproduced
Paris 1973-1, no. 51, reproduced
Bielefeld 1979, no. 149, reproduced (not in exhibition)
Paris 1982, no. 40, reproduced color p. 145 (not in exhibition)

Philadelphia Museum of Art, A. E. Gallatin Collection

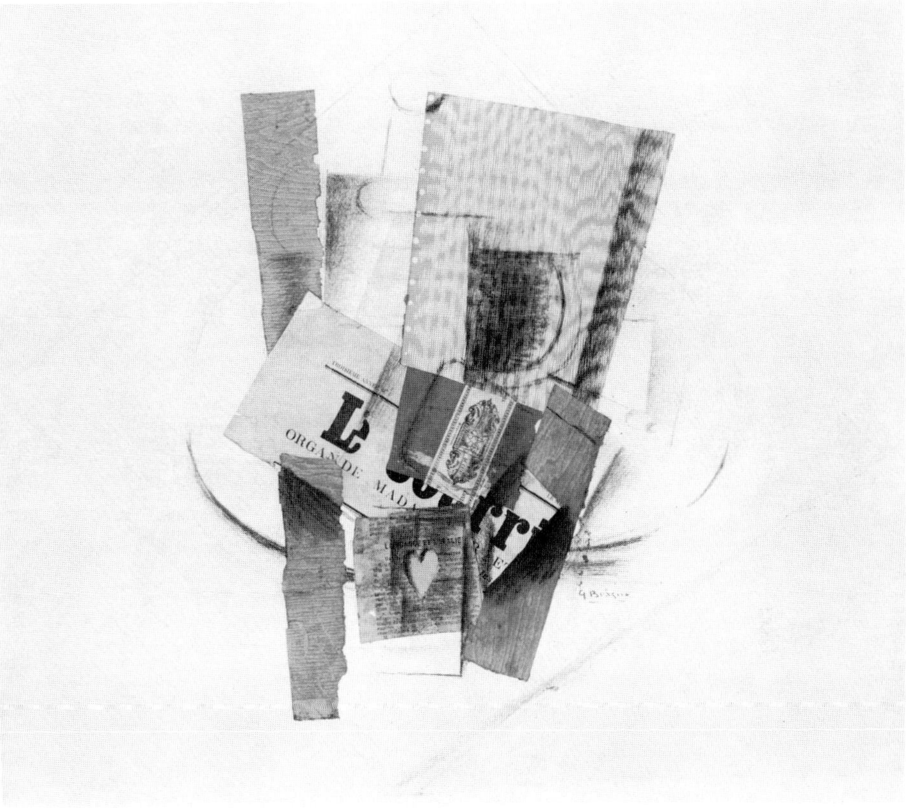

Once again objects are set out—in a fan shape—on a *gueridon* (small, three-legged table). The drawn oval, elongated and shaded, is not only a planar surface, but is in itself a space, with its own depth, inscribed in a lozenge. The drawing, more and more transparent, allows itself to be impregnated with the most refined colors and textures. New experiments work on the edges—irregular borders torn from the top and a thin band of *faux bois* paper which limits the composition at left, the white-dotted edge from the piece of painted *moiré* paper, another edge of this same piece of painted paper lined with a band of drawn shadow. The newspaper becomes a playing card, pierced with a cut-out heart; everything converges on this little empty space. I.M.-F.

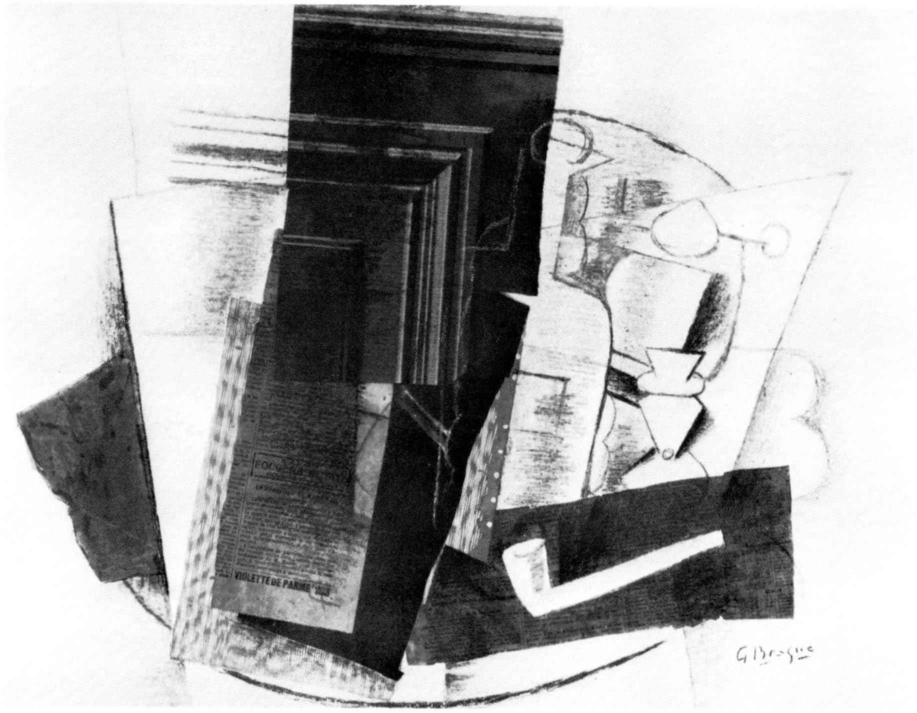

See plate 8

44.

Bottle, Glass and Pipe
(Bouteille, verre et pipe)
(Violette de Parme)

1914
beige cardboard, painted paper, black paper, newspaper, on paper
48 x 64 (18 15/16 x 25 3/16)
Signed, lower right: *G Braque*
CGP 41

Provenance
Galerie Louise Leiris, Paris
Collection Sir Edward and Lady Hulton, London, around 1955
Collection Marlborough Fine Art Ltd., London, 1981
Present collection, 1981

Literature
Gieure 1956, reproduced color pl. 30
Paulhan 1956, reproduced p. 69
Elgar 1958, reproduced color pl. 14
Golding 1959, p. 109, reproduced color pl. 8
Habasque 1959, reproduced color p. 78
Chevalier 1961, reproduced color p. 6
Rosenblum 1966, p. 96, reproduced pl. 49
Tono 1967, reproduced color
Pouillon 1970, reproduced color pl. V
Carrà 1971, reproduced no. 130
Schwartz 1971, p. 102, reproduced p. 103
Cogniat 1976, reproduced fig. 13b
Mangin (Worms de Romilly) 1982, no. 224, reproduced

Exhibitions
Paris 1953, no. 159
Edinburgh 1956, no. 39, reproduced pl. 10
Munich 1963, no. 41, reproduced pl. 37
Zurich 1968, unnumbered, reproduced p. 55
Bielefeld 1979, no. 172, reproduced (not in exhibition)
Paris 1982, no. 41, reproduced color p. 147

Private collection

The complexity of the composition and of the materials used here is very great, and in some ways exemplary of the last series of *papiers collés* made before the war.

The central axis (placed slightly askew, as almost always) is composed uniquely of pasted and superimposed papers. Two drawn "wings" balance this axis; the whole is contained in an oval.

The formal and spatial paradoxes are multiplied, making of the collage a "seeing machine" of unequaled subtlety. Two of them are as follows: the *faux bois* paper with moldings occurs in the last position in the collage (on top, if one reconstitutes the successive steps in this way):

1) the white background—the paper seems to be covered with a coating that makes of it a worked pictorial background, less neutral than the white paper left as such, as in the first *papiers collés;*
2) thick beige paper;
3) painted paper with a *moiré* design—Braque once again has emphasized the dotted border of this paper, and these white dots recall dots of gouache which are going to appear in other *papiers collés,* and start the return to painted textures and to color;
3 bis) black paper;
4) newspaper;
5) *faux bois* paper with moldings.

Thus, placed uppermost for the eye of the spectator, this last figure is in fact a background, as its drawn prolongation at left and the phantomlike form of the bottle indicate.

Another paradox: the contour of the pipe is cut out of the newspaper, so well that the pipe "imposes itself by its absence" as John Golding has stated; and that in the successive planes, it is "under" the newspaper (Golding 1959, 109). [Actual quote from Golding: ". . . since one is conscious of the physical, tactile existence of the newspaper, one might almost say that one is made aware of the pipe by its absence."] But Braque has shaded it in such a way that it seems to be brought forward by a purely optical effect which has nothing to do with *trompe l'oeil.*

In the last analysis, there are plenty of games in Braque's work, but games which are situated exclusively in a formal and pictorial space and which are not immediately discoverable. It is as if the game is to be discovered through a mirror, behind the precise mechanism of a harmony which first commands attention. The best example of this is *Bottle, Glass and Pipe,* where one discovers the parricide of Montreuil buried between the *Fougère Royale* (Royal Fern) and the *Violette de Parme* (Violet of Parma). I.M.-F.

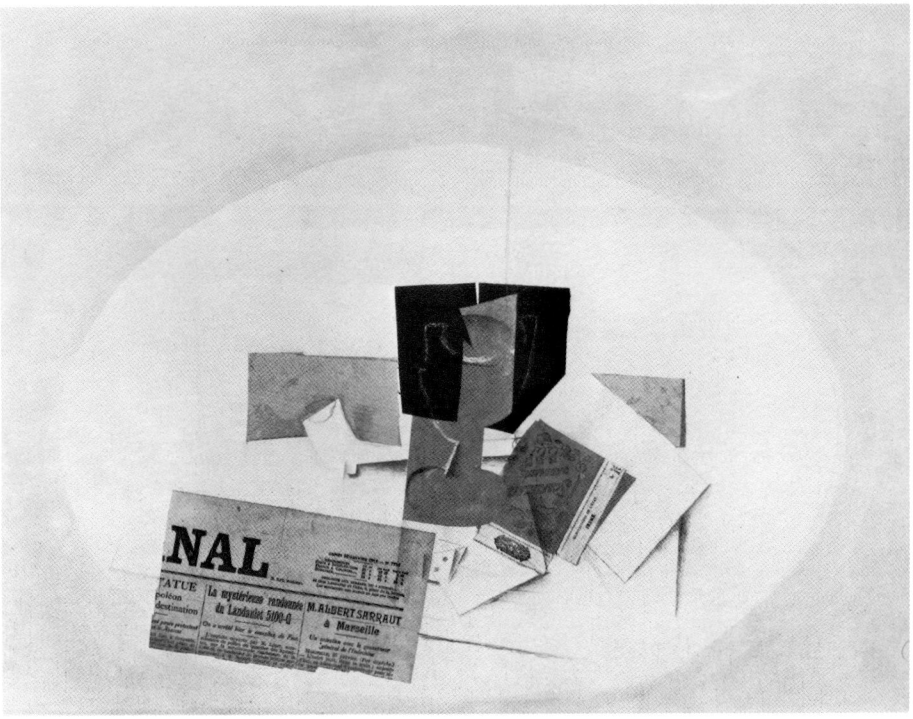

45.

Pipe, Glass and Die
(Pipe, verre et dé)
(Journal)

1914
charcoal, *faux bois* paper, black paper, green paper, newspaper, wrapper from cigarette package, on paper
50 x 60 (19 5/8 x 23 5/8)
CGP 46

Provenance
Galerie Kahnweiler, Paris
Possibly 4th Kahnweiler sale, 1923, no. 6, *"Nature morte"* (53 x 60 cm), for 160F
Collection Raoul La Roche
Collection Thomas Speiser, Basel
Present collection, 1981

Literature
Tono 1967, reproduced color no. 58
Mathey 1968, reproduced p. 158
Carrà 1971, no. 133, reproduced
Mangin (Worms de Romilly) 1982, no. 234, reproduced color on cover

Exhibitions
Basel 1962, no. 21, reproduced
Paris 1963, reproduced color no. 27
Munich 1963, no. 48, reproduced pl. 44
Basel 1968, no. 21, reproduced color
Humlebaeck 1969, no. 211, reproduced color p. 17
Minneapolis 1975, no. 61, reproduced p. 59
Basel 1976, no. 9, reproduced color
Bielefeld 1979, no. 147, reproduced (not in exhibition)
Paris 1982, no. 46, reproduced color p. 157

Kunstmuseum Hannover mit Sammlung Sprengel, Hannover

In this series, as compared to the first *papiers collés,* and according to a course which has been developing progressively, one finds the reversal of the respective presences of the drawing and the pieces of pasted paper. If the drawn structure was at first of prime importance, it now only punctuates an arrangement of cut-out forms.

There is also a reversal in respect to color (in the common sense of the word) used with less parsimony. In this very pure and very beautiful *papier collé,* one has the impression that Braque has allowed himself to cut directly into the color: as Matisse will do much later and in another context (the glass, for example, is cut from green paper with an almost imperceptible humor). The composition, on the whole, is constructed of large flat areas, clearly differentiated, without transitions, somewhat in the manner of Gris. In any case the luminous space, as well as the oval frame determined by a modulated stone tone, is only found in Braque's world.

I.M.-F.

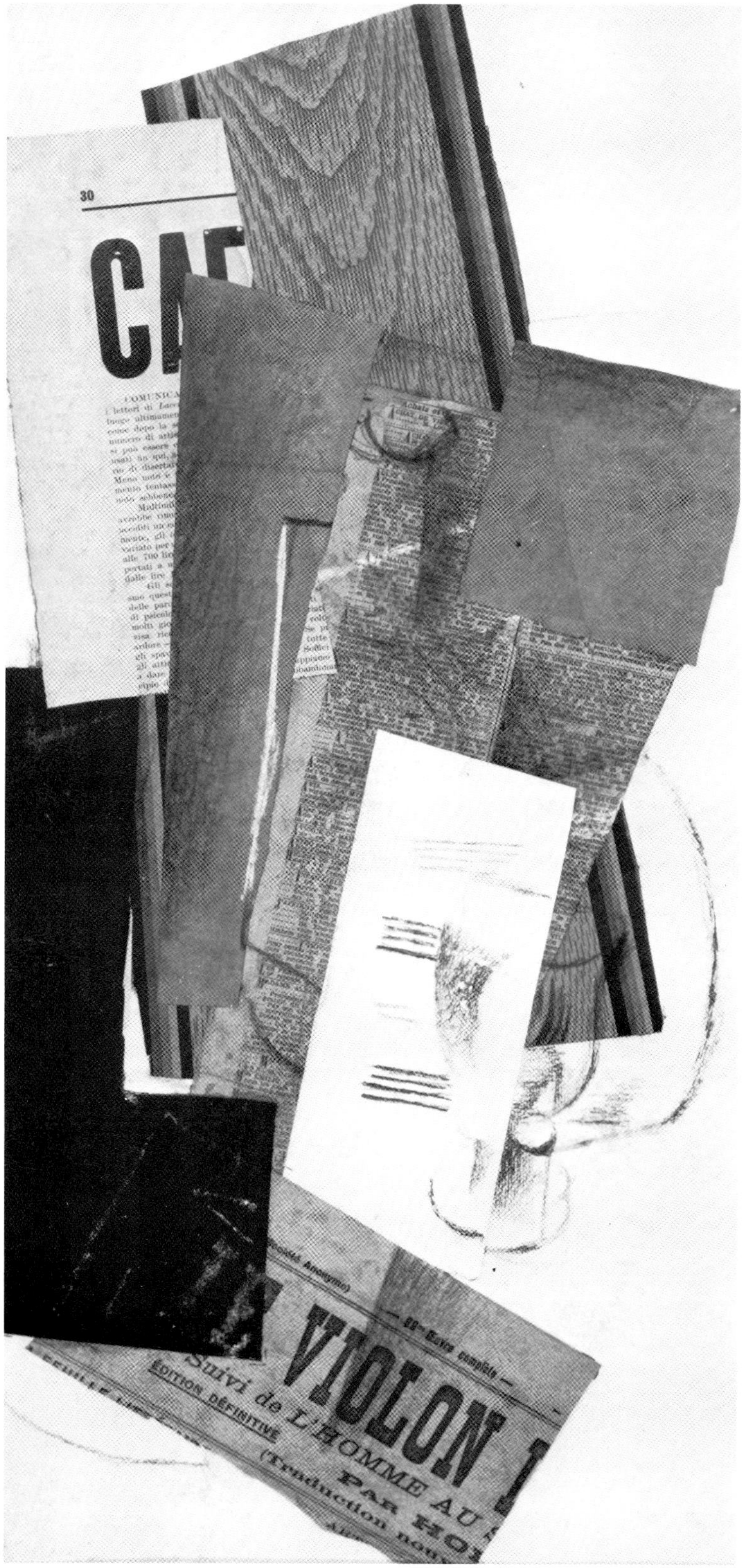

See plate 1

46.

Glass, Bottle and Newspaper (Le violon)

(The Violin; Glass, Carafe and Newspaper; Bottle and Glass)

1914
faux bois paper, colored papers (green, white), newspaper, on paper
62.5 x 28.5 (24 5/8 x 11 1/4)
Signed on verso: *G Braque*
CGP 45

Provenance
Galerie Kahnweiler, Paris
Collection Raoul La Roche

Literature
Vallier 1962, reproduced color pl. 11
Fumet 1965, reproduced color p. 50
Mullins 1968, reproduced color p. 47, ill. 29
Cogniat 1970, reproduced color p. 26
Cooper 1970, reproduced color p. 187, pl. 206
Carrà 1971, reproduced no. 114
Cogniat 1976, reproduced color pl. 15
Wescher 1979, p. 24, reproduced color pl. 4
Mangin (Worms de Romilly) 1982, no. 233, reproduced color

Exhibitions
Paris 1961, no. 21
Basel 1962, no. 22
Paris 1963, no. 25, reproduced
Munich 1963, no. 39, reproduced pl. 35
Zurich 1968, unnumbered, reproduced p. 58
Humlebaeck 1969, no. 210, reproduced color
Los Angeles 1970, no. 38
Paris 1973, no. 55, reproduced
Saint Paul 1980, no. 62
Paris 1982, no. 45, reproduced color p. 155

Private collection

This is one of the only cases, to our knowledge, where Picasso and Braque—almost at the same time, but at a point when they were working far away from each other—used the same formal elements, namely fragments of the magazine *Lacerba,* but with very different and hardly comparable results (see fig. 79).

Lacerba, at the beginning of 1914 (Picasso used the cover of the issue dated 1 January 1914, Braque a page from the 15 January 1914 issue), had just modified its typography and begun to use exaggeratedly high, thick, and very striking letters. The particular form of the letters perhaps played a role in Braque's choice of a format which was unusually stretched out. I.M.-F.

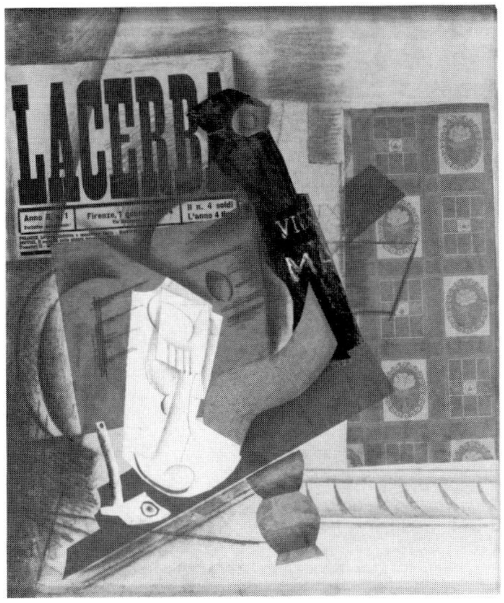

79. Pablo Picasso (Spanish, 1881-1973), *Lacerba*, 1914, chalk, oil and *papier collé* on fine linen. The Peggy Guggenheim Collection, Venice; The Solomon R. Guggenheim Foundation, New York.

80. Page from *Lacerba*, 15 January 1914.

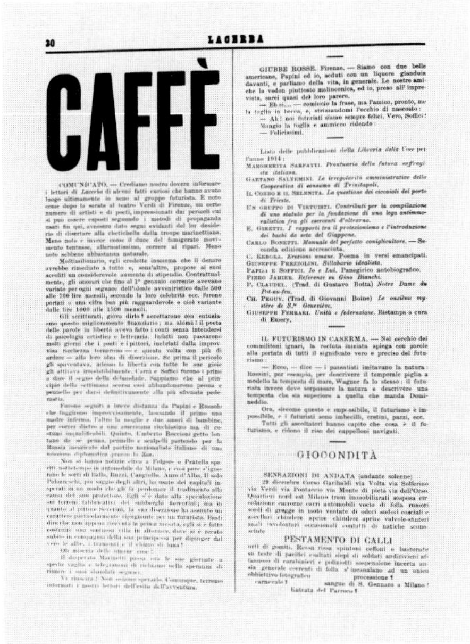

30 LACERBA

CAFFÈ

COMUNICATO. — Crediamo nostro dovere informare i lettori di *Lacerba* di alcuni fatti curiosi che hanno avuto luogo ultimamente in seno al gruppo futurista. È noto come dopo la serata al teatro Verdi di Firenze, un certo numero di artisti e di poeti, impressionati dai pericoli cui si può essere esposti seguendo i metodi di propaganda usati fin qui, avessero dato segni evidenti del lor desiderio di disertare alla chetichella dalla troupe marinettiana. Meno noto è invece come il duce del famigerato movimento tentasse, allarmatissimo, correre ai ripari. Meno noto sebbene abbastanza naturale.

Multimilionario, egli credette insomma che il denaro avrebbe rimediato a tutto e, senz'altro, propose ai suoi accoliti un considerevole aumento di stipendio. Contrattualmente, gli onorari che fino al 1° gennaio corrente avevano variato per ogni seguace dell'ideale avveniristico dalle 500 alle 700 lire mensili, secondo la loro celebrità ecc. furono portati a una cifra ben più ragguardevole e cioè variante dalle lire 1000 alle 1500 mensili.

Gli scritturati, giova dirlo! accettarono con entusiasmo questo miglioramento finanziario; ma ahimè! il poeta delle parole in libertà aveva fatto i conti senza intendersi di psicologia artistica e letteraria. Infatti non passarono molti giorni che i poeti e i pittori, inebriati dalla improvvisa ricchezza tornarono — e questa volta con più di ardore — alla loro idea di diserzione. Se prima il pericolo gli spaventava, adesso la libertà con tutte le sue gioie gli attirava irresistibilmente. Carrà e Soffici furono i primi a dare il segno della debandade. Sappiamo che al principio della settimana scorsa essi abbandonarono penna e pennello per darsi definitivamente alla più sfrenata pederastia.

Furono seguiti a breve distanza da Papini e Russolo che fuggirono improvvisamente, lasciando il primo una madre inferma, l'altro la moglie e due amori di bambine, per correr dietro a una americana ricchissima ma di costumi inqualificabili. Quinto, Umberto Boccioni gettò lontano da se penna, pennello e scalpelli partendo per la Russia incaricato dal partito nazionalista italiano di una missione diplomatica presso lo Zar.

Non si hanno notizie circa a Folgore e Pratella spariti nottetempo in automobile da Milano, e così pure s'ignorano le sorti di Balla, Buzzi, Cangiullo, Auro d'Alba. Il solo Palazzeschi, per saggio degli altri, ha usato dei capitali insperati in un modo che gli fa perdonare il tradimento alla causa del suo protettore. Egli s'è dato alla speculazione sui terreni fabbricativi dei subborghi fiorentini; ma in quanto al pittore Severini, la sua diserzione ha assunto un carattere particolarmente ripugnante per un futurista. Basti dire che non appena ricevuta la prima mesata, egli si è fatto costruire una sontuosa villa in [illegible], dove si è recato subito in compagnia della sua principessa per dipinger dal vero le albe, i tramonti e il chiaro di luna!

Oh miseria delle umane cose!

Il disperato Marinetti passa ora le sue giornate a spedir vaglia e telegrammi di richiamo nella speranza di riunire i suoi sbandati seguaci.

Vi riuscirà? Non osiamo sperarlo. Comunque, terremo informati i nostri lettori dell'esito dell'avventura.

—

GIUBBE ROSSE. Firenze. — Siamo con due belle americane, Papini ed io, seduti con un liquore gianduia davanti, e parliamo della vita, in generale. Le nostre amiche la vedon piuttosto malinconica, ed io, preso all'imprevista, sarei quasi del loro parere.

— Eh sì... — comincio la frase, ma l'amico, pronto, me la taglia in bocca, e, strizzandomi l'occhio di nascosto:

— Ah! noi futuristi siamo sempre felici. Vero, Soffici?

Mangio la foglia e ammicco ridendo:

— Felicissimi.

—

Lista delle pubblicazioni della *Libreria della Voce* per l'anno 1914:

MARGHERITA SARFATTI. *Prontuario della futura suffragista italiana.*

GAETANO SALVEMINI. *Le irregolarità amministrative della Cooperativa di consumo di Trinitapoli.*

IL CORBO E IL SELENITA. *La questione dei ciccaioli del porto di Trieste.*

UN GRUPPO DI VIRTUISTI. *Contributi per la compilazione di uno statuto per la fondazione di una lega antimmoralistica fra gli esercenti d'oltrarno.*

E. GIRETTI. *I rapporti tra il protezionismo e l'introduzione dei bachi da seta del Giappone.*

CARLO BONETTI. *Manuale del perfetto coniglicoltore.* — Seconda edizione accresciuta.

C. REBORA. *Erezioni umane.* Poema in versi emancipati.

GIUSEPPE PREZZOLINI. *Sillabario idealista.*

PAPINI E SOFFICI. *Io e Lui.* Panegirico autobiografico.

PIERO JAHIER. *Referenze su Gino Bianchi.*

P. CLAUDEL. (Trad. di Gustavo Botta) *Notre Dame du Pot-au-feu.*

CH. PEGUY. (Trad. di Giovanni Boine) *Le onzième mystère de S.te Geneviève.*

GIUSEPPE FERRARI. *Unità e federazione.* Ristampa a cura di Emery.

—

IL FUTURISMO IN CASERMA. — Nel cerchio dei commilitoni ignari, la recluta iniziata spiega con parole alla portata di tutti il significato vero e preciso del futurismo:

— Ecco, — dice — i passatisti imitavano la natura: Rossini, per esempio, per descrivere il temporale piglia a modello la tempesta di mare, Wagner fa lo stesso: il futurista invece deve sorpassare la natura e descrivere una tempesta che sia superiore a quella che manda Domineddio.

Ora, siccome questo è impossibile, il futurismo è impossibile, e i futuristi sono imbecilli, cretini, pazzi, ecc.

Tutti gli ascoltatori hanno capito che cosa è il futurismo, e ridono il riso dei cappelloni navigati.

—

GIOCONDITÀ

SENSAZIONI DI ANDATA (andante solenne)

29 dicembre Corso Garibaldi via Volta via Solferino via Verdi via Pontaccio via Monte di pietà via dell'Orso Quartieri nord est Milano tram immobilizzati sospesa circolazione carrozze carri automobili vocio di folla rumori sordi di gregge in moto ventate di odori sudori cosciali e ascellari chiudere aprire chiudere aprire valvole-sfinteri anali involontari occasionali contatti di natiche sconosciute

PESTAMENTO DI CALLI

urti di gomiti. Ressa rissa spintoni ceffoni e bastonate su teste di pacifici esaltati siepi di soldati andirivieni affannosi di carabinieri e poliziotti sospensione incerta ansia generale correnti di folla s'incanalano ad un unico obbiettivo fotografico processione!

carnevale! sangue di S. Gennaro a Milano!

Entrata del Parroco!

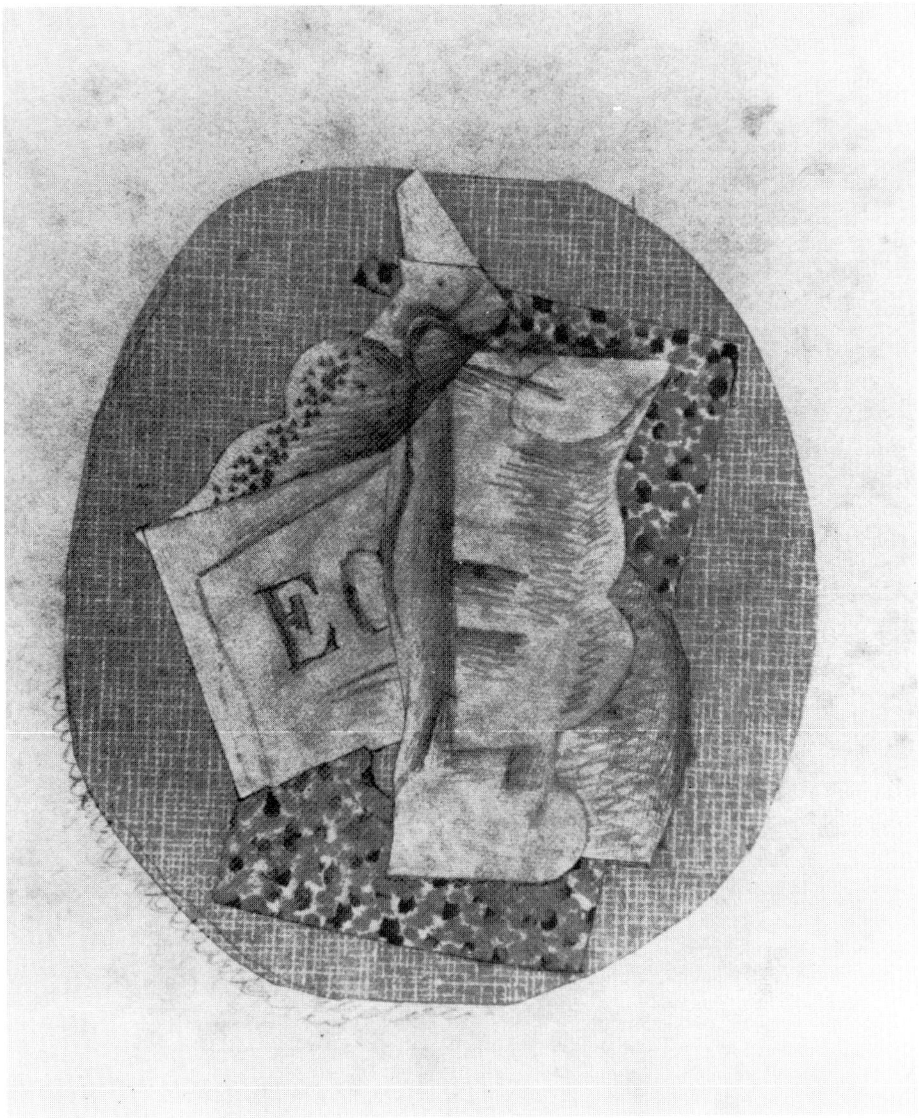

47.

The Glass (Le verre)

1914

pencil, paper heightened with gouache, painted paper, on gray paper

34.5 x 43.5 (13 5/8 x 17 1/8) (with bottom paper)

CGP 49

Provenance

Collection Dr. F. J. Bossard, Paris (until 1973)

Literature

Mangin (Worms de Romilly) 1982, no. 244, reproduced

Exhibitions

Paris 1963, reproduced color

Oslo 1964, no. 8, reproduced

Saint-Paul 1980, no. 293

Paris 1982, no. 49, reproduced p. 163 (not in exhibition)

Location unknown

48.

The Package of Tobacco
(Le paquet de tabac)
(Still Life; Glass and Package of Tobacco)

1914
pencil, charcoal, chalk, paper heightened with gouache and cut out, newspaper clipping, cigarette wrapper, on heavy cardboard
35 x 27.7 (13 13/16 x 10 7/8)
Signed on back, in charcoal: *G. Braque*
CGP 50

Provenance
Galerie Kahnweiler, Paris (no. 1206)
Collection Mrs. Gilbert W. Chapman
Present collection, 1947

Literature
Isarlov 1932, no. 199
Carrà 1971, reproduced no. 140
Mangin (Worms de Romilly) 1982, no. 243, reproduced

Exhibitions
Seattle 1973
Bielefeld 1979, no. 152, reproduced (not in exhibition)
Paris 1982, no. 50, reproduced color p. 165

The Art Institute of Chicago, Gift of Mrs. Gilbert W. Chapman

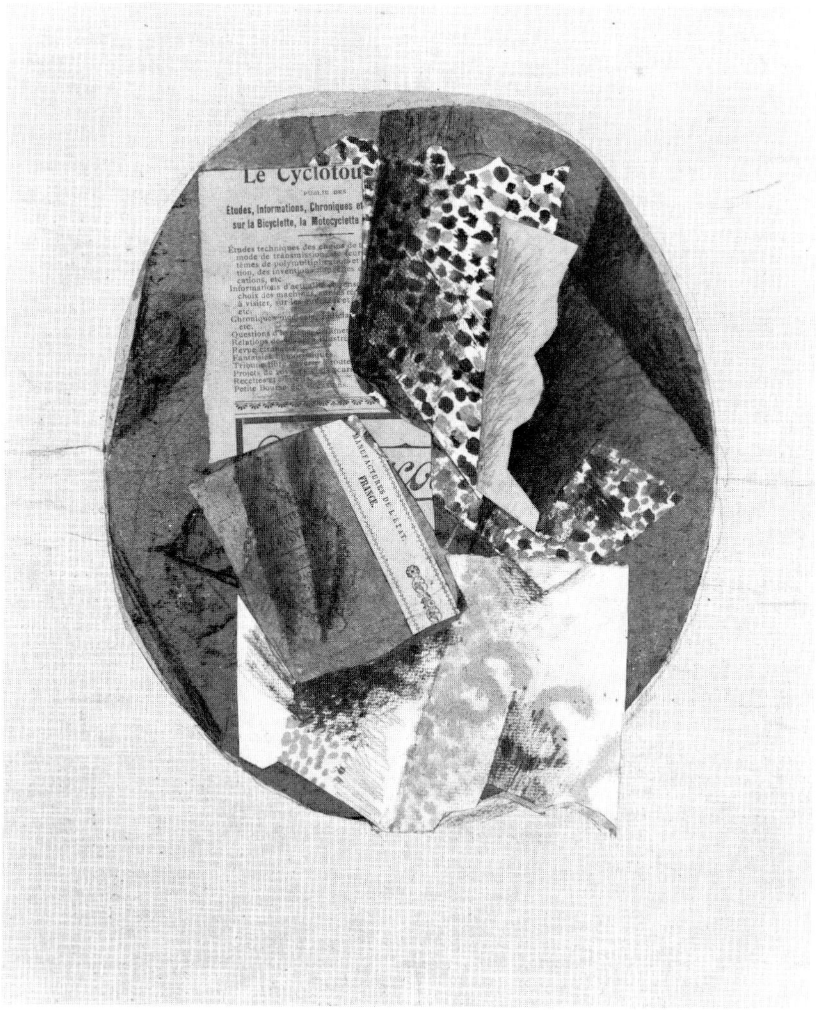

Both the oval composition of paper cut-outs and the frame which is an integral part of it are entirely invested with woven materials and colors. Not only does Braque renounce the transparency of the white paper background, but also he abandons all drawing (in the sense of line, grid, and structure).

Now at the end of this course of development, *papier collé* appears to be reinvested by painting; by the means proper to painting: thus Braque is significantly on the way to replacing, in part, papers which are mechanically imprinted (which allowed him, in the beginning, to dissociate form and color) with "painted papers" of his own, covered with gouache dots, then cut out and pasted down (see also *Still Life with Musical Instruments,* cat. no. 49, and *Bottle of Rum,* cat. no. 51).

The gouache dots act as a transition between mechanical repetition and the unique color of the painting: they bring about a return to painting. I.M.-F.

49.

Still Life with Guitar
(Nature morte aux instruments de musique)

1914
pencil; newspaper; beige, white, and black papers, heightened with gouache; *faux bois* paper, on paper
63 x 47 (24 3/4 x 18 1/2)
CGP 51

Provenance
Galerie Kahnweiler, Paris
Collection Raoul La Roche
Collection Thomas Speiser

Literature
Vallier 1962, reproduced color pl. 1
Fumet 1965, reproduced color p. 45
Mathey 1968, reproduced p. 158
Cogniat 1970, reproduced color p. 15
Carrà 1971, reproduced no. 134
Mangin (Worms de Romilly) 1982, no. 231, reproduced color

Exhibitions
Paris 1961, no. 20, reproduced
Basel 1962, no. 23, reproduced
Paris 1963, no. 28, reproduced color on cover
Basel 1968, no. 20, reproduced color
Humlebaeck 1969, no. 212, reproduced color
Minneapolis 1975, no. 60, reproduced color p. 58
Basel 1976, no. 8, reproduced color
Bielefeld 1979, no. 166, reproduced color (not in exhibition)
Paris 1982, no. 51, reproduced color p. 167

Galerie Beyeler, Basel

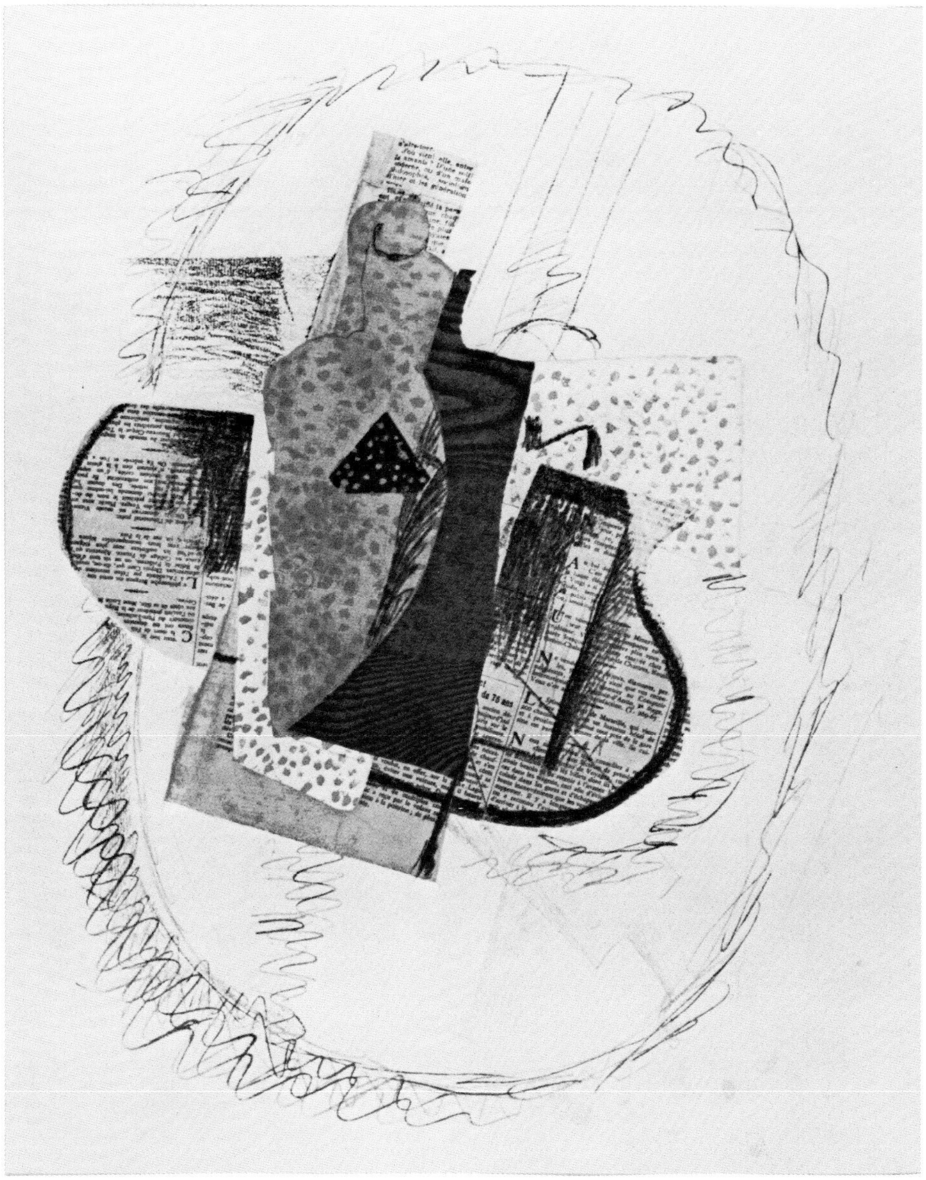

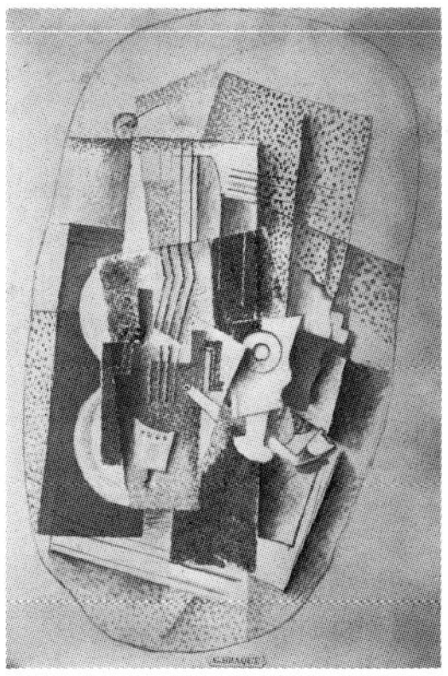

81. Braque, *Musique,* 1914, oil on canvas. Bequest of Katherine S. Dreier, Milford, Connecticut, to The Phillips Collection, Washington, 1953.

We can date this collage with some certainty, from the newspaper element at the center left. Although this fragment remains unidentified, its text concerns the election of Henri Bergson to the French Academy, which occurred on 10 January 1914, thus giving us a *terminus a quo* for the work. Its composition, in which the objects read as if set on overlapping vertical planes, is not so clearly used in other collages but does appear in paintings of this period, including the Phillips Collection's *Music* (fig. 81). Indeed, this oil also features dotted areas in secondary or background passages, much like those found in the *Still Life with Musical Instruments.* Its irregular oval border, which more closely resembles that found in this collage than in Braque's other paintings, suggests a direct connection exists between *Music* and *papier collé.* E.A.C. jr.

50.

Composition (L'as de coeur)

(The Ace of Hearts)

1914
black pencil, cut-out white cardboard, on beige cardboard
30 x 41 (11 13/16 x 16 1/8)
CGP 48

Provenance
Galerie Kahnweiler, Paris
Collection Raoul La Roche

Literature
Fumet 1965, reproduced color p. 52
Carrà 1971, no. 135, reproduced
Draeger 1971, reproduced color p. 121
Mangin (Worms de Romilly) 1982, no. 246, reproduced color

Exhibitions
Paris 1961, no. 22, reproduced
Paris 1963, no. 26, reproduced
Saint-Paul 1980, no. 63
Paris 1982, no. 48, reproduced color p. 161

Private collection

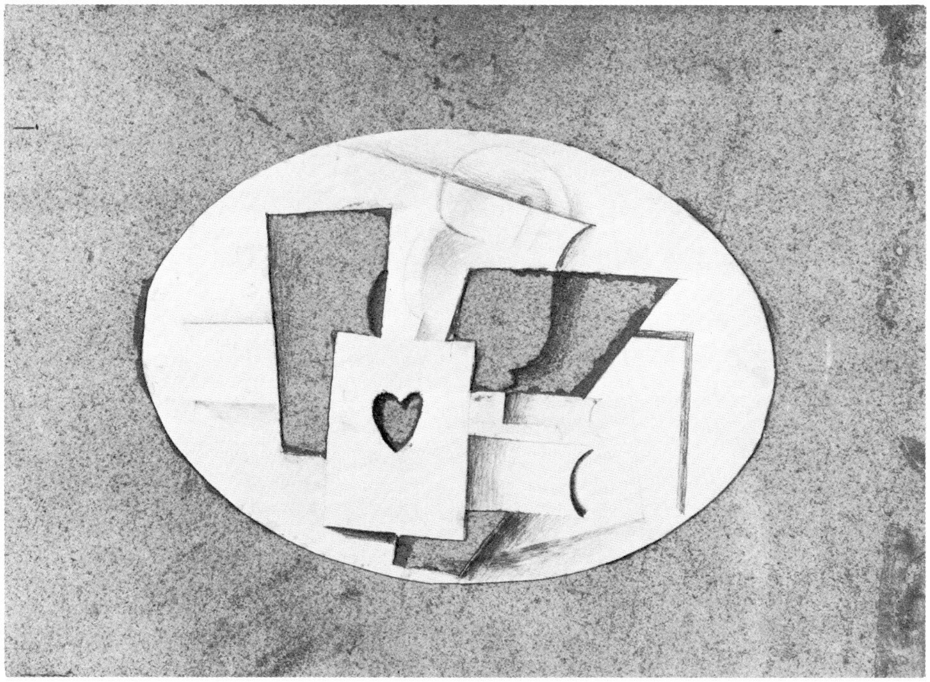

51.

The Bottle of Rum
(La bouteille de rhum)

1914
charcoal, newspaper, beige paper, wrapping paper, black paper, heightened with gouache, cut out, on cardboard
65.5 x 46.5 (25 3/4 x 18 5/16)
CGP 52

Provenance
Studio of the artist

Literature
Descargues 1973, reproduced color p. 32
Mangin (Worms de Romilly) 1982, no. 241, reproduced color

Exhibitions
Paris 1982, no. 52, reproduced color p. 169

Private collection

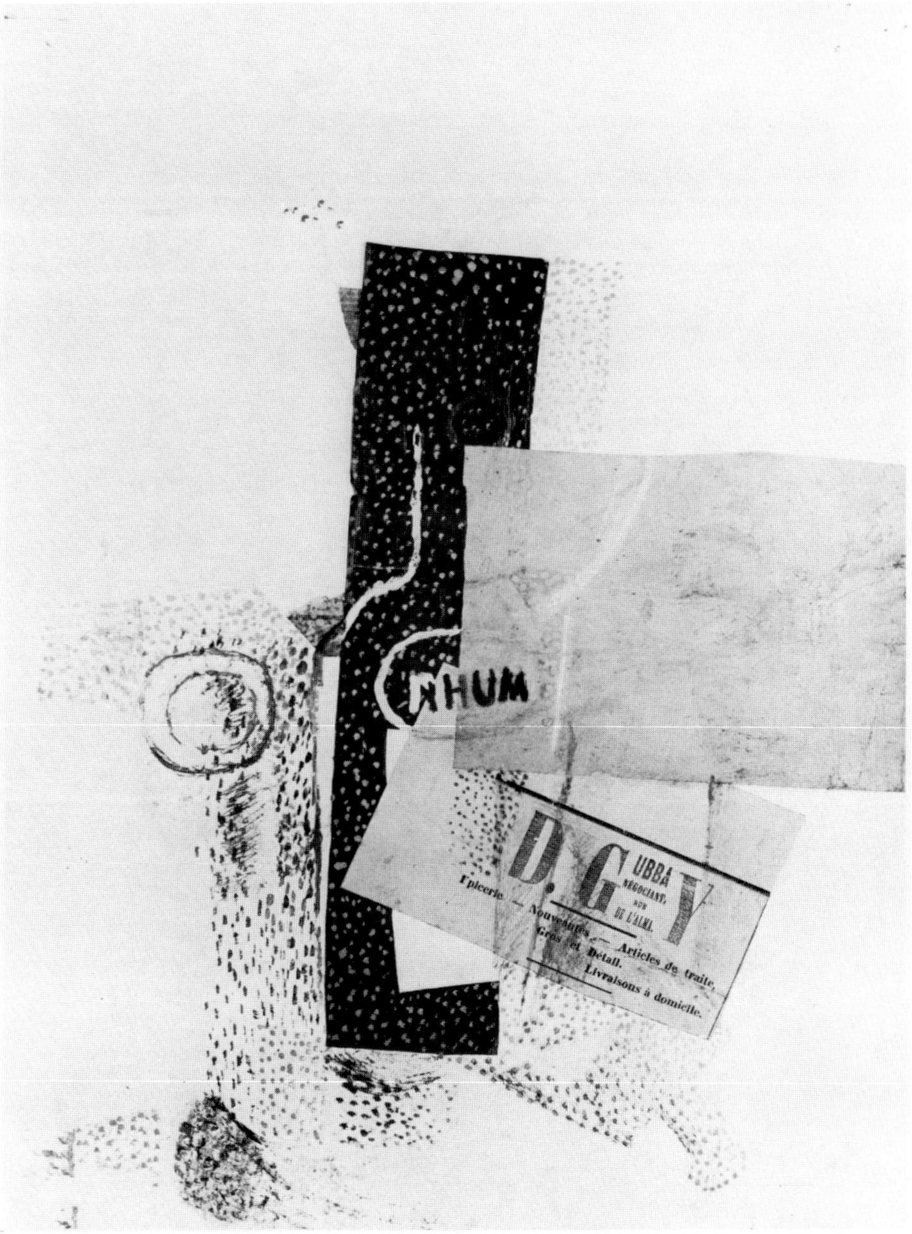

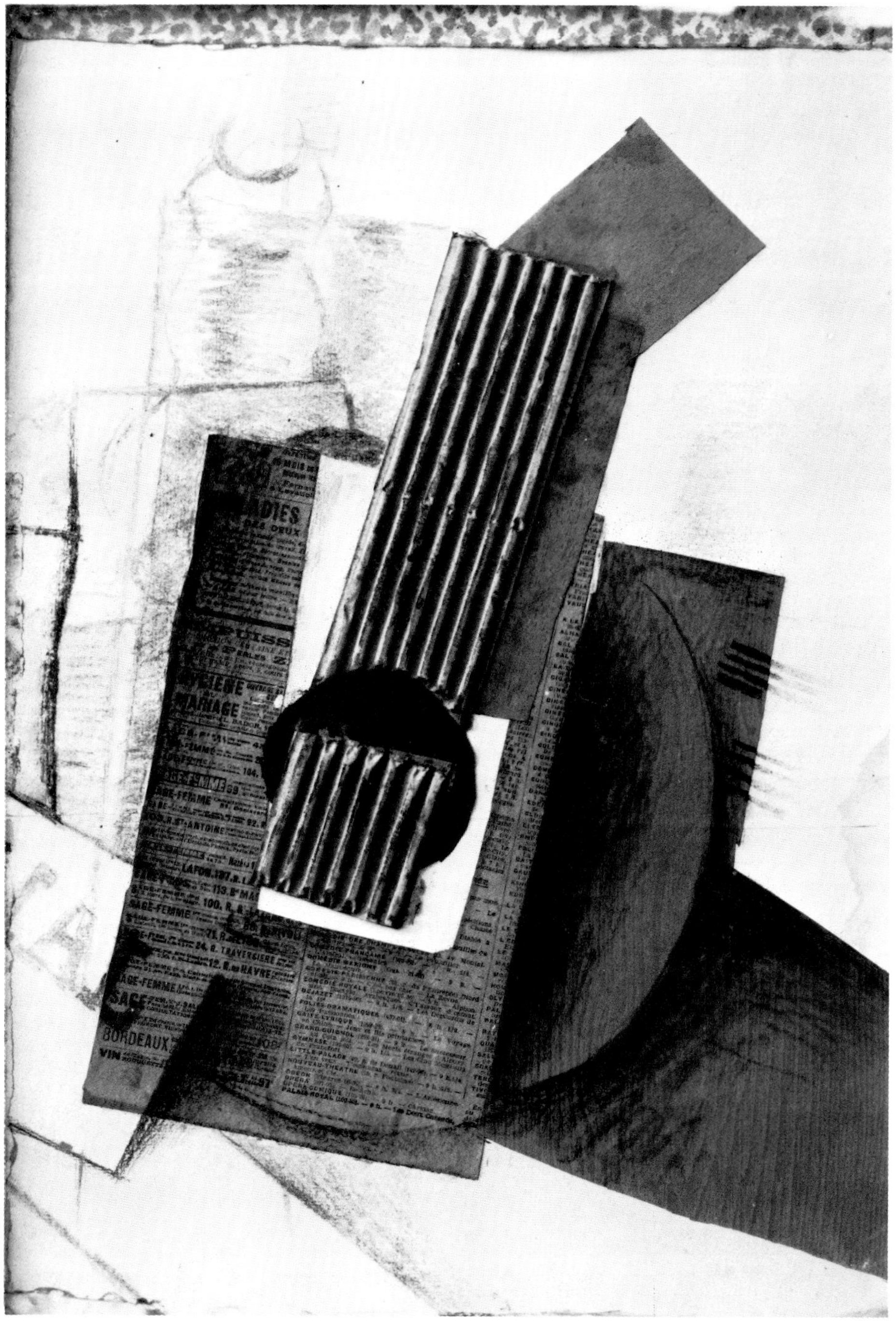

See plate 4

52.

The Mandolin (La mandoline)

(Still Life with Guitar)

1914

charcoal, gouache, *faux bois* paper, newspaper, corrugated cardboard, on paper

50 x 32 (19 5/8 x 12 5/8)

CGP 47

Provenance

Galerie Kahnweiler, Paris (no. 1207)
Collection Antoine Coutrot, until 1965
Werner Rusche, Cologne
Present collection, 1965

Literature

Janneau 1924, p. 56
Einstein 1931, reproduced p. 349
Isarlov 1932, no. 200, p. 20
Zervos 1933, reproduced p. 27
Zervos 1938, reproduced p. 234
Einstein 1934, reproduced pl. XXXVI
Carrà 1971, reproduced no. 143
Wescher 1979, p. 24
Mangin (Worms de Romilly) 1982, no. 242, reproduced

Exhibitions

Rio de Janeiro 1954, no. 9
Zurich 1968, unnumbered, reproduced p. 57
Bielefeld 1979, no. 138, reproduced color (not in exhibition)

82. Braque, *Guitare, pipe et cartes à jouer*, 1917, oil on canvas. Bergen Billedgalleri, Norway.

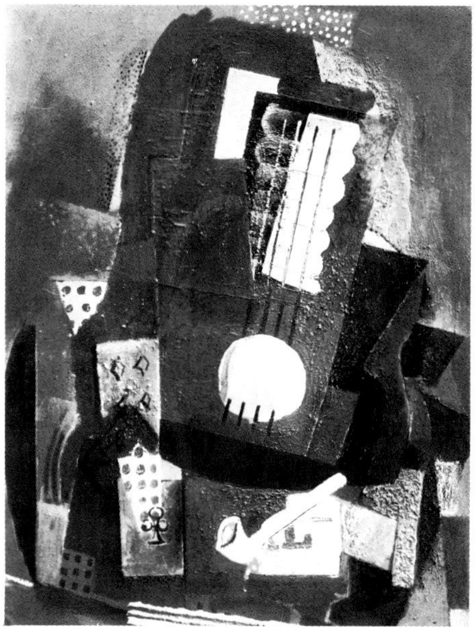

Stuttgart 1981, no. 6, reproduced color p. 4
Paris 1982, no. 47, reproduced color p. 159
(not in exhibition)

Ulmer Museum, Ulm

The corrugated cardboard does not need to be heightened with charcoal shadows: it contains a succession of shadow and light in itself, and the sculptor Henri Laurens used it in his *papiers collés* because of its eminently tactile qualities. After the war Braque also (and perhaps under the influence of Laurens) gave it a major place in his last series of *papiers collés.*

The other irregular band of paper covered with colored gouache dots brings the mandolin forward; it is certainly also the reintervention of painting, with its own means. These speckled textures are found in Picasso's work from the beginning of 1913, but are systematically repeated during the winter of 1913-1914. Braque doubtless began to use them at about the same time, the end of 1913 or beginning of 1914.

I.M.-F.

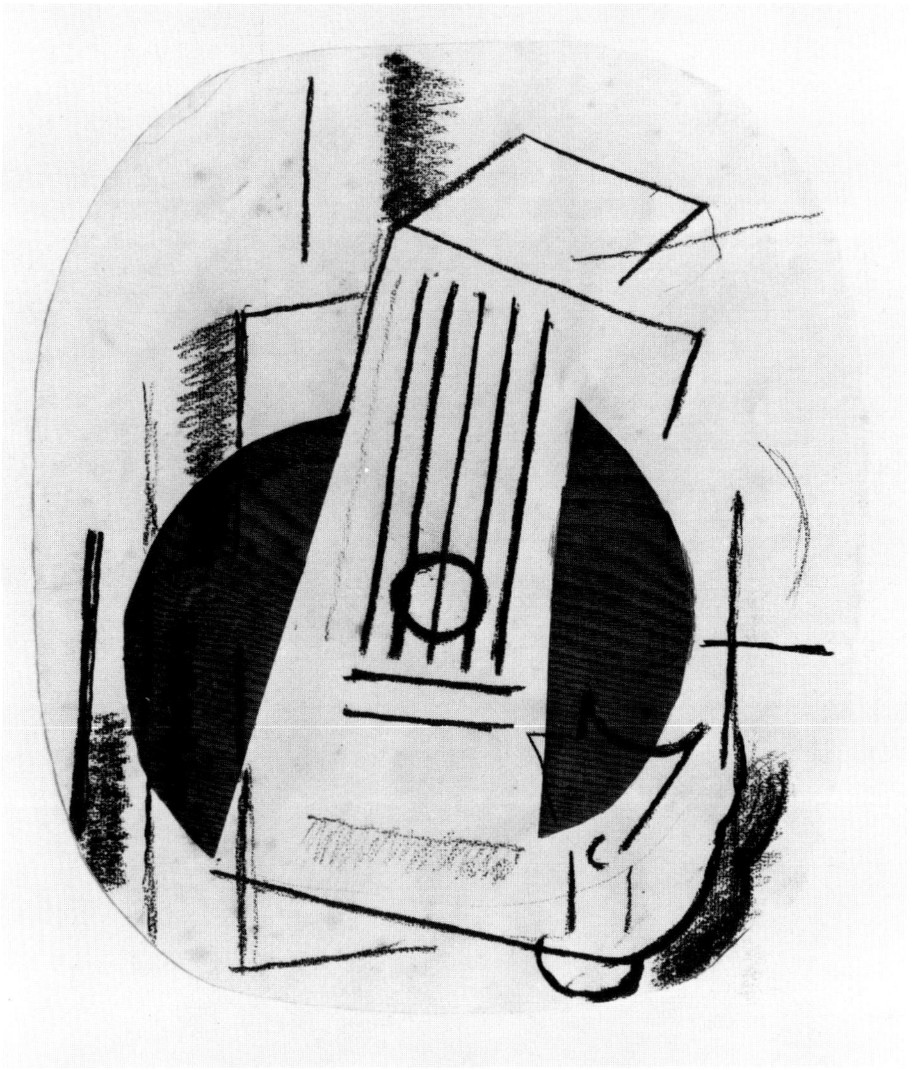

53.
Papier collé

1913
charcoal, *faux bois* paper, on paper
34 x 28 (13 3/8 x 11)
not in CGP

Provenance
Collection C. and F. Friedrich-Jezler

Kunstmuseum, Winterthur

None of the preparators of this catalogue has examined this work. Its short provenance and lack of exhibition history also presents a difficulty, as earlier opinions by scholars are wanting. The guitar relates to others represented in previous collages, especially cat. no. 3, and the size and more specialized oval format can be connected to an earlier series of such works (cat. nos. 18-22). Other aspects of the composition, especially its simplified drawing and boxlike shaping of the objects, suggest this work is later in the sequence, perhaps one of Braque's first postwar efforts, as similar shaping occurs in cat. nos. 54 and 54bis. E.A.C. jr.

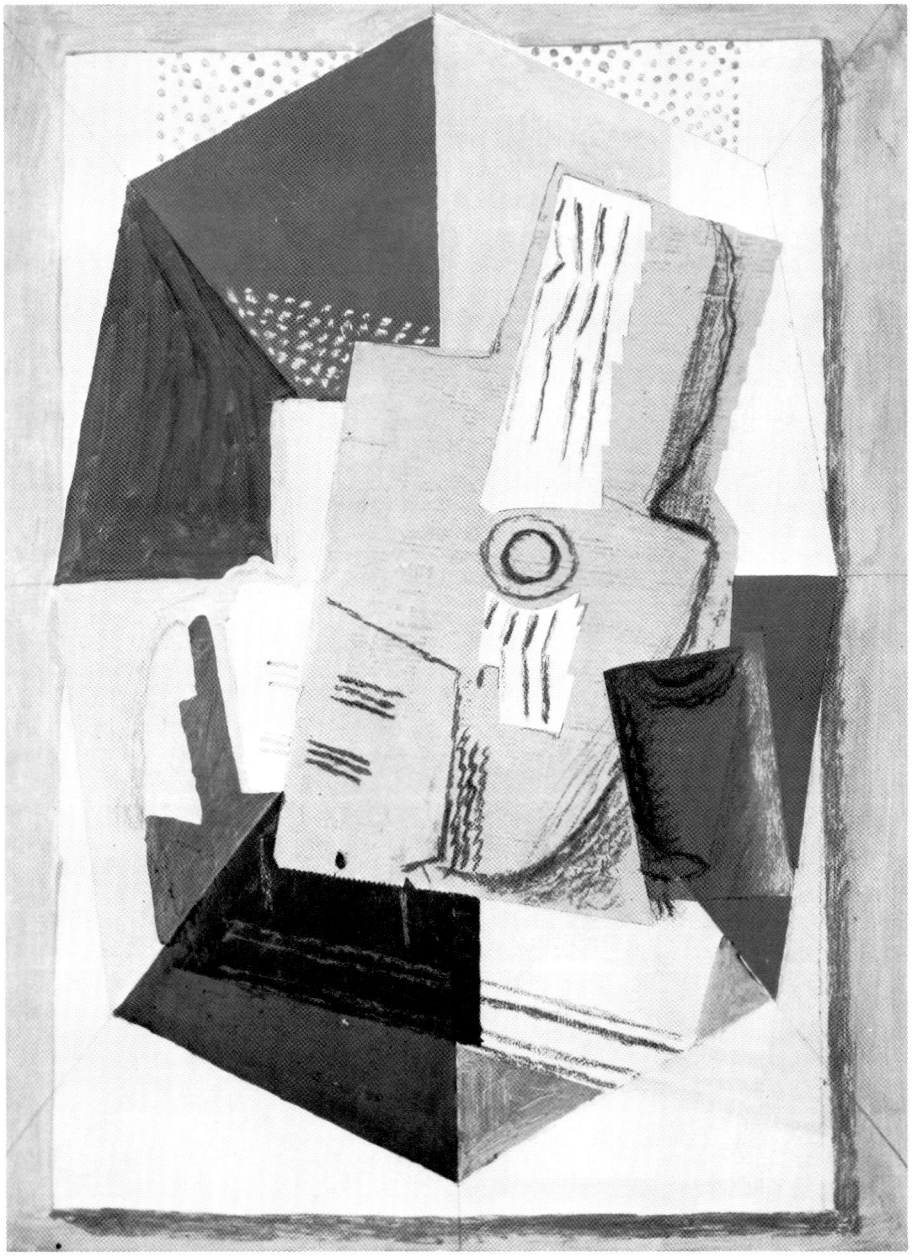

54.
Guitar (Guitare)

1918
newspaper, gouache, on cardboard
63.5 x 47 (25 x 18 1/2)
CGP 56

Provenance
Galerie Léonce Rosenberg (no. 132-50-84)
Collection Ferdinand Howald

Literature
Isarlov 1932, no. 230
Gieure 1956, reproduced
Mangin 1973, no. 34, reproduced

Exhibitions
Bielefeld 1979, no. 173, reproduced (not in exhibition)
Paris 1982, no. 56, reproduced color p. 176 (not in exhibition)

Columbus Museum of Art, Columbus, Ohio. Gift of Ferdinand Howald.

The (news)paper guitar is covered by painting. How better to say that the series is finished? I.M.-F.

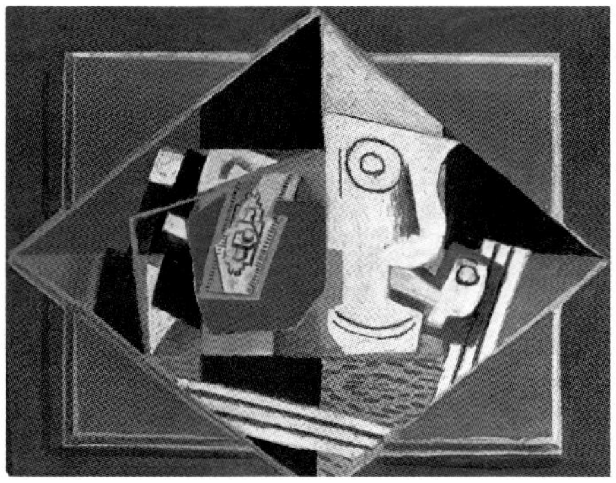

83. Braque, *Nature morte géometrique,* 1917, oil on canvas. Rijksmuseum Kröller-Müller, Otterlo, The Netherlands.

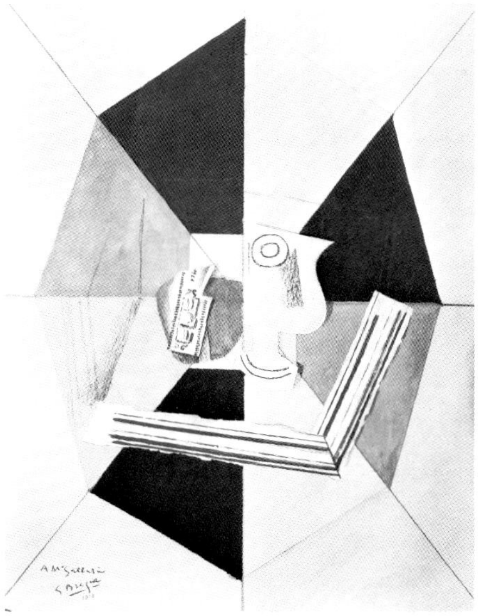

84. Braque, *The Cup,* 1917-1918, oil on cardboard. Philadelphia Museum of Art, The A. E. Gallatin Collection.

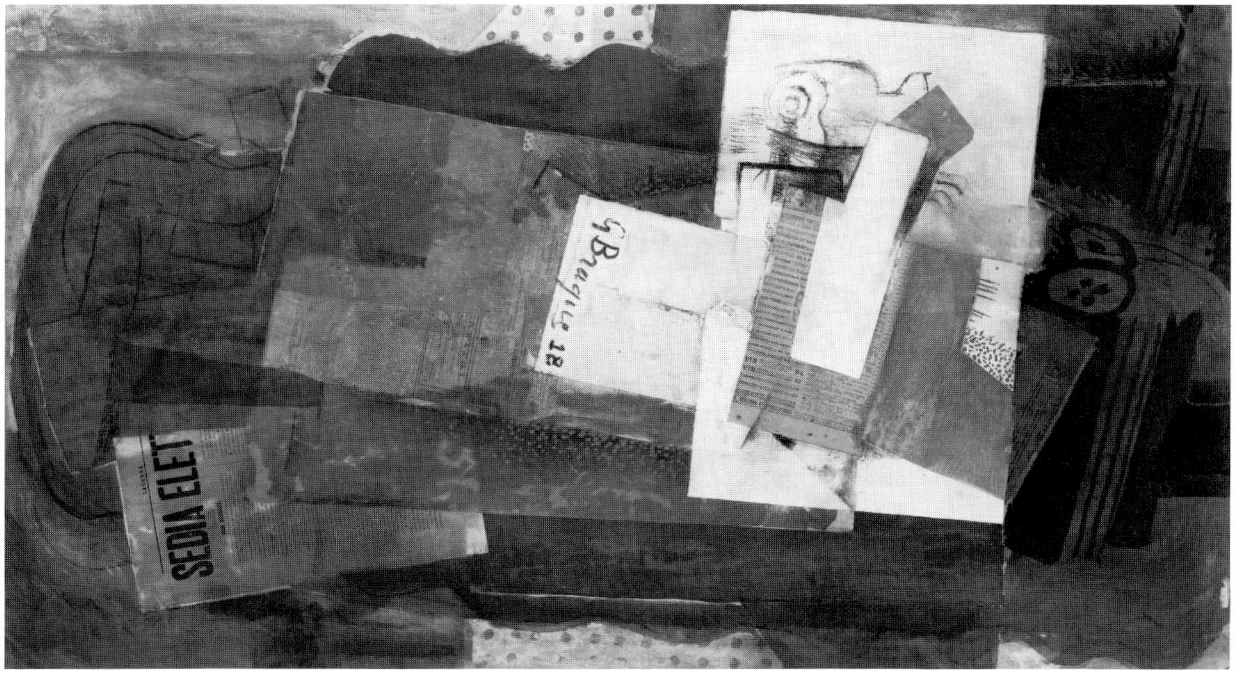

54 bis.
Still Life

1914?/1917-1918?
oil, gouache, paper and charcoal, on canvas
75.6 x 133 (29 3/4 x 52 3/8)
Signed, center (may refer to painting on reverse): *G Braque 18*
not in CGP

Provenance
Collection Louise and Walter Arensberg, Hollywood
Present collection, 1954

Literature
Kahnweiler 1945, reproduced p. 116
Arensberg Collection 1954, no. 27, reproduced
Valsecchi 1971, no. 150
Kushida 1975, reproduced color pl. 14

Exhibitions
Cincinnati 1962, reproduced

Philadelphia Museum of Art

This long, horizontal collage, the biggest of Braque's oeuvre, was left unfinished in 1918 when he turned the canvas to a vertical position and painted a still life on the verso. The signature and date at the center—"G Braque 18"—refer to this painted composition on the other side. In the collage we find numerous items represented by many different elements of pasted paper as well as painted paper; this use of paint correlates to that seen in cat. no. 54, and boxlike shaping of objects is also shared by these works. The massing of items and the fact that they are placed on a table dates no. 54bis with the later, more ample still lifes of 1917-1918. However, the piece of paper at the lower left is a page from the journal *Lacerba,* akin to an element from this same publication used earlier in *Glass, Bottle and Newspaper* (cat. no. 46). E.A.C. jr.

55.
Bottle and Musical Instruments
(Bouteille et instruments de musique)

1918
gouache, various papers, corrugated cardboard, on cardboard
52 x 76 (20 1/2 x 29 7/8)
CGP 55

Provenance
Collection Dr. G. T. Reber, Lausanne
Collection René Gaffé

Literature
Mangin 1973, no. 36, reproduced

Exhibitions
Basel 1933, no. 74, reproduced
Paris 1982, no. 55 reproduced p. 175 (not in exhibition)

Private collection

This *papier collé* has an exact painted equivalent: *Nature morte (Still life;* fig. 85).

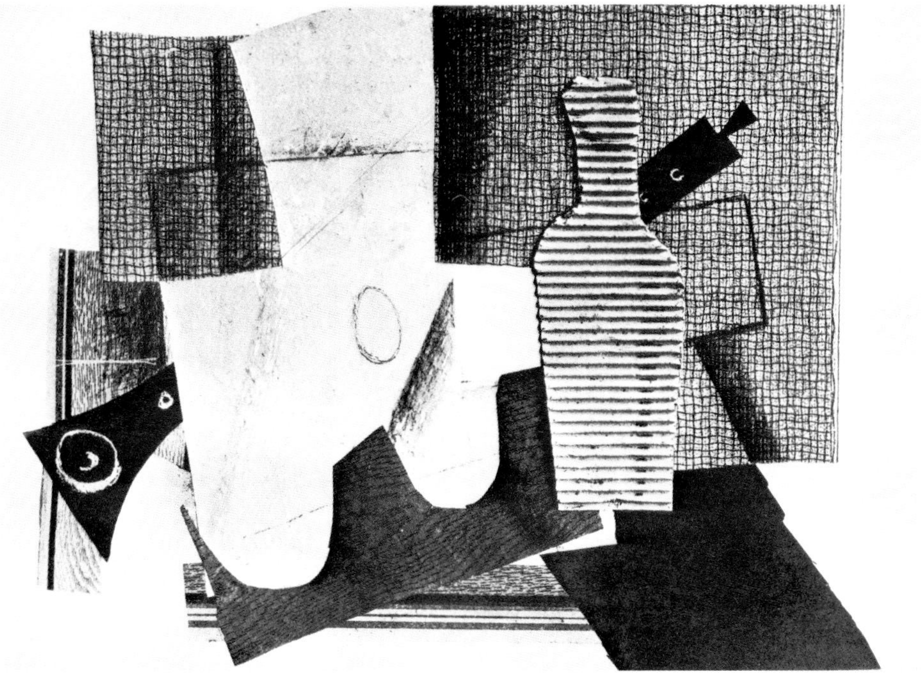

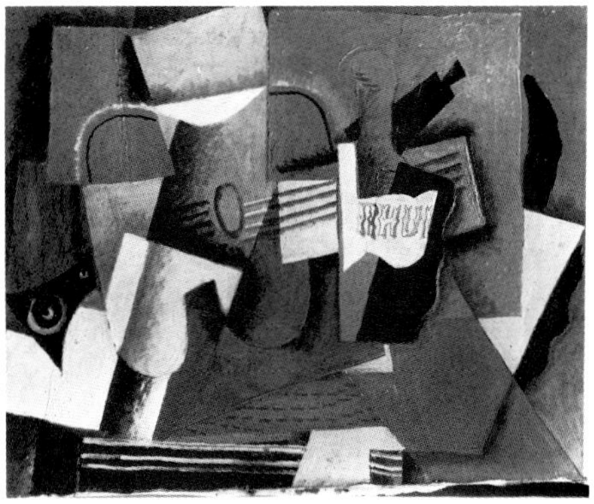

85. Braque, *Nature morte*, 1917-1918, oil on canvas. Location unknown. Photo: Archives Photographiques, Paris.

56.
Still Life with Flute
(Nature morte à la flûte)
(Duet for Flute)

1912-1913?/1914?/1917-1918?
paper, pencil, gouache, on cardboard
52 x 75 (20 1/2 x 29 1/2)
Signed, lower left: *G Braque*
(signature affixed in 1962 at time of purchase by Pulitzer)
CGP 53

Provenance
Studio of the artist (until 1916)
Sergei Diaghilev, Paris
Léonide Massine, Paris
Galerie l'Oeil, Paris (in 1961)
Collection Joseph Pulitzer, Jr., St. Louis (acquired 3 April 1962)
Present collection, 12 December 1969

Literature
Damase 1963, reproduced p. 26
Fumet 1965, reproduced color p. 55
Bernier 1967, reproduced p. 34
Carrà 1971, reproduced no. 136
Chetham 1971, no. 148, pp. 360-362, reproduced p. 361
Mangin (Worms de Romilly) 1982, no. 247, reproduced color

Exhibitions
Paris 1961, no. 13 reproduced
St. Louis 1968, no. 9
Cambridge 1971, no. 148
Bielefeld 1979, no. 170 reproduced (not in exhibition)
Paris 1982, no. 53, reproduced p. 171 (not in exhibition)

Fogg Art Museum, Cambridge, Gift of Mr. and Mrs. Joseph Pulitzer, Jr.

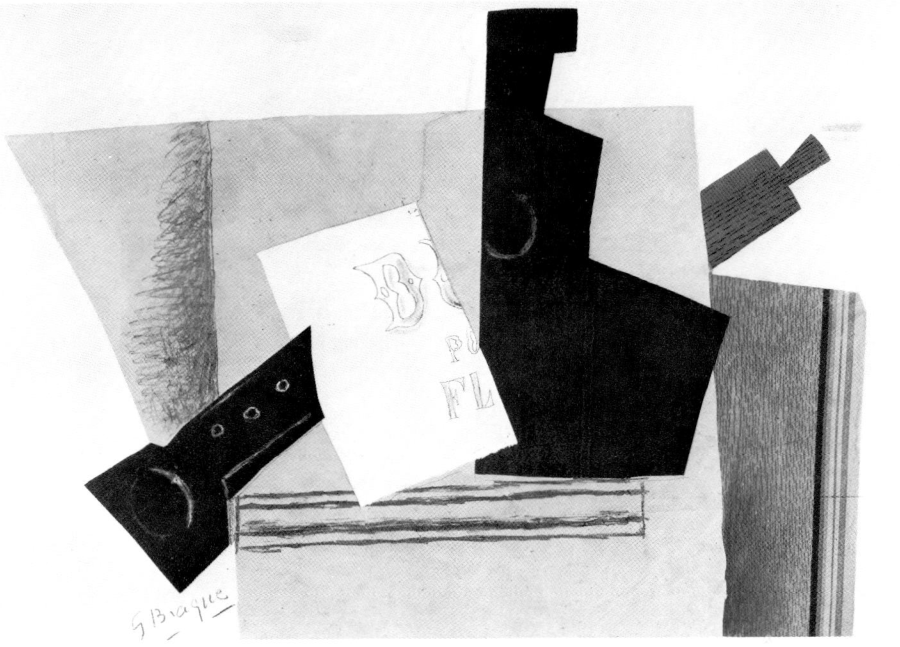

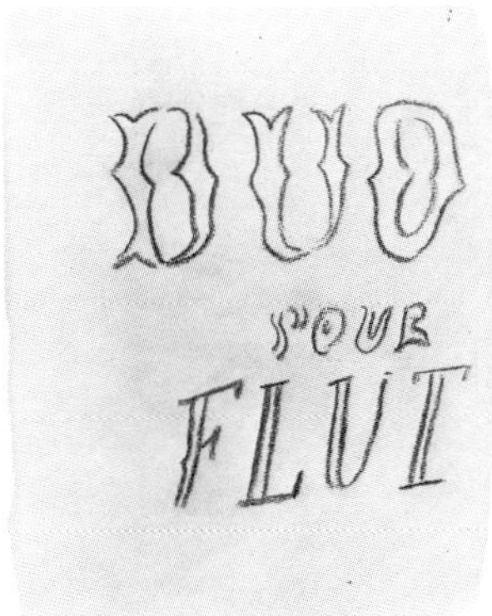

86. Braque, unused fragment with inscription "DUO POUR FLUT." Photo: Archives Laurens.

The dating of this collage presents a major problem. It is one of the handful of works where Braque commented directly about the object. Rosamond Bernier twice visited Braque in 1961 and 1962, taking *Duet for Flute* with her. She recalled that during the first of these visits Braque said of the work, "Look at it, look at this very beautiful collage! I haven't seen it since 1916. . . . I did this at the end of 1912 and January 1913. I liked it so much that I hung it in my dining room. It was still there when I came back, wounded, from the front" (Bernier 1967).

However, while the paper elements used in this collage—*faux bois,* white, and black paper—do accord with the kinds of this period, their shapings do not. In works of 1912-1913 the paper elements either are cut so as to serve as silhouetting background areas, or they are more abstract shapes, which refer to the object only by their imitation of the material of its surface. In *Duet for Flute,* however, Braque has clearly cut the various papers into the shapes of the objects being represented, for example the two components of the flute (or clarinet?) or the bottle. Furthermore, where the 1912-1913 works use multiple lines with subtle shadings in the white ground, no such passages appear in this collage.

Indeed, the closest stylistic parallels for *Duet for Flute* are the two later collages, cat. nos. 55 and 57, dating 1917-1918. This is especially true of the latter, which has not only a similarly cut-out musical instrument, but also the same compositional massings of forms at the center of the work. For these reasons we question Braque's recollection of this work, and in particular its 1912-1913 date. The collage might date from 1914, (which would allow it to be in the living room upon his return), but if so it would still fall out of any realtionship with Braque's other works of this period. In this regard, however, we should note that Picasso did make a similar cut-out black bottle in his *Glass and Bottle of Bais,* which does date from 1914 (Daix 684).

An unused fragment, also bearing the phrase *"Duo pour flut",* still exists (fig. 86). E.A.C. jr.

57.

Guitar and Clarinet
(Guitare et clarinette)

(Musical Forms; Musical Instruments)

1918
charcoal, gouache, *faux bois* paper, colored papers, corrugated cardboard, pencil, on gray-blue cardboard
76.9 x 95.3 (30 1/4 x 37 1/2)
Signed on verso
CGP 54

Provenance
Galerie Léonce Rosenberg, Paris (no. 119-57-19)
Collection Marius de Zayas
Collection Louise and Walter Arensberg, Hollywood
Present collection, 1954

Literature
Bissière 1920, reproduced pl. 4
Bulletin de l'Effort moderne, November 1925, no. 19
Raynal 1927, reproduced p. 87
Isarlov 1932, no. 229
Zervos 1933, reproduced p. 36-37
Einstein 1934, reproduced pl. L
Hope 1949, p. 64, reproduced p. 60
Arensberg Collection 1954, no. 26, reproduced color
Greenberg 1958, reproduced color p. 46
Russell 1959, pp. 21, 122, reproduced pl. 26
Richardson 1961, reproduced color pl. 16
Art International 1962, reproduced p. 41
Rosenblum 1966, p. 104, reproduced pl. 65
Haftmann 1968, reproduced p. 91
Mullins 1968, p. 86, reproduced p. 87
Carrà 1971, reproduced no. 156
Draeger 1971, reproduced color p. 129
Mangin 1973, no. 35, reproduced color
Judkins 1976, reproduced p. 447
Fortunescu 1976, reproduced pl. 23
Wescher 1979, p. 29

Exhibitions
Chicago 1939, no. 23 or 24
New York 1949, no. 18, reproduced
Edinburgh 1956, no. 46, reproduced pl. 21g
Cincinnati 1962, unnumbered, reproduced
Munich 1963, no. 54, reproduced pl. 50
New York 1964, no. 33, reproduced
Paris 1973-1, no. 61, reproduced color
Paris 1982, no. 54, reproduced color p. 173
(not in exhibition)

Philadelphia Museum of Art, The Louise and Walter Arensberg Collection

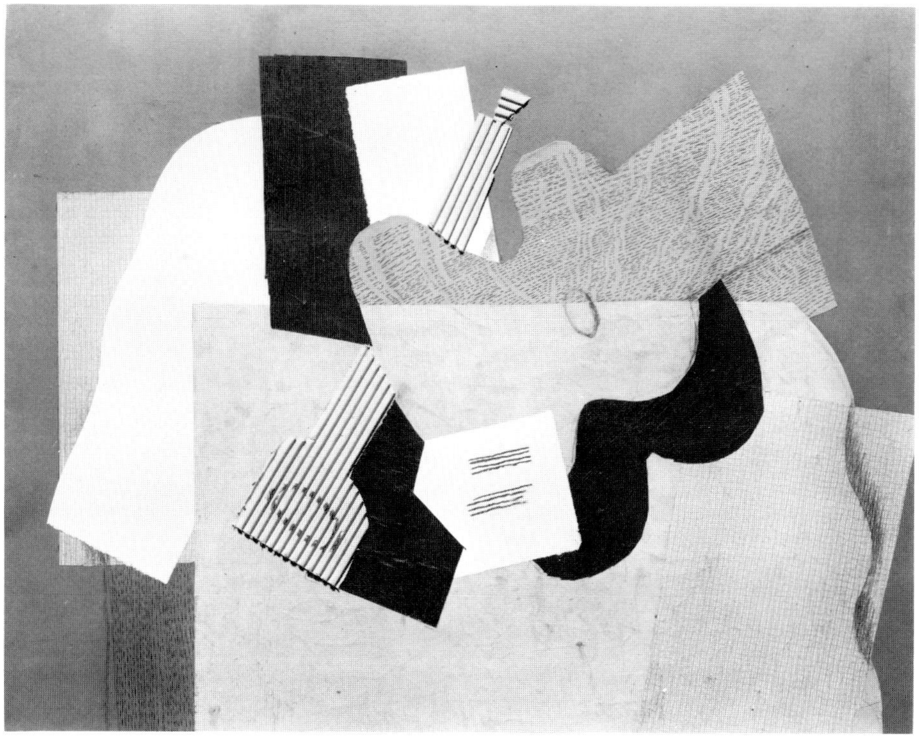

Inventory of Materials

The following summary inventory shows both the variety and frequency of use of the twelve different kinds of paper elements Braque pasted into his collages. It is interesting to note that *papier faux bois* (imitation woodgrain paper), which was the spark for the invention of this medium, appears throughout the sequence of collages, including the postwar works. Furthermore, it is employed in over 80 percent of the *papiers collés.* Braque's use of other decorative wallpapers, either *galon de papier peint* or *papier peint,* perhaps surprisingly occurs infrequently, while paper printed in solid colors appears in almost all of the works, including two where it is the sole collage element (cat. nos. 25-26). Plain white paper appears in only 20 percent of the works and is the only element in the extraordinary decoupaged composition (cat. no. 50) where cut-out elements are set against a field of tan color. We traditionally regard newspaper elements as part of a classic cubist still life, whether painted or collaged, and indeed they do occur in seventeen of the *papiers collés.* This lettered material is joined by two cinema programs and one journal; five works use cigarette packages. Twenty-two works use only one kind of material, while the five most complex pictures each use five different papers. E.A.C. jr.

PAPIER FAUX BOIS
(imitation woodgrain paper)
in 46 works

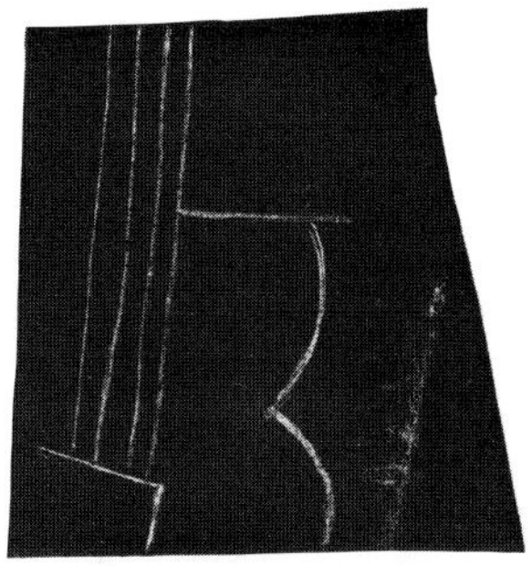

PAPER PRINTED OR DYED WITH COLOR
in 26 works

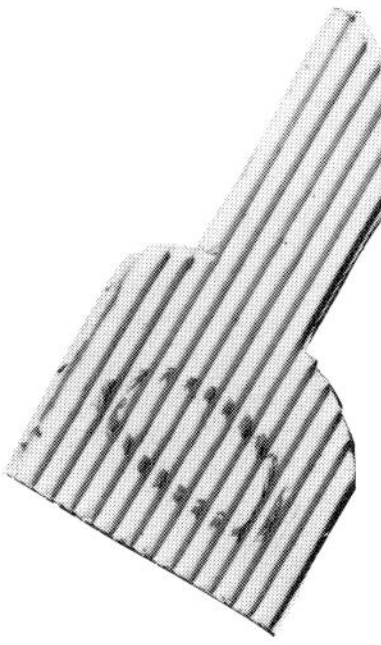

CORRUGATED CARDBOARD
in 3 works

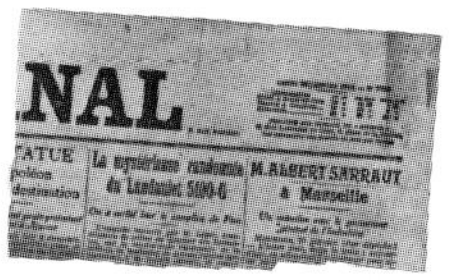

NEWSPAPER
in 17 works

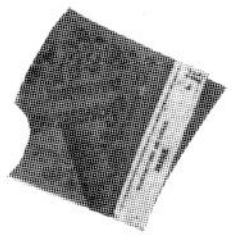

CIGARETTE PACKAGES
in 5 works

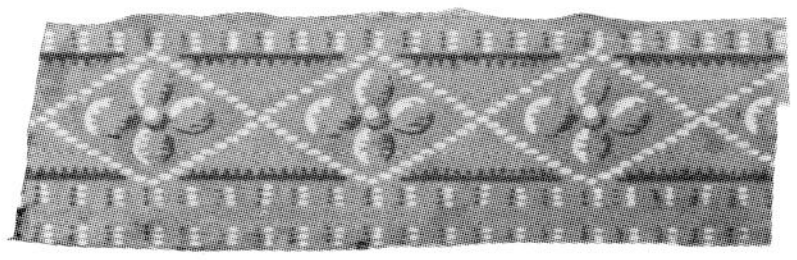

GALON DE PAPIER PEINT
(decorative border paper)
in 2 works

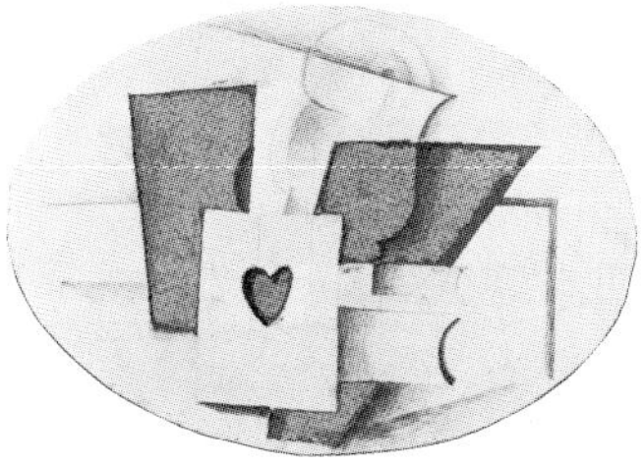

UNPAINTED WHITE PAPER
in 9 works

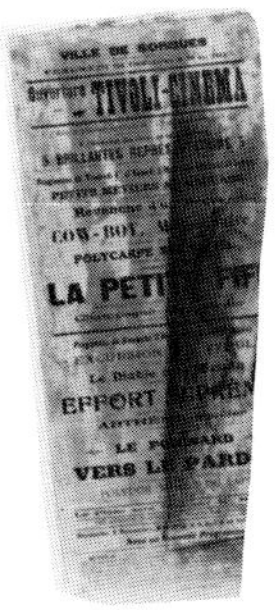

CINEMA PROGRAMS
in 2 works

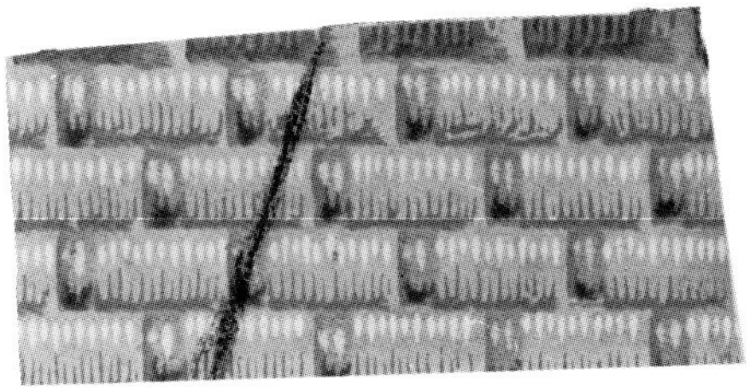

PAPIER PEINT (patterned wallpaper)
in 7 works

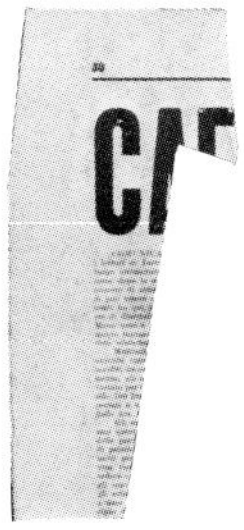

JOURNAL
in 1 work

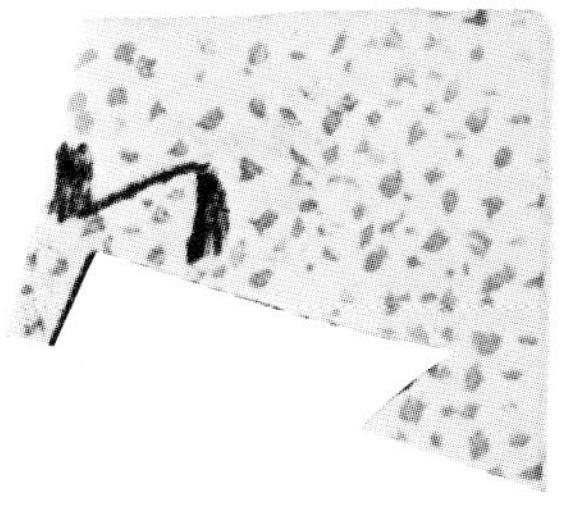

PAPER PAINTED WITH COLOR
in 4 works

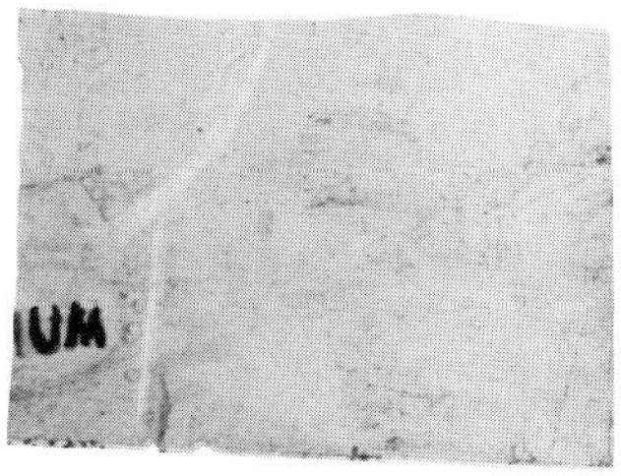

WRAPPING PAPER
in 1 work

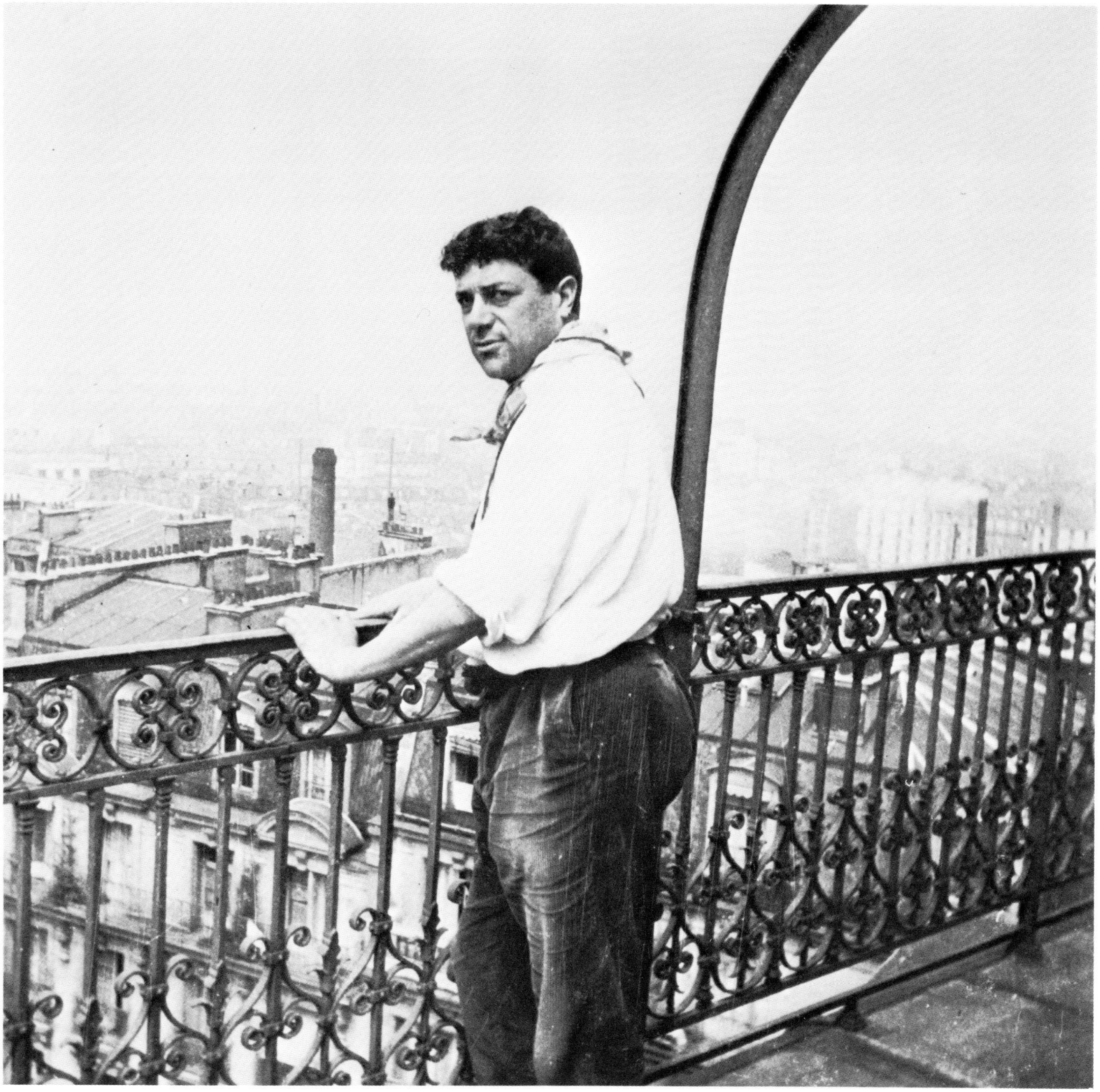

87. Georges Braque on the terrace of his studio at the Hôtel Roma in Paris at Montmartre, 1913. Photo: Archives Laurens.

GEORGES BRAQUE: CHRONOLOGY AND CRITICAL REVIEW

Trinkett Clark

1882 On 13 May, Georges Braque is born to Charles and Augustine Johanet Braque in Argenteuil-sur-Seine. Charles Braque and his father share a house-painting business in Argenteuil-sur-Seine. The family resides at 40, rue de l'Hôtel Dieu. Charles Braque is an amateur artist, often taking his son with him on sketching outings.

c.1890 In order to expand the family business, Charles Braque moves his family to Le Havre, where they reside at 33, rue Jules Lecesne.

1893 Braque enters the Lycée in Le Havre, showing a great interest in the outdoors and athletics rather than academics. He is given flute lessons by Gaston Dufy, the brother of Raoul.

c.1897 Braque begins drawing classes in the evening at the Ecole des Beaux-Arts in Le Havre, with Monsieur Courchet, first drawing from plaster casts of antique sculpture and later from models.

1899 At age seventeen, Braque withdraws from the Lycée and becomes an apprentice to one of his father's house-painting colleagues, Monsieur Roney, in Le Havre. He continues his evening classes, where he is beginning to paint.

1900 In order to reduce his three-year military requirement to one year, Braque must qualify as an artist or "artist-craftsman." He decides to continue his apprenticeship as a "peintre-décorateur" in Paris, under the guidance of Monsieur Laberthe, and resides in Montmartre (rue des Trois Frères), attending art classes at the Cours Municipal at Les Batignolles under Guignolet.

During Braque's apprenticeship, he learns the process of painting *papier faux bois* and other simulations, in order to produce the effects of marble, wood grain, and other expensive surfaces. He also learns the skill of hand-lettering and sign painting.

1901 In October, Braque begins his year of military service. Stationed in Le Havre, he obtains the rank of a non-commissioned officer.

1902 Braque and his parents agree that he should devote all of his time to his art. In late 1902 he settles in Montmartre (rue Lepic), enrolling in the Académie Humbert. He makes the acquaintance of Francis Picabia and Marie Laurencin.

1903 In the fall Braque enters the Ecole des Beaux-Arts under the tutelage of Léon Bonnat. After two months, Braque finds that he cannot tolerate the academic structure of this institution, and returns to the Académie Humbert.

During this time, Braque makes frequent visits to the Musée du Louvre, where he is attracted to ancient Egyptian and Greek sculpture, as well as the work of Corot, his favorite artist at the time, and Poussin. From visits to the Musée du Luxembourg and the galleries of Vollard and Durand-Ruel, Braque becomes familiar with the impressionists, experiencing a great affinity for the work of Monet, van Gogh, Sisley, Renoir, Seurat, and Cézanne.

1904 Summer is spent in Honfleur, where Braque meets or becomes reacquainted with Raoul and Jean Dufy (as the Dufys were from Le Havre, Braque might have known them before), Maurice Raynal, and a son of Pissarro.

In the fall, Braque leaves the Académie Humbert, renting a studio on the rue d'Orsel in order to work on his own.

1905 Braque is introduced to the work of the fauve painters at the Salon d'Automne. With his friends Raoul Dufy and Othon Friesz (also from Le Havre), he begins to move within the fauve circle.

1906 In March Braque exhibits seven paintings at the Salon des Indépendants. In the summer, he travels to Antwerp with Friesz, painting his first fauve works. After searching for an area with bright light and vivid colors, he goes in October to L'Estaque. This is the first of several visits to sites where Cézanne painted.

1907 Braque returns to Paris in the spring, entering six recent paintings in the Salon des Indépendants (all of these are sold); at the opening of the exhibition in March, he is introduced to Matisse, Derain, Marquet, Vlaminck, Von Dongen, and other artists. He spends late spring and summer at La Ciotat, returning to L'Estaque for the month of September. In October, Braque returns to Paris. Exhibits at the Salon d'Automne. Daniel-Henry Kahnweiler, a Paris dealer, purchases several pictures from him, and subsequently obtains a contract for his entire production. Braque meets Guillaume Apollinaire, who takes him to Picasso's studio where he encounters *Les demoiselles d'Avignon* (fig. 3) for the first time. This painting, as well as an exhibition of works by Cézanne at the Salon d'Automne, influences Braque in December, when he begins to paint his *Grand nu* (fig. 2) turning away from the fauve pictures of earlier years.

1908 Braque spends the summer at L'Estaque. His paintings begin to reflect the influence of Cézanne. In October, seven of his paintings are rejected by the jury of the Salon d'Automne. In November, the Galerie Kahnweiler holds a one-man exhibition featuring twenty-seven paintings by Braque, with a catalogue introduction written by Apollinaire. In the 14 November 1908 edition of *Gil Blas,* Louis Vauxcelles writes:

> Braque is a very bold young man. The striking examples set by Derain and Picasso have encouraged him. Perhaps also he has been too much obsessed by the style of Cézanne and his memories of the static art of the Egyptians. He constructs metallic and deformed figures which have a terrible oversimplification. He mistreats form, reduces everything, sites, figures and houses to geometric outlines, to *cubes.* But since he is working in good faith, let us not make fun of him. Let us wait and see.
>
> Hope, 1949, 33.

1909 In the 16 January 1909 issue of *Mercure de France* Apollinaire writes:

> Visibly [Braque] proceeds from a geometric *a priori* to which the entire field of his vision is submitted and he attempts to translate the whole thing by combinations of a few absolute forms. Before his paintings of women people have cried out in horror: "hideous, monstrous!" That sort of remark is spoken too hastily. Where we think we are looking for a feminine figure because the catalogue reads "female nude" the artist has seen only geometric harmonies which for him are a complete expression of nature. For him this female figure was merely a pretext for containing those harmonies in certain lines, and putting them into relation with certain tonalities. In these three realms he searches equally and uniquely for these harmonies. No one was less concerned than he with the psychology of his subject and I believe a stone would move him as much as a face. He has created a new personal alphabet of which each character has universal acceptance. Before declaring it to be a hideous grimace tell me if you have really grasped it, if you have understood the decorative intentions. Hope 1949, 33.

In March Braque participates in the Salon des Indépendants, entering two canvases. Louis Vauxcelles, writing about the exhibition in the 25 May 1909 edition of *Gil Blas,* calls the two landscapes "bizarreries cubiques." This is Braque's last appearance in the Salon until 1920; after meeting with increasingly unfavorable reactions, the group of artists affiliated with Kahnweiler decides not to enter works in the various salons. Summer at La Roche Guyon (another Cézanne site) and Carrières-St. Denis.

Braque and Picasso become close friends.

In December Braque paints *Nature morte, violon et cruche* (fig. 44), in which a *trompe l'oeil* nail is painted in the upper center. Henry Hope later writes of the significance of this new element:

> . . . one discovers a curiously incongruous detail—a large nail, with a cast shadow, as if it fastened the canvas to the wall.
> . . . the nail was an innovation that caused much discussion among Braque, Picasso and their friends.

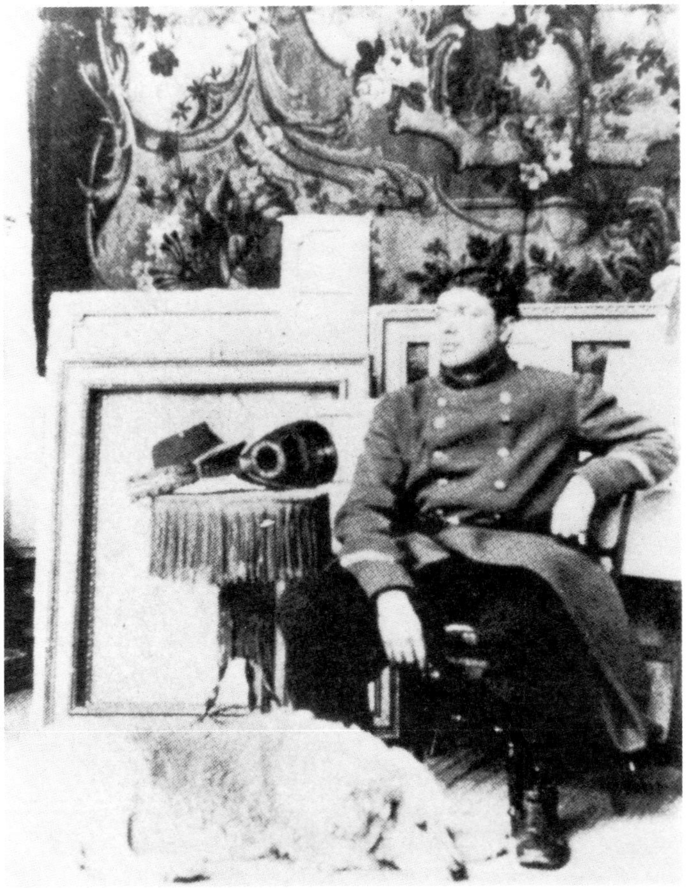

88. Braque in his studio in Paris, 1909 (?).

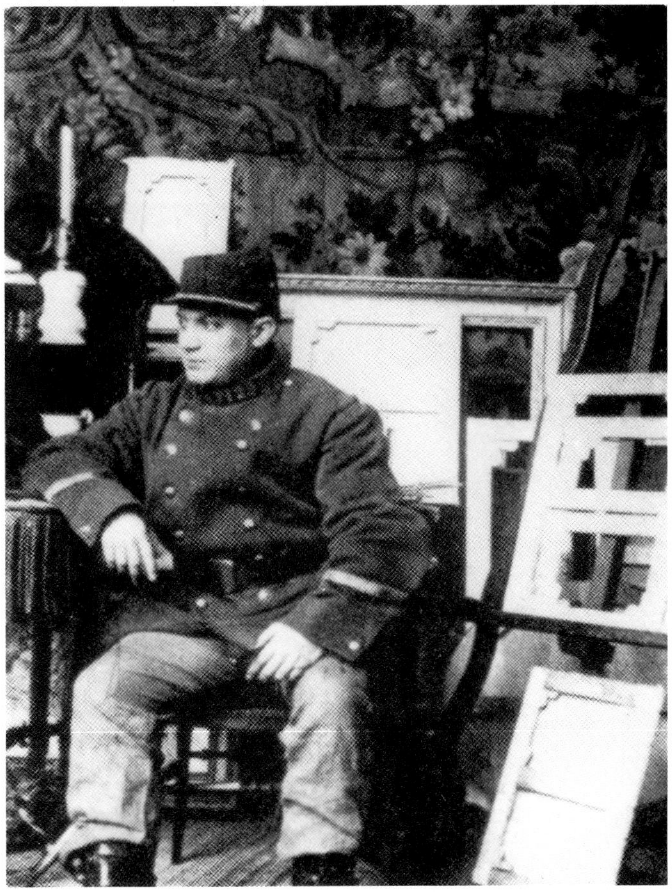

89. Picasso wearing Braque's uniform, 1909 (?).

Kahnweiler argued that this revealed a new significance in their painting. It was held to be a sudden evocation of reality, in the midst of their bold departure from material appearances. Now that we can see not only what preceded, but also what followed, it appears as a logical step toward later developments in cubism. Hope 1949, 49.

1910 Beginning of high analytical cubism.

Braque begins to put letters in his paintings (fig. 50), although of a rather free-flowing character. Summer at L'Estaque. Paints first oval pictures.

Jean Metzinger writes about Braque in the October-November issue of *Pan*:

Braque, who fashions new signs with joy, does not commit errors of taste. The new word does not deceive us! I can, without diminishing the innovative audacity of this painter, compare him to Chardin and to Lancret. Metzinger 1910.

1911 Paints *Le Portugais* (fig. 9), using stenciled letters for the first time. Hope writes of these letters:

But this serene world of formal harmonies is rudely interrupted by a group of stencilled letters and numbers. This is the first appearance of these irrelevant and conspicuous symbols which were later so widely used. . . .

Braque had known how to do hand lettering since his apprentice days, but the sudden appearance of these letters in the midst of a cubist composition can only be explained as another attempt to evoke reality— like the *trompe l'oeil* nail. It might be compared to the introduction of mechanical sounds into music, or advertising slogans into poetry. In addition to the shock value of the irrelevant BAL & 10, 40, there is also a decorative effect, and these letters were to be much used for this purpose by Picasso, Gris and most of all by Braque himself.

Hope 1949, 52-53.

Summer at Céret with Picasso.

In October, upon his return to Paris, Braque meets Henri Laurens, who will become a close lifelong friend.

In the 8 October edition of *The New York Times,* Gelett Burgess writes about cubist painting in Paris:

There is Georges Braque who paints nudes with square feet and right-angled shoulders. Before one of his weird productions, a woman with a balloon-shaped stomach, we remarked "a wild place fit for dreams but no place for mother." Hope 1949, 159.

1912* Braque marries Marcelle Lapré.

On 12 January Braque is once again at Céret. From August until mid-November (?), Braque is at Sorgues sur l'Ouvèze. Along with his wife, he lives in the villa Bel Air, on the road to Entraigues. Picasso, with his friend Eva, resides in the villa Les Clochettes.

In the beginning of August Braque and Picasso make a short trip to Marseilles: "After having bought all the *nègres* (African sculpture), and shown the town to Picasso, I returned to Sorgues where I am living. I am anxious to work . . ." wrote Braque to Daniel-Henry Kahnweiler (postcard arrived in Switzerland, where Kahnweiler was staying, on 11 August 1912).

In the beginning of September (about the 13th), Picasso makes a trip to Paris and back. It is at this point that Braque buys the *faux bois* paper in Avignon which he uses in the first *papier collé* (cat. no. 1).

Toward the end of September (?), Braque writes to Kahnweiler: "Complete calm: I am trying to profit from it as much as possible. I am working a lot. Since my arrival I have worked on a rather large oil (1.60 m), a woman in which I have innovated painting with sand. In short I am very happy to be here. Picasso told me about his trip to Paris. . . ."

*Portions of the chronology from 1912-1917 provided by Isabelle Monod-Fontaine.

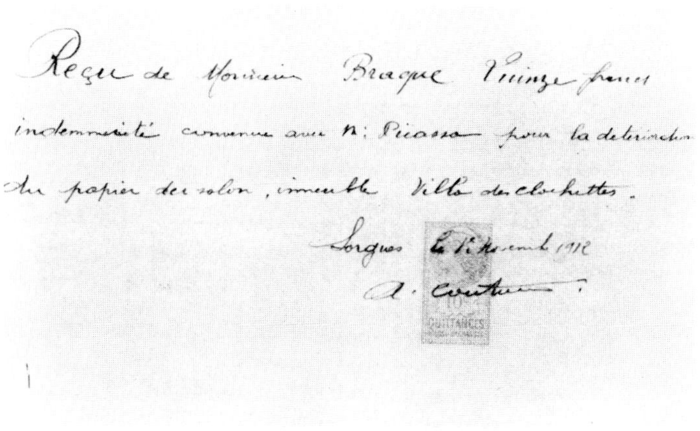

90. Receipt given to Braque for some paper which he and Picasso would use in their *papiers collés,* 1 November 1912, Sorgues.

At the beginning of October, Picasso returns to Paris. He writes almost immediately to Braque (9 October): "I am using your latest paperistic and powdery procedures. . . ."

At the end of October, Braque is still at Sorgues. He writes to Kahnweiler on 30 October: "My dear friend, I was counting on seeing you before your departure. I do not expect to return home until the same time as you on the 15th. That will be just time for me to finish what I am working on. We are having wonderful weather. Most cordially yours, G. Braque."

A month later Braque sends (from Paris) his letter/contract to Kahnweiler.

1913 Guillaume Apollinaire gives a lecture in Berlin in January at the Galerie Der Sturm. His thoughts are subsequently published in *Der Sturm* as "Die moderne Malerei." It is one of the earliest writings in which the medium of collage is mentioned.

Picasso and Braque incorporated in some of their pictures letters from labels and other printed matter, because label, notice and advertisement play a very important aesthetic role in the modern city and are well-suited for incorporation into works of art.

Apollinaire in Fry 1966, 113.

Braque leaves Paris in June.

After a visit to Picasso in Céret (where Juan Gris and Max Jacob are as well), Braque returns to Sorgues in July, and lives there until mid-November, as evidenced by several letters to Kahnweiler.

2 October 1913: "Before I leave I am sending you the paintings which I have finished. I would also like very much to see them in Paris framed and in place because here I only have frames in paper and that is not very satisfactory. It has been a long time since I have had news of Picasso. . . ."

Autumn 1913: "My departure for Paris is approaching. I would very much like to return in about three weeks so I will not begin anything more, as I need to finish the paintings and drawings, then paste afterwards."

12 November 1913: "I am working enough, I am making big drawings with which I am happy, and I have abandoned oil painting for the moment. The weather for several days now has been gray like in Paris, so I have chosen to work at night. I am well established in a barn where I have installed all the lights I need."

Guillaume Apollinaire publishes *Les peintres cubistes. Méditations esthétiques.* In his essay, Apollinaire writes:

Here, then, is Georges Braque. His role was heroic. His art calm and splendid. He is a serious craftsman. He expresses a beauty full of tenderness, and the pearly lusters of his pictures play on our senses like a rainbow. This painter is angelic.

He has taught the aesthetic use of forms so hidden that only certain poets had intimations of them. These luminous signs flare around us, but only a handful of painters have grasped their plastic significance. The work, particularly in its plainest realizations, contains a multiplicity of aesthetic elements which, no matter how new, are always in accord with the sentiment of the sublime, that which enables man to put order in chaos: what looks new must not be scorned, nor what is dirty, nor what we use, not even the imitation wood or marble of house painters. These appearances seem trivial, but when action requires, a man must begin with them.

I detest artists who are not of their time, and, just as the language of the people was for Malherbe the proper language of his period, the means of the artisan, of the house painter, should be the most vigorous material expression of painting to the artist.

Georges Braque should be called "the verifier." He has verified all the innovations of modern art, and will verify still others. Appollinaire 1913-2, 25.

Three works by Braque are included in the Armory Show in New York (which travels to Chicago and Boston), marking the first time Braque's work is seen in America.

1914 Braque spends the summer at Sorgues, and it is there that the mobilization surprises him. He is assigned to the 224th infantry regiment.

Braque and Picasso are exhibited together in New York at Alfred Stieglitz's gallery, "291."

André Salmon writes a sequel to his 1912 book *La jeune peinture française* (Paris) called *La jeune sculpture française* (not published until 1919, Paris). In it he relates the following:

The painter, Georges Braque, a fervent disciple of Picasso, comes from the class of artisans who have prospered, entrepreneurs on a considerable scale. His family painted, or saw to the painting of, the interior walls of nearly all the buildings constructed in Le Havre at the end of the last century. I am convinced that Georges Braque owes some of his most brilliant qualities to his descent from such a family.

One day he was talking with Picasso about the things that cannot be imitated in a painting. This is a favourite theme of the modern artists. Should one, if one is painting a newspaper held in someone's hands, take pains to reproduce the words PETIT JOURNAL, or reduce the business to sticking a part of the newspaper itself on to the picture? This led to praise for the skill of the house-decorators who extract large amounts of marble and precious wood from imaginary quarries and forests. . . .

Fry, 1966, 140.

1915 Kahnweiler, having been forced to leave Paris during the war because of his German citizenship, lives in Switzerland. During this "exile" he writes *Der Weg zum Kubismus,* which is published in Munich in 1920. The impact of the invention of *papiers collés* is not yet evident, but he writes:

These two artists [Picasso and Braque] are the great founders of Cubism. In the evolution of the new art, the contributions of both are intimately related, often hardly distinguishable. Friendly conversations between the two afforded the new method of painting many advances which one or the other first put into practice. Both deserve credit; both are great and admirable artists, each in his own way. Braque's art is quieter, Picasso's is nervous and turbulent. The lucid Frenchman Braque and the fanatically searching Spaniard Picasso stand together.

Kahnweiler 1915-1920, 6.

Braque is severely wounded on 11 May at Carency by an exploding shell. He is trepanned while still at the front and remains in a coma for forty-eight hours. He spends his convalescence at Sorgues. Then he is assigned to Bernay in Eure by April 1916.

In a letter dated 1 June 1915, Juan Gris writes to Kahnweiler:

You asked about Braque. He has been seriously wounded but is now out of danger. Yesterday he was brought to a hospital here [Paris]. I expect to see him tomorrow. He was hit in the head by shrapnel and has been trepanned. We knew that he had been wounded, but for a whole fortnight we did not know just what had happened. While he was on the danger list he kept it all quiet. He's a wonderful person. I have been terribly worried on his account because, as you know, I am very fond of him.

Letters of Juan Gris (1913-1927), Collected by Daniel-Henry Kahnweiler. Translated and edited by Douglas Cooper (London, 1956), 29 (no. XXXV).

1916 Braque organizes his life between Sorgues and Paris, after having been conditionally discharged from the army, and begins to recover slowly. He is awarded for his bravery with the *Croix de Guerre* and the *Légion d'Honneur.*

1917 On 15 January a banquet is organized in Paris by Braque's friends to celebrate his recovery.

Braque begins to paint again and becomes more and more friendly with Gris and Laurens. In December an article by Braque, "Pensées et réflexions sur la peinture" is published in the review *Nord-Sud* which is under the direction of his friend, Pierre Reverdy. Braque writes:

A painter trying to make a circle would only make a ring. Possibly the look of it may satisfy him but he will have doubts. The compass will restore his certainty. The *papiers collés* in my drawings have also given me a kind of certainty.

Trompe-l'oeil is due to *anecdotal* accident that makes its effect through the simplicity of the facts.

The *papiers collés,* the imitation wood—and other elements of the same nature—which I have used in certain drawings, also make their effect through the simplicity of the facts, and it is this that has led people to confuse them with *trompe-l'oeil,* of which they are precisely the opposite. They too are simple facts, but *created by the mind* and such that they are one of the justifications of a new figuration in space. Fry 1966, 147-148.

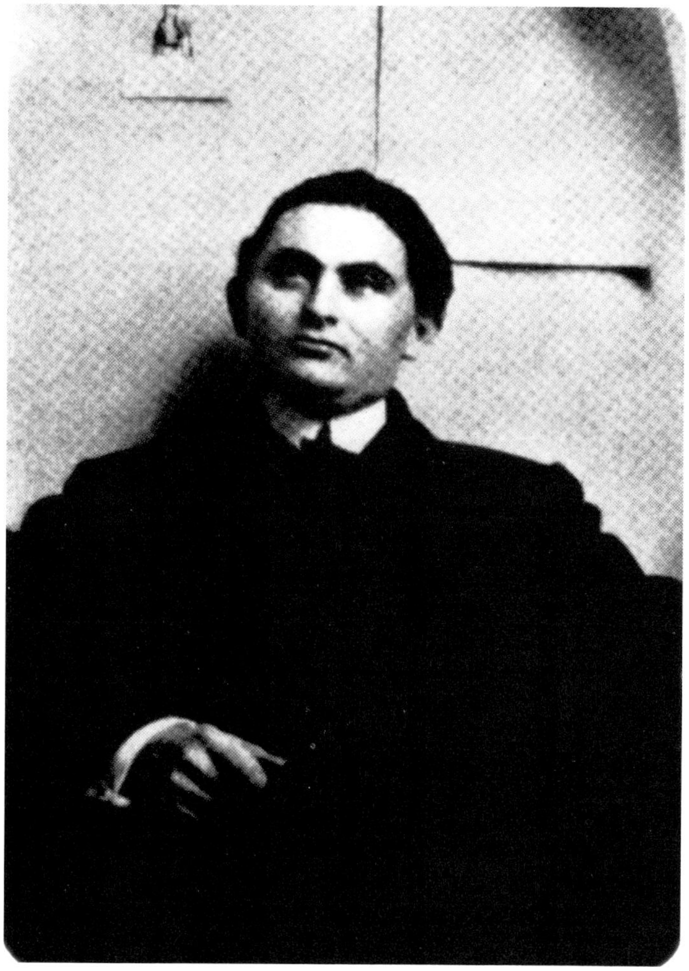

91. D.-H. Kahnweiler, photographed by Picasso in his studio at 11, boulevard de Clichy, 1912.

Léonce Rosenberg becomes Braque's dealer in the absence of Kahnweiler.

1918 Rosenberg opens his Galerie de l'Effort Moderne, where many of the cubist artists exhibit their work.

Braque's work at this time reflects a growing interest in color; his canvases are filled with large flat areas of varied hues.

1919 *Exposition Braque* at the Galerie de l'Effort Moderne, 5 to 31 March.

1920 Daniel-Henry Kahnweiler opens the Galerie Simon in Paris, once again serving as Braque's dealer.

Braque executes his first permanent sculpture, using plaster.

Roger Bissière publishes *Georges Braque*:

> Braque in fact inherited methods and tricks of the trade which are perhaps the fundamental essence of painting, or at any rate its most solid basis. He spent his youth watching others patiently laboring to create imitation wood or marble, he was taught the complicated art of applying paint in thin and thick coats, he learnt from his father's workmen not only the science of mixing colors so as to produce a particular tone, but also how best to apply it, and finally he mastered lettering and line-work.
>
> . . . Braque is perhaps the first of the moderns to sense the poetry inherent in fine craftsmanship, in a work elaborated with love and patience and owing nothing to any preconceived sensibility. He realizes that a human handiwork, long and lovingly caressed by its maker will in the end bear traces of the care which attended its creation and reveal some indefinable but touching sign of humanity."
>
> Bissière in Cooper 1972, 36 and 37.

Léonce Rosenberg publishes *Parlons peinture* (Leyden); *Le cubisme et la tradition* (Paris).

1921 *1re vente Kahnweiler,* Paris, Hôtel Drouot, 13-14 June, no Braque *papiers collés* included, but this was the first of four sales which dispersed the collection of Kahnweiler.

Maurice Raynal publishes *Georges Braque* which reproduces *Le Courrier* and *Compotier et verre.*

2me vente Kahnweiler, Paris, Hôtel Drouot, 17-18 November (public viewing 16 November), one *papier collé* (cat. no. 36) included among thirty-eight works by Braque.

Collection Uhde—Tableaux Modernes, Paris: Hôtel Drouot, 30 May 1921, one *papier collé* (cat. no. 1) is sold.

1922 Braque moves from Montmartre to Montparnasse, where he lives on the avenue Reill.

3me vente Kahnweiler, Paris, Hôtel Drouot, 4 July 1922, eighteen works by Braque, three *papiers collés* sold.

1923 *Collection Henri Kahnweiller, Tableaux Modernes, Quatrième et Dernière Vente,* Paris, Hôtel Drouot, 7-8 May (public exhibition 6 May). Nos. 1-56 were works on paper by Braque. Among these were twenty-one (according to Monod-Fontaine) *papiers collés* which included the following: 1) *Nature morte* (cat. no. 19); 2) *L'as de pique* (cat. no. 18); 3) *La bouteille de Marc* (cat. no. 21); 4) *La guitare* (cat. no. 22); 5) *L'Arlequin* (cat. no. 5); 6) *Nature morte* (probably cat. no. 45); 8) *L'as de trèfle* (cat. no. 30); 9) *Le damier* (cat. no. 31); 10) *Le violon* (probably cat. no. 27); 11) *La guitare* (cat. no. 29); 12) *Nature morte* (probably cat. no. 33); 13) *Violon et pipe* (cat. no. 38); 14) *Flûte et verre* (cat. no. 28); 18) *Le compotier* (cat. no. 2); 19) *L'as de pique* (probably cat. no. 10); 21) *Le bock* (cat. no. 17); 37) one of nineteen drawings from lot 22-40 (cat. no. 8—according to Douglas Cooper); 39) one of nineteen drawings from lot 22-40 (cat. no. 14); 43) one of six drawings from lot 41-46 (cat. no. 11); 46) one of six drawings from lot 41-46 (cat. no. 6).*

*Lot 47-56 included ten drawings among which there were several *papiers collés* (according to the sales catalogue). I have been unable to determine which of these ten works were actually *papiers collés.*

1924 Paul Rosenberg becomes Braque's dealer; holds exhibition of Braque's works from 2 to 21 May.

1925 Diaghilev commissions Braque to make the décor for the ballet *Zephyre et Flore.*

1930 Louis Aragon writes "La peinture au défi," which accompanies an exhibition of collages presented by the Galerie Goemans in Brussels. Only one *papier collé* by Braque is exhibited (cat. no. 43), but Aragon's essay is really the first major publication which focuses solely on the medium/technique and history of collage.

1931 Christian Zervos writes "Le classicisme de Braque," *Cahiers d'Art* 6(1931): 35-40.

Tristan Tzara writes "Le papier collé ou le proverbe en peinture," *Cahiers d'Art* 6(1931): 61-74:

> The *papier collé,* with so many different aspects, marks in the evolution of painting, the most poetic and revolutionary moment, an impulse moving toward the most viable hypothesis, a great intimacy with daily realities, the invincible affirmation of the temporary and temporal and perishable matters, the sovereignty of the idea. Tzara 1931, 64.

Braque begins to spend summers in Varengeville, where he builds a house.

1932 Christian Zervos writes "Georges Braque et le développement du Cubisme," *Cahiers d'Art* 7(1932): 13-27, mostly focusing upon Braque's later works.

In the spring issue of *Orbes* George Isarlov writes "Georges Braque," in which he includes a list of works by Braque from 1906-1929; a list of exhibitions from 1906-1929; a list of collections containing works by Braque; and a short bibliography. This article was also released in a separate volume as *Georges Braque* (Paris: José Corti).

1933 *Georges Braque,* Basel: Kunsthalle Basel, 9 April to 14 May 1933. This marks the first major retrospective exhibition of Braque's work (183 items).

Christian Zervos publishes a special issue of *Cahiers d'Art* devoted to Braque on the occasion of the exhibition in Basel. Essays by Apollinaire, Roger Bissière, André Breton, Jean Cassou, Blaise Cendrars, H. E. Ede, Carl Einstein, A. Lhote, André Salmon, A. Soffici, and Zervos.

1934 Carl Einstein publishes *Georges Braque,* in which he writes about the significance of the *papiers collés*:

> Through this medium, the painter succeeded in separating the vision of forms from the conventional components of objects. At the same time, the "collages" signified the end of the analytical phase of cubism. Braque was pushed toward this process by the need to create a synthetic form, independent of professional tricks.
>
> These works, whose importance is still unrecognized by most people, contain besides a very significant element. These "papiers collés" exhibit a total indifference with regard to technique; they constitute a rupture with painting's "beau morceau," a break which took place at a moment when, before a painting, people only wondered with more or less competence if it was well or badly painted. Paintings had finished being despiritualized, transformed into trinkets. But the work of art which succeeds from the technical point of view, the painting whose craft is praised first, represents in human terms, only ineptitude, devoid of importance. How often technical prejudice has obstructed the way toward original creation; technical success constitutes a limit in this sense, that emotion is translated into painting, only in the measure that the means of the craft allow it. . . . technical "successes" appear to us as rigid "belle peinture," scarcely capable of expressing elementary emotions, and in front of which pain sinks to stupidity and vision is devalued to dilettantism. It is from this overestimation of the technical factors that an inept aesthetic idealism was born, art for inhuman art.
>
> It is precisely in the "papiers collés" that one destroyed the technical subterfuge and attempted to reduce paintings to their simplest vision. One sensed that wherever "belle peinture" showed its teeth, spontaneous intuition and vision were "fichus" [done for]. In these "papiers collés," vision triumphed from the technical success. The way was now more widely open for the advent of a visionary primitivism. Einstein, 1934, 101.

1936 Alfred H. Barr, Jr., writes in the exhibition catalogue *Cubism and Abstract Art:*

> The development of Cubism during its first six years from 1906 to 1912 has been called analytical because of the progressive tearing apart or disintegrating of natural forms. Throughout this progression color had been gradually eliminated, especially in the work of Braque and Picasso; and the method of applying paint had been generally in the Cézanne-Impressionist tradition of hatching or flecking combined with frequent plain or unpainted surfaces as in Cézanne watercolors or oils. But in the midst of this tradition of technical modesty, heresies began to appear, mostly through the inventiveness of Braque. . . . As early as 1910 in a still life he had introduced a foreshortened nail with an illusionistic shadow, a trick, a *trompe-l'oeil.* In the following year he began to paint imitation textures and letters. . . . Sometimes the letters were associated with a newspaper or a sheet of music but as often they formed fragmentary independent words. These textures and letters contributed not merely to the variety of forms and surfaces but also to what might be called Cubist realism—that is, an emphasis not upon the reality of the represented objects but upon the reality of the painted surface. . . . [The] texture further adds to their independent reality so they may be considered not a breaking down or analysis, but a building up or synthesis. The difference in point of view is made clear by the addition in 1912 of *collage,* the pasting of strips of paper, bus tickets, newspapers, playing cards etc. upon the canvas as part of the composition. This was a logical culmination of the interest in simulating textures

and a further and complete repudiation of the convention that a painter was honor-bound to achieve the reproduction of a texture by means of paint rather than by the short cut of applying the texture itself to his canvas. In this way, paradoxically, the Cubists, having destroyed in their paintings the image of the natural world, began to apply to their paintings actual fragments of the natural world. Barr 1936, 78.

1939 *Georges Braque Retrospective Exhibition,* the first major traveling retrospective of Braque's works in the United States; four *papiers collès* are included. Essays by Henry McBride, Duncan Phillips, and James Johnson Sweeney. Begins sculpting in stone.

1940 Braque spends the spring in Varengeville. After the German invasion, he goes to Limousin, and the Pyrenees. In the fall Braque returns to Paris, where he stays for the duration of the war.

1943 Albert E. Gallatin publishes *Georges Braque, Essay and Bibliography* (dedicated to Brancusi), in which he writes of Braque's *papiers collés:*

> . . . Braque began to experiment with pictures entirely composed of pieces of paper pasted on cardboard, black paper, colored papers, some containing designs, pieces of newspaper, fragments of wall paper, and so on, the composition thus created being completed with deft touches of charcoal; these in time became known as *papiers-collés* or *collages.* . . . Many of these *collages* of Braque are perfect expressions of his genius; he once told the writer that he considered them to rank among his choicest work. Such an example as . . . "Le Courrier," or "The Package of Tobacco," is in the purest French tradition of taste and elegance. It contains the undiluted essence of his rare art at its best and fairly breathes distinction and style, the latter quality, no doubt, being the crowning glory of genuine aesthetic expression. The shapes and moulds which Braque employed in these creations, as well as in his paintings of this period, were so strangely beautiful and unknown, that Apollinaire was moved to say that only certain poets had surmised them.
> Gallatin 1943, n.p.

1945 Braque is made an officer of the Légion d'Honneur.

1946 Jean Paulhan publishes *Braque le patron* in which he quotes Braque:

> I attempted to obtain relief, without trompe-l'oeil. I was told: it is sufficient to use shadows. No, what counts at first sight, it is the idea that one makes for oneself. If I set a piece of white paper on this blotter, I see it before I see the blotter. I see it in relief. Upon that basis, I searched. I made some sculpture in paper, and when Picasso wrote me, he called me: my old friend Vilbure [Wilbur]. Because of Wright. It made him think of airplanes. Then, I introduced sculpture on canvas. These were my first *papiers collés.* With them, color came back to me all at once. I no longer had to force it. The struggle was always there, but it took place without me, on the canvas. Ah, I was very happy. Paulhan 1946, 37.

1948 Douglas Cooper writes *Braque: Paintings, 1909-1947:*

> Cubism was an attempt to penetrate by plastic means to the very essence of objects by representing them not as they appear on a given day and at a given time, but as they exist constantly in themselves and in the human mind.
>
> This preoccupation explains the Cubists' choice of subject-matter. For since they were creating a new pictorial language which would allow them to represent their subjects completely, it was simpler to begin with glasses, bowls, bottles, and musical instruments. To these straightforward inanimate objects Braque has remained true. . . . No single painter has lavished more care and technical mastery on describing in terms of oil paint the unassuming objects which compose our daily life. No painter has loved them more or known them better. Though Braque works with his intelligence rather than with his passions, his art is neither devoid of lyricism nor of sensuousness. . . . Braque, too, knows better perhaps than anyone today the importance of tactile values. "Ce n'est pas assez de faire voir ce qu'on peint. Il faut encore le faire toucher." No one has a greater sense of *matière* and how it can be varied: for instance, his brilliantly evocative use of pasted papers in the period 1910-1914, his use of lettering, newspapers and sheets of music, the ever-varied though recurrent use of 'graining' in marble and wood, the sand or sawdust which is often mixed with his paint.
> Cooper 1948, 6.

1949 Henry Radford Hope, in the catalogue for the *Georges Braque* exhibition at the Cleveland Museum of Art and the Museum of Modern Art, New York, writes about *papier collé:*

> Who made the first collage? This is a question which will never find a satisfactory answer unless it

is stated in the same evolutionary terms. For it was in this atmosphere of cubist theory and under the same impulses that the first papiers collés or collages were made. Picasso, whose extraordinary talent and passion make him as much a draftsman as a painter, and as much a sculptor as a draftsman, had many times experimented with sculpture. At that moment he had been experimenting with painted metal and possibly other materials. Braque in the meantime had been making paper sculpture, folding it into shapes like certain geometric details in his paintings. None of these has survived but we can guess what they looked like from the fact that Picasso in a letter . . . addressed Braque as *"Mon vieux Vilbure,"* referring to Wilbur Wright. These paper sculptures seem to have suggested possible adaptations to painting which led to the making of the first collage.

As Braque remembers it, this was at Sorgues in September of 1912. Picasso had already returned to Paris. He and Marcelle stayed on at the *Villa Bel Air.* His eye was attracted by some wallpaper at an Avignon shop, printed to resemble the close grain of quartered oak. He bought some, took it to the studio and began experimenting with it. The first composition he made with this papier collé or glued-on paper, was on a sheet of drawing paper about two feet high, upon which he pasted the strips of the wood-grain paper. He then drew a simple composition in charcoal. He sketched a bunch of grapes, a goblet, and beneath the grapes a suggestion of a compote dish upon a table. One of the strips was placed at the bottom where it suggests the table drawer. Another was neatly cut out to fit the curve of the fruit bowl. The drawing was extended across some of the pasted strips and the letters ALE and BAR were added.

Soon Braque made other collages, at first preferring to use only black strips, as in the *Black and White Collage*. Later he added newspaper, sometimes cutting it into the shape of a guitar. Picasso was quick to follow the device; indeed it is possible he may already have produced collages in material other than paper.

Braque, then, made the first papier collé, but who knows what discussions preceded it, what mutual ideas and inspiration, what forgotten remarks or sketches led up to the discovery?

Hope 1949, 60, 62, 64 (continuous).

In the preface to this exhibition catalogue, Jean Cassou writes:

Picasso's cubism is Spanish: one occasion among others which he has seized, and will continue to seize, for the affirmation of his imperious and inexhaustible, fantastic and provocative genius. Braque's cubism, on the other hand, is French: a manifestation of unified personality, a search for reason and for method, an expression of a natural and naturally exquisite taste. The collages of the former are a kind of paradox as to the fundamentals of the painter's art; those of the latter reveal only his fervent and modest love of the materials in question, his submissiveness to whatever they inspire.

Hope 1949, 7.

1951 Braque is made a commander in the Légion d'Honneur.

1952 Braque is commissioned by the Musée du Louvre to paint a ceiling for the room housing Etruscan art.

1954 Dora Vallier writes "Braque, la peinture et nous" in *Cahiers d'Art* (1954): 13-24. The text of this article appears again in *G. Braque* (Basel: Editions Beyeler, 1968). In this publication Braque speaks of color and the *papiers collés:*

The final grasp of colour came about with the 'papiers collés.' This is a fact which critics have never really understood. There it was possible to clearly dissociate colour from form and to see its independence in relation to form. And that was the main point: colour affects the beholder simultaneously with form, but has nothing to do with it. I did my first papiers collés in 1914 before I went off to the war. How did I come by the idea? But it's not an "idea." I don't know what to call it. It's a sort of revelation. I wrote in my notebooks: "Science progresses by accumulating repetitions." Precisely in this sense, what I call revelation is the opposite extreme of scientific discovery. . . . true discovery, as I understand it, can only be made outside science. When you have science, you have things reaching their predestined goal, there is no revelation. . . . You see, when I was very close to Picasso, there was a time when we had difficulty in distinguishing our own canvasses. Later, when the revelation had become deeper, differences appeared. Revelation is the only thing that no-one can take away from you. Braque 1968, n.p.

Braque executes a series of stained glass windows for a church at Varengeville.

1956 Braque is awarded a Doctorate honoris causa at Oxford University.

Braque's health begins to decline.

1958 Clement Greenberg writes "The Pasted Paper Revolution."

The collage played a pivotal role in the evolution of Cubism, and Cubism had, of course, a pivotal role in the evolution of modern painting and sculpture. As far as I know, Braque has never explained quite clearly what induced him, in 1912, to glue a piece of imitation wood-grain paper to the surface of a drawing. Nevertheless, his motive, and Picasso's in following him (assuming that Picasso did follow him in this), seems quite apparent by now—so apparent that one wonders why those who write on collage continue to find its origin in nothing more than the Cubists' need for renewed contact with "reality."

. . . [Braque] made his first collage, *Fruit Bowl,* by pasting three strips of imitation wood-grain wallpaper to a sheet of drawing paper on which he then charcoaled a rather simplified Cubist still-life and some *trompe-l'oeil* letters. Cubist space had by this time become even shallower, and the actual picture surface had to be identified more emphatically than before if the illusion was to be detached from it. Now the corporeal presense of the wallpaper pushed the lettering itself into illusioned depth by force of contrast. But at this point the declaration of the surface became so vehement and so extensive as to endow its flatness with far greater power of attraction. The *trompe-l'oeil* lettering, simply because it was inconceivable on anything but a flat plane, continued to suggest and return to it. And its tendency to do so was further encouraged by the placing of the letters in terms of the illusion, and by the fact that the artist has inserted the wallpaper strips themselves partly inside the illusion of depth by drawing upon and shading them. The strips, the lettering, the charcoaled lines and the white paper begin to change places in depth with one another, and a process is set up in which every part of the picture takes its turn at occupying every plane, whether real or imagined, in it. The imaginary planes are all parallel to one another; their effective connection lies in their common relation to the surface; wherever a form on one plane slants or extends into another it immediately springs forward. The flatness of the surface permeates the illusion, and the illusion itself re-asserts the flatness. The effect is to fuse the illusion with the picture without derogation of either—in principle.

Greenberg 1958, 48.

A major exhibition of works by Braque is held at the Venice Biennale (109 works).

1959 John Russell writes *Georges Braque,* in which he discusses the invention of the *papier collé:*

. . . the two years before the war were unprecedentedly rich in technical invention. Much of this invention flowed logically from the introduction of flat forms (stencilled letters initially) into the pictures painted in 1911. But the letters were not important merely for their flatness: there was also the consideration that they were visitor-objects, intruders from the world of everyday fact. This gave them a double importance for painters whose aim was to produce pictures which would co-exist with nature on terms of equality. In the struggle to achieve this, the traditional blandishments of the illusionist-painter had been discarded, one by one; the hermetic-cubist pictures which eventually resulted contrived, none the less, to give a full and profound experience both of space and of the sensuous and tactile reality of objects. Colour, was, however, the great casualty of these procedures; and so, when Picasso and Braque settled down to work at Sorgues, near Avignon, in July 1912, their main object was to find a valid way of re-introducing into their pictures an element of constructive colour. That colour and form should be dissociated was axiomatic, and must somehow be demonstrated.

. . . both painters were anxious . . . to arrive at a less penitential variety of picture-substance without relapsing into the trumpery attractions, as they saw them, of *la belle peinture.* Neither Braque nor Picasso was of a nature to keep for long to the total sobriety of *matière* which is characteristic of hermetic cubism. And as Braque has always had an almost religious regard for the original substances from which the world is made up . . . he began at this time to mix alien matter into his pigments: ashes from his stove, sand, wood-shavings, metal-filings, tobacco. But the notion that colour *is* texture did not solve the immediate problem, though it gave Braque a new instrument, and one which he has used to marvellous effect in more recent times. Something other than the cross-breeding of paint was clearly needed; and it was in the autumn of 1912, after Picasso had left Sorgues, that Braque hit on the solution. . . . We can really only appreciate the originality of [*Fruit-Dish and Glass*] if we remember the kind of painting which was most admired, in 1912, by the grandees of the day: the sumptuous Edwardian manipulations of paint, the dressed-up and high-lit fraudulence.

The *Fruit-Dish and Glass* which Braque drew and constructed in September 1912, is technically one of the most un-sumptuous pictures ever set before the public; it consists merely of a number of strips of wallpaper, cut and pasted on to a sheet of white paper, with a minimum of charcoal drawing to relate them to one another and to the composition as a whole. . . . In so far as, in this revolutionary work, the false has been made true (the "imitation," i.e., been regenerated as a "true" account of the experience of wood), the *Fruit-Dish and Glass* has an almost philosophical importance in the history of art. More empirically, it meant that "real" matter could thenceforward be introduced into paintings. Not merely would such intruder-objects not be "incongruous," but they would present an entirely new source of interplay between art and reality.

Braque was extremely scrupulous, not to say precautionary, in his use of the new method. Where Picasso's instinctive dynamism led him to an ever greater exuberance in the exploitation of the *papier collé,* Braque rarely used more than a telling minimum of charcoal drawing in any picture which included pasted paper; and, in general his *papiers collés* are tranquil, and at times even seraphic, in tone. . . . Artists have striven throughout history to provide a unique experience which cannot be counterfeited or experienced through any other means; and here,in the *papiers collés* executed between September 1912 and the outbreak of war, Braque proves that this experience can be made up of the humblest of elements, and that those elements can turn out, by the intensity of their transformation, to have as great an effect upon us as any of the tours-de-force of *la belle peinture.*

Russell 1959, 17-19.

John Golding publishes *Cubism: A History and an Analysis, 1907-1914,* in which he writes:

The invention of *collage* struck the most violent blow yet at traditional painting, and particularly at the idealized and romantic conception of the "work of art" as the expression not only of technical skill but also almost of some absolute beauty. Now the Cubist painters were constructing works of art from odd bits of material—one might almost say from bits of rubbish—generally considered to have no aesthetic value, and not even to serve any good or useful purpose. And the invention of *collage* was, to a large extent, a revolt against slickness of brushwork and other forms of technical facility. Sabartés quotes Picasso as saying, "we sought to express reality with materials we did not know how to handle, and which we prized precisely because we knew their help was not indispensable to us, that they were neither the best nor the most adequate."

. . . *collage* was the logical outcome of the Cubists' conception of their works as self-contained, constructed objects. For the Cubist *collages* and *papiers collés* are in a sense exactly that—objects built up of various different substances and materials, a protest against the conventional oil painting proudly displayed on an easel or elaborately framed on a wall. . . .

It is, however, necessary to make a distinction between *collage* in general and the Cubists' use of a particular kind of *collage,* namely *papier collé.* It is characteristic that Picasso should have invented *collage,* which was subsequently to be used by Dadaists as a weapon to destroy all art, and by the Surrealists to achieve the most disconcerting and disturbing of psychological effects, while Braque should have been the author of the first *papier collé,* an equally original pictorial technique at the service of more purely formalistic ends.

. . . the fragments of *papier collé* . . . can be said to exist on three levels. They are flat, coloured, pictorial shapes. They represent or suggest certain objects in the picture by analogies of colour and texture or by the additions of keys or clues. Thirdly, and this is the aspect of *papier collé* that most relates it to other forms of Cubist *collage,* the pieces of paper exist as themselves, that is to say that one is always conscious of them as solid, tactile pieces of extraneous matter incorporated into the picture and emphasizing its material existence. . . .

But it should be emphasized that while *papier collé* involved new methods of work and intitiated almost at once a new phase in the art of Picasso and Braque, it did not involve any fundamental change of aesthetic. *Papier collé* was, in part at any rate, an experiment designed to solve certain problems that the painters were concerned with in their creation of the style. It was not a fortuitous discovery that altered their view of the world around them, but rather a technical invention that conditioned the appearance of their paintings. Or, to put it differently, while *papier collé* affected their pictorial vision, the nature of the movement remained unchanged. Cubism continued to be an art of realism; its subject-matter remained the same, as did the interests and intentions of the painters. It has already been seen to what extent *collage* and *papier collé* were the natural result of the painters' aesthetic beliefs. As new techniques they speeded up the natural reaction from an austere, complex form of art towards a simpler, clearer kind of painting into which sensuous values could be re-introduced.

Golding 1968, 103-106, 117-118.

1960 Robert Rosenblum writes *Cubism and Twentieth Century Art,* discussing Braque's discovery of 1912:

If collage, with its material references to nonartistic realities, acted as an antidote to the growing illegibility of so many Cubist works of 1911, it nevertheless enriched considerably the paradoxes involved in the Cubist dialectic between art and reality. It effected, moreover, a profound reorganization of the very structure of Cubist painting. In the first place, the size of these clippings is now larger than those increasingly small and diffuse pictorial units of 1911, and therefore begins to establish a simpler and more readily grasped pattern of fewer and bolder shapes. Thus, in opposition to the painted works preceding them, these early collages are compositionally lucid and extremely restricted in the number of their pictorial elements. But, more important still, the technique of pasting so strongly emphasizes the two-dimensional reality of the picture surface that even the few vestiges of traditional illusionism clinging to earlier Cubist painting—the vibrant modeling in light and dark, the fragmentary diagonals that create a deceptive space—could not survive for long. Rapidly, the luminous shimmer and the oblique disposition of planes in earlier Cubism were to be replaced by a new syntax in which largely unshaded planes were to be placed parallel to the picture surface. In the case of actual collage, the placement was quite literally on top of the opaque picture surface, thereby controverting another fundamental principle of Western painting since the *quattrocento,* if not earlier— namely, that the picture plane was an imaginary transparency through which an illusion was seen. Rosenblum 1960, 70.

A Braque retrospective exhibition is held at the Kunsthalle in Basel.

1961 John Richardson writes *Georges Braque,* in which he discusses the significance of the invention of *papier collé:*

The advantage of *papier collé* was that it enabled [Braque] to separate the pictorial functions of form, as represented by drawing, and colour as represented by pieces of cut paper; it also enabled him to represent an object . . . by an exact equivalent as itself. At the same time, it opened the door to a new range of tactile effects, injected an extra measure of reality into pictures and undermined the cult of *belle peinture* by establishing the artists' right to make a work of art with the humblest materials. Going still further, this discovery meant that Braque was able to cross the traditional barrier between sculpture and painting, because his picture became what he and Picasso called a *tableau-objet*—that is to say, something which is not a mirror-image of nature or a wall-decoration, but an autonomous object with an identity of its own.

Instead of being acclaimed for his inventiveness and daring, Braque was accused by colleagues and critics alike of defiling the noble medium of oil-paint and of perversely ennobling the tricks and materials of a decorator. Granted, Braque . . . paved the way unintentionally for many of the freakish and frivolous experiments in texture and *matière* which plague us today: the burnt burlap of Burri, the sandy wastes of Tapies, the torn blue-jeans of Arthur Dove, or the stuffed birds of Rauschenberg. But, by and large, Braque's imaginative approach has enriched and widened the artist's technique and been responsible for many valuable developments in the work of men as disparate as Gris, Laurens, Boccioni, Schwitters, Arp, Ernst, Miró and de Staël. Richardson 1961, 17-18.

The Musée du Louvre holds an exhibition, *L'atelier de Braque.*

1962 Harriet Janis and Rudi Blesh write *Collage: Personalities, Concepts, Techniques,* in which they say:

The violent shock has faded from cubist collage and a kind of mellow beauty has taken its place—a measure of the revolution in seeing that it helped to win. Today it is classic in every sense, yet has not become dated as its newspaper clippings have. It constantly yields new meanings. Its principles and patterns are constantly being discovered by new generations of artists. Its drama of *vrai et faux* is the eternal drama engaging the generations. Georges Braque was clear about this. He knew that the bits of glued paper and imitation wood were compositional facts. Janis and Blesh 1962, 24.

1963 Braque dies on 31 August at the age of eighty-one. A state funeral is held in the Cour Carrée du Louvre, at which André Malraux makes an address. Braque is buried at Varengeville.

A retrospective exhibition of Braque's works is held at the Haus der Kunst in Munich.

Georges Braque: Papiers collés, 1912-1914 is held in Paris at the Galerie Maeght. The catalogue is published in *Derrière le Miroir,* no. 138, with an essay by Stanislas Fumet.

Twenty *papiers collés* are exhibited—this marks the first time so many *papiers collés* are brought together since the fourth Kahnweiler sale in 1923.

1966 Edward F. Fry publishes *Cubism,* in which he relates the history of cubism, and includes valuable, and often rare, documentary texts which provide the reader with the critical reactions which the cubists received from 1905 through the 1920s. Of the invention of *papier collé*, Fry says:

In Braque's first *papier collé* the strips of paper *signify* both the colour and the texture of an object, while the forms and interrelations of objects are indicated by means of the vocabulary of lines and planes perfected during the previous two years. Since 1910 Braque and Picasso had dispensed with closed form; so now, with *papier collé,* the strips of pasted paper were not restricted to the contours of the objects they signified. The artist was now free to compose the strips of paper in a *papier collé* according to a scheme of pattern and colour aesthetically independent of all realistic intent, even while these same coloured or patterned papers conveyed information about the objects depicted. . . . These pieces of pasted paper also eliminated all vestiges of illusionistic space; the *papier collé* is concretely and absolutely flat. But these paper strips could also, when the artist so desired, express spatial relations directly, by overlapping each other or by their relation to lines drawn over or under them. And, as in 1910-11 cubism, a spatial ambiguity which itself denied illusionism could be created by means of mutually interlocking strips, overlapping each other in one sequence at a given point of juncture but in a different sequence at a second point. Lines and planes indicating the formal qualities of objects could be drawn across, or separate from, the paper strips, so that both the colour and the form of an object might be described. The previously existing dilemma of local colour versus *chiaroscuro* was thereby eliminated; and with the discovery of a technique involving neither brushwork nor oil pigment, the cubist break with previous artistic methods and attitudes was virtually complete. Fry 1966, 27-28.

1968 Herta Wescher writes, in her book *Die collage* (published in English in 1979 as *Collage*), about Braque's subjects in his *papiers collés:*

Mostly the subjects were musical instruments, the violins, guitars, and mandolins that also turn up so often in Braque's oil paintings from 1910-13 . . . . Braque explained this partiality by the fact that he had always been surrounded by musical instruments and that their volumes could fit in so harmoniously in the still lifes that preoccupied him at the time. As a third reason he alleged that if you touched them you could wake these instruments to life. Wescher 1979, 22.

1970 Douglas Cooper writes the catalogue accompanying the exhibition *The Cubist Epoch* (Los Angeles County Museum of Art and The Metropolitan Museum of Art).

The technique of *papiers collés* assumed a growing importance for both artists firstly because it enabled them to inject a new kind of realism into their art, but secondly because it was yet another defiance of the cult of *belle peinture* and of the belief that fine art was inseparable from a use of fine materials. Moreover, this technique was an ironic comment, like the *trompe-l'oeil* rendering of a nail in early Cubist paintings, on the conventional notion that reality could only be properly rendered through eye-fooling images created by the hand of a highly skilled artist. By establishing that reality could be pictorially re-created with only the humblest materials, the technique of *papiers collés* reinforced the idea of the *tableau-objet.* It also transformed the ideas of Braque and Picasso as to the relationship between color and form. More importantly, it led them to the conclusion that they could create their own pictorial reality by building up towards it through a synthesis of different elements. Thus in the winter of 1912-13 a fundamental change came about in the pictorial methods of the true Cubists. Whereas previously Braque and Picasso had analyzed and dissected the appearance of objects to discover a set of forms which would add up to their totality and provide the formal elements of a composition, now they found that they could begin by composing with purely pictorial elements (shaped forms, planes of color) and gradually endow them with an objective significance. Cooper 1970, 188.

Nicholas Wadley discusses Braque's *papiers collés* in his book *Cubism.*

Braque's development between 1912 and 1914 was no less considered and coherent. The incorporation of extraneous elements into drawing and painting (wood-graining, sand and sawdust, and finally collage) were part of a single pursuit for him. . . . The new substances allowed him to exploit the determining effect of texture on colour. . . .
Wadley, 1970, 85.

1973 A major exhibition, *Georges Braque,* is held in Paris at the Orangerie des Tuileries (16 October 1973 to 14 January 1974). Seven *papiers collés* are included.

1979 *Georges Braque* is shown in Madrid at the Fundación Juan March, with catalogue essays by André Chastel, Jean Paulhan, Jacques Prévert, Pierre Reverdy, Georges Salles, and Christian Zervos.

1980 *Georges Braque,* another major retrospective, is held in Saint-Paul at the Fondation Maeght, with catalogue essays by Francis Ponge, Jean Paulhan, Claude Esteban, and Nicolas Calas. Nine *papiers collés* are included.

1982 *Braque: Les papiers collés* is held in Paris, Centre Georges Pompidou/Musée national d'art moderne (15 June to 27 September 1982). Forty-one *papiers collés* are assembled in honor of the one-hundredth anniversary of Braque's birth. At the same time, the Centre Georges Pompidou presents a second exhibition of works by Braque from its collection.

BIBLIOGRAPHY

"The focusing of color arrived with *papiers collés.* This is a fact that criticism has never well understood," said Braque in 1954. Indeed, the first discoverable allusions to *papiers collés* refer only to their most anecdotal aspects, seeing in them only amusing provocation, *trompe l'oeil,* or, at best, an investigation of material and an injection of raw reality (even Apollinaire, from the spring of 1913, in the short sentence added to the proofs of *Les peintres cubistes,* or Tabarant in *L'Action* of 1 March 1914, or Coquiot in *Cubistes, futuristes, passéistes,* which appeared in 1914).

However, an important text by Braque appeared in 1917 in *Nord-Sud,* "Pensées et réflexions sur la peinture" ("Thoughts and Reflections on Painting"), which contained a very clear explanation: *"Papiers collés, faux bois*—and other elements of the same nature—which I used in certain drawings assert themselves also by the simplicity of the deeds and it is this which made them be confused with *trompe l'oeil,* of which they are precisely the contrary. These are also simple deeds, but they are created by the mind and are one of the justifications of a new figuration in space."

A manuscript page in Reverdy's hand, which served as an elaboration of the published text, contains—for the passage about *papiers collés*—some interesting variants (figs. 92a and b).(Notably the explicit opposition between a "simple fact by coincidence"—the reproduction in *trompe l'oeil* of a pencil placed on white paper would only be the illusion of reality due to a coincidence, that of light and shadow— and a "simple fact without coincidence"—the *faux bois.*)

These "Pensées" would have great repercussions, at least among the painters and their friends (M. Raynal, J. E. Blanche, D.-H. Kahnweiler, Juan Gris).

After the Uhde and Kahnweiler sales (1921-1923), which put a large number of *papiers collés* on the market (almost all of Braque's) and brought about a critical revision of cubism, the first serious attempts to evaluate the contribution of *papiers collés* appeared one after the other: Aragon's famous preface, entitled "La peinture au défi" ("Painting in Defiance"), to the exhibition of collages organized by the Galerie Goemans in 1930 (Aragon had seen the *papiers collés* as early as 1918—cf. the text published in *Le Film* and recently repeated in the anthology edition of his writings on art); then the illustrated article by Tzara published in 1931 in *Cahiers d'Art,* "Le papier collé ou le proverbe en peinture" ("Pasted Paper or the Proverb in Painting"). Thereafter Zervos in 1933 and Carl Einstein in 1934 published important series of reproductions of Braque's *papiers collés* and restored them to their place in the history of cubism.

Between 1940 and 1953, Jean Paulhan worked out a series of texts on Braque, cubist space, and modern painting (figs. 93a and b), now gathered together in *La peinture cubiste* (published by Denoël Gonthier, 1970). He confirmed what Zervos had suggested in 1932 when he mentioned in *Cahiers d'Art* the letter of 9 October 1912 sent by Braque to Picasso: that Braque was the inventor of the process of *papier collé;* he set out the circumstances of this discovery, and after conversations and correspondence with Braque, he began to limit the specificity of *papier collé* and its role as "mediator" between the cubism of 1911 and that of 1913.

One must also cite the important article of Greenberg, "The Pasted Paper Revolution" *(Art News,* 1958) and the fundamental works of Golding *(Cubism: A History and an Analysis, 1907-1914,* 1959); Rosenblum *(Cubism and Twentieth Century Art,* 1961); Fry *(Cubism,* 1966); and Cooper *(The Cubist Epoch,* 1977), which define the chronology of Picasso, Braque, and Gris; republish the principal contemporary critical texts; and form the basis of all further study.

Finally, Pierre Daix published in 1979 the second volume of his catalogue raisonné *Le Cubisme de Picasso* and proposed a reclassification of Picasso's *papiers collés.*

Apollinaire 1913-1

Guillaume Apollinaire. "Die moderne Malerei," *Der Sturm* (February 1913): 272. In this essay (which he first delivered as a lecturer at the Galerie Der Sturm in Berlin) Apollinaire mentions collage.

Apollinaire 1913-2
Guillaume Apollinaire. *Les peintres cubistes. Méditations esthétiques.* Paris: Figuière, 1913 (one of the first references published on the cubists and *papiers collés,* under an amended form shown on the proofs; see the re-edition in 1980 with an introduction and annotations by L.C. Breunig and J. -Cl. Chevalier, Editions Hermann/Savoir). This treatise was published in three issues of *The Little Review:* 8(Spring 1922): 7-19; 9(Autumn 1922): 41-59; 9(Winter 1922): 49-60, as "Aesthetic Meditation on Painting: The Cubist Painters," translated by Mrs. Charles Knoblatich, for the Société Anonyme. See also *The Cubist Painters, Aesthetic Meditation 1913.* Translated by Lionel Abel. The Documents of Modern Art, vol. I. New York: George Wittenborn, Inc., 1949 and 1962. When there is a reference to this text in our publication, we refer to the 1962 version.

Aragon 1918
Louis Aragon. "Du décor." *Le Film* (16 September 1918). Reprinted in *Aragon, ecrits sur l'art moderne.* Paris: Flammarion, 1981.

Aragon 1930
Louis Aragon. "La peinture au défi." Preface to an exhibition of *papiers collés* presented by the Galerie Goemans, Brussels, 1930. Text printed in Aragon 1965.

Aragon 1965
Louis Aragon. *Les collages.* Paris: Hermann, 1965. Contains a reprint of Aragon 1930.

Arensberg Collection 1954
The Louise and Walter Arensberg Collection, 20th Century Section. Philadelphia Museum of Art, 1954.

Art International 1962
"Homage to Georges Braque." *Art International* 6 (November 1962). Two *papiers collés* reproduced.

Art News 1966
"Seven Decades 1895-1965." *Art News* 65 (May 1966). One *papier collé* reproduced.

Ashbery 1963
John Ashbery. "Paris Notes." *Art International* 7 (1963). One *papier collé* reproduced.

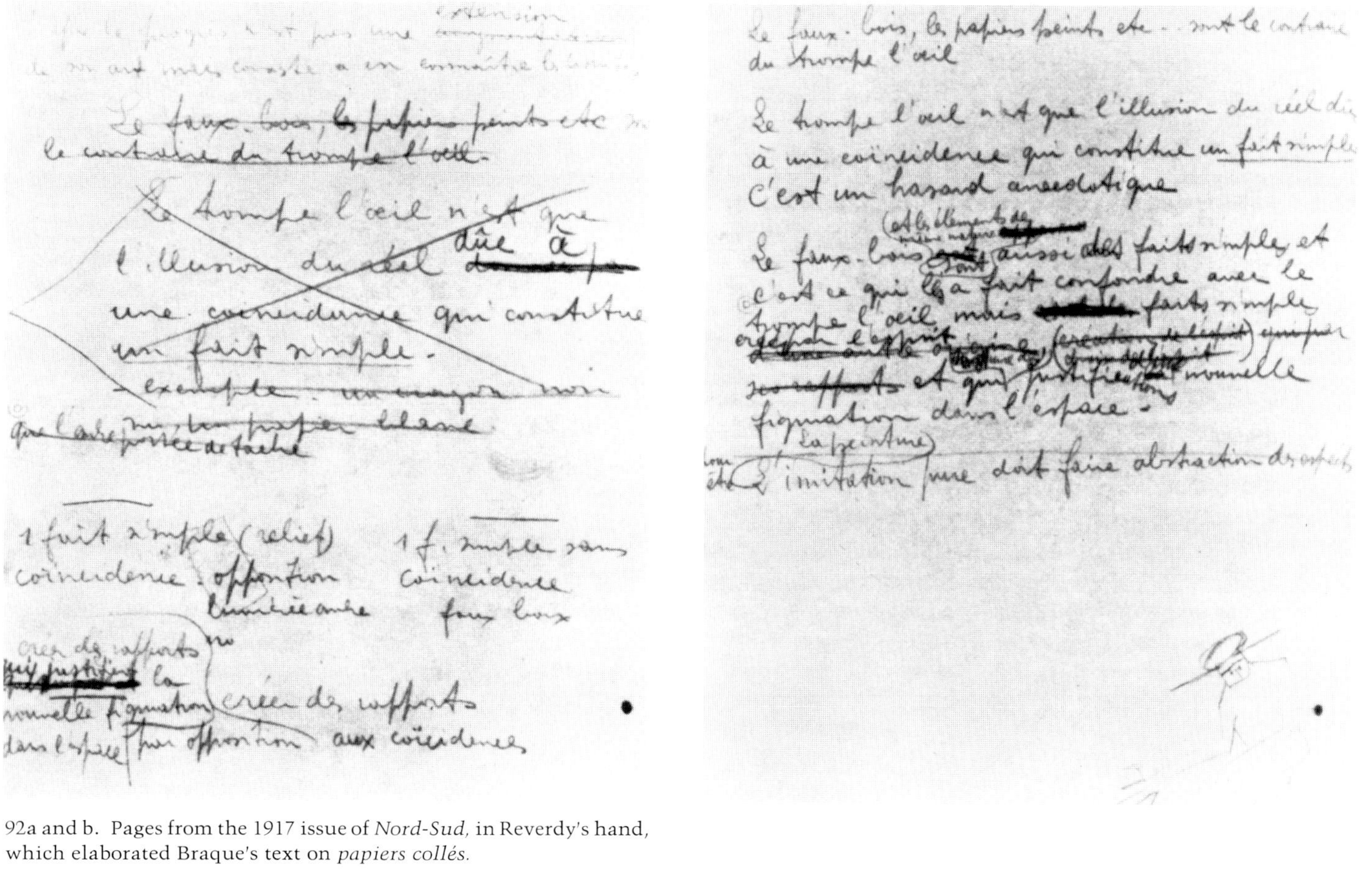

92a and b. Pages from the 1917 issue of *Nord-Sud,* in Reverdy's hand, which elaborated Braque's text on *papiers collés.*

Barr 1936
Alfred H. Barr, Jr. *Cubism and Abstract Art.* New York: The Museum of Modern Art, 1936. Reprinted in 1964.

Berne Joffroy 1973
André Berne Joffroy. "Jean Paulhan devant Braque." *Les nouvelles littéraires* (15 October 1973).

Bernier 1967
Rosamond Bernier. "Une collection du Middle West." Remarks recorded with Joseph Pulitzer and Rosamond Bernier, *L'Oeil* 156 (December 1967): 30-39.

Bissière 1920
Roger Bissière, *Georges Braque.* Paris: Editions de l'effort moderne, 1920. Text reprinted in the *Bulletin de l'effort moderne* 3 (March 1924): 11-14.

Braque 1917
Georges Braque. "Pensées et réflexions sur la peinture." *"Nord-Sud* 10 (December 1917): 3-5. Published in English, Fry 1966, 148-149 (translation by Jonathan Griffen).

Braque 1968
G. Braque. Basel: Editions Beyeler, 1968. Includes Vallier 1954, *Braque, Painting and Us,* Remarks and Recollections by Dora Vallier (translated by Sonia Joyce Rouve), as well as *Thoughts by Georges Braque,* Selected from his Note-Book "The Day and the Night."

Breton 1928
André Breton. *Le surréalisme et la peinture.* Paris: Librairie Gallimard, 1928. One *papier collé* reproduced.

Breunig 1972
Guillaume Apollinaire. *Apollinaire on Art: Essays and Reviews 1902-1918.* Translated by Susan Suleiman. Edited by Leroy C. Breunig. The Documents of 20th-Century Art. New York: The Viking Press, 1972.

Buckley 1981
Harry E. Buckley. *Guillaume Apollinaire as an Art Critic.* Ann Arbor: UMI Research Press, 1981.

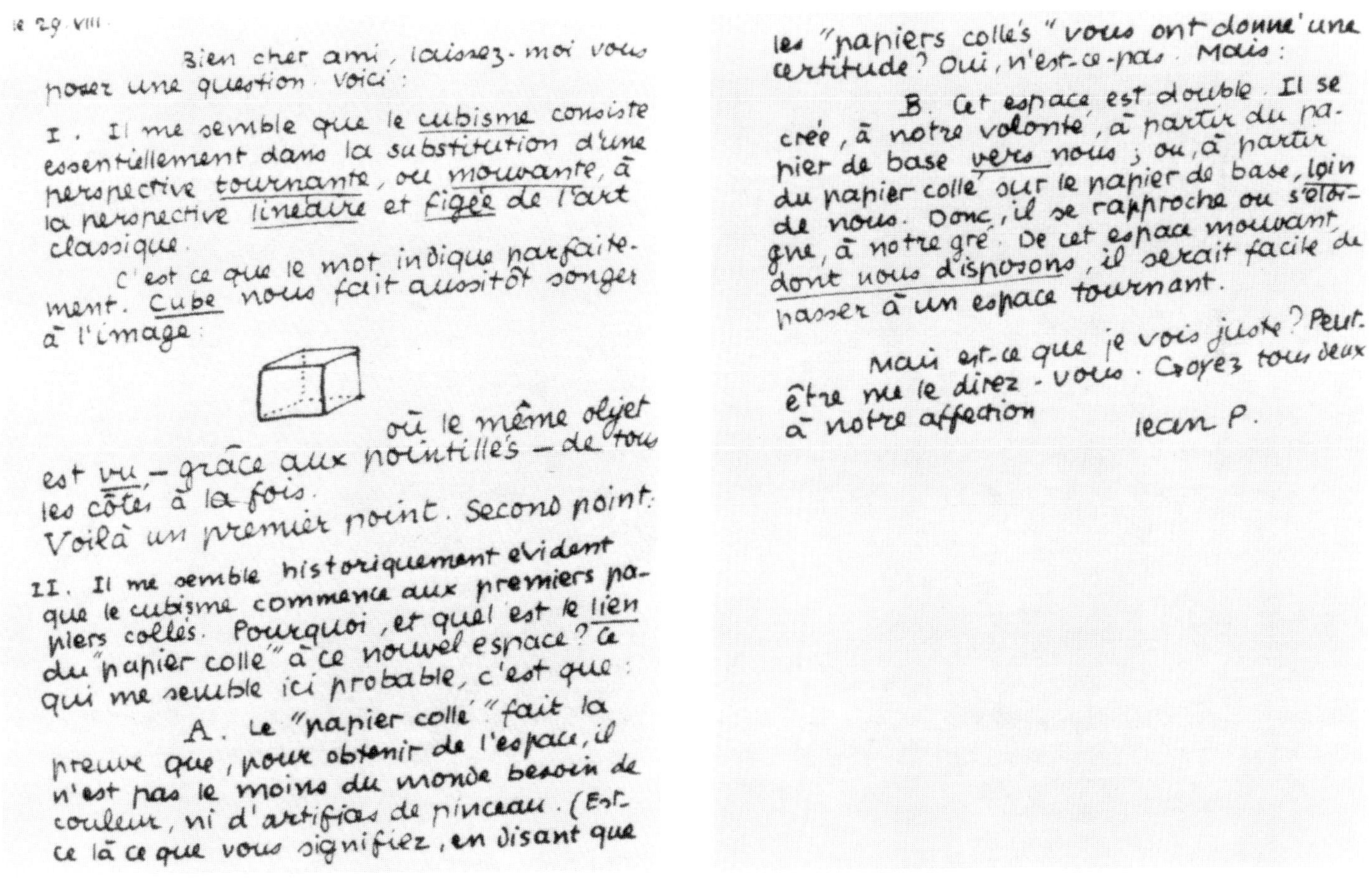
le 29 VIII

Bien cher ami, laissez-moi vous poser une question. Voici :

I. Il me semble que le cubisme consiste essentiellement dans la substitution d'une perspective tournante, ou mouvante, à la perspective linéaire et figée de l'art classique.

C'est ce que le mot indique parfaitement. Cube nous fait aussitôt songer à l'image :

où le même objet est vu – grâce aux pointillés – de tous les côtés à la fois.

Voilà un premier point. Second point :

II. Il me semble historiquement évident que le cubisme commence aux premiers papiers collés. Pourquoi, et quel est le lien du "papier collé" à ce nouvel espace ? Ce qui me semble ici probable, c'est que :

A. Le "papier collé" fait la preuve que, pour obtenir de l'espace, il n'est pas le moins du monde besoin de couleur, ni d'artifices de pinceau. (Est-ce là ce que vous signifiez, en disant que les "papiers collés" vous ont donné une certitude ? Oui, n'est-ce-pas. Mais :

B. Cet espace est double. Il se crée, à notre volonté, à partir du papier de base vers nous ; ou, à partir du papier collé sur le papier de base, loin de nous. Donc, il se rapproche ou s'éloigne, à notre gré. De cet espace mouvant dont nous disposons, il serait facile de passer à un espace tournant.

Mais est-ce que je vois juste ? Peut-être me le direz-vous. Croyez tous deux à notre affection

Jean P.

93a and b. Pages from one of Paulhan's manuscripts, in which the medium of *papier collé* is discussed.

Buffet Picabia 1938
Gabrielle Buffet Picabia. "Matières plastiques." *Vingtième siècle* 1 (May-June 1938).

Cabanne 1963
Pierre Cabanne. *L'épopée du cubisme.* Paris: La table ronde, 1963.

Cabanne 1980
Pierre Cabanne. "Braque à la Fondation Maeght." *Le Matin* (9 July 1980).

Carrà 1971
Massimo Carrà. *L'opera completa di Braque (1908-1929).* Milan: Rizzoli Editore, 1971. Twenty-six *papiers collés* reproduced. French edition, Flammarion, 1973, with an introductory text by Pierre Descargues.

Cartier 1956
J. A. Cartier. "Poétique de Braque." *Le jardin des arts* (December 1958).

Cassou 1956
Jean Cassou. *Braque.* Paris: Flammarion, 1956.

Cassou 1959
Jean Cassou. *Georges Braque.* Barcelona: Editorial Timun Mas, 1959. Three *papiers collés* reproduced.

Chetham 1971
Charles Scott Chetham. *Modern Painting, Drawing and Sculpture Collected by Louise and Joseph Pulitzer, Jr.* Cambridge: Fogg Art Museum, 1971.

Chevalier 1961
Denys Chevalier. "Georges Braque." *Aujourd'hui art et architecture* 34 (December 1961): 4-12.

Cogniat 1970
Raymond Cogniat. *Georges Braque.* Paris: Flammarion, 1970. Three *papiers collés* reproduced.

Cogniat 1976
Raymond Cogniat. *Georges Braque.* Paris: Nouvelles éditions françaises, 1976. Seven *papiers collés* reproduced.

Cooper 1948
Douglas Cooper. *Braque: Paintings, 1909-1947.* London: Lindsey Drummond, Ltd., 1948. The same plates were issued in a French edition with text by Jean Grenier. Paris: Les éditions du chêne, 1948.

Cooper 1956
Douglas Cooper. "Georges Braque: The Evolution of a Vision," in the exhibition catalogue which accompanied *G. Braque: An Exhibition of Paintings.* Arranged by the Arts Council of Great Britain in association with the Edinburgh Festival Society.

Cooper 1970
Douglas Cooper. *The Cubist Epoch.* London: Phaidon Press, 1970. Five *papiers collés* reproduced. Published in association with the Los Angeles County Museum of Art and The Metropolitan Museum of Art (see exhibitions).

Cooper 1972
Douglas Cooper. *Braque: The Great Years,* Chicago: The Art Institute of Chicago, 1972 (see exhibitions).

Daix 1971
Pierre Daix. "Du nouveau sur Braque et Picasso." *Les lettres françaises* (15 December 1971). One *papier collé* reproduced.

Daix 1979
Pierre Daix. *Le cubisme de Picasso.* Catalogue raisonné of paintings, *papiers collés,* and assemblages, 1907-1916. Text by Pierre Daix, catalogue by Daix and Joan Rosselet. Neuchâtel: Editions ides et calendes, 1979.

Damase 1963
Jacques Damase. *Georges Braque.* London: Blanford Press, 1963. One *papier collé* reproduced.

Descargues 1973
Pierre Descargues. "Braque à l'Orangerie." *L'Oeil* 219 (October 1973): 32-42.

Dorival 1966
Bernard Dorival. "La préemption de l'état à la 2e vente Lefèvre." *La revue du Louvre* 2 (1966): 111-120. One *papier collé* reproduced.

Draeger 1971
G. Braque de Draeger. Texts by Francis Ponge, Pierre Descargues, André Malraux. Paris: Draeger Editeur, 1971. Seven *papiers collés* reproduced. Also published as *G. Braque.* Translated by Richard Howard. New York: Abrams, 1971.

Einstein 1931
Carl Einstein. *Die Kunst des 20. Jahrhunderts.* Berlin: Im Propyläen Verlag, 1931.

Einstein 1934
Carl Einstein. *Georges Braque.* Paris: Editons des chroniques du jour, 1934.

Elgar 1958
Frank Elgar. *Braque 1906-1920.* London: Methuen and Co., Ltd., 1958. One *papier collé* reproduced.

Fermigier 1973
André Fermigier. "Le parti pris des choses." *Le monde* (19 October 1973).

Flanner 1957
Janet Flanner. *Men and Monuments.* New York: Harper, 1957.

Fry 1966
Edward Fry. *Cubism.* London: Thames and Hudson, 1966. Also published as *Le cubisme.* Brussels: La Connaissance, 1966.

Fumet 1965
Stanislas Fumet. *Georges Braque.* Paris: Maeght Editeur, 1965. Six *papiers collés* reproduced.

Gallatin 1933
Gallery of Living Art, A. E. Gallatin Collection. New York University, 1933. One *papier collé* reproduced.

Gallatin 1936
Museum of Living Art, A. E. Gallatin Collection. New York University, 1936. One *papier collé* reproduced.

Gallatin 1943
Albert E. Gallatin. *Georges Braque.* New York. George Wittenborn, Inc., 1943. One *papier collé* reproduced.

Gamwell 1980
Lynn Gamwell. *Cubist Criticism.* Ann Arbor: UMI Research Press, 1980.

George 1921
Waldemar George. "Braque." *L'esprit nouveau* 6 (1921): 638-656.

Gieure 1956
Maurice Gieure. *Georges Braque.* Paris: Editions Pierre Tisné, 1956. Four *papiers collés* reproduced.

Golding 1959
John Golding. *Cubism: A History and an Analysis, 1907-1914.* New York: George Wittenborn, Inc., 1959. Two *papiers collés* reproduced. Second printing, London, 1968.

Granville 1980
Pierre Granville. "L'austère cantate de Braque." *Le Monde* (24 July 1980).

Greenberg 1958
Clement Greenberg. "The Pasted Paper Revolution." *Art News* (September 1958): 46-49, 60.

Greenberg 1961
Clement Greenberg. *Art and Culture, Critical Essays.* Boston: Beacon Press, 1961. See essays on "Collage" and "Braque."

Grenier 1948
Jean Grenier. *Braque: Peintures, 1909-1947.* Paris: Les éditions du chêne, 1948. The same plates were issued in an English edition with text by Douglas Cooper. London: Lindsey Drummond, Ltd., 1948.

Guiney 1972
Mortimer Guiney. *Cubisme et littérature.* Geneva: Georg, 1972.

Habasque 1959
Guy Habasque. *Le cubisme.* Geneva: Editions d'art Albert Skira, 1959.

Haftmann 1968
Werner Haftmann. *Painting in the Twentieth Century.* London: Lund Humphries, 1968.

Henning 1977
Edward B. Henning. "The Cubist Collection at The Cleveland Museum of Art." *Apollo* (January 1977). One *papier collé* reproduced.

Hope 1949
Henry Radford Hope. *Georges Braque.* New York: The Museum of Modern Art, 1949 (see exhibitions). Ten *papiers collés* reproduced.

Huser 1980
France Huser. "Grandeur et décadence d'un peintre." *Le nouvel observateur* (19-25 July 1980).

Isarlov 1932
George Isarlov. *Georges Braque.* Paris: José Corti (collection Orbes, no. 3), 1932.

Janis and Blesh 1962
Harriet Janis and Rudi Blesh. *Collage: Personalities, Concepts, Techniques.* Philadelphia and New York: Chilton Company, Book Division, 1962.

Janneau 1924
Guillaume Janneau. *L'art cubiste.* Paris: Editions d'art Charles Moreau, 1924.

Jouffroy 1980
J. P. Jouffroy. "Et le grand Braque." *L'humanité dimanche* (15 August 1980).

Judkins 1976
Winthrop Judkins. *Fluctuant Representation in Synthetic Cubism: Picasso, Braque, Gris, 1910-1920.* New York and London: Garland Publishing, 1976.

Kachur 1980
Lewis Kachur. "Cubism and Related Movements." *Arts Magazine* 54 (January 1980): 13.

Kahnweiler 1915/1920
Daniel-Henry Kahnweiler. *Der Weg zum kubismus.* Munich: Delphin-Verlag, 1920. Written in 1915, but not published until 1920. Published in English as *The Rise of Cubism.* Translated by Henry Aronson. The Documents of Modern Art. New York: Wittenborn, Schultz, Inc., 1949.

Kahnweiler 1950
Daniel-Henry Kahnweiler. *Les années héroiques du cubisme.* Paris: Editions Braun et Cie, 1950.

Kahnweiler 1954
Daniel-Henry Kahnweiler. "Cubism: The Creative Years." *Art News Annual* 53(November 1954): part 2.

Kahnweiler 1961
Daniel-Henry Kahnweiler. *Mes galeries et mes peintres.* Paris: Editions Gallimard, 1961. Published in English as *My Galleries and Painters.* Translated by Helen Weaver. The Documents of 20th Century Art. New York: The Viking Press, 1971.

Koepplin 1968
Dieter Koepplin. *Das grosse Buch der Graphik.* Edited by von Boekdorff and F. Winzer. 1968.

Koepplin 1969
Dieter Koepplin. *Kubismus, Zeichnungen und Druckgraphik aus dem Kupferstichkabinett Basel.* Basel: Kunstmuseum, 1969. Four *papiers collés* reproduced.

Laude 1973
Jean Laude. "Picasso et Braque 1910-1914: la transformation des signes." *Université de Saint Etienne, Travaux IV, Le Cubisme.* Saint Etienne, 1973.

Lejard 1949
André Lejard. *Braque.* Paris: Editions Fernand Hazan, 1949. One *papier collé* reproduced.

Le Point 1953
"Braque." *Le Point* 46 (October 1953). Contains articles by Stanislas Fumet, Georges Limbour, Georges Ribemont-Dessaignes. One *papier collé* reproduced.

Leymarie 1961
Jean Leymarie. *Braque.* Geneva: Editions d'art Albert Skira, 1961.

Life 1949
"Georges Braque." *Life International* (6 May 1949).

Mackworth 1961
Cecily Mackworth. *Guillaume Apollinaire and the Cubist Life.* London: John Murray, Ltd., 1961.

Mangin (Worms de Romilly) 1982
Nicole Mangin (Worms de Romilly). *Catalogue de l'oeuvre de Georges Braque, peintures 1908-1915.* Paris: Editions Maeght, 1982.

Marcus 1973
Susan Marcus. "The Typographic Element in Cubism, 1911-1915: Its Formal and Semantic Implications." *Art International* 17 (May 1973).

Masini 1969
Lara Vinca Masini. *Georges Braque.* Florence: Sadea Sansoni, 1969. Two *papiers collés* reproduced.

Mathey 1968
François Mathey. "La trinité cubiste, Braque, Picasso, Gris." *L'Arte Moderna* 4. Milan: Fratelli Fabbri Editori, 1968.

Metzinger 1910
Jean Metzinger. "Note sur la peinture." *Pan* (October-November 1910): 649-652.

Mullins 1968
Edwin Mullins. *Braque.* London: Thames and Hudson, 1968. Six *papiers collés* reproduced.

Paulhan 1946
Jean Paulhan. *Braque le patron.* Geneva and Paris: Editions des Trois Collines, 1946.

Paulhan 1952
Jean Paulhan. *Braque le patron.* Paris: Gallimard, 1952.

Paulhan 1956
Jean Paulhan. "Georges Braque, le patron des cubistes." *Le nouveau fémina* (February 1956). One *papier collé* reproduced.

Paulhan 1970
Jean Paulhan. *La peinture cubiste.* Paris: Denoël/Gonthier, 1970. One *papier collé* reproduced. Reprint of various texts by Paulhan, compiled by J. C. Zylberstein.

Ponge 1946
Francis Ponge. *Braque le réconciliateur.* Geneva: Editions d'art Albert Skira, 1946.

Pouillon 1970
Nadine Pouillon. *Braque.* Paris: Le musée personnel, 1970. Two *papiers collés* reproduced.

Der Querschnitt 1924
Der Querschnitt 4(1924). One *papier collé* reproduced.

Raynal 1921
Maurice Raynal. *Georges Braque.* Rome: Editions "Valori Plastici," 1921. Two *papiers collés* reproduced.

Raynal 1924
Maurice Raynal. *Georges Braque.* Rome: Editions "Valori Plastici," 1924. Reprint of text from 1921, with different plates. Three *papiers collés* reproduced.

Raynal 1927
Maurice Raynal. *Anthologie de la peinture en France de 1906 à nos jours.* Paris: Editions Montaigne, 1927. Two *papiers collés* reproduced.

Raynal 1953
Maurice Raynal. *Peinture moderne.* Geneva: Editions d'art Albert Skira, 1953.

Read 1960
Herbert Read. *Histoire de la peinture moderne.* Paris: Aimery Somogy, 1960.

Richardson 1959
John Richardson. *Braque.* London: Penguin Books, 1959. One *papier collé* reproduced.

Richardson 1961
John Richardson. *Georges Braque.* Paris: La bibliothèque des arts, 1961; and Milan: Silvana editions d'art, 1961.

Rosenblum 1960
Robert Rosenblum. *Cubism and Twentieth Century Art.* New York: Harry N. Abrams, Inc., 1960. Four *papiers collés* reproduced.

Russell 1959
John Russell. *Georges Braque.* London: Phaidon Press, 1959. Two *papiers collés* reproduced.

Saucet 1976
Jean Saucet. *Panorama du cubisme.* Paris: Editions Filipacchi, 1976. One *papier collé* reproduced.

Schwartz 1971
Paul Waldo Schwartz. *Cubism.* London: Thames and Hudson, 1971.

Seitz 1961
William C. Seitz. *The Art of Assemblage.* New York: The Museum of Modern Art, 1961.

Soby 1957
James Thrall Soby. *Modern Art and the New Past.* Norman, Oklahoma: University of Oklahoma Press, 1957.

Les soirées de Paris 1914
Les soirées de Paris (15 April 1914). Dedicated to Braque. One *papier collé* reproduced: first and only reproduction of a *papier collé* by Braque before the war.

Steegmuller 1963
Frances Steegmuller. *Apollinaire, Poet among the Painters.* New York: Farrar, Straus and Company, 1963.

Teyssèdre 1973
Bernard Teyssèdre. "De l'audace au bon métier." *Le nouvel observateur* (22 October 1973).

Time 1949
"Georges Braque." *Time* (2 May 1949). One *papier collé* reproduced.

Tono 1967
Yoshiaky Tono. *Picasso-Braque.* Tokyo: Zanbo Press, 1967 (Gendai Sekai Bijutsu Zenshu no. 7).

Tzara 1931
Tristan Tzara. "Le papier collé ou le proverbe en peinture."*Cahiers d'Art* 2 (1931): 61-74. Five *papiers collés* reproduced.

Vallier 1954
Dora Vallier. "Braque, la peinture et nous." *Cahiers d'Art* (1954). Remarks by Braque collected by Vallier.

Vallier 1962
Dora Vallier. *Georges Braque, 10 oeuvres* (preceded by "Braque, la peinture et nous"). Basel: Editions Phoebus, 1962.

Wadley 1970
Nicholas Wadley. *Cubism.* London and New York: The Hamyln Publishing Group Limited, 1970.

Wescher 1953
Herta Wescher. "Les collages cubistes." *Art d'aujourd'hui* 4 (May-June 1953): 33-43.

Wescher 1979
Herta Wescher. *Collage.* New York: Harry N. Abrams, 1979. Translation of *Die collage.* Cologne: Du Mont, Schauberg, 1968.

Will-Levaillant 1973
Françoise Will-Levaillant. "La lettre dans la peinture cubist." *Université de Saint Etienne, Travaux IV, Le Cubisme.* Saint Etienne, 1973

Wolfram 1975
Eddi Wolfram. *History of Collage.* London: Studio Vista, 1975.

Zervos 1933
Christian Zervos. *Georges Braque.* Paris: Editions Cahiers d'Art, 1933.

Zervos 1938
Christian Zervos. *Histoire de l'art contemporain.* Paris: Editions Cahiers d'Art, 1938.

EXHIBITIONS

What the Uhde and Kahnweiler sales just after the First World War were is well known: the precipitate liquidation of hundreds of cubist works (the seized property of D. H. Kahnweiler alone amounted to more than 1,500 pieces) belonging to "German nationals," works which by virtue of the Treaty of Versailles the French state had the right "to retain and liquidate." We shall not dwell upon the rather catastrophic consequences of these massive sales for the artists themselves and ultimately for the state which, as seller, did not acquire a single piece and thoughtlessly allowed an inestimable patrimony to be dispersed.

With regard to Braque's *papiers collés,* the fourth Kahnweiler sale (7-8 May 1923) is the most interesting for us since the near totality of these works appeared there in twenty numbers and three lots (see figs. 94 and 95; only some isolated examples were dispersed in preceding sales and very few had apparently been sold before the war).

This sale can therefore be considered the first and, until now, the only occasion ever offered for taking stock of the ensemble of Braque's *papiers collés.* To some extent it was the first exhibition. But under what conditions! An article by Robert Desnos (in *Paris-Journal,* May 1923) vividly recreates both the atmosphere of this sale and the evident indignation of a public composed of amateurs and poets.

The Last Kahnweiler Sale

How a drawing (unsigned) by Braque measuring 37 x 46 cm. can become a drawing (signed) by Picasso measuring 24 x 31 cm.

The last paintings from the Galerie Kahnweiler were dispersed last 7-8 May at the Hôtel Drouot by the ministry of M. Zapp, in charge of seizure and liquidation, assisted by the president of the auction house, and by M. Durand-Ruel, expert.

The exhibition was made in scandalous fashion: the paintings were stacked without order; rolled drawings were folded in boxes; others, in rolls, were carefully sealed so than no one could see them; still others were enclosed in baskets or hidden behind the platform. All in an indescribable filth and mess which would justify the worst reprisals from the painters concerned: MM. Braque, Derain, Vlaminck, Gris, Léger, Manolo, and Picasso.

The hanging, especially, bore witness to an incompetence of commercial servility which merits insult. Vlaminck's paintings occupied one large partition. Derain had a small room at the back. As for Braque, Gris, Léger, and Picasso, they shared, the four of them, the third wall. The sale was no less exasperating. The auctioneer, doubtless a man of the best society, allowed himself sly jokes about the works that he sold, sly jokes which in any case revealed only a very restricted intelligence. He was imitated in this by his assistants who systematically presented paintings the wrong way, crumpled the drawings, scraped *papiers collés* and paintings with sand on the table, and did not spare the buyers their taunts. It would be something if these fellows, who several times tried the patience of the audience, realized that these paintings were not made for asses and that only silence can excuse imbecility. Numbers were stuck onto the canvases themselves, some bore fresh stains and on one of them, one could swear that there were shoe marks.

The eternity of a work matters little to me. All paintings and books could be burned tonight and I would be in no way diminished. But the moment that someone takes such license with something I love, I truly do not see why I should abstain from defiling the postage stamps of the *Renaudière* or scraping my boots on the books of the Comte de Montesquiou. I would do so very willingly on a copy of *Illuminations,* in which that ridiculous lordling includes a "very severe critic," or on his correspondence with the grotesque Marcel Proust!

The sale was relatively lively. The admirable *papiers collés* and paintings by Braque excited the buyers. These were works of the great period, the most moving and the most moved that I know by this painter, serious and respectful of mysteries. Especially noteworthy was the *Violon et verre* (no. 142: *Violin and Glass*), although it is difficult to choose from such a remarkable ensemble. The *Deux soeurs (Two Sisters)*, the more seductive *Arbres (Trees)*, and the *Baigneurs (Bathers)* by Derain fetched high bids. I prefer *Le rideau* (no. 159; *The Curtain)* to those, a sinister and disturbing painting which went unnoticed. The elevated prices attained by the Vlamincks did not at all disturb the monotony of their march past: postcards in color or still lifes for the barracks at Nanterre, there is not one which does not bear witness to an ordinary talent. The prices for Gris were elevated. As for the Picassos, they are admirable for their scandal and freedom of spirit. They have borne these fifteen years without aging and condemn the new hackneyed stuff that the second-rate cubists want to inflict on us today.

I especially noticed the *Nature morte* (no. 73; *Still Life), La citronnade (The Lemonade), Nature morte (Lacerba) (Still Life), Buffall Bill, Tête de jeune fille* (340-347; *Head of a Young Girl), La Pointe de la Cité*, and *La nature morte* (no. 360; *The Still Life)* doubled up with a *Scène galante (Gallant Scene)*, were also coveted.

For my part I was tempted only by Braque and Picasso; I had remarked a charcoal drawing cited in the catalogue under number 20 as Braque, unsigned, and which I had taken right away for a Picasso. Surprised, I showed it to my friend Paul Eluard, who confirmed my doubt. The drawing was pretty, I risked nothing in buying it, and so I entrused it to Paul Eluard who obtained it for 37 francs plus charges. Having arrived at home, I unframed the drawing so that I could go show it to the two presumed authors and ask their opinion. I removed the backing, then some newspapers from 1913 dealing with my friend Rirett Maîtrejean, and finally I came to the drawing. I noticed first that the catalogue measurements of 37 x 46 cm. were those of the cardboard mat and not those of the drawing, which measured only 24 x 31 cm. Upon closer examination, I saw that it was signed on the back—and signed *Picasso.* The question was resolved. The attribution to Braque had been only a guess and under these conditions, one may well think that the same was true of other numbers and that other buyers found themselves in the same situation. Thus is illustrated the commercial value of the paintings and the conscience of the expert.

Robert Desnos

We know, thanks to the *Gazette de l'Hôtel Drouot* (of 15 May 1923; fig. 96), the prices attained by Braque's *papiers collés:*

One will recall only that on 30 November 1912, in the letter-contract that he sent to his dealer D.-H. Kahnweiler, Braque fixed the following prices for "drawings with wood paper, marble or any other accessory": 75 francs for an Ingres sheet, 50 francs for the half and quarter sheet.

Let us note, finally, that besides this dispersion of 1923, the only other important gathering of Braque's *papiers collés* was organized in 1963 by the Galerie Maeght (with twenty *papiers collés*).

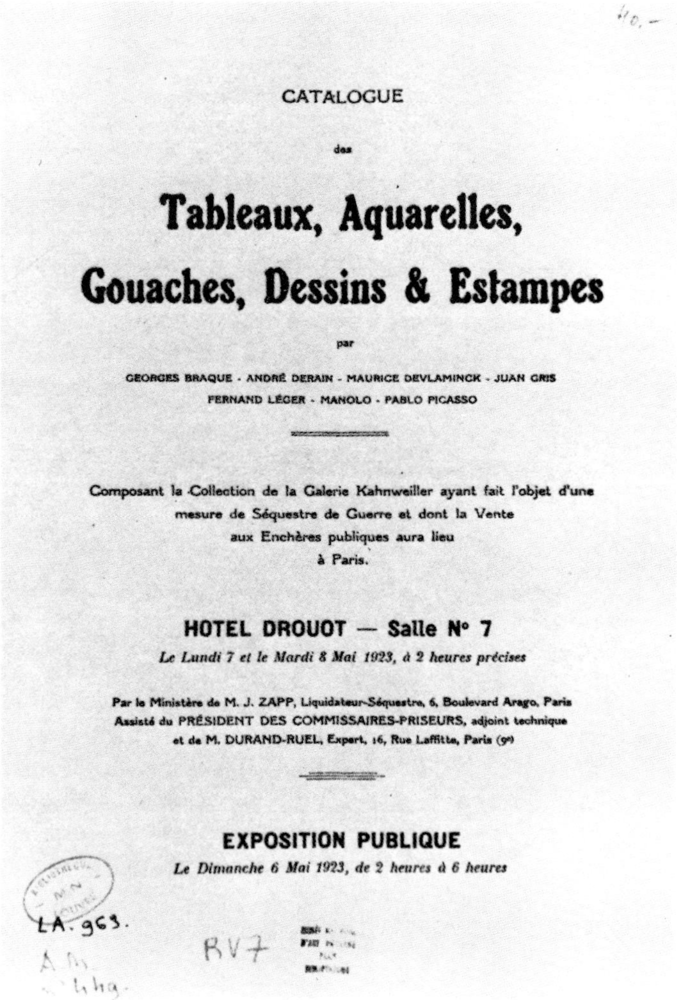

CATALOGUE

des

Tableaux, Aquarelles,

Gouaches, Dessins & Estampes

par

GEORGES BRAQUE - ANDRÉ DERAIN - MAURICE DEVLAMINCK - JUAN GRIS
FERNAND LÉGER - MANOLO - PABLO PICASSO

Composant la Collection de la Galerie Kahnweiler ayant fait l'objet d'une mesure de Séquestre de Guerre et dont la Vente aux Enchères publiques aura lieu à Paris.

HOTEL DROUOT — Salle N° 7

Le Lundi 7 et le Mardi 8 Mai 1923, à 2 heures précises

Par le Ministère de M. J. ZAPP, Liquidateur-Séquestre, 6, Boulevard Arago, Paris
Assisté du PRÉSIDENT DES COMMISSAIRES-PRISEURS, adjoint technique
et de M. DURAND-RUEL, Expert, 16, Rue Laffitte, Paris (9e)

EXPOSITION PUBLIQUE

Le Dimanche 6 Mai 1923, de 2 heures à 6 heures

94. Page from the catalogue for the fourth Kahnweiler sale, 7-8 May 1923.

Sales which included papiers collés by Braque

Uhde sale 1921

Sale of goods of war which were sequestered during the war.

Collection Uhde—Tableaux Modernes.

Paris, Hôtel Drouot, 30 May 1921 (one *papier collé*).

Second Kahnweiler sale 1921

Sale of German goods which were sequestered during the war.

Collection Henry Kahnweiler. Second sale.

Paris Hôtel Drouot, 17 and 18 November 1921 (on view to the publc, 16 November 1921) (one *papier collé*).

Third Kahnweiler sale 1922

Sale of German goods which were sequestered during the war.

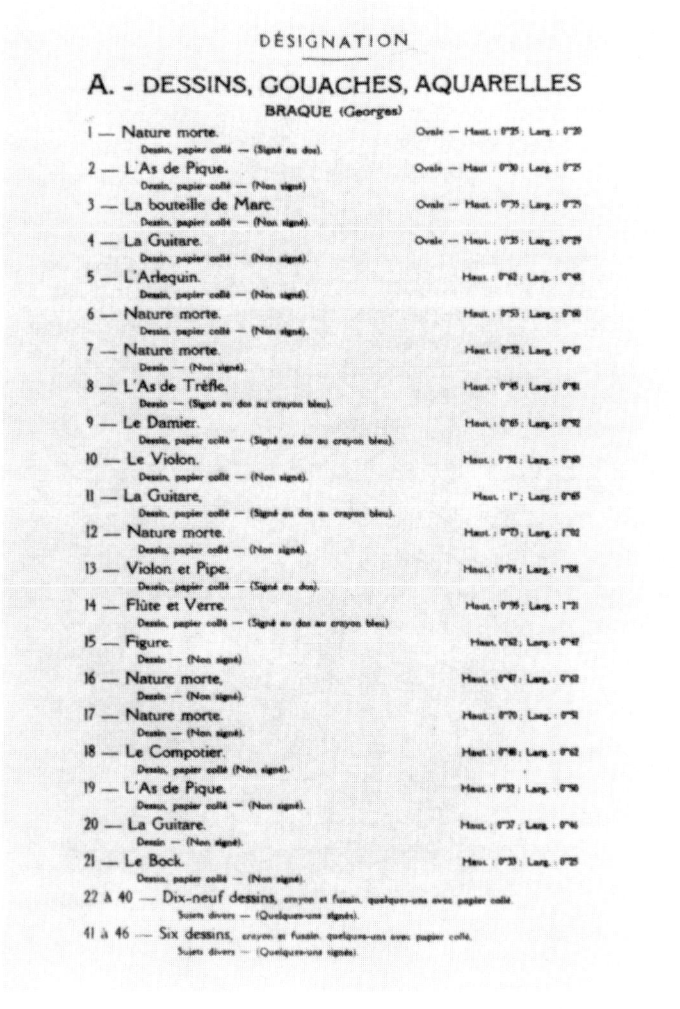

DÉSIGNATION

A. - DESSINS, GOUACHES, AQUARELLES

BRAQUE (Georges)

1 — Nature morte. Ovale — Haut. : 0m25 ; Larg. : 0m20
Dessin, papier collé — (Signé au dos).
2 — L'As de Pique. Ovale — Haut : 0m30 ; Larg. : 0m25
Dessin, papier collé — (Non signé)
3 — La bouteille de Marc. Ovale — Haut. : [illegible] ; Larg. : [illegible]
Dessin, papier collé — (Non signé).
4 — La Guitare. Ovale — Haut. : 0m35 ; Larg. : 0m29
Dessin, papier collé — (Non signé).
5 — L'Arlequin. Haut. : 0m62 ; Larg. : 0m48
Dessin, papier collé — (Non signé).
6 — Nature morte. Haut. : 0m53 ; Larg. : [illegible]
Dessin, papier collé — (Non signé).
7 — Nature morte. Haut. : [illegible] ; Larg. : [illegible]
Dessin — (Non signé).
8 — L'As de Trèfle. Haut. : [illegible] ; Larg. : [illegible]
Dessin — (Signé au dos au crayon bleu).
9 — Le Damier. Haut. : [illegible] ; Larg. : [illegible]
Dessin, papier collé — (Signé au dos au crayon bleu).
10 — Le Violon. Haut. : [illegible] ; Larg. : [illegible]
Dessin, papier collé — (Non signé).
11 — La Guitare. Haut. : 1m ; Larg. : 0m65
Dessin, papier collé — (Signé au dos au crayon bleu).
12 — Nature morte. Haut. : [illegible] ; Larg. : [illegible]
Dessin, papier collé — (Non signé).
13 — Violon et Pipe. Haut. : [illegible] ; Larg. : [illegible]
Dessin, papier collé — (Signé au dos).
14 — Flûte et Verre. Haut. : [illegible] ; Larg. : [illegible]
Dessin, papier collé — (Signé au dos au crayon bleu)
15 — Figure. Haut. 0m62 ; Larg. : 0m47
Dessin — (Non signé)
16 — Nature morte. Haut. : 0m47 ; Larg. : [illegible]
Dessin — (Non signé).
17 — Nature morte. Haut. : 0m70 ; Larg. : [illegible]
Dessin — (Non signé).
18 — Le Compotier. Haut. : [illegible] ; Larg. : [illegible]
Dessin, papier collé (Non signé).
19 — L'As de Pique. Haut. : [illegible] ; Larg. : [illegible]
Dessin, papier collé — (Non signé).
20 — La Guitare. Haut. : 0m37 ; Larg. : [illegible]
Dessin — (Non signé).
21 — Le Bock. Haut. : [illegible] ; Larg. : [illegible]
Dessin, papier collé — (Non signé).
22 à 40 — Dix-neuf dessins, crayon et fusain, quelques-uns avec papier collé.
Sujets divers — (Quelques-uns signés).
41 à 46 — Six dessins, crayon et fusain, quelques-uns avec papier collé.
Sujets divers — (Quelques-uns signés).

95. Page from the catalogue for the fourth Kahnweiler sale, which lists lots 1 to 46, many of which are *papiers collés*.

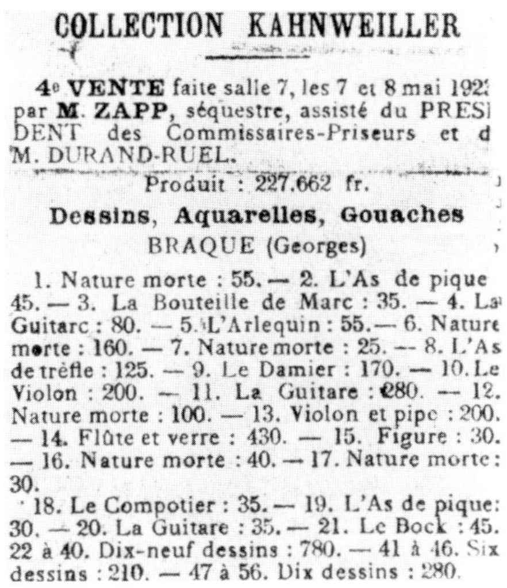

COLLECTION KAHNWEILER

4e VENTE faite salle 7, les 7 et 8 mai 192[illegible] par M. ZAPP, séquestre, assisté du PRESIDENT des Commissaires-Priseurs et de M. DURAND-RUEL.

Produit : 227.662 fr.

Dessins, Aquarelles, Gouaches

BRAQUE (Georges)

1. Nature morte : 55. — 2. L'As de pique 45. — 3. La Bouteille de Marc : 35. — 4. La Guitare : 80. — 5. L'Arlequin : 55. — 6. Nature morte : 160. — 7. Nature morte : 25. — 8. L'As de trèfle : 125. — 9. Le Damier : 170. — 10. Le Violon : 200. — 11. La Guitare : 280. — 12. Nature morte : 100. — 13. Violon et pipe : 200. — 14. Flûte et verre : 430. — 15. Figure : 30. — 16. Nature morte : 40. — 17. Nature morte : 30.

18. Le Compotier : 35. — 19. L'As de pique : 30. — 20. La Guitare : 35. — 21. Le Bock : 45. 22 à 40. Dix-neuf dessins : 780. — 41 à 46. Six dessins : 210. — 47 à 56. Dix dessins : 280.

96. Page from the 15 May 1923 issue of the *Gazette de l'Hôtel Drouot* listing the prices attained by Braque's *papiers collés* at the fourth Kahnweiler sale.

Collection Henry Kahnweiler. Third sale.

Paris, Hôtel Drouot, 4 July 1922 (three *papiers collés*).

Fourth Kahnweiler sale 1923

Sale of German goods which were sequestered during the war.

Collection Henry Kahnweiler. Fourth and last sale.

Paris Hôtel Drouot, 7 and 8 May 1923 (twenty-one *papiers collés* and three lots, nos. 22 to 40; 41 to 46; and 47 to 54 (including drawings and *papiers collés*).

Zoubaloff sale 1935

Collection Jacques Zoubaloff.

Paris, Hôtel Drouot, 27-28 November 1935 (one *papier collé*).

Exhibitions which included papiers collés by Braque

Brooklyn 1926

An International Exhibition of Modern Art, assembled by the Société Anonyme. Brooklyn: The Brooklyn Museum, 19 November 1926 to 1 January 1927.

Paris 1930

La peinture au défi (exposition de collages). Paris: Librairie José Corti, March 1930. Catalogue by Louis Aragon.

Brussels 1931

L'art vivant en Europe. Brussels: Palais des Beaux Arts, 25 April to 24 May 1931 (one *papier collé*).

Basel 1933

Georges Braque. Basel: Kunsthalle, 9 April to 14 May 1933 (four *papiers collés*).

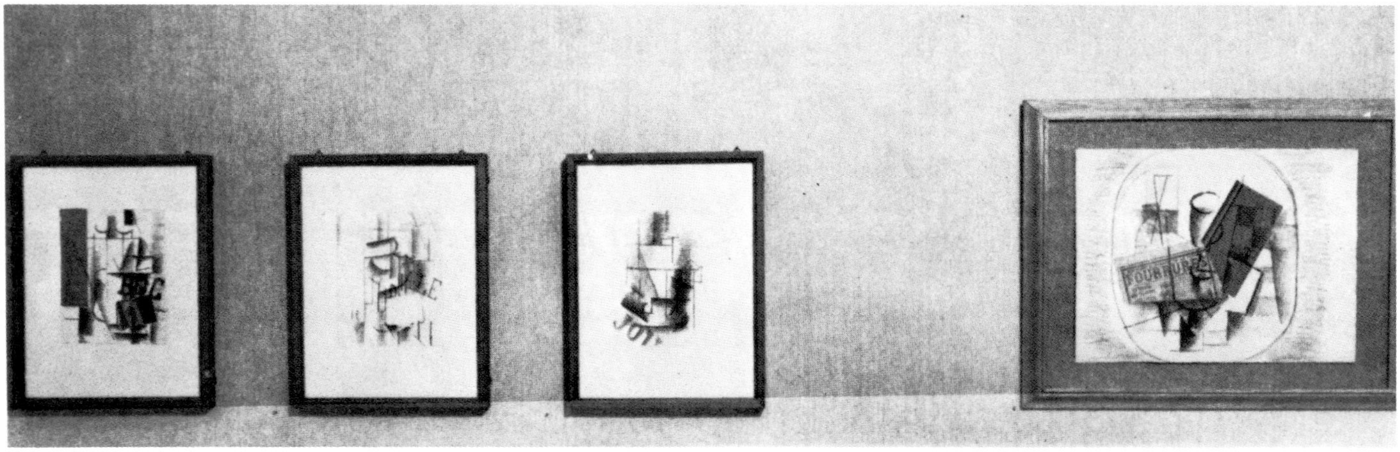

97. *Braque, papiers collés,* an exhibition at the Galerie Maeght, Paris, 1963. Photo: Archives Galerie Maeght.

New York 1936
Cubism and Abstract Art. New York: The Museum of Modern Art, 1936 (one *papier collé*).

Chicago 1939
Georges Braque Retrospective Exhibition. Chicago: Arts Club of Chicago, 2 to 27 November 1939 (four *papiers collés*). The exhibition traveled to Washington: Phillips Memorial Gallery, 6 December 1939 to 6 January 1940; and San Francisco: San Francisco Museum of Art, 6 February to 6 March 1940.

Paris 1945
Le cubisme 1911-1918. Paris: Galerie de France, 25 May 1945.

Freibourg 1948
Georges Braque. Freibourg-im Brisgau: Paulusaal, October 1948, introduction by Elfried Schulze (one *papier collé*).

New York 1948
Collage. New York: The Museum of Modern Art, 21 September to 5 December 1948.

Chicago 1949
20th Century Art from the Louise and Walter Arensberg Collection. Chicago: The Art Institute of Chicago, 20 October to 18 December 1949.

New York 1949-1
Georges Braque. New York: The Museum of Modern Art, 29 March to 12 June 1949 (six *papiers collés*). The exhibition opened first in Cleveland: The Cleveland Museum of Art, 25 January to 13 March 1949, but it was apparently organized by MOMA. Catalogue by Henry Radford Hope.

New York 1949-2
Cubism. New York: Buchholz Gallery, 5 to 30 April 1949.

Paris 1952
*L'oeuvre du XXe siècle.*Paris: Musée national d'art moderne, May to June 1952 (one *papier collé*).

Tokyo 1952
Exposition des oeuvres de Georges Braque, organisée par le Musée national de Tokyo et le Journal Yomiuri. Tokyo: National Museum, September to October 1952 (one *papier collé*).

Berne 1953
Braque. Berne: Kunsthalle, 25 April to 31 May 1953 (two *papiers collés*).

Paris 1953
Le cubisme 1907-1914. Paris: Musée national d'art moderne, 30 January to 9 April 1953 (four *papiers collés*).

Zurich 1953
Georges Braque. Zurich: Kunsthaus Zurich, 7 June to 19 July 1953 (five *papiers collés*).

Rio de Janeiro 1954
Exposição do Cubismo. Rio de Janeiro: Museu de Arte Moderna, 1954 (one *papier collé*).

Edinburgh 1956
Georges Braque, An Exhibition of Paintings. Edinburgh: The Royal Scottish Academy, 18 August to 15 September 1956 (seven *papiers collés*). The exhibition traveled to London: The Tate Gallery, 28 September to 11 November 1956. Arranged by the Arts Council of Great Britain in association with the Edinburgh Festival Society; catalogue essay, "Georges Braque: The Evolution of a Vision," by Douglas Cooper.

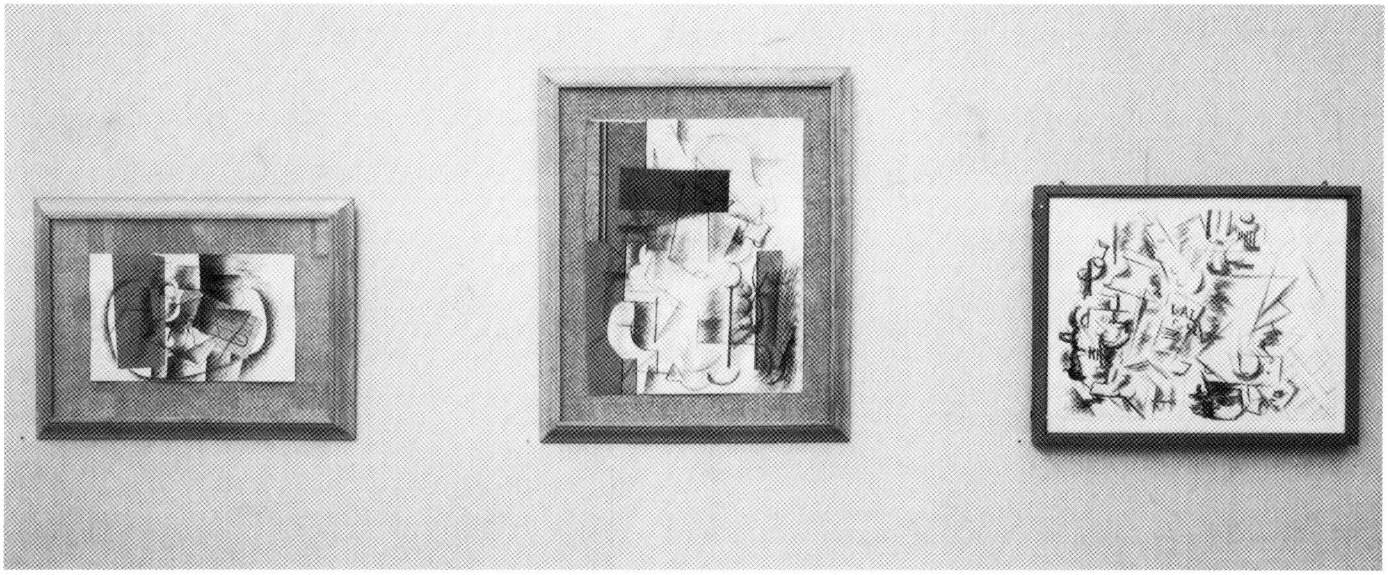

98. Galerie Maeght exhibition, 1963. Photo: Archives Galerie Maeght.

London 1957
XIX and XX Century European Masters. London: Marlborough Fine Art Ltd., October to December 1957 (one *papier collé*).

Houston 1958
Collage International. Houston: Contemporary Arts Association, 1958.

New York 1958
10th Anniversary Exhibition. New York: The Sidney Janis Gallery, 29 September to 1 November 1958.

Paris 1958
Les Soirées de Paris. Paris: Galerie Knoedler (M. Knoedler and Co.), 16 May to 30 June 1958 (one *papier collé*).

Rome 1958
Georges Braque. Rome: Ente Premi Roma, Palazzo Barberini, November 1958 to early 1959 (one *papier collé*).

Basel 1960
Georges Braque. Basel: Kunsthalle, 9 April to 29 May 1960 (three *papiers collés*).

Paris 1960
Les Sources du XXe siècle (les arts en Europe de 1884 à 1914). Paris: Musée national d'art moderne, 4 November 1960 to 23 January 1961 (two *papiers collés*).

The Hague 1961
Collection Thompson uit Pittsburght. The Hague: Haags Gemeentemuseum, 17 February to 9 April 1961 (one *papier collé*).

New York 1961
The Art of Assemblage. New York: The Museum of Modern Art, 2 October to 12 November 1961 (two *papiers collés*). The exhibition traveled to Dallas: The Dallas Museum of Contemporary Arts, 9 January to 11 February 1962; and San Francisco: San Francisco Museum of Modern Art, 5 March to 13 April 1962.

Paris 1961
L'atelier de Braque. Paris: Musée du Louvre, November 1961 (nine *papiers collés*).

Basel 1962
Le Cubisme. Basel: Galerie Beyeler, May to July 1962 (five *papiers collés*).

Cincinnati 1962
Homage to Georges Braque, an exhibition to honor the artist on the occasion of his eightieth birthday. Cincinnati: The Contemporary Arts Center, 22 September to 22 October 1962 (three *papiers collés*). The exhibition traveled to Chicago: The Arts Club of Chicago, 6 November to 6 December 1962; and Minneapolis: The Walker Art Center, 20 December to 20 January 1963.

Paris 1962
Le Cubisme. Paris: M. Knoedler et Cie, 9 October to 10 November 1962.

Basel 1963
Die Schenkungen Raoul La Roche. Basel: Kunstmuseum, 16 March to 28 April 1963 (four *papiers collés*).

Munich 1963
Georges Braque. Munich: Haus der Kunst, 18 October to 15 December 1963 (seven *papiers collés*).

Paris 1963
Georges Braque, papiers collés 1912-1914. Paris: Galerie Maeght, May 1963 (twenty *papiers collés*).

Honfleur 1964
Hommage à Georges Braque. Honfleur: Salle des expositions du Grenier à sel, 26 July to 31 August 1964 (one *papier collé*).

New York 1964
Georges Braque, An American Tribute. New York: Saidenberg Gallery (for fauvist and cubist art), 7 April to 2 May 1964 (five *papiers collés*).

Oslo 1964
Georges Braque 1882-1963. Oslo: Kunstnernes Hus, 14 November 1964 to 3 January 1965 (four *papiers collés*). The exhibition traveled to Bergen: Kunstforening, 15 January to 7 February 1965.

Paris 1964
Collection André Lefèvre. Paris: Musée national d'art moderne, March to April 1964 (one *papier collé*).

Saint-Etienne 1964
Cinquante ans de "collages." Saint-Etienne: Musée d'art et d'industrie, 1964 (one *papier collé*).

Lille 1965
Apollinaire et le Cubisme. Lille: Palais des Beaux Arts, 3 April to 4 May (one *papier collé*).

Geneva 1967
Jean Paulhan et ses environs. Geneva: Galerie Krugier, April 1967 (one *papier collé*).

Le Havre 1967
Georges Braque. Le Havre: Nouveau Musée du Havre, 15 April to 31 May 1967 (one *papier collé*).

Paris 1967
Autour de Cubisme. Paris: Galerie Jean-Claude Bellier, 3 May to 30 June 1967 (one *papier collé*).

Basel 1968
Georges Braque. Basel: Galerie Beyeler, July to September 1968 (three *papiers collés*).

Houston 1968
Look Back: An Exhibition of Cubist Paintings and Sculptures from the Menil Family Collection. Houston: University of St. Thomas, 13 March to 13 September 1968. The exhibition traveled to Kansas City: Nelson Gallery of Art—Atkins Museum, 1 October to 1 November 1968; Montreal: The Montreal Museum of Fine Arts, Le Musée des Beaux-Arts de Montreal, 6 November to 5 December 1968; Providence: Museum of Art, Rhode Island Shool of Design, 8 January to 16 February 1969; Waltham, Mass.: Rose Art Museum, Brandeis University, 23 February to 23 March 1969; Berkeley: University Art Museum, University of California, 29 April to 1 June 1969; Raleigh: The North Carolina Museum of Art, 22 June to 7 September 1969; Minneapolis: The Minneapolis Institute of Arts, 24 September to 26 October 1969; Indianapolis: Herron Museum of Art, 9 November 1969 to 1 January 1970 (one *papier collé*).

St. Louis 1968
Works of Art of the Nineteenth and Twentieth Centuries, collected by Louise and Joseph Pulitzer, Jr. St. Louis: City Art Museum of St. Louis, 23 January to 24 March 1968 (one *papier collé*).

Zurich 1968
Collagen. Zurich: Kunstgewerbemuseum, 8 June to 18 August 1968 (five *papiers collés*).

Humlebaeck 1969
Georges Braque, Henri Laurens. Humlebaeck: Musée de Louisiana, March 1969 (four *papiers collés*).

New York 1969-1
Twentieth Century Art from the Nelson Aldrich Rockefeller Collection. New York: The Museum of Modern Art, 26 May to 1 September 1969 (one *papier collé*).

New York 1969-2
A Selection of Drawings, Pastels and Watercolors from the Collection of Mr. and Mrs. Lester Francis Avnet. New York: New York Cultural Center, 9 December 1969 to 25 January 1970.

Basel 1970
Collection Marie Cuttoli, Henri Laugier, Paris. Basel: Galerie Beyeler, October to November 1970.

Los Angeles 1970
The Cubist Epoch. Los Angeles: Los Angeles County Museum of Art, 15 December 1970 to 21 February 1971 (five *papiers collés*). The exhibition traveled to New York: The Metropolitan Museum of Art, 7 April to 7 June 1971.

Rouen 1970
Collection de Menil, oeuvres cubistes. Rouen: Musée des Beaux Arts (one *papier collé*). The exhibition traveled to Chambéry: Musée des Beaux Arts; Toulouse: Musée des Augustins; Nantes: Musée des Beaux Arts; and Lille: Palais des Beaux Arts (same exhibition as Houston in 1968, which subsequently traveled to eight American museums).

Saint-Paul 1970
Pierre Reverdy à la rencontre de ses amis. Saint-Paul-de-Vence: Fondation Maeght, summer 1970 (one *papier collé*).

Amsterdam 1971
Kubisme, Tekeningen en prenten vit het Kupferstichkabinett, Basel. Amsterdam: Stedelijk Museum, 17 April to 31 May 1971 (three *papiers collés*).

Chicago 1972
Braque: The Great Years. Chicago: The Art Institute of Chicago, 7 October to 3 December 1972. Catalogue essay by Douglas Cooper.

Santa Fe 1972
Look Back: An Exhibition of Cubist Paintings and Sculptures from the Menil Family Collection. Santa Fe: The Museum of New Mexico, 1972-1973. The revised exhibition (see Houston 1968) traveled to Austin: Art Museum, The University of Texas at Austin, 1973.

Bordeaux 1973
Les cubistes. Bordeaux: Galerie des Beaux Arts, 4 May to 1 September 1973 (two *papiers collés*). The exhibition traveled to Paris: Musée d'art moderne de la ville de Paris, 26 September to 10 November 1973.

Paris 1973-1
Georges Braque. Paris: Orangerie des Tuileries, 16 October 1973 to 14 January 1974 (nine *papiers collés*).

Paris 1973-2
Oeuvres cubistes, Braque, Gris, Léger, Picasso. Paris: Galerie Berggruen, 1973 (two *papiers collés*).

Seattle 1973
International Impurity. Seattle: University of Washington, 1973.

Paris 1974
Jean Paulhan à travers ses peintres. Paris: Galeries Nationales du Grand Palais, 1 February to 15 April 1974 (four *papiers collés*).

Rome 1974
Braque. Rome: Accademie di Francia, Villa Medici, 15 November 1974 to 20 January 1975 (one *papier collé*).

Minneapolis 1975
Picasso—Braque—Léger, Masterpieces from Swiss Collections. Minneapolis: The Minneapolis Institute of Arts, 30 October 1975 to 4 January 1976. The exhibition traveled to Houston: Sarah Campbell Blaffer Gallery, University of Houston, 17 January to 7 March 1976; and San Francisco: San Francisco Museum of Modern Art, 19 March to 4 May 1976.

Basel 1976
Autres dimensions (collages, assemblages, reliefs). Basel: Galerie Beyeler, June to September 1976 (two *papiers collés*).

Marcq en Baroeul 1978
G. Braque. Marcq en Baroeul: Fondation Anne et Albert Prouvost à Septentrion, 7 October 1978 to 21 January 1979 (one *papier collé*).

New York 1978
A Treasury of Modern Drawing, The Joan and Lester Avnet Collection. New York: The Museum of Modern Art, 1978 (one *papier collé*).

Washington 1978
Aspects of Twentieth-Century Art. Washington, D.C.: National Gallery of Art, 1 June 1978 to 4 September 1978 (one *papier collé*).

Bielefeld 1979
Zeichnungen und Collagen des Kubismos, Picasso, Braque, Gris. Bielefeld: Kunsthalle, 11 March to 29 April 1979 (seven *papiers collés*).

Basel 1980
Lettres et chiffres. Basel: Galerie Beyeler, March to May 1980 (one *papier collé*).

New York 1980
Homage to Kahnweiler. New York: Saidenberg Gallery, 26 April to 14 June 1980 (one *papier collé*).

Paris 1980
Donation Masurel. Paris: Musée du Luxembourg, 14 March to 25 May 1980 (one *papier collé*).

Rome 1980
Apollinaire et l'Avanguardia. Rome: Galleria Nazionale d'Arte Moderna, 30 November 1980 to 4 January 1981 (one *papier collé*).

Saint-Paul 1980
Georges Braque. Saint-Paul-de-Vence: Fondation Maeght, 5 July to 30 September 1980 (ten *papiers collés*).

Philadelphia 1981
Drawings from van Gogh to Matisse. Philadelphia: Philadelphia Museum of Art, 21 February to 10 May 1981.

Stuttgart 1981
Georges Braque, Ausstellung Zum 100. Geburtstag. Stuttgart: Staatsgalerie Stuttgart, 22 November 1981 to 31 January 1982 (one *papier collé*).

Paris 1982
Georges Braque: les papiers collés. Paris: Centre Georges Pompidou, Musée national d'art moderne, 17 June to 27 September 1982 (forty-one *papiers collés*).

Washington 1982
Georges Braque: The Late Paintings (1940-1963). Washington, D.C.: The Phillips Collection, 9 October to 12 December 1982; will travel to San Francisco: California Palace of the Legion of Honor; Minneapolis: The Walker Art Center; Houston: The Museum of Fine Arts.